E. G. [illegible]

HOUSE...... No. 15.

REPORT OF THE COMMISSIONERS

APPOINTED TO

INQUIRE INTO THE EXPEDIENCY OF REVISING
AND AMENDING THE LAWS

RELATING TO

TAXATION AND EXEMPTION THEREFROM.

JANUARY, 1875.

BOSTON:
WRIGHT & POTTER, STATE PRINTERS,
79 MILK STREET (CORNER OF FEDERAL).
1875.

REPORT.

To the Honorable the Senate and the House of Representatives:

The following Resolve was passed by the last General Court, and approved June 18, 1874:—

Resolved, That the governor and council be and they are hereby authorized to appoint a commission consisting of three suitable persons to sit during the recess of the legislature, to inquire into the expediency of revising and amending the laws of the state relating to taxation and the exemptions therefrom, with authority to call witnesses, and to report in full, in print, to the next general court.

Resolve authorizing the commission.

Such a Commission was constituted by our appointment thereto, on the 22d of July. In the time since intervening (altogether too limited for so large and difficult an undertaking) we have given the matter the most careful attention in our power, and submit the following Report:—

Commission appointed.

The subject of taxation is one of the most important which can claim the attention of the legislator, and it is as difficult as it is important. The course of the state upon this matter touches the welfare, and brings good or ill to every man, woman and child within its borders, and leads to results often so intricate and always so various, that it needs the clearest and most comprehensive vision of the statesman to foresee them. Hardly any practical question of the state requires greater caution in its admin-

The general subject of taxation.

istration. No change could be adopted in any established system of taxation, without some resulting evil. There may be a good commensurate with the evil, and even more than sufficient to compensate therefor, in which case changes would, of course, be wise. But as any change must necessarily involve the unsettlement of some time-adjusted pressure, requiring for any new tax imposed and any old one repealed a fresh adjustment, with many inconveniences certain and many inequalities probable during the process, a wise man will not lightly propose it, whatever the existing system may be. Especially where a tax system has been long followed by an increasingly prosperous community, any radical changes should be most carefully weighed before they are adopted.

Brief outline of the revenue system of Massachusetts.

Briefly outlined, the revenue system of Massachusetts is this: Territorially, the state is divided into counties, the counties into towns and cities. There are also minor municipal corporations, as school districts and fire districts with territorial limits, and parishes composed of persons only.

These divisions and sub-divisions, among which the central unit is the town or city, are availed of in order to apportion the burden of raising the revenue and of facilitating its collection.

Independently of direct taxation, the Commonwealth has a revenue founded in part upon the ancient prerogatives of the government which it succeeded, but mainly derived from sinking funds, lands, fees collected incidentally in the administration of the government and the courts of justice, the regulation of corporations and of business, and from its reformatory and correctional institutions. It derives much larger sums from excise-taxes imposed on its own corporations, and those doing business within its limits, and from the tax on non-resident shares in national banks. When more revenue is needed than these sources yield, the legislature enacts a law imposing and apportioning among the towns and cities a tax large enough to meet the deficiency, and holds them responsible for its prompt payment into the public treasury.

The several counties also have a considerable revenue received from the courts, in fees, fines, and forfeited recognizances, and from licenses and the like. If, in any county, this proves inadequate, a county tax or deficiency bill is granted it by the legislature, and imposed upon and apportioned among the towns and cities within the county. That the towns and cities may not fail to pay these county and state taxes, provision is made for their separate assessment and collection by the local officers, unless voluntarily blended with the local taxes.

The town, in open meeting of its inhabitants, and the city, through its city government, appropriate money for authorized purposes, and vote to raise it by tax. Such votes are certified to assessors, chosen by the towns and cities, who lay, upon the polls and estates within the place, all such taxes, either separately or with the county and state taxes, for which they have received warrants.

The school districts, in open meetings, make appropriations and vote taxes, which are certified to the town assessors, and laid by them upon the polls and estates of the districts.

Fire districts also make appropriations and vote taxes, which, if the district is in a single town, are certified and assessed in like manner; but if in more than one town, by assessors and collectors of the district.

Parishes have like power to grant money and vote taxes, but such taxes are assessed and collected by officers of the parish upon the polls of its members, their real estate within the state, and their personal property wherever it may be.

The theory governing the apportionment and assessment is, that all who are bound to contribute to the common charges should do so in proportion to ability. The rules applying this theory to the actual assessment are, that a reasonable part of the tax, not exceeding one-sixth, and not more, in the case of any individual, than two dollars, shall be assessed in respect of polls,—the remainder in proportion to the valuation of estates, certain income being included in this valuation.

Every tax when laid is committed by the assessors, with their warrant, to the collector, and in its collection he is authorized to use the compulsory processes of the law.

Persons aggrieved by over-valuation of their estates may petition the assessors for abatement, and if it is refused, may appeal to the county commissioners.

Illegal or void taxes, if paid under protest, may be recovered by suit.

From the operation of this system certain persons, corporations and estates are wholly or partially exempted, for various reasons and by different methods; and the laws enunciating, construing and enforcing it are contained in several articles of the bill of rights and constitution, the eleventh and twelfth chapters of the general statutes, and in many subsequent enactments.

Ch. 70, Res. of 1874.

The resolve directing us to "inquire into the expediency of revising and amending the laws of the state relating to taxation and the exemptions therefrom" opened a very wide field.

Circulars issued by commissioners.

Feeling that if there were just grounds of complaint with the practical working of the present system, the officers charged with its administration would be able to point them out, and perhaps suggest the remedy, we issued to them a circular, a copy of which will be found in the Appendix, page 305. We have received in reply many valuable communications, some of which are given in the Appendix, and others are referred to in the body of our report.

Aware that similar commissions had been created in neighboring states, we have endeavored to understand the results of their labors, that you might profit by their experience.

We also addressed a circular to the secretaries of all the states, asking for copies of compilations and reports upon this subject, and of statutes and documents more recent than those to be found in the state library. This circular was very generally responded to and documents forwarded to us from almost every state, from Maine to California, and from Minnesota to Texas. We regret that we have been unable to carry out the plan we had in view, in obtaining them, viz., to present to you a clear idea of the theory and results of the revenue system of every state.

In many of them recent revisions have been either enacted or reported by commissions. Commissions are now sitting in Virginia and New Hampshire. From several of the states have come suggestions for an inter-state commission upon the subject, and the legislature of Maine has passed a resolve looking in the same direction.

Limitation of taxation.

There are certain clear limits within which our tax levies are bounded by the constitution of Massachusetts and the constitution and laws of the United States. The constitution of Massachusetts gives to the legislature power "to impose and levy proportional and reasonable assessments, rates and taxes, upon all the inhabitants of, and persons resident, and estates lying within, the said Commonwealth; and also to impose and levy reasonable duties and excises upon any produce, goods, wares, merchandise and commodities whatsoever, brought into, produced, manufactured, or being within the same, . . . for the public service, in the necessary defence and support of the government of the said Commonwealth, and the protection and preservation of the subjects thereof, according to such acts as are or shall be in force within the same. And in order that such assessments may be made with equality, there shall be a valuation of estates within the Commonwealth, taken anew once in every ten years at least, and as much oftener as the General Court shall order."

Constitution of Mass. c. 1, § 1. Art. IV.

From these provisions, three restrictions upon the legislature are clear.

First. The taxes imposed must be proportional and reasonable.

Second. They must be levied for objects within the general purposes enumerated.

Third. The assessments must be laid upon a valuation renewed, at least, every ten years.

Added to these are the restrictions to which Massachusetts, as well as every other state of the Union, is subjected by the constitution and laws of the United States.

McCulloch v. Maryland, 4 Wheaton, 316. Dobbins v. Erie, 16 Pet. 435; or 1 Howard, 370. Palfrey v. Boston, 101 Mass. 329.

It has been adjudged by the supreme court that the state governments have no right to tax any of the constitutional means employed by the government of the Union to execute its constitutional powers, nor to retard, impede, burden, or in any manner control the operations of the constitutional laws enacted by Congress, to carry into effect the powers vested in the national government. The reason for this adjudgment is, that the power to tax would involve the power to destroy; and the power to destroy might defeat and render useless the power to create.

Constitution of the U. S., Art. I. § 8. Brown v. State of Maryland, 12 Wheaton, 419. Low v. Austin. 13 Wallace, 29. Almy v. State of California. 24 Howard, 169. Case of state freight tax. 15 Wallace, 232.

Under the power given to Congress to regulate commerce, it has been decided that no state may tax or impose restrictions upon the sale of imported goods while in their original packages and in possession of the importer (a restriction which does not apply to goods imported and in the hands of the retail trader); and, also, that no tax can be imposed on the transportation of goods from one state to another.

Constitution of U. S. Art. I. § 9.

In express terms, the Federal constitution declares that no state shall, without the consent of Congress, lay any imposts or duties on imports or exports, except what may be absolutely necessary for executing its inspection laws.

Ib. Art. I. § 8.

Still farther, the power given to Congress to borrow money on the credit of the United States, has been decided to imply that a state tax on stock issued for loans made to the United States is unconstitutional, because it is a tax on this power of Congress. All taxing by any state of the bonds of the United States, is therefore repugnant to the Federal constitution, and could not even be granted by Congress to any state.

Weston v. city council of Charlestown, 2 Pet. 449.

Constitution of U. S., Art. I. § 10.

By the constitution of the United States, also, no state may pass any law impairing the validity of contracts, on which ground certain provisions in the revenue laws of some of the states have been set aside.

But constitutions are themselves subject to a higher right, even the right which determined how they should be made; and, beyond these restrictions set by the constitution of Massachusetts and that of the United States, it becomes us to inquire if any bounds are also determined by the original right of taxation itself.

State tax on foreign-held bonds. 15 Wallace, 300.

The individual person has no inalienable rights except that to his own righteousness. His property, his labor, his liberty, his life, are not inalienably his. He may forfeit them by his own act, or the state may require them for its own needs, in which cases the individual yields them justly to the state. The state may demand every thing which belongs to a man, except his manhood and his moral integrity, which he has no right ever to surrender.

Theory of contract between state and citizen.

Now this supreme right of the state to every required service of its subjects, is often supposed to rest on some implied contract, whereby the subject is bound to render some service to the state, as a recompense for the service which the state has rendered him. The state protects a man in his person and his property, and furnishes him many means of enjoyment, from which the inference is easy, that a man should pay the state his proportional equivalent. In this view the state stands to its citizens in a relation somewhat like that of an insurance company to its policy-holders. Pay me so much money, and I guarantee you so much protection.

But this view does not hold. It has two great fallacies. Waiving the question whether every one has ever made such a contract, and whether the state could release any one therefrom should he claim to set up for himself, such a notion would surely estop the state from demanding the whole property or the life of its subjects in any case where these were not forfeited by crime; and it would fairly permit a claim for indemnity wherever the state had failed to protect. We may, therefore, set this view aside.

The true theory of taxation.

A man is taxed not to pay the state for its expense in protecting him, and not, in any respect, as a recompense to the state for any service in his behalf, but because his original relations to society require it. All the enjoyment which a man can receive from his property comes from his connection with society. Cut off from all social relations, a man's wealth would be useless to him. In fact, there could be no such thing as wealth without society. Wealth is what may be exchanged, and requires for its very existence a community of persons with reciprocal wants. Gold and silver to any amount is not wealth till it is put into the hands of some member of society, and becomes a means wherewith he can serve others, and receive some service from them in return. But not only are the enjoyment and even the existence of wealth wholly a social creation; not only would they cease entirely if men were only individuals, living each one alone or apart from others; but in like manner all social progress gives an increasing value to wealth, and a man's possessions grow in worth as he grows in the intimacy, and perhaps, also, in the intricacy, of his relations to his kind. It is wise and right, therefore, for an individual to contribute of his wealth whatever the true interests of society may require; and this he does, not as a payment for the gifts which society has conferred, —the creature does not serve his creator in payment for his creation,—but because the law of his own well-being or perfection summons him thus to do.

Constitution of Mass., Part 2d, ch. 1, § 1, Art. IV.

From this it follows that, in the admirable language of the constitution of Massachusetts, "proportional and reasonable assessments should be imposed and levied upon all the inhabitants of, and persons resident, and estates lying within the Commonwealth."

It is very difficult to determine in every case, what are "proportional and reasonable assessments." This has probably never yet been perfectly done. Every system of taxation yet devised is liable to the charge of more or less injustice. Until the spirit which loves one's neighbor as one's self is everywhere felt, and the great command, "Render unto Cæsar the things which are Cæsar's," is loyally and universally obeyed, individuals will contrive to throw burdens upon others which they themselves ought to bear, and human selfishness and greed will render the practical working of any scheme of taxation often oppressive, however wisely and justly the scheme may have been conceived. The most important point, therefore, for a state, in matters of taxation, as in all its procedure, relates to the honesty, purity and unselfishness of its subjects.

Relation of public indebtedness to taxation.

We cannot but view it as an injustice, though, doubtless, often not regarded as such, that both the Commonwealth herself, and the municipalities embraced within her jurisdiction, are so willing to incur pecuniary obligations which those of a future time will have to pay. If it be said that these are often for benefits which the future will enjoy, it cannot be denied that they often involve burdens also, quite disproportionate to the benefits received, while in many cases the future is taxed for the payment of debts which are only a curse without any compensation. We find the outstanding debt of Massachusetts, January 1, 1874, to be, $28,477,804. Added to this are the debts of the various cities and towns, aggregating at the same date, $67,277,188, making a sum total of $95,754,992, or 4.58+ per cent. of the entire valuation of the Commonwealth. The available resources for meeting the *state* debt we find to be $13,448,800, which amount deducted, leaves the *net* debt of the Commonwealth $15,029,004. This sum added to the debt of the municipalities decreases the total indebtedness to $82,306,192, or 3.94+ per cent. of the valuation. The formidable amount of municipal liability is also offset, to some extent, by sinking funds applicable to their payment, the aggregate of which we have not been able to ascertain. In some of the larger cities we know that they exist to a considerable amount. But making a reasonable deduction for these funds, and allowing for an increase of liability in the form of *county* debts,

—the statistics of which we have not investigated,—the indebtedness of our cities and towns has reached an amount that is out of proportion to their present resources, and, if allowed to continually increase, will retard, not only their progress, but the prosperity of the Commonwealth.

That these debts, so serious in amount, have very often been improvidently incurred, for objects unnecessary or unprofitable, will be admitted by every one, as will also the fact that the tendency to run into debt which these figures disclose, is a wrong fraught with many dangers. The unparalleled growth of expenditure, the country through, which, not satisfied with eating up the proceeds of generous taxes, has plunged alike, the nation, the state, the county, the town, and almost every lesser municipality, into debt, ought to be recognized as one of our gravest public perils. But we fear there is no evidence of the diminution of this tendency, which, on the contrary, rather threatens to increase, and which we cannot but think is a matter calling for legislative interference, by the enactment of a statute which shall forbid any municipality to incur a debt beyond a certain fixed per cent. of the assessed value—at the time—of the property taxable for its payment. We recommend, also, that municipalities be required to provide that, for every debt created without special legislative sanction, taxation shall at once commence for a sinking fund, that shall meet the principal of the debt when due.

Recommendation for limitation of indebtedness and for creation of sinking funds.

Poll-Taxes.

While poll-taxes are regarded as wise and just, we find a very considerable dissatisfaction with our present system respecting them, a dissatisfaction based upon the fact that in many places the voters assessed for poll-taxes only, outnumber all the rest. The majority, in such cases, are restrained by no fear of increasing their own taxes when the question of extravagant or large expenditure is to be decided, directly, in the town meeting, or indirectly, in the choice of members of the city government. The poll-tax being limited to two dollars, the voter who has nothing else to pay, does not feel the burden of his vote for a new town hall, or a costly school-house, or public park, and may decide the question of such expenditures quite contrary to the judgment or the wish of those who must pay the taxes necessary thereto. If he is a laborer, the very vote which puts a new mortgage on his neighbor's farm, or factory, or dwelling-house, may give him employment, with the best of wages and a sure paymaster.

The value of a direct pecuniary stake on the part of every voter in the amount of appropriations voted, as a means of enforcing that economy in expenditure which alone can secure what all economists agree is the best tax, "that which is least in amount," was recognized in that provision of our law which declares that the assessors shall assess upon the polls, as nearly as may be, one-sixth part of the whole sum to be raised.

In the ideal New England community, where each voter and tax-payer was the head of a family, had a "settling lot" equal in area and value to that of his neighbor, an equal share in the common lands, and a pew in the meeting-house, perhaps the whole tax might have been justly and proportionably levied as a capitation, or poll-tax, while no great inequality was produced in raising the whole one-sixth of the tax in this manner, even after the people had departed quite extensively from the earlier New England type. But changes wrought by the growth of villages and cities, and the increase of trade and manufactures, made so much difference in the abilities of citizens to contribute to the public charges, that it became necessary to limit the tax to one dollar and fifty cents, and again, in 1862, to two dollars.

Anc. L. and Ch. p. 70, c. 21, § 3. 1828, 143, § 3. 1830, 151, § 2. R. S. c. 7, § 27. 1859, 157. 1862, 158.

How far short the tax falls, at this limit, from the one-sixth of the whole tax raised, will be seen from the following figures:—

Amount of tax on polls.

YEAR.	Total Tax.	One-Sixth Total Tax.	No. of Polls.	Actually assessed on Polls.
1870, . .	$21,922,569 00	$3,653,761 00	357,339	$757,734 00
1871, . .	22,063,946 00	3,677,324 00	374,079	782,753 00
1872, . .	22,911,883 00	3,818,647 00	396,784	825,250 00
1873, . .	25,153,399 00	4,192,233 00	408,131	854,250 00

A very large proportion, nearly one-half, of the polls of the Commonwealth is embraced in its cities, the figures for 1873 being as follows:—

No. of polls in state.

Whole number of polls in the state, ...	408,131
" " " " cities, ...	197,687
" " " " towns, ...	210,444

In our largest city the whole number of polls assessed in 1874 was 84,684, of whom 66,415, or over 78 per cent., were assessed on polls only. Undoubtedly, the proportion of voters who pay only a poll-tax is liable, in many places, to be so large, that some general provision is highly desirable for impressing them with a sense of direct pecuniary responsibility for their votes. While the voter in a city cannot throw his ballot directly for or against any certain scheme, yet his power to elect or reject the city officers by whom appropriations are ordered, is hardly inferior to the direct vote cast by a citizen of a town; and there would seem to be the same propriety and advantage in making each feel and bear a certain share of the burdens which great expenditures impose. How many loans of municipal credit have been voted to railroads, which would have been withheld, had the voters who favored them known that their taxes would thereby be increased! Extravagance is as likely to result from careless power over one's neighbor's purse, as is economy likely to follow the necessity of caring for one's own.

Two methods have been proposed for the end desired. The first is to rate the poll-tax at a certain valuation in making up the assessment. Under this method, the person now taxable for his poll, merely, would be entered on the lists at a fixed sum, say $200 or $300, which sum would be carried into the valuation, and on which a tax would be assessed, when the rate should be determined, equal to the amount assessed upon the same amount of real or personal property. This tax would then vary with the rate,—each fresh expenditure swelling its amount. If the assumed valuation were $200, and the rate $10 per thousand, the tax would equal the present maximum poll tax. If the rate were $15 per thousand, it would be $3; if $20 per thousand, $4, and so on. In Monroe, which has the highest rate this year, $41, the poll tax would be $8.20, while in Nahant, with a rate of $5, it would be $1. Whether this would be a just tax in Monroe may be doubted.

The difficulties in this plan seem to be,—

First. The different standards of valuation in the different towns would make it difficult to determine upon an assumed valuation for the poll, which should work substantially equal results throughout the state.

Second. The presence in the valuations of the several cities and towns of these assumed valuations set upon polls, but representing no actual property, would disturb the equalization of the state tax.

Third. There are tax-payers who would be slow to understand the system, and, failing to comprehend it, would not recognize its justice. When the collector presented the tax bill, or they examined the valuation lists and found themselves taxed upon a valuation of two hundred dollars, or any other sum, they would insist that they had no such amount of property, and were therefore entitled to an abatement.

The other system, suggested by the assessors of Marblehead, makes the minimum poll-tax two dollars, and provides that, when the amount of a town tax to be assessed exceeds one per cent. of the valuation of the previous year, the poll tax shall be increased twenty-five per cent., or to two dollars and fifty cents. When the amount to be raised equals or exceeds one and one-half per cent. of the valuation of the previous year, the poll-tax shall be increased fifty per cent., or to three dollars; and when the amount to be raised equals or exceeds two per cent. of the valuation of the previous year, the poll-tax shall be doubled, that is, raised to four dollars.

Under this plan there would be four rates or grades of poll-taxes,—two dollars, two dollars and fifty cents, three dollars and four dollars,—depending upon the proportion which the money voted to be raised bears to the last ascertained valuation of the town. The voter who paid a poll-tax only, would then have a plain and obvious pecuniary interest in keeping down expenditures.

There may, perhaps, be some question whether both of these schemes are not open to criticism, as being contrary to the provision of the constitution respecting "proportional and reasonable assessments." The point is, whether the assessment of an inhabitant upon his poll, at an assumed valuation, in the one case, and, in the other, at a sum determined by the proportion which the amount to be raised bears, not to the whole taxable estates which are to share the burden, but to the valuation of the previous year, is "proportional" in the sense of the constitution.

But it is difficult to see how either of the proposed plans is more open to this objection than the system now in vogue, and which, in substance, has always been in use in the state, both before and after the adoption of the constitution.

A brief glance at the history of the tax in the state will show that the legislature have been in the habit of fixing the poll-tax at an arbitrary sum, or not to exceed an arbitrary limit, either year by year or by general acts.

The rules for assessment and exemption of persons and estates were formerly set down in the several yearly acts granting taxes; and the general direction to assessors, found in chapter 50 of the acts of 1785, section 1, for the assessment of the state tax, is:—

"And the assessors so chosen and sworn, shall assess the polls of, and estates within such town or district, their due proportion of any tax, according to the rules set down in the act for raising the same, and make perfect lists thereof," etc. 1 General Laws of Mass. ed. of 1823, p. 217.

The manner of apportioning and assessing town, county and other rates is thus prescribed in section eight of the same act:—

"Sect. 8. *And be it further enacted*, That all county, town, district, precinct, plantation and parish rates and taxes shall be assessed and apportioned by the assessors of the several towns, districts, plantations, precincts and parishes within this Commonwealth, upon the polls of, and estates within the same, according to the rules that shall, from time to time, be prescribed and set, in and by the then last tax-act of the general court; and such assessors shall cause attested copies," etc., etc. Ib. p. 221-2.

In 1812 and 1813 the poll-tax was twenty-seven cents, with a proviso that it should not exceed one-third part of the whole tax. From 1813 to 1822 it was fourteen cents, with proviso that it should not exceed one-sixth of the whole. This, of course, must be understood to be the poll-tax ordered as part of the state tax; and the several tax acts directed that, "in the assessment of all county, town, parish, or society taxes, the assessors . . . shall assess the polls therein in the same proportion as they may be assessed to pay a state tax." But no poll-tax should be more than one-third or one-sixth of the whole.

In 1829, by the act known as chapter 143 of the year 1828, many matters of assessment were regulated by perpetual act; and, by section three, the assessors were required to assess one-sixth of all taxes upon polls, with a proviso that the whole amount of poll-taxes on any person in any one year, for city, town and county purposes, highway taxes excepted, should not exceed one dollar and fifty cents.

The act of 1859, chapter 157, confined the exception relating to highway taxes to those separately assessed.

Recommendation.

Believing that it is wise and not unconstitutional, we recommend the adoption of a system of taxing polls which shall make the poll-tax increase with the increase of expenditure, and allow it to diminish with its reduction. We regard that to be the best system, for the purpose, which shall fix a minimum and maximum amount of the tax, and make it vary between these amounts with the rate of taxation on property, year by year.

In order to enable the legislature to fix justly the minimum and maximum amounts, and the variations between them, it ought to be able to determine, at least approximately, the proportional ability which the average able-bodied poll-tax-payer, with no taxable property, has to contribute to the public charges,—an interesting problem, for which there are materials more or less valuable, but which your Commissioners have not had sufficient time to elaborate.

If one-sixth of the whole tax of 1873 ($4,192,253) had been imposed upon the 408,131 polls of that year, the poll-tax would have been ten dollars and twenty-seven cents to each person. There were only two towns in the state in 1873 in which the poll-taxes were less than two dollars, and sixty-eight towns in which, by assessing the highway tax separately, the poll-taxes were brought above that sum.

The repeal of the present limitation of the maximum amount would, in most cases, allow the poll-tax to go to a figure which would be clearly unreasonable, while the substitution of a limit, say double in amount, or four dollars, would be to say that, in the great majority of places, the poll-tax should be fixed at that sum.

The adoption of either of the proposed plans would tend, incidentally, to the equalization of valuations through the state, by making them more closely approach the legal standard. While the result now obtained is creditable to the assessors, it is well known that there are some towns whose policy it is to systematically undervalue their estates, for the purpose of escaping their fair share of the state and county taxes. These towns are, however, compelled to spend money, and the result is, that, owing to the low valuation, rates are high. If, in such towns, the poll-tax could be either assessed upon an assumed valuation, or made to increase with the rate of taxation, there would at once be found a body of citizens, powerful in number at least, whose interest would impel them to see to it that valuations should be fairly made.

The practice of assessing highway taxes separately is, no doubt, due to the fact, that towns are thereby enabled practically to increase the poll-tax beyond the two-dollar limit. Since the repeal of the law allowing these taxes 1871, c. 298. to be "worked out," there is, apparently, no other reason for assessing them separately. But, even if legal, this course is indefensible, as the expense of highways ought to be borne by property in a much larger proportion than many other expenses of government.

The Taxation of Personal Property.

While it is by no means clear that under the constitution of the state, it would be possible for the legislature (Constitution of Mass., part 2d, c. I., § I., art. 4.) to exempt personal property from taxation, yet as that instrument is capable of amendment, and as the expediency of such exemption has been a matter of earnest discussion, we have considered the question and present our views thereupon.

All political economists agree that the real estate of a community should be taxed either by a direct assessment or by rating it upon its rental value. But many and conflicting opinions are held with regard to the expediency of the assessment of the various classes of personal property which make so large a part of the wealth of every civilized community. Citizens of our own state have entertained and expressed the opinion that has found official indorsement at the hands of a commission

First Report of New York Commissioners proposing system for that state.

in our sister state of New York* that the difficulties in the way of an equal assessment of personal estate have become so great, that whatever views we may entertain as to the justice of the theory that all property should be taxed, we must yield to the necessary limitations of the case, and frame our revenue laws accordingly. These limitations are supposed to arise in part from the complex nature of the government under which we live, partly from the ease with which personal estate can be moved or concealed, and partly also from the limitations, legal or equitable, incident to the double taxation deemed to exist, when the property, being within the jurisdiction of one state while the owner resides in another, is liable to assessment in both states,—or when a personal estate is assessed, in the form of debts due, or credits, based upon property, which also is assessed to the debtor who has possession.

It is thought we can escape all these limitations by ceasing from direct taxation of personal property, and levying assessments only upon real estate or upon "tangible property and fixed signs or property." Houses and lands cannot be spirited away, nor a man's general style of living be altogether hid, therefore let the assessor only note these evident facts and lay his assessment accordingly. By this means it is claimed, we shall escape the "odious inquisitorial system" which assessments of personal property so often involve; we shall no longer be offering a premium to deception and dishonesty; we shall escape all double taxation, and all doubtful cases between the state and the national government; we shall secure greater efficiency and economy in our financial administration; and, since "all taxes equate and diffuse themselves, if levied with certainty and

Second Report, p. 47.

* Report of the Commissioners—*David A. Wells, Edwin Dodge* and *George W. Cuyler*—appointed to revise the laws for the assessment and collection of taxes in the state of New York. *Albany*, 1871.

Second Report of the same commissioners, with a code of laws relative to assessment and taxation. *Albany*, 1872.

uniformity upon tangible property, and fixed signs of property, they will, by a diffusion and repercussion, reach and burden all visible and also all invisible and intangible property, with unerring certainty and equity."

This scheme having been very ably presented by the New York commissioners, is now receiving a favorable regard in some influential quarters, and strong influences are undoubtedly at work to secure its adoption in that wealthy and powerful state. We will not venture any prediction as to whether these influences are likely or not to succeed, but as there is a possibility of their success, it becomes us to look carefully at the probable result.

Probable effect of the adoption of such a system.

What, then, would be likely to follow in any state which should adopt this method of taxation, and what would be the probable effect upon Massachusetts should such a system be adopted by New York?

Undoubtedly the method has the merit of simplicity and economy of administration. At the first sight it looks well. It would certainly save us much confusion, many perplexities, and innumerable disputes. It would also remove the many inequalities now existing which rise from the peculiar relation of the states to the Federal government.

Since there is much personal property that the government of the United States forbids the individual states to tax, while much is also exempt—though following no uniform law—by the customs or statutes of the different states, an owner of personal property, which is subject to taxation, can change his property at any time into some form exempt from taxation, and thus openly and legally escape his assessments.

All such possibilities, and the consequent inequalities of taxation, together with all fraudulent concealments are clearly obviated by levying the taxes only upon "tangible property and fixed signs of property." Such taxes increasing the burdens upon real estate would have a tendency to diminish its value and thus would be likely to exercise a salutary restraint upon the disposition to speculate in this kind of property.

Moreover, if personal property should be exempt from taxation in an adjoining state like New York, with such close mercantile and social connections with ourselves, such property, if Massachusetts should still continue to tax it, would doubtless have a tendency to betake itself to the more favored locality, and there is certainly ground of inquiry whether the business interests of this community would not thus be gravely threatened, and whether we should not be obliged in self-defence to allow a similar exemption ourselves.

We call the attention of the legislature to these arguments in favor of the system proposed, and beg leave, also, to state the reasons which prevent us from recommending its adoption by this Commonwealth.

Why it should not be adopted here.

We are obliged to take issue at the outset with the eminent authority which insists upon the tendency of "all taxes to equate and diffuse themselves." Such a doctrine has some plausibility. In certain cases taxes will undoubtedly equalize and diffuse themselves; but as a uniform doctrine it is condemned by facts and justified by no sound economical theory. Instead of diffusing themselves, the tendency of taxes is to stay where they are laid,—in other words, the tendency is, that they must be paid by the actual persons upon whom they are levied. Granted that these persons are glad to shift them to some other shoulders if they can, but these other shoulders surely do not covet the burden, and will not receive it unless forced thus to do. It is not thus a natural and easy process for taxes to diffuse themselves, but wherever it is done it requires effort and meets with resistance.

Moreover, if the diffusion of taxes be granted in a given instance; if, for example, a wealthy landholder finding an increasing taxation upon his land raises his rents in a corresponding degree, and thus the tax is not paid by himself but by his tenant, who, in turn, perhaps raises the price of his products proportionately, and thus spreads the tax in a still wider diffusion, the important question arises whether this diffusion is an equal and a just one. It only needs to be closely contemplated to be seen that such a diffusion of taxes might include a very unequal distribution of burdens. If the land in question lie in some crowded locality, specially advantageous for business or dwellings, there would be two classes from whom the owner of the land might probably exact his increasing tax in an increasing rental. The prosperous merchant might perhaps be willing to pay the larger rent, though whether he could reimburse himself by a larger price upon his goods would depend upon other conditions, and would be by no means certain. The poor day-laborer, also, obliged to live near the business centers where work abounds, might also be forced to pay this additional burden; but that he could relieve himself by demanding a corresponding addition to his wages would not at all follow. It would be at least as possible, and, in fact, more likely that the addition to his rent would be followed by a decrease of his previous comforts. But the class able to migrate would be likely to go where they could find cheaper rents, or would be only prevented from doing so by the landlord assuming for himself the burden of the additional tax, or laying it upon others instead of upon them. There would be no equality in the diffusion.

But, added to this, there is another point to be noticed. In this shifting of burdens there is not apt to be an exact equivalence. It is quite likely that the party rolling off the burden will seek to transfer to another a little more than has been laid upon himself. It is natural for him to try to make a profit in the exchange. Thus when the United States government laid a tax of one-eighth of a cent upon each passenger carried in street cars, the proprietors simply added one cent to the fare of each passenger, from which they paid to the government one-eighth and retained seven-eighths themselves. This was, to be sure, a shifting and diffusing of the tax, but with results to those on whom the burden ultimately fell, of which they could properly complain. This illustrates what is likely to be true in all such cases. The burden grows by the shifting. If the landlord is able to increase his rents in order to release himself of some heavier tax upon his land, the increase of the rent is likely to be more than the increase of the tax; and if his tenant is a merchant, or a manufacturer, who endeavors to roll off his burdens upon his customers by charging a heavier price for his goods, his increasing prices are likely to be greater than his increasing rental, and thus the more perfectly the taxes diffuse themselves by this shifting process, the less is the diffusion to be desired.

Still farther, it can hardly be doubted that in this shifting process a disproportionate burden always falls upon the poor. They have no such resources for "shifting" that the wealthier classes possess, and the burdens which have come to settle upon them with this accumulated pressure they are without any means to alleviate.

The whole system of the New York commissioners hinges upon this theory of the natural and equable diffusion of all taxes, and ceases to swing if this hinge be wanting. But as the system has so many advocates urging it with vigor and with much plausibility of statement, we deem it our duty to give in detail the results we have reached from a careful examination of its several positions, and the conclusions which appear from a patient and extended calculation into which we have entered, and which show what would be the effects of its practical application.

A prominent argument urged in favor of the exemption of personal property from taxation, is, that real estate derives its sole value from the amount of personal property expended upon it, and the demand of personal property to possess and use it. Thus the taxation of all land values is a virtual taxing of personal property, upon which, therefore, there should be imposed no other tax. But not only is the general position here assumed unsound, but, even if it were correct, the inference derived from it is fallacious. The value of real estate, like all other value, is the product of labor, and is exactly measured by the amount of labor which it represents. That which costs no labor may be very desirable and useful,—like the air or sunshine,—but it has no value; *i. e.*, it cannot be exchanged for anything,—no one will give anything for it, since every one has all that he needs without any effort. But the value of wealth is seen in the efforts necessary to produce it. Without labor there never could be any wealth. In this respect there is no distinction between real estate and personal property. Both are equally, and in the same way, the product of labor. The reason why a good farm or garden, in the neighborhood of a good market, is more valuable than the same sort of land farther off, or why a lot in a crowded city is worth more than one in the open country, is not because the market-farm is better stocked with personal property, nor because a larger amount of personal property surrounds and presses to occupy the city lot, but because in each case the location is a saving of labor,—in other words, because the advantages which the location gives could only be gained in another less valuable location by an exactly corresponding amount of labor. A city lot is valuable, one is apt to say, according to the number of inhabitants in the city, or the amount of business done there; but all this means that its value consists in its capacity to save labor; *i. e.*, its value is exactly measured by the amount of labor which would elsewhere be necessary to gain the same advantages. The position, therefore, that real estate derives its sole value from the amount of personal property expended on it, is not sound.

But, if it were correct, the inference derived from it is fallacious. For, if personal property confers value upon real estate, this is surely not its sole function. Personal property may have a value quite independent of the real estate which it may occupy, and may, therefore, be taxed for this value without any double taxation.

4

Double relation of the citizen to national and state government considered.

We give full weight to the difficulties in this matter which rise from the double relation of the citizen to the national and state governments; but we are not willing to exaggerate them, and we cannot allow that the different states are thereby estopped from taxing personal property to anything like the degree which the New York commissioners claim. Whatever decision the supreme judicial tribunal of the nation shall lay upon Massachusetts, this Commonwealth will not be slow to accept. Massachusetts has always rendered prompt obedience to the constitution and laws of the nation, as expounded by the highest national court. But Massachusetts is not bound to accept the decisions of the courts of other states where they conflict with the judgments of her own courts, neither need she change her long established revenue system to accord with a verdict, not yet pronounced, of the supreme court of the United States. The power of the legislature and the executive officers of some of the states of our Union has been restrained by the action of their own courts, which have declared that certain classes of personal property, which have been assessed in Massachusetts from its earliest history, cannot in those states be legally taxed. It might be profitable to place against these decisions, those of the tribunals of our own Commonwealth, sustaining assessments similar in character, were it not for the fact that however we may differ from the declared opinions of the highest courts of New York or California, it is the undoubted right of the citizens of those, or any other state, to live under such administration of government as best meets their wishes. If the organic laws of the several states were identical, it would be strange if, with nearly forty independent courts, the decisions upon any given point were uniform. But with constitutions and laws framed to suit the views and interests of the several sovereignties, it is remarkable that, on a subject so important as taxation, the decisions of so many states should be in substantial accord.

Hoyt. v. the Commissioners of New York. 23 N. York, 240.

Parker Mills v. Commissioners of New York. 23 N. York, 242.

San Francisco Savings and Loan Co. v. Austin. 46 California, 415.

The points thus far covered by the judicial decisions of the United States, which limit the legislative action of the different states, we have already noted, and it does not seem to us either necessary or wise that our own tax system, in so far as we still judge it to be sound in principle, and still find it to be satisfactory in its workings, should be now changed in order to accommodate itself to decisions of the supreme court of the United States, which, even if some anticipate them as probable, have not yet been actually given. When the action of the United States, or any of our sister states, makes a change in our system necessary, we may safely leave to the people and legislators, at the time, the performance of the duty which would then be laid upon them. Recent decisions would seem to indicate that the United States supreme court has found the limitations of its own rule, and that the states, within the restrictions now laid upon them, will be permitted to frame such assessment laws as best subserve their interests. Unnecessary to change our system on account of United States decisions.

In deciding the case of Lane County *v.* Oregon, Chief Justice Chase declared that,— 7 Wallace, p. 77.

"In respect to *property*, *business*, and *persons* within their respective limits, the power of taxation of the states remained and remains entire. It is, indeed, a concurrent power, and, in the case of a tax upon the same subject by both governments, the claim of the United States as the supreme authority must be preferred; but with this qualification, it is absolute. The extent to which it shall be exercised, and the mode in which it shall be exercised, are all equally within the discretion of the legislatures to which the states commit the exercise of the power. That discretion is restrained only by the will of the people, expressed in the state constitutions, or through elections, and by the condition that it must not be so used as to burden or embarrass the operations of the national government. There is nothing in the constitution which contemplates or authorizes any direct abridgment of this power by national legislation. To the extent just indicated, it is just as complete in the states as the like power, within the limits of the constitution, is complete in Congress."

Union Pacific Railroad v. Penniston, 18 Wallace, 29.

And, in a case decided within the last year, Justice Strong, delivering the opinion of the court, after referring to the case above quoted, re-affirms the principle that,—

"The taxing power of a state is one of its sovereign attributes; that it exists independently of the constitution of the United States, and underived from that instrument, and that it may be exercised to an unlimited extent upon all *property*, *trades*, *business*, and *avocations*, existing, or carried on, within the territorial boundaries of the state, except so far as it has been surrendered to the Federal government, either expressly or by necessary implication, are propositions that have often been asserted by this court, and in thus acknowledging the extent of the power to tax belonging to the states, we have declared that it is indispensable to their continued existence. No one ever doubted that, before the adoption of the constitution of the United States, each of the states possessed unlimited power to tax, either directly or indirectly, all *persons* and *property* within their jurisdiction, alike by taxes on polls, or duties on internal production, manufacture, or use, except so far as such taxation was inconsistent with certain treaties which had been made; and the constitution contains no express restriction of this power, other than a prohibition to lay any duty of tonnage, or any impost, or duty on imports or exports, except what may be absolutely necessary for executing the state's inspection laws."

Can our laws for assessment of personal property be executed?

But can our laws respecting the assessment of personal property be executed?

We are told by a certain class of political economists that, if all the courts, both national and state, should, instead of restraining the action of executive officers, aid them to the utmost of their power in the execution of all tax laws that might be framed by the state governments, the operation of natural laws, and the ease with which large amounts of personal property can be concealed by those who seek to evade their share of the public burdens, would render all efforts on the part of the most efficient officials of no avail in the attempt to assess an equal tax. If this position could be proved, it would still be a question whether it would not be the duty of the state to maintain as vigorous a conflict as possible with those who refuse to obey her laws; and, even if she failed to achieve that uniform assessment which is the ideal standard, approximate as closely to it as her power would permit.

But has the Commonwealth been brought to the condition of being compelled to consider if it is possible to execute her laws in relation to the assessment of personal property?

That personal property in Massachusetts, declared by her laws to be subject to taxation, does in some degree escape assessment, it is impossible to deny. The most vigilant of assessors cannot find it all, and there are not wanting those in every community, willing to invoke the name of their Creator to the truth of a statement which is a falsehood and a fraud. There are not wanting officers who shut their eyes to the facts they have sworn to observe, in the supposed interests of the locality of which they are residents, and help the possessors of wealth to act the lie they dare not utter.

The numerous boards of equalization common in other states, but unknown to Massachusetts law, attest the fact that this Commonwealth has, to say the least, no larger share of such officials than falls to the lot of other communities. But when the laws against burglary, arson, and homicide are always executed, and when no thief, incendiary or murderer escapes the penalty of his crime, it will, perhaps, be time to consider if the state will give up her attempt to equally assess all property, and, yielding to the difficulties of the case, place her burdens where they cannot be evaded, and extort her revenue from those too powerless to resist. But if it shall be found that the laws of this state have been executed in the past, and that, notwithstanding the restrictions placed upon the assessment of personal estate by the authority of the United States, it still bears over thirty per cent. of the burden of taxation, it would seem clearly not impossible to compel the holders of this class of property to contribute materially to the general expense.

Argument from the collection of United States taxes in Massachusetts.

Whatever may be the opinion of the people of Massachusetts as to the equity of an income tax, it will be admitted that this tax, as levied by the United States, with its accompanying assessments for internal revenue, was not popular with the people of this or of any other section of the country. After the war of the rebellion had been brought to a successful issue, public sentiment, as represented by "the press," all over the country, demanded its repeal. Unpopular as it was, however, the people of Massachusetts, in the United States fiscal year ending June 30, 1868, were assessed a tax exceeding eighteen millions of dollars upon personal property and income, much of it incorporeal, and most of it depending on the oath of the person assessed for the amount of the assessment, and it was collected with a loss of less than two per cent., as shown by the following table:—

	Assessments.	Collections.
District No. 1,	$1,192,390 95	$998,155 64
2,	1,069,015 10	1,115,909 07
3,	5,445,568 67	5,104,626 57
4,	1,773,171 99	1,798,537 96
5,	1,077,218 77	1,071,755 77
6,	1,772,490 19	1,683,457 17
7,	2,070,189 57	1,989,092 67
8,	1,533,716 67	1,528,267 22
9,	897,284 69	948,553 75
10,	1,352,549 68	1,615,176 92
Total,	$18,183,596 28	$17,853,523 74

But it may be objected that this large tax was taken from the people by the power of the United States, upon whose government and officers the people of any section have but an indirect influence, and that it would have been as useless for the people of the state to have resisted or evaded the tax, as for a citizen of a town to contend against the tax of the Commonwealth enforced by the sheriff's officer. There may be force in the argument. Then let us see with what weight a personal-property tax can be laid, and with what vigor collected, in a community where all the executive officers, both assessors and collector, are elected by a government which, in its turn, is elected by the citizens who must pay the taxes. It will be admitted that, the larger the municipality, the more difficult it is to closely assess or collect any tax that can be evaded. In the country, where every citizen is personally acquainted with every inhabitant, evasion can be made practically impossible. The best place to hide from the tax-gatherer is not the wilderness, but the great city. With its facilities for concealment, years will sometimes elapse before its tax list of a given year will be considered closed, and the balance uncollectible. Under these conditions, take the statistics of our largest city, and see if it is impossible to assess and collect a personal property tax.

From collection of personal property tax in Boston.

In the year 1870, the tax of Boston was based upon 56,926 polls, a valuation of $365,593,100 real, and $218,496,300 personal estate,—a total of $584,089,400. The rate was 1.53 per cent., or $15.30 on the $1,000. The warrant committed to the collector amounted to $9,052,841.21. It was the largest tax that had ever been, at that date, assessed in the city. The rate had risen from 1.37 per cent. for the preceding year, and the conditions for a favorable collection were below the average. On the first day of May, 1874, there remained of this tax uncollected upon the books of the treasurer, $92,992.49, or 1.026 per cent. of the whole amount committed to him to collect. Admitting that the real estate tax is collected in full, the amount uncollected, as against polls and personal estate, rises to 2.785 per cent. of the sum assessed against those two items of the levy. But as nearly all the alien polls, and those of some of the citizens, are claimed to be uncollectible, except at an expense exceeding the amount of the tax; and, as it appears that of the $92,992.46 not yet realized, that $53,040 are due on polls, it shows that of the amount of $3,342,993.39 (over 36 per cent. of the entire tax levy assessed upon personal estate as defined by Massachusetts), only 1.193 per cent. of the whole sum remains uncollected.

With such results, it cannot be claimed that it is impossible to execute laws requiring personal property to be assessed.

The policy or impolicy of assessing personal property.

But it is said by those who believe that personal property should not be assessed: "If the state can make and execute such laws, it is suicidal to do so. Your own best interests are sacrificed in attempting an equality of assessment which, at best, is only approximately attainable. If you have prospered, it has not been because of your action, but in spite of it. Your prosperity would have been greater and your people happier, if you had followed the better way which we have marked out; and if you do not walk in this path, others will, and your wealth, and, consequently, your power, will pass away, to find a place where wiser laws prevail." If these views could be demonstrated, the state would be wanting in that regard for the best interests of its citizens,—which is one of its highest duties,—as well as in common prudence, if it did not at once abandon its methods and shape its policy by better plans.

It has been said that many men, apparently in perfect health, carry within them the seeds of that disease which, ultimately, will lay them low. But we should not advise a man to begin to take unpalatable medicine before the symptoms of sickness appear.

It may be that the Commonwealth, in her policy of compelling personal property to bear its share of the common charges, has planted the seeds of her own decay; but it would seem to be only prudent to postpone the bitter experience of raising needed revenues by levying unequal assessments, until necessity shall compel such action. Meanwhile her citizens, while carefully guarding her well-being, may be pardoned if they congratulate themselves that the state as yet shows no signs of decay.

By the census of 1870,* in the family of thirty-seven sister states, while but three were smaller in area than our own, only three could show a larger valuation of real and personal estate, and only six could show a larger population.

The area of the states exceeding our own in the number of their inhabitants, so greatly exceeds the area of this Commonwealth, that the most populous and wealthy of them all contains within in its borders but a little more than one-half the number of persons to the square mile that are supported upon the soil of Massachusetts. The state that leads the Union in population and wealth has but three times as much accumulated capital as Massachusetts, although its more fertile soil covers more than four times the area of the Commonwealth, and contains within its limits one of the noblest rivers of the continent, —which divides its territory from north to south,—and has for more than half a century been divided from west to east by one of the great artificial highways of the world.

With such evidences of general prosperity, with a constantly increasing valuation throughout the Commonwealth,† which even the destruction of the business

* Area by Census, 1870.		Valuation by Census, 1870.		Population by Census, 1870.		
				Total.		To Sq. Mile.
Mass.,	7,800 sq. m.	N. York,	$6,500,841,264	N. Y.,	4,382,759	65.90
				Penn.,	3,521.951	50.26
Conn.,	4,750 sq. m.	Penn., .	3,808,340,112	Ohio, .	2,665,260	49.55
				Ill., .	2,539,891	15.37
Del.,	2,120 sq. m.	Ohio, .	2,235,430,300	Mo., .	1,721,295	10.44
				Ind., .	1,680,637	29.24
R. I.,	1,306 sq. m.	Mass., .	2,132,148,741	Mass.,	1,457,351	127.50

† Aggregate of valuations by assessors, for the whole State:—

1870, ...	$1,417,127,376	1873, ...	$1,763,429,990
1871, ...	1,497,351,686	1874, ...	1,831,601,165
1872, ...	1,696,599,969		

Loss by the great fire in Boston, November 9 and 10, 1872, . $75,000,000

centre of her chief city and the exceptional financial derangement of the present time have not materially checked, it will be well to wait until the indications of disease or decay become somewhat marked before we leave a path that has led to results thus far successful.

First report of New York commissioners. The first report of the New York commissioners (February, 1871) recommended that all laws in relation to taxes assessed by authority of the state, be repealed; and that, for the purpose of obtaining the necessary revenue for the state, certain corporations should be taxed by methods very similar to those in use in Massachusetts. For the remainder of the scheme, the commissioners recommended that the legislature adopt one of two plans, either of which, they were of opinion, would make a just and equal assessment.

First plan. The first of these plans was to assess all *land* at *one-half* of its market value, and all *buildings* at their *full* value. Second plan. The second plan was to assess all *real estate* (land and buildings) at *one-half* their value, and then to tax the occupier of every building, whether owner or tenant, on three times the annual rental of the estate. In other words, assuming ten per cent. of the full value to be the gross rental of the estate, three times its rental, added to the fifty per cent., or the amount of its assessment as realty, would make an *occupied* estate stand in the scale for taxation at *eighty per cent.* of its value, and *unoccupied* real estate at *fifty per cent.* of its value.

Second report. By the second report, made in February, 1872, the commissioners would seem to have abandoned their previous plans, for, without reference to them, they proceed to lay down their objections to existing systems in substantially the same form as in their first report, and give, Third plan. as *the* plan which they endorse, the recommendation that moneyed corporations be taxed as under existing laws, that *land and buildings* be taxed at *full value*, and that all occupiers of buildings, for whatever purpose used, be assessed upon three times the rental value of their premises,—confining the area of the land assessed for rental value to that immediately connected with the buildings. Under each of these plans, all property, of every kind and nature, other than that included in the several schemes, would be free from all taxes.

Result of first plan shown.

When the first report of the commissioners was made public, their plans were tested by the valuations made in the city of Boston, on the first day of May preceding, for the tax of the current year. The results obtained were as follows: The assessment of May, 1870, in Boston, was based upon 56,926 polls,—$365,593,100 real, and $218,496,300 personal estate,—total valuation, $584,089,400. The amount of the warrant committed to the collector was $9,050,419.82, and the rate of tax $15.30 on a thousand. Actual cases were taken as representatives of classes, beginning with those who had the minimum amount of property, as found among the tax-payers, and ascending the social scale to the wealthiest citizens. The result which the supposed assessment of a tax of $9,050,419, upon the first plan of the commissioners (which required all land to be taken at half value and all buildings at full value), and which produced a valuation of $258,661,713 and a rate of $34.60 per thousand, as placed against the actual assessment of the tax against the same persons under the Massachusetts system, was as follows:—

OCCUPATION.	Real Estate.	Personal Estate.	Total Valuation.	Taxes at $15.30 per $1,000.				Buildings at full value and land at 50 per cent. of value.	Taxes at $34.60 per $1,000.	Taxes decreased.	Per cent. of decrease.	Taxes increased.	Per cent. of increase.
				Poll.	Real.	Personal.	Total.						
Merchant, . .	$150,000	$550,000	$700,000	$2 00	$2,295 00	$8,415 00	$10,712 00	$104,000	$3,598 40	$7,113 60	66	-	-
Capitalist, . .	148,000	1,000,000	1,148,000	2 00	2,264 40	15,300 00	17,566 40	109,100	3,774 86	13,791 54	78	-	-
Lawyer, . .	70,600	400,000	470,600	2 00	1,080 18	6,120 00	7,202 18	48,900	1,691 94	5,510 24	76	-	-
Merchant, . .	57,000	250,000	307,000	2 00	872 10	3,825 00	4,699 10	44,250	1,531 05	3,168 05	67	-	-
Merchant, . .	40,000	255,000	295,000	2 00	612 00	3,901 50	4,515 50	30,250	1,046 65	3,468 85	77	-	-
Cashier, . .	10,000	2,000	12,000	2 00	153 00	30 60	185 60	8,600	297 56	-	-	$111 96	60
Clergyman, .	7,200	1,000	8,200	2 00	110 16	15 30	127 46	6,200	214 52	-	-	87 06	68
Lawyer, . .	9,200	2,000	11,200	2 00	140 76	30 60	173 36	7,850	264 69	-	-	91 33	53
Public Officer, .	6,400	1,500	7,900	2 00	97 92	22 95	122 87	6,000	207 60	-	-	84 73	69
Mechanic, . .	2,100	-	2,100	2 00	32 13	-	34 13	1,850	64 01	-	-	29 88	88

A test of the second plan is shown in the following table. This plan requires real estate (land and buildings) to be taken at *one-half* its value, and occupants of buildings to be assessed on three times their rental value. Allowing ten per cent. (the proposed rate) as the annual rental value of each improved estate, and four per cent. for the annual rental value of unimproved vacant land, marshes and flats, the rental valuation was found to be $100,792,066,—half the value of the real estate, $182,796,-550,—the total valuation $283,588,616, and the rate to raise the required amount of tax, $31.50. The result obtained was as follows:— Result of second plan shown.

[The column of total tax at $15.30 is transferred from preceding table]

Occupation.	Total tax at $15.30, as by preceding table.	Fifty per ct. value of real estate.	Three times rental val. of dwellings.	Total taxable valuation by proposed plan.	Amount of tax at $31.50.	Taxes decreased.	Per ct. of decrease.	Taxes increased.	Per ct. of increase.
Merchant, .	$10,712 00	$75,000	$45,000	$120,000	$3,780 00	$6,932 00	65	-	-
Capitalist, .	17,566 40	74,000	44,400	118,400	3,729 60	13,836 80	79	-	-
Lawyer, .	7,202 18	35,300	21,180	56,480	1,779 12	5,423 06	75	-	-
Merchant, .	4,699 10	28,500	17,100	45,600	1,436 40	3,262 70	69	-	-
Merchant, .	4,515 50	20,000	12,000	32,000	1,008 00	3,507 50	78	-	-
Cashier, .	185 60	5,000	3,000	8,000	252 00	-	-	66.40	35
Clergyman, .	127 46	3,600	2,160	5,760	181 44	-	-	53.98	43
Lawyer, .	173 36	4,600	2,760	7,360	231 84	-	-	58.48	34
Pub. Officer,	122 87	3,200	1,920	5,120	161 28	-	-	38.41	31
Mechanic, .	34 13	1,050	630	1,680	52 92	-	-	18.79	55

Why, during the twelve months that elapsed between the time of making their first and second report, the commissioners should have abandoned their previous plans, and recommended one based upon a *full valuation of land and buildings*, they do not explain. Possibly the injustice of assessing a given amount invested in buildings twice as much as the same amount invested in land, and the unquestionable effect of fixing a disproportionate amount of the burden of a state tax based upon such a valuation upon the cities and larger towns, may have induced the change. As applied to the city of Boston this third plan of the commissioners, to assess all real estate (land and buildings) at *full value*, and all occupiers of buildings at three times their rental value, produced a valuation of real estate of $365,593,100,—rental value, $100,792,066,—total, $466,385,166. Rate per thousand, to raise $9,050,-419,—$19.45. By this scheme the reduction in the rate, as compared with the second plan, was met by an exactly corresponding increase in the amount of real estate held for assessment. The table showing its results as to the amount of tax, is the almost exact counterpart of the table that shows the effect of the second plan.

Result of the third plan shown.

OCCUPATION.	Total tax at $15.30, as by preceding table.	Full value of real estate.	Three times rental val. of dwellings.	Total taxable valuation by proposed plan.	Amount of tax at $19.45.	Taxes decreased.	Per ct. of decrease.	Taxes increased.	Per ct. of increase.
Merchant, .	$10,712 00	$150,000	$45,000	$195,000	$3,782 75	$6,929 25	65	-	-
Capitalist, .	17,566 40	148,000	44,400	192,400	3,740 78	13,825 62	79	-	-
Lawyer, .	7,202 18	70,600	21,180	91,780	1,785 16	5,417 02	75	-	-
Merchant, .	4,699 10	57,000	17,100	74,100	1,441 24	3,257 86	69	-	-
Merchant, .	4,515 50	40,000	12,000	52,000	1,011 40	3,504 10	78	-	-
Cashier, .	185 60	10,000	3,000	13,000	252 85	-	-	67.25	36
Clergyman,	127 46	7,200	2,160	9,360	182 15	-	-	54.69	43
Lawyer, .	173 36	9,200	2,760	11,960	232 52	-	-	59.16	34
Pub.Offic'r,	122 87	6,400	1,920	8,320	160 82	-	-	37.95	31
Mechanic, .	34 13	2,100	630	2,730	53 09	-	-	18.86	55

The preceding tables have of necessity been based upon the assumption that the tax of the state was apportioned among the cities and towns as provided by the law in force in 1870.

Other results of the plans of the N. Y. commissioners.

The second and third plans would undoubtedly raise the taxes of all the persons whose valuations are shown in the tables (above the amount there indicated), and of all others in cities and towns, who like them live upon house-lots to a considerable extent, by reason of the large amount of unoccupied land in farming districts which would not be held for the rental tax.

By the first plan, the rates of some of these persons would be materially raised by the practical exemption of nearly one-half the value of a farm, or of any land where its value formed a large percentage of the value of the whole estate.

By the second and third plans, the amount being raised by a per cent. increase upon all the classes represented, there would be a remittance of taxes to the farmers and to the speculators in town lots and other unoccupied land—the former of whom would be partly and the latter wholly free from the rental tax.

By the first plan the amounts remitted largely to the farmers and speculators would be shared in, to some extent, by the most valuable estates in the thickly-settled communities, where a large proportion of their value is in the land. Of course, in every case the amounts remitted to any class must be made up by the others.

One thing is common to all the plans proposed,—they discriminate heavily against the occupiers of buildings. Want of equality in plans.

Even if the New York commissioners can demonstrate that taxation under their plans can be made with *uniformity* among *classes*, it is not easy to see, with such results as these tables have given (which were taken from, or based on, the valuations of Boston, because her statistics were easily attainable), how they can convince themselves, or any one, that assessments can be made by their methods, that will produce *equality* among the *citizens* of the Commonwealth.

In this connection it may be well to see what some of those who have to deal with this subject in older countries have to say upon this question.

Imperial taxation in England, which corresponds for this nation, to the sums raised by assessments of all kinds Imperial taxation in England.

for the revenue of the United States, bears but lightly on real estate.

Report and speeches on lo- local taxation. Geo. J. Goschen, M. P. London, 1872, pp. 36–7.

By a table in the report of the President of the Poor Law Board to the Lords of the Treasury, it appears that out of a total revenue for England and Wales for the year 1868, amounting to £46,653,000, less than £5,700,000, or 12.17 per cent. of the whole tax was based upon real estate. Of the remaining £41,000,000, over £30,000,-000 were collected from customs and excise. This large amount was derived through duties upon imports, and by methods similar to those of the United States internal revenue,—mainly from wines, distilled and fermented liquors, tea, coffee, sugar and tobacco. Of the £5,677,000 which is charged on the real estate, £1,785,000 is an income tax based on rents received, which the owners are prohibited by law from placing upon their tenants by any contract. The items of £571,000 for succession duty, £1,033,500 for stamps upon deeds, and £143,000 for a portion of probate duty, would seem difficult of transfer to the occupiers. We may assume, then,—in order to give every weight to the argument,—that the remaining items of £1,082,000 for land tax, and £1,062,000 for house tax,—a total of £2,144,000, or about 4⅓ per cent. of all,—is the amount of imperial tax carried by the occupiers of England and Wales.

The amount of local taxation, corresponding to our state, county and town taxes, for the same year, for that part of Great Britain, was £16,600,000.

Henry Fawcett, M. P., in the "Fortnightly Review," May, 1873.

These taxes are thus described: "With a few exceptions, all local taxation is confined to levying rates on land, houses and business premises. The exceptions to which I refer are certain tolls and dues, and in a few instances some commodity, such as coal, is subjected to a special local tax. It often happens, however, that the toll or due is simply the price charged for a distinct service rendered, and therefore can hardly be regarded as taxation." "In such a case, it would be as unfair to consider these charges as taxes as it would be to consider as taxation the price paid for a telegram, or for the postage of a letter."

England seems to be no exception to the rule that local taxation is pressing upon every civilized community with ever-increasing force.

The popular discontent, with added burdens, compelled the British government to give special attention to the matter.

The report of the President of the Poor Law Board affirms that the great burden of the rates rests upon the occupiers. From the effect of ancient laws, drawn in the interest of owners of the soil, and of judicial decisions under them, nearly all of the *increase* of the rates for many years has been borne by the occupiers.

Report, etc., Geo. J. Goschen, M. P. London, 1872.

As stated in the speech of Mr. Goschen in the House of Commons, in April, 1871, on "the local government and house-rating bill," "If the taxation upon real property were divided into two portions, it would be found that the rates have increased infinitely more upon houses than upon land." In his report he states that "house property in England is very heavily taxed."

P. 182.

P. 50.

As a measure of reform the bill of the government may be briefly outlined as follows:

It was proposed that numerous local boards, each assessing its own rate, should be abolished, and all local taxes be assessed by one board of assessors in each parish,—adopting practically for the English unit, "the parish," our methods as applied to "towns." It was also proposed to yield from the imperial, for the benefit of the local revenues, the house tax, amounting to about $5,000,000 annually. As a further measure of relief for the occupiers, it was proposed to sweep away certain exemptions which the soil had enjoyed under the Act of Queen Elizabeth, and other ancient laws, and to compel the land to contribute, by providing that one-half of the increase of rates should be borne by the owner, whose contract with his tenant, if he should attempt to oblige him to carry the whole burden, was to be declared void.

Reform bill of the English government.

Rental values.

The local rates in England have always been levied upon rental values, and the government did not propose to change the method, except in the case of a large landed estate, where four per cent. of market value was to be taken in lieu of the rental value; as it was rightly claimed that the actual rental of such an estate was not a fair index of its true value.

English government plan similar to that of N. Y. commissioners.

It will be observed that the plan is strikingly similar, if not identical in its effect, to that proposed by the New York commissioners.

Report, etc., Geo. J. Goschen, 1872, p. 204.

This similarity of method probably did not escape the notice of the English minister; for, in his speech, after quoting the plans of the commissioners with approbation, he says: "Mr. Wells concludes that the house a man lives in is the best test of what he can pay, *pointing to England as offering a model system of local taxation because it has adopted that test.*"

In his attempt to persuade the country that his scheme should be adopted, he did not assert, as do the New York commissioners, that the burden would be *equitably* adjusted, as our citizens understand the term, but, offering his system as the best possible under existing circumstances, did "not claim or admit that local or indeed any taxation should be adjusted by a rule-of-three sum."

p. 148.

R. Dudley Baxter, "Review of Report on Local Taxation," London, 1874.

The view that taxes laid upon real estate, to be diffused through the occupier, are not equitably adjusted, finds expression through a gentleman of acknowledged ability as a statistician, who, in a review of the government report above quoted, expresses his opinion in these words: "Rates reach everybody, and every one is interested in their diminution. They fall heaviest on the deserving poor, who are struggling to keep above pauperism. They press with great severity on working men who own and occupy their own land and houses."

The New York commissioners, as one of their strongest arguments for the discontinuance of taxation upon all personal property, rely upon the fact that the states of the American Union alone impose this class of assessments; and that all European countries, and notably England, have long since outgrown such methods, and that there is no probability of their ever again being adopted where once laid aside. Yet it is a singular fact that the bill of the English ministry was defeated under the lead of those who did not share this view.

In the volume containing the report of Mr. Goschen, will be found a speech delivered by him, February 28, 1871, in opposition to a resolution of Sir Massey Lopes, that declared—

"That, inasmuch as many of the existing and contemplated charges on the local rates are for national purposes, and that it is neither just nor politic that such charges should be levied exclusively from one description of property (viz., houses and land), this house is of opinion that it is the duty of the government to inquire forthwith into the incidence of imperial as well as local taxation, and take such steps as shall insure that *every description of property* shall equitably contribute to all national burdens." Report, etc., Geo. J. Goschen, 1872, p. 177.

In the same work will be found an important letter from Julian Goldsmid, Esq., M. P., in which that gentleman says, "I can see no reason why those who derive large incomes from *personal property* should not pay something more than income tax towards the national burdens." p. 144.

The views of these members, and of those who acted with them, commanded a sufficient number of votes in the House of Commons to prevent the passage of the government bill. Bill withdrawn May 8, 1871. Hansard's Debates, 3d series, vol. ccvi., p. 399.

It would certainly be a remarkable incident if the Parliament of England should be found imposing personal-property taxes at a time when some of the states of our Union are discontinuing their use.

It would seem, at first view, that the vast amounts of money needed for local taxation could not be raised unless the large amounts of personal property held by the wealthy are directly assessed. But a very slight examination of the statistics available, will convince any who doubt the fact, Can large revenues be obtained from the middle and poorer classes.

that the money can be raised if the people will bear the burden.

National income of the United Kingdom, R. Dudley Baxter. London, 1868.

Mr. Baxter, in a recent work, has estimated the *annual* income of the United Kingdom at £814,119,000. Of this enormous sum, larger than the national debt of Great Britain, he puts the income of those persons who receive annually not exceeding £300 each, at £516,915,000, or sixty-three per cent. of the whole amount.

Essays on political and social science. Wm. R. Greggs. Vol. 2. London, 1853. Vol. 1, p. 247.

Another writer states that, at the period at which he wrote, "The exemption of all houses under £20 (annual rent), and all incomes under £150, exempted six-sevenths of all dwellings, and nine-tenths of all incomes in the country, from direct taxation."

Auditor's report city of Boston, 1870–71, p. 277.

To take an illustration from our own locality. In 1870, of the 27,384 dwellings in Boston, 22,681, or eighty-three per cent. of the whole number, were under $10,000 in value; 16,089, or fifty-nine per cent. of all, were under $5,000 valuation, It was found, as nearly as possible, that one-half of the *value* of these dwelling-houses was in the hands of the middle and less favored classes. The aggregate of all above and all below $10,000, was $89,000,000, for each class respectively.

It is into the great classes of the poor and those of moderate means that indirect taxes diffuse themselves in the exact proportion of the necessary expenditure of their members; and from these classes will always come the great bulk of any revenue based upon consumption.

An English observer of the incidence of British taxation, expresses his view of the probable result of their methods in the following remark :—

Cobden and modern political opinion. James E. Thorold Rogers. London, 1873, p. 215.

"It may seem a sinister prediction, but I feel persuaded that nothing but the acquiescence, at no distant date, in a genuine property tax, will silence the demand for such fiscal claims as those with which Mr. Mill has identified himself in the programme of the Land Tenure Reform League. The property classes may find it expedient to come to terms in good time. Confiscation is an ugly word, but it may be retaliated, for there is no confiscation more gross and more irritating, when it is once understood, than that which leaves untaxed the luxury of the rich, and visits the earnings of the poor with crushing exactions."

Without further comment, we may leave the report of the New York commissioners. If the people of that state desire for themselves the experience of England in the distribution of their local burdens, they can unquestionably attain that object by adopting methods similar to those which have long been in use in that country. But it may be observed, that it is unfortunate for those among us who believe in such schemes, and desire their success and perpetuity, that their disproportionate burden will fall upon a class, outnumbering, in the ratio of three to one, all others in the community, and in whose hands is lodged the political power of the country.

But, in passing from the topic, it is proper to notice that, as yet, none of the recommendations of the commissioners have been adopted, and that the comptroller of the state, in his last report, expresses the opinion that—

Report of comptroller of New York, January 1, 1874.

"The people are becoming sensitive and uneasy under the increasing burden of taxation; and if, in addition to this burden, already grievous to be borne, those upon whom it is imposed are made aware that it is unfairly and unequally imposed, that those who are most able to bear it are allowed to escape it, in whole or in part, it requires no great amount of prophetic intelligence to predict that the time is not far distant, when the people will rise up against this injustice and oppression, and will refuse to enforce the collection of taxes so unfairly, unequally and inequitably imposed." "The object the legislature should seek to accomplish is, to distribute the burden of taxation equally upon the taxable property of the state, and, if possible, compel all property, real and personal, to be assessed its full value." "It is obvious that any other rule makes taxation unequal, and unjust."

p. 49.

While the state assessors, who act as a board of equalization, remark, that—

Report of state assessors of New York, January 21, 1874, p. 14.

"It is safe to say that the majority of farms yield less than five per cent. of their value, while much personal property aggregated in insurance, trust, safe-deposit and other companies and banks, pay semi-annual dividends of five per cent. over and above all taxes and expenses, and accumulate large sums in surplus, or dividends, far beyond seven per cent. Instead of exempting all personal property from taxation, as has been proposed, we find a very general feeling, we may say a demand, outside the larger cities, that some system of taxation, either by license or other mode, shall be devised to release the real estate from the burden now so onerous. Much can be done in that direction with our present law, if the proper means are used to enforce it."

Plan of City Commissioner Andrew, of New York, Oct. 6, 1874.

George H. Andrews, Esq., one of the commissioners of taxes and assessments of New York city, in a recent address before the committee on ways and means of his state assembly, while objecting to the plan of Mr. Wells and his associate commissioners, advocated that the state take to itself the full revenue of its corporations, exempting, however, manufacturing companies from all assessment other than the taxation of their real estate. For local purposes, for the needed revenue of cities and towns, his scheme proposes the taxation, at full value, of the real estate,—all other property to be exempt.

As public attention has been somewhat attracted to this plan, we would say that its effect can be easily estimated as applied to our Commonwealth.

Its effect if applied in Massachusetts.

As the revenue from our Massachusetts corporations and national banks closely approximates the amount of our state tax, its immediate effect, so far as the whole Commonwealth is concerned, is as though there were no state tax, and the whole amount of county and town assessments were borne by real estate. The only qualification this statement requires, is occasioned by the proposed exemption of manufacturing corporations. To the extent that there might be value in the shares above the worth of the real estate of the companies, such exemption would add to the weight of local taxation, by a state tax, to supply the deficiency. Its effect in relieving cities and towns of state taxation on the one hand, and on the other of depriving them of revenue from these corporations in the proportion as their citizens are stockholders, is shown by a table in the Appendix, page 554. Like the plan of the New York commissioners, its burden is diffused in proportion to consumption; and it is open to the same objections that lie against their methods.

Plan to tax "tangible things" only.

Another scheme of taxation which, as yet, has not received official endorsement, but which by many citizens is believed to be the best solution of the difficulties that surround this subject, is a proposition to assess real and personal estate uniformly, but *to tax tangible things* only. This plan proposes to exempt all bonds, notes, mortgages, shares, debts, or other *evidences* of property, and assess only the *actual property itself* in the place where it is located.

William Endicott, Jr., Esq., has prepared a paper upon this view of the subject, which will be found in the Appendix, page 407.

It is easy to see that under this plan, a class of citizens of large property would contribute nothing to the revenues of the state, except the indirect tax upon them through their expenditure. The loss of the direct tax they now pay under our present system would, consequently, have to be made up by a heavier assessment of the owners of *tangible* property.

This plan is less objectionable than those we have been considering, because to the extent that personal estate is held for assessment, the real estate of the occupiers (owner or tenant) is relieved from direct taxation.

Probable results of the adoption of new methods in adjoining States.

It does not seem to us to be a matter of special anxiety to the people of this Commonwealth, if any of these proposed systems of taxation should become the methods of adjoining states. The results which we have indicated as likely to follow their adoption, would be likely also, in our judgment, to secure their reversal. If personal property should be exempt from taxation in New York while still taxable here, the tendency of this class of wealth to forsake us would find much opposition in other tendencies, also strong. There is always a considerable reluctance of capital to emigrate. To secure its transfer from one locality to another requires large inducements. There are persons with large wealth who, in order to escape a high rate of taxation in the place where they have been wont to reside, acquire a residence, fictitious or real, in some place where the rate is lower. But honesty is a strong check with many people against such a course; and where honesty is wanting, social pride is likely to interpose a strong counteracting pressure; while a removal of residence, for such a purpose, beyond the bounds of the state, would find many hindrances which it would need strong and very clear advantages to overcome.

But the effects of new systems elsewhere should be closely observed, and the best interests of our people, as a whole, should govern our policy.

Massachusetts rule of assessment, General Court, Boston, May 14, 1634, vol. 1 of Records, p. 78.

More than two hundred years ago our fathers enacted as the equitable rule of assessment, that, "It is further ordered that, in all rates and public charges, the town shall have respect to levy every man according to his estate, and with consideration of all other his abilities whatsoever, and not according to the number of his persons." Under the principle then laid down we are governed to-day, and our ancient Commonwealth should not be among the first to abandon methods under which she has prospered.

Recommendation on taxation of personal property.

We are therefore of opinion that if the legislature has the power under the constitution to exempt personal estate from taxation, it is not expedient that such exemption should be made.

The Tax on Income.

No one of our taxes reveals so great a lack of uniformity in its construction and enforcement, and such a wide difference of opinion as to its worth, as is found with reference to the income tax. This tax has always held a prominent place in our system of taxation. Some of the early tax acts convey the impression that, substantially, the whole tax contemplated was in the nature of an income tax,—it being arbitrarily assumed that the income from certain kinds of property would be as rated in the act, while the valuation of each person for assessment was arrived at by adding to the assumed income his actual gains in other ways. In such acts, unimproved lands were directed to be entered at two per cent. of their actual value, and improved land and personal estate at six.

The following extract from a law of 1646 will show that the design of this tax was to reach an ability which would otherwise escape :—

"And for all such persons as, by the advantage of their arts and trades, are more enabled to help bear the public charge than common laborers and workmen, as butchers, bakers, brewers, victualers, smiths, carpenters, taylors, shoemakers, joiners, barbers, millers, and masons, with all other manual persons and artists, such are to be rated for returns and gains, proportionable unto other men, for the produce of their estates." Anc. L. and Ch. p. 70.

But, while every tax act, from colony times to the present day, has plainly and explicitly required the taxation of income, as a matter of fact, income is taxed in but very few places in the state; and the revenue derived from its assessment, either by the municipalities or the state, is very inconsiderable, as will be seen by the following statement made up by the tax commissioner, from the copies of the valuation lists for 1873, on file in his office :—

Number of towns giving income,	41
" " " " income and personal property,	5
" " " " salary,	3
" " " " excess of salary,	1
" " " " no income,	273
" " " not heard from,	17
	340

As will be seen from this table, in a great majority of places the assessors make no mention whatever of income in their valuation lists. In others, the tax is only assessed upon incomes derived from salaries and the learned professions. We have also ascertained that, in still others, a deduction is made of the amount of income invested in property, in respect of which the person taxable for income is taxable on the first day of May.

In one town, having some 14,000 inhabitants, a valuation of fully $8,400,000, and containing many prosperous merchants and manufacturers, only thirteen persons—and these cashiers, lawyers, clergymen, physicians, a mill-agent and an actuary—were assessed for income in 1874, on a total valuation of $15,121. When asked why the merchants and manufacturers were not assessed in like manner, the assessors replied that, "whenever they made up the lists, if a merchant or manufacturer had made any money during the year, they raised the valuation of his estate"; thus, in effect, taxing his income with a deduction for property taxable, purchased with the income.

A doubt whether the gains of a trader, merchant, manufacturer or other person who uses, in business, property, subject to taxation, were not exempted from taxation under the clause, "but no income shall be taxed which is derived from property subject to taxation," may also have contributed to the present want of uniformity in assessing this tax. This point has, however, been decided by the supreme judicial court, and the validity of the tax on such gains affirmed.

G. S. chap. 11, § 4.

Wilcox v. Middlesex, 103 Mass. 544.

Expediency of repeal considered.

In view of the great discrepancies existing in the construction and application of this portion of the law in the few places where any attempt even is made to enforce it, of the small amount of revenue obtained from it, and of its entire disregard in so great a portion of the Commonwealth, much doubt has been felt as to the expediency of retaining it on the statute-book. Construed differently in different and, perhaps, adjoining places,—enforced here, and allowed there to remain a dead letter,—it, no doubt, works hardship, inequality and injustice.

The considerations which withhold us from recommending its repeal are, that, without it, many inhabitants of ability would escape direct taxation, and many others would contribute, not in proportion to ability, but to property in possession only; and that, properly construed and uniformly and thoroughly administered, it works no injustice, but perfects our system, and insures that every inhabitant "shall contribute proportionably to his ability, to all common charges." Income-tax should be retained.

However unpopular an income tax is,—and we admit that it is extremely so,—and however irregular and inefficient its administration,—all which, in the actual fact, it would be difficult to exaggerate,—it seems to us that no one can clearly understand this tax without admitting both its economy and its justice. "The subjects of every state," says Adam Smith in his *Wealth of Nations*, "ought to contribute to the support of the government, as nearly as possible, in proportion to their respective abilities,—that is, in proportion to the revenue they enjoy under the protection of the state. In the observation or neglect of this maxim consists what is called the equality or inequality of taxation." Our whole tax system rests upon this principle. Every citizen or other male inhabitant of mature age, not a pauper, must be presumed, even if without realized property, to have a certain ability, in respect of which we assess his poll-tax. Then the man who has a much greater ability, but who is not possessed of lands or chattels, of stocks or money, yet whose "faculty" has brought him in $10,000 during the year, has as much ability to contribute to the common charges as the owner of property of that value, and our law accordingly assesses him in respect to this ten thousand dollars' worth of ability, and calls it a tax upon income. But there are many others who, although they have property to some extent, are yet able to a greater extent to contribute, because during the year they also, by their skill, acquire absolute gains, some portion of which they are reasonably sure to have expended during the same year. When these persons have been assessed upon this result of their ability, or their income, we have in theory compelled all to contribute according to their abilities, and the result is a just and equal taxation,—a taxation theoretically laid where it ought finally to rest,—needing no uncertain and obscure process of diffusion and adjustment.

It is, of course, impossible, even if it were desirable, that the assessor should be always in the field, or that taxes should be imposed weekly or monthly. The amount of property which the person has in possession or ownership on the first day of May is taken as the fair index or measure of that which he has acquired and retained, and in respect of which he certainly has ability to contribute. Adding to this a sum equal to the proceeds of his skill or faculty applied in a trade, profession, salaried occupation or business, if he has realized or is reasonably sure to realize such proceeds, and you have the full measure of his ability in respect of property. To the taxes imposed in respect of property, add further the reasonable poll-tax, and the state will demand of its inhabitants equally in proportion to ability. Omit the tax in respect of acquired or realized property, or the poll-tax, or that in respect of the property which faculty is reasonably sure to bring, and some are burdened unjustly, while others unjustly escape.

It is clear, aside from all theories of diffusion of taxes, and of their re-imposition by citizens upon each other without the aid of collector or constable, that if no assessment is made upon the citizen in respect of his income, those who have no accumulated property on the assessment day will go untaxed, although it is certain that they have owned, absolutely, great amounts during the past year, and reasonably certain that they will acquire as great or greater amounts during the year to come. This fact, of income realized in the immediate past, and morally sure in the immediate future, constitutes an ability, in respect of which a state, demanding of its inhabitants according to ability, must assess a tax. The same gains secured and to be secured by the merchant are no less an ability, additional to that which is measured by his realized or accumulated property, and in respect to which, also, the state, if it imposes equal and proportional burdens, must assess to him a tax.

Nor is it true that if such income should be taxed, all income, as well from property taxed, as from an annuity or profession, business, etc., should also be included. The ability derived from mere property is no greater in the hands of one than of another. Bank stock held by the greatest merchant yields no more dividend than if in the estate of an infant or a lunatic. When the state has assessed the capital once in the average time of assessment, it has levied the full contribution which the ability of its owner ought to bear in that respect, and the income, without further deduction, is the owner's share. But the gains of the merchant, or trader, or manufacturer, are not of the same nature as the interest of money, or the dividends of stocks, or the yield of land, or rent of buildings. The gain is due to the skill of the man, rather than to the property to which he may apply it, and is an ability of which, for purposes of taxation, the gain or income is a fair measure. Still less can receipts from mere salaries or from professional employment be compared, in this respect, with dividends, or interest money, or rents, from property once taxed. But even if consistency requires the taxation of income from property taxed, it is no valid reason why other income should be exempt.

In connection with this, also, comes the question as to the proper amount of income to be exempted in all cases. *Proper amount to be exempted.*

Under the revised statutes no amount whatever was exempted. Nor did the law contain the provision that no income should be taxed which is derived from property subject to taxation. But in 1849 it was enacted that "income from any profession, trade or employment, shall not be construed to be personal estate for the purposes of taxation, except such portion of said income as

R. S. 7, § 4.

Acts of 1849, c. 149.

shall exceed the sum of six hundred dollars per annum; *provided, however*, that no income shall be taxed which is derived from any property or estate which is the subject
G. S. 11, § 4. of taxation." Similar exemptions are provided for in
1866, c. 48. the general statutes. In 1866 the exemption was raised to one thousand dollars, and the income of the previous year declared to be that which is taxable. The exemption was raised to its present limit (two thousand dol-
1873, c. 354. lars) in 1873.

The last change, certainly, was a compromise—the result of an attempt wholly to repeal the law; but in our opinion so large an exemption, if any incomes are to be taxed, is wholly indefensible.

The theory upon which any exemption is justifiable is, that the state ought not, by taxation, to take away from one what he needs to procure the fair necessaries of life. The average income, which the average inhabitant, having, must wholly expend to procure his living, is not to be diminished by taxation. If it is so diminished, the incentive to work is taken from him, and the deficit must, besides, be made up to him by the public in poor rates or in charity. And this amount being thus necessarily exempted to those who have no more, must also be exempted to all, that there may be equality, But beyond this amount, thus necessarily expended, the exemption cannot be allowed to go, unless, for the purpose of encouraging thrift and saving, a further exemption be made of such an amount as is capitalized, or of an amount greater than the necessary exemption, in order that it may be capitalized. But direct rewards for thrift, in the way of exemption from taxation, are hardly necessary in our community, and could not be so managed as to avoid inequality and injustice. The exemption, therefore, should not exceed the sum reasonably necessary for subsistence. Those who, by proper economy, could contribute to the common charges, should be required to do so.

We recommend that the sum exempted be reduced from two thousand to one thousand dollars. Recommendations.

We also recommend the adoption of some means to insure the enforcement of this tax throughout the state, equally, and upon a uniform construction. For this purpose no more efficient measure can be devised than the adoption of the plan, elsewhere recommended, for a central supervising department of taxes, with agents in the several municipalities.

In our opinion, that construction of the present law is correct which makes no deduction for taxable property purchased with the income of the year, and we have no doubt that such would be the ruling of such a department.

The apparent inequality in assessing, without deduction, incomes derived from business requiring the use of large amounts of capital which is taxed as property, should, in our opinion, be removed. We, therefore, also, recommend a change in the law, so as, in such cases, to allow a deduction from the gross income of a sum equal to six per cent. of the assessed value of the property employed in the business from which the income is derived. This change will equalize the operation of the tax, and remove what seems to be a discrimination against trade and manufactures in the present system. Further recommendation.

The determination of the total amount of the annual income of the inhabitants of the state, and its sources and distribution, opens a wide and interesting field for profitable inquiry. The materials for a comprehensive and intelligent investigation of these questions are not ample, adequate or accessible. The bureau of statistics of labor has made many investigations and reported many valuable facts and figures, but it is impossible to satisfactorily determine from its reports the income of those of our people even, whom it calls "wage-laborers." In addition, we have the United States census and the various public documents of our own state. But without a more careful enumeration of the different trades and employments, and many other statistics, we can arrive at nothing better than conjecture. The state census, about to be taken, will afford an opportunity to procure many valuable statistics bearing upon this point, and might easily be made to afford the data necessary to solve the problem.

See Appendix, p. 562.

We append a table showing the results of the United States income tax in Massachusetts while it was in force, in various forms, from 1862 to 1872. It will be seen that the total collections were about $38,000,000. During the same period the town, county and state taxes locally assessed in Massachusetts were about $187,000,000. Had this sum been assessed upon the same incomes which paid the United States, the rates must have been raised about 500 per cent. Should an attempt be made to raise all revenue, local, state and national, by means of an income tax, it is plain that there would be need to extend the assessment at once to very small incomes. The income of the manual-labor classes of England is shown to be greater than that of the upper and middle classes combined. The earnings of labor are probably larger, relatively, in Massachusetts than in England. But it will be long before a serious attempt is made to apportion the public expense upon income exclusively, or, indeed, to collect it by means of any one tax, however simple, just and economical such a plan may appear in theory.

Baxter's national income.

Of the United States Tax upon Legacies and Successions to Real Estate.

United States tax on legacies and successions.

From the experience of the general government in raising an internal revenue, we gain information as to the operation of another tax, sufficiently valuable to induce us to speak of it in this connection.

A tax was imposed by Congress, in 1862, upon legacies and distributive shares of personal estate. A corresponding duty upon successions to real estate was added in 1864, when some changes were also made in the rates of the legacy tax. These taxes were in force until October 1, 1870. We append a table, showing the collections under them, so far as shown in the reports of the commissioners of internal revenue, from 1863 to 1874, inclusive. Some small amount should be added for taxes yet in process of collection. The table is of collections shown in the annual reports of the commissioners for the year ending June 30. It will be seen that in Massachusetts these taxes yielded a total of nearly $2,000,000, and that the revenue from them during the latter part of the period in which they were in force, considerably exceeded $300,000 annually. The gross amount of property which became actually subject to the tax was, without allowance for exemptions, $133,885,926, being a yearly average of $14,776,214. Estimating the whole property in the Commonwealth at $2,000,000,000, it would all pass under the operation of such a tax in about one hundred and thirty-five years. Certainly all the property of a community would not come under the operation of such a tax in the ordinary life of a generation, while, in the same period, many estates would be subjected to it more than once. It will also be seen that such a tax would not be proportional in the sense in which that term is applied to ordinary taxes. If, therefore, the state should ever wish to use it as a source of revenue, it must be imposed as a duty or excise upon the settlement of estates; and it should not be adopted except it be continued for so long a time as is necessary to secure substantial equality. The rates also must be such as will not furnish too great inducements for evasion, by means either of ante-mortuary gifts or removals from the state.

Appendix, p. 566.

Savings Banks.

Savings banks.

Three important questions have presented themselves with reference to the taxation of these institutions under the present system:—

Tax on deposits.

1st. Whether the rate at which their deposits are now taxed is sufficiently high.

Complaints of many places of the use of banks as a method to escape taxation.

2d. Whether the complaint is just which many places make—generally those smaller and poorer in personal property—that, by the present system, they are deprived of the proportional contribution to common charges which their citizens should make in respect of personal property.

Rebate to savings banks for tax on national bank stock.

3d. Whether the rebate to savings banks, of the taxes upon bank shares held by them, gives them such special inducements to purchase shares in national banks, that their price is raised to others, who take them subject to taxation,—producing uncertainty and want of uniformity in the national bank tax, and, ultimately, a very considerable loss of revenue therefrom.

In regard to tax on deposits—history of the system.

1862, c. 224, § 4.
1863, c. 164.
1865, c. 267.
1868, c. 315.

First. The present system came into use in 1862, the tax being then fixed at the rate of one-half of one per centum on the amount of deposits. This rate was changed in 1863 to three-fourths of one per centum, was reduced in 1865 to one-half, and was again increased, in 1868, to three-fourths, where it has since remained. The tax is paid semi-annually,—one-half of the rate being assessed on the deposits of the six months preceding the first day of May, the other half on the deposits of the next six months,—and finds its way into the treasury within ten days from the first Mondays of June and December.

Prior to the enactment of the law of 1862, depositors in savings banks were taxable on the amount of their deposits on the first day of May, as money at interest,—the amount of the deposit being one of the items which the assessors should include in making up the valuation of personal estate,—and no tax was levied upon the savings bank directly, unless it owned real estate.

Under this method no tax was levied on the deposits of non-residents, widows, unmarried females, etc., exempted by the tenth clause of section 5 of chapter 11 of the General Statutes, or of persons exempted by the other clauses of the same section. Doubtless, a large number of deposits also escaped taxation through failure of the assessors to discover that they belonged to residents of their respective places, and some were perhaps offset by indebtedness of the depositor to others.

The amount realized from the taxation of these deposits before the adoption of the present system was very small. The whole amount assessed for taxation in 1861 was $9,655,796. The results of the present system, as shown by the auditor's reports, are as follows:—

Abstract of assessors' returns for 1861, prepared by the secretary of the Commonwealth.

Year.	Amount of Tax.	Rate per $1,000.
1862,	$228,683 21	$5 00
1863,	400,080 01	7 50
1864,	452,399 29	7 50
1865,	364,591 36	5 00
1866,	311,848 33	5 00
1867,	361,889 35	5 00
1868,	570,065 86	7 50
1869,	771,998 10	7 50
1870,	927,254 91	7 50
1871,	1,097,332 13	7 50
1872,	1,329,709 89	7 50
1873,	1,454,719 46	7 50

Amount of tax and rates.

How the rate adopted in the act of 1862 (one-half of one per cent.) was arrived at, is not apparent. There would seem to be but little connection between the rates at which these deposits have been assessed under that and subsequent acts, and the average rate of taxation in the state.

Stated in the usual manner, as so much per thousand dollars, the figures are as follows:—

Year.	Rate of Savings Bank tax per $1,000 of deposits.	Average rate in the Commonwealth.	Year.	Rate of Savings Bank tax per $1,000 of deposits.	Average rate in the Commonwealth.
1862, . .	$5 00	$10 02	1869, . .	$7 50	$14 92
1863, . .	7 50	11 81	1870, . .	7 50	15 47
1864, . .	7 50	14 28	1871, . .	7 50	14 74
1865, . .	5 00	16 94	1872, . .	7 50	13 50
1866, . .	5 00	14 51	1873, . .	7 50	14 26
1867, . .	5 00	16 39	1874, . .	7 50	15 67
1868, . .	7 50	13 16			

The average rate of taxation in the state for 1861, which was the last tax assessed before the passage of the law of 1862, was $8.82 per thousand, while the rate fixed in that enactment for the deposits was only $5. The general rate for 1862,—the aggregates for that year being before the legislature when it raised the savings bank tax to $7.50 per thousand, in April, 1863,—was $10.02. And, although the general rate rose from $11.81, in 1863, to $14.28, in 1864, the savings bank rate was reduced, in May, 1865, to $5,—or a little more than one-third of the rate which the last published table of aggregates showed was prevailing through the state. The subsequent rise in the bank rate to $7.50, in 1868, was made at a time when the general rate seems to have become permanently lower than that which obtained when the tax on deposits was reduced to $5. The explanation of the rates adopted for this tax must, therefore, probably be sought elsewhere than in an attempt to proportion them to the general rate prevailing in the Commonwealth.

It will also be noticed that the legislature of 1863, which raised the savings bank rate, was compelled to increase the amount of the state tax, the levy for that year being $2,396,568, against $1,797,516 in 1862. But, on the other hand, the legislature of 1865 reduced the savings bank rate, although it was necessary to make the state tax in that year $4,700,000, against only $2,396,463 in 1864; and the legislature of 1868 increased the savings bank rate to its present amount, although they were enabled to adopt a state tax of $2,000,000 only for 1868, in place of $5,000,000, which had been raised in 1867.

It is thus clear that it has not hitherto been the policy of the state to regulate the rate of this tax in accordance with either the general rate of taxation, or the magnitude of the annual deficiency bill, or state tax. Should it be so regulated? Policy of state.

If there were no tax at all upon the deposits, either under the present system, or assessed directly to the depositors, the banks would be used to a great extent by those who seek to escape taxation. If the rate is so low that a depositor, although taxed, is yet assessed at a rate perceptibly lower than that which his estate, otherwise invested, would be made to pay, the effect is an evasion of taxation, less in amount, but as bad in its degree.

Especial care must always be taken to guard against institutions or methods which may enable those who have abundant means, combined with leisure, ingenuity and the disposition, to evade taxation. The worst effect, perhaps, of the exemption of government bonds, is the facility with which they may be used to screen other property.

The chief difficulty in the assessment and collection of a fair tax on personalty in New York, seems to be in the multitude of forms entitled to exemption into which it can be turned.

If, then, the savings banks are being used, or can be used, by people who ought not to escape their proportion of the burden, as a cover or means of escaping partially from taxation, such a remedy should be applied as will make their future use for such purposes impracticable.

The claim of the savings banks themselves is, that the present rate compels them to pay a tax equal to the amount which would be realized by the assessment of such of their deposits as are taxable to their owners in the places where they reside, taking into account the great Appendix, p. 427.

number of depositors who would be exempt, and also those who, but for the banks, would hold their savings in non-taxable bonds.

They deny that they are being made use of to any appreciable extent by wealthy depositors, or to any extent for the purpose of evading taxation, and aver that an increase of the rate would compel them to diminish the amount of their dividends, which, in its turn, would lead to a rapid and great lessening of deposits, carrying with it again a loss in the power of the banks to aid trade, manufactures, and the building of homes, by means of their loans.

Ownership of deposits.

The ownership of the bulk of the savings bank deposits has been a vexed question, and one which can hardly now be considered as settled. His Excellency Governor Claflin, in his address to the legislature of 1871, remarked that,—

> "It is very evident that a large share of this increase (over the amount of the previous year) is not the savings of labor. . . . . Each year shows more deposits by capitalists. . . . . The accumulations of capitalists will in the end find their way largely into these institutions."

Sen. Doc. No. 309, 1871.

The senate committee on expenditures, to whom this portion of the address was referred, say, in their report, that they "have endeavored to ascertain how far the banks are open to the charge of becoming the depositories of capitalists, placing large sums in them for the purpose of evading taxation"; and they find that, with regard to a large part of the sum of $51,616,774, on which, out of a total deposit of $135,745,097.54, they were taxed by the United States, in 1870, as on deposits exceeding $500, "it is undoubtedly true that it does belong to people able to take care of their own property, and who put it into the banks to secure the high rates of interest, and the exemption from taxation."

Report on Statistics of Labor, 1872, pp. 293-338.

The bureau of statistics of labor discusses the question at length in its report for 1872. The conclusion there arrived at is, that "the great bulk of depositors is from the wage classes, and it is equally evident that the great sums generally credited to them are not the savings of wage labor, but are the results of profit upon labor in some form," and "that not the Boston banks alone are the receptacles of the deposits of the wealthy, but that the country savings banks are as largely used by the same class."

Report on Statistics of Labor, 1872, p. 332.

Ib. p. 318.

The banks, however, did not acquiesce in this conclusion, and an order of the legislature directed its committee on banks and banking to investigate that part of the report of the bureau relating to savings banks. This committee reported a resolve declaring that the inferences of the bureau are "based upon insufficient returns and data, and are not properly substantiated by the facts in the case." But the resolve, after having been engrossed in the Senate, was rejected in the House by a vote of 71 to 69.

Sen. Doc. 1872, No. 300. Sen. Jour. p. 376. House Jour. p. 504.

The bureau, in its next report, gives an elaborate review of the hearing before the committee, and discusses the point at issue at still greater length; and again in the report for 1873, reaches substantially the same conclusion, namely: "That manufacturers, traders and lawyers use these banks instead of banks of discount as a place of safety and convenience,—that capitalists, and persons living upon their income, use these banks to escape taxation, and the care necessitated by other investments."

Report on Statistics of Labor, 1873, pp. 129–228

Ib. p. 228.

The fifth annual report of the bureau will also be found to contain a number of tables and returns bearing upon the same question, but which hardly enable a precise answer to be yet given to the question as to "how great an extent the deposits are the property of capitalists."

Ib. 1874, Part VII. pp. 203–247.

In connection with this it may be useful to compare the deposits with the total property of the state, as returned by the local assessors, for the purpose of ascertaining whether their increase is out of proportion to the increase of the common fund.

Deposits compared with total valuation.

Year.	Deposits.	Total Valuation.
1861,	$44,785,439 00	$861,547,583 00
1862,	50,403,674 00	858,980,326 00
1863,	56,883,828 00	897,150,983 00
1864,	62,557,604 00	901,883,103 00
1865,	59,936,482 52	991,841,901 00
1866,	67,732,264 31	1,081,316,001 00
1867,	80,431,583 71	1,165,893,413 00
1868,	94,838,336 54	1,220,498,939 00
1869,	112,119,016 64	1,341,069,403 00
1870,	135,745,097 54	1,417,127,376 00
1871,	163,704,077 54	1,497,351,686 00
1872,	184,797,313 92	1,696,599,969 00
1873,	202,195,343 70	1,763,429,990 00
1874,	217,452,120 84	1,831,601,165, 00

From the table it will be seen that while the savings bank deposits of 1874 have increased nearly fivefold since 1861, the whole taxable property of the Commonwealth, locally assessed, has but little more than doubled itself during the same period. It is not, however, safe to conclude from these figures, that the enormous increase of these deposits is due to the use of the savings banks by capitalists.

It is, perhaps, indisputable, that in those countries of the Old World, where the power of legislation is and has long been in the hands of the wealthy, taxation has been so adjusted as to bear most heavily upon the poor. Their homes and living are largely taxed, while great fortunes invested in personalty escape altogether, making as a consequence the rich richer, and the poor poorer. But it has been usual to claim that, in our more favored land, under a system which aims to compel contributions from its citizens in proportion to their ability, however their property may be invested, it is not true that the rich are growing richer, and the poor poorer; but that the poor, if industrious and frugal, are largely and constantly adding to their accumulations. If this should be found to be the true explanation of a large portion of the increase in savings bank deposits, it would be a very strong argument in favor of the practical justice of our whole system of taxation, as well as of the rate adopted for the taxation of this class of property.

But the question of increasing this rate was directly in issue in 1871, and was thoroughly considered, and deliberately settled by the legislature in the negative. The governor's address contains the following passage:— Question of rate in issue in 1871.

"The rate of taxation on deposits in these institutions is only about one-half the average rate of the state. Owing to the great changes in our financial affairs, the drift of these institutions is to become ordinary money-corporations, and it is a question whether such a great relief from the public burdens is longer justifiable. An increase of the tax would also tend to check the establishment of new banks, where there are enough already for the accommodation of the public." Sen. Doc. 1871, No. 1, p. 24.

This portion of the address was referred by the Senate to its committee on expenditures, who had it under consideration during the greater part of the session, and reported that any further legislation looking to an increase of the rate was inexpedient. The grounds of the report were that the deposits, if taxed in the hands of their owners, would not naturally or legally pay a greater amount in taxes than under the present system and rate, while to increase it, many poor men would be made to pay a heavier tax on property which should be exempted, in order that a few capitalists might be made to pay their share. The committee also cite with approval a passage from the report of the commissioner of savings banks for 1869, in which he says "the present rate of taxation, with such taxes as are paid to the general government, and necessary expenses of banks, seems to be as high as can be paid by a majority of them, without endangering their future success." Pub. Doc. 1870, No. 8, p. 117.

Aside from the disputed question whether the capitalists are the owners of the great proportion of the increased deposits of the last few years, there are two considerations which should be kept in view in determining the question of an increase of the rate. It is quite likely that one of these will be found to counterbalance the other; and if so, we would not advise an increase in the rate.

First consideration as to increase of rate of tax on deposits in savings banks.

1. At the time of the discussion, in 1871, the savings banks were subject to a heavy tax, imposed on their deposits by Congress, for the benefit of the general government, and which has been taken off.

U. S. Stat. at Large, vol. 12, p. 470.

The first internal revenue act, passed July 1, 1862, section 82, imposed a duty of three per centum upon all dividends of savings banks paid to their depositors, and on all sums added to their surplus or contingent funds.

Ib. vol. 13, p. 277.

By the act of Congress of June 30, 1864, section 110, this duty was exchanged for a tax of one twenty-fourth of one per centum per month, or one-half of one per centum per year, on deposits.

Ib. vol. 14, p. 137.

By the act of July 13, 1866, the act of 1864 was so amended that savings banks were exempted from the duty "on so much of their deposits as they have invested in securities of the United States, and on all deposits less than five hundred dollars made in the name of any one person."

Ib. vol. 17, p. 256.

No further change was made by Congress until June 6, 1872, when the exemption from tax on deposits of less than five hundred dollars, made in the name of one person, in savings banks, was extended to deposits so made, of not exceeding two thousand dollars.

This provision wholly exempted our banks, as they held no deposits exceeding two thousand dollars, in the name of one person.

The amounts paid by the savings banks to the United States, while these laws were in force, were very considerable, but it is impossible to ascertain their amount from the reports of the commissioners of internal revenue, because the receipts of that department, from the various taxes upon banks, are not separately shown in the public reports.

The Massachusetts Senate committee on expenditures, in their report above referred to, state the amount of the tax paid the preceding year (1870) to have been $258,-083.37. As the deposits of the banks increased after that date, and no change was made in the rate of the United States tax until it was taken off in 1872, we may safely conclude that the banks are now relieved from the payment of at least $250,000 yearly to the general government,—or, in other words, of a sum about equal to one-half of the total expense of their management in 1873.

It should, however, be remarked, that the savings banks were probably liable to another tax, of a small amount, under the United States internal revenue laws, from the passage of the act of July 13, 1866, until June 22, 1874, although the rulings of the commissioners of internal revenue were to the contrary.

The act of July 13, 1866, section 9, imposed a tax of five per centum upon all dividends, and also upon all sums made or added during the year to their surplus or contingent funds, with a proviso that the interest paid to depositors in savings banks should not be considered as dividends. This provision was substantially reënacted in the act of 1870, July 14th.

U. S. Stat. at Large, vol. 14, p. 138.

Ib. vol. 16, p. 260.

Until 1872 the construction of these statutes by the department was, that sums added to their surplus funds by savings banks were not taxable. In that year, however, a new construction was adopted, by which such sums were taxable; and the supreme court of the United States, in a recent decision, has sustained the last ruling and given judgment for the United States in an action brought for the recovery of such a tax. The act of 1872 seems to have made no change in the law; but, at the last session of Congress, an act was passed which provides that no further collection of internal revenue taxes shall be made on the earnings of savings banks,—and they are thus completely relieved from national taxation.

19 Wallace, 227.

Act of Congress, June 22, 1874. U. S. Stat. at Large, vol. 18, p. 194.

2. The rate of interest which savings banks can obtain

Second consideration as to increase of rate, etc.

upon their investments is already much less than they have received since the commencement of the war, and will probably diminish in the future, especially if the legislature should see fit, in accordance with the recommendations of the savings-bank commissioner, to restrict still further their investments. That officer makes such a recommendation in his report for 1873, and accompanies it with another, that in view of the restrictions upon their investments, "and as the state, in collecting its tax upon the deposits, has an assessment upon a full and not an estimated value," "and, also, as much of the deposit would, by law, be exempt from taxation if not held by savings banks," "the banks should be relieved from tax upon so much of their deposits as is invested in United States bonds."

Pub. Doc. 1874, No. 8, pp. 6, 7.

In regard to complaints of many places of the use of banks as a method to escape taxation.

Second. But if the rate at which deposits are now taxed is not increased, it is very desirable that some method be devised which will put an end to the use of these banks as a means by which the rich can escape taxation, and which will enable the towns to receive a fair contribution from the property of their citizens, so invested.

The complaint from the towns that they are crippled by the loss of the tax is quite general and forcible. One assessor says :—

"I think deposits in savings banks ought to be taxed for local purposes, above three hundred dollars. Our valuation is small. We have thousands of dollars in savings banks which we cannot touch."

Another says :—

"In our city there are many capitalists who invest their money in savings banks, considering it the best investment they can make, as they thereby avoid taxation."

Another :—

"It seems to me that no part of the laws on taxation needs amending more than that relating to savings banks. Under our present rate of taxation ($20.30), unless the above law is amended, we shall have no money to tax."

Again:—

"We would suggest that every person having more than five hundred dollars deposited in institutions for savings, should be taxed by the local assessors, for the full amount of all their deposits in any and all such institutions."

And every board of assessors, which expressed an opinion upon this subject, agreed in complaining of the effect of the present law.

On the other hand, it will not do to give up taxing the banks, and go back to the old method of assessing depositors merely. The efficiency of the present system is shown by the great amount of revenue received under it. That it has not been oppressive upon depositors is demonstrated by the great and growing increase in the amount of deposits. Its constitutionality has been upheld both by the state and Federal courts; and it is in the line of policy adopted by the state, of assessing corporations for their franchises.

5 Allen, 428. 12 Allen, 312. 6 Wallace, 611.

But it was not the design of the savings bank to afford a place of investment for the funds of the capitalist, or a cover to shield him from the burden of equal taxation; nor did the legislature intend, by the present law, to disturb the adjustment of the weight of taxation between real and personal estate in towns.

Remedy proposed.

These evils can be remedied by allowing local assessors to include in every person's valuation of personal property for assessment, any and all deposits which he has in savings institutions, in excess of one thousand dollars, and cured without injustice to anybody. For all moneys in excess of one thousand dollars, which the assessors can show really belong to a citizen of their town, let him be taxable in the same way, and at the same rate as for his other personal property, whether the deposits are in one or several banks, in his own name or that of his wife, or child, or of himself as trustee. The capitalist would soon leave the bank to those for whom the gratuitous services of its officers were intended. The town whose citizen had invested all his money in bank deposits, could still claim a contribution from him to the town charges in respect of the excess of his deposits above one thousand dollars; the banks themselves could not complain that their ability to make dividends was taken away by increased taxes; nor would such a tax be open to the technical charge of illegality, on the ground of its being double taxation. The present tax has been repeatedly decided to be, not a property but a franchise tax, and hence it is entirely competent to impose another tax upon the depositor as owner of the deposit, notwithstanding the bank is taxed for its franchise. The poor depositor would not pay a mill more by reason of such a change in the law, and the capitalist would be justly dealt with, if thus made to pay a fair price for the use of facilities designed, not for him, but for his laborer or poor neighbor.

In regard to the rebate to savings banks for tax on national bank stock.

Third. It is now the practice to pay to savings banks the amount of the taxes paid to the collector, by national banks, on account of shares in such banks owned by the savings banks. This is equivalent to the payment, by the national bank to the savings bank, of an extra dividend, equal in amount to the tax, on all shares held by it, over and above the usual dividends which it pays to its ordinary stockholders. The result is that the savings banks can afford to pay more for national bank stock than other purchasers, and are constantly bidding up its price in the market against other buyers, who are compelled to pay upon it a more than usually onerous tax; for so well does the machinery work that national bank stock is sure to be assessed upon its full market value. The higher the market value, the greater is the tax which the common owner has to pay, and the greater the extra dividend which the savings bank receives. This cannot properly be called a refunding of the tax, since it has never been paid by the savings bank. The money is paid first by the national bank to the collector of the place where it is located, and is remitted or accounted for by that place to the treasurer of the Commonwealth, and by him paid over to the savings bank owning the shares. As rapidly as the national bank stock is acquired by the savings banks, just so rapidly are the proceeds of the national bank tax diverted from the treasuries of the towns and cities, into the coffers of the savings banks. Since the working of the system became apparent, the increase in the number of shares in national banks held by savings banks has been rapid. The amount held by the 175 banks in 1873 was $21,733,490.44, against $16,972,805.21 held by the 172 banks in 1872,—an increase of 28 per cent. in a single year.

The state of affairs which would exist if the savings banks should purchase all the stock of the national banks, and thereby divert into their own vaults the entire revenue now derived from the national bank tax by the state and its towns and cities, is not pleasant to contemplate, but serves forcibly to show the impolicy of continuing the present exemption.

The true policy is to make such a tax as the national bank tax, uniform upon all owners of its stock. If, then, a savings bank, charitable association, poor widow, or college, should invest in it, they would do so understandingly, and whatever other taxes they might pay, or to whatever exemptions they might be entitled, they could have no just ground for complaint. Recommendation.

Discount for Prompt Payment.

One test of a system of taxation is the promptness and completeness with which the sums assessed are collected. If a large percentage of the tax reaches the treasury without delay the system is efficient, and most likely just. Discount for prompt payment.

Before this merit, however, is conceded, the method of collection must be examined. If the returns of a town or city show but a small amount of delinquent taxes, we must still inquire what sums have been abated because uncollectible, and what discounts have been allowed for prompt payment, before we can determine the real worth or efficiency of its system.

Working of our system of collection.

What amount or proportion of the taxes of the Commonwealth become delinquent and remain uncollected? No reliable data are known to us by which this question can be answered as to the whole state. In reply to the general inquiries of our circular to assessors and collectors, no complaint was made of the working of the system of collection generally. The tax upon real estate seems to be collected throughout the state without delay or difficulty, if collectors attend to their duties as they ought. Nor is there reason to suppose that there is great loss of the taxes laid upon personalty, or delay or difficulty in their collection. Difficulty in this particular would be found, if at all, in Boston and the larger cities. In them the population is more changeable, masses of personalty larger, and more easily concealed and transferred, and the facilities for evasion of demands of all kinds, greater than in the country.

It will be remembered that the immense loss of taxes assessed upon personalty in New York city, is one of the facts upon which Mr. Andrews, and others, found an argument for the entire exemption of personalty. The figures, as given by him in a recent address before a committee of the New York assembly, are as follows :—

Year.	Tax on personalty uncollected.	Representing assessment.
1870,	$902,376 27	$40,105,612 00
1871,	1,044,343 11	48,110,908 00
1872,	1,487,706 49	51,282,523 00
1873,	1,099,634 14	43,985,360 00

The following table shows the amount of uncollected taxes assessed upon personalty in the city of Boston :—

TABLE *showing the Amount of Tax on Personalty uncollected in the city of Boston, from 1864 to 1870, and the Percentages which the same bears to the whole Amount assessed on Personalty for those years: it being estimated that the whole Tax on Real Estate is collected, and that 32 per cent.* of the Poll-Tax is uncollected.*

YEARS.	Total warrant committed to collector, including tax on real and personal estate and polls.	Amount of tax on personal estate.	Amount of tax on polls.	Amount of warrant outstanding, May 1, 1874.	Amount of tax on personal estate outstanding, May 1, 1874.	Percentage of total tax outstanding, May 1, 1874.	Percentage of tax on personal estate, outstanding May 1, 1874.
1864, ...	$4,500,168 55	$2,000,122 08	$65,664 00	$31,948 72	$10,936 24	0.71	0.54
1865, ...	5,946,642 52	2,690,169 22	69,408 00	9,904 94	–	0.166	–
1866, ...	5,469,592 58	2,464,736 69	68,384 00	47,594 56	25,711 68	0.87	1.04
1867, ...	6,970,604 40	3,012,555 20	71,544 00	64,260 25	41,366 17	0.922	1.37
1868, ...	6,170,165 87	2,533,036 17	96,832 00	61,311 65	30,325 41	0.994	1.19
1869, ...	7,632,006 41	2,977,197 89	102,390 00	108,358 56	75,593 76	1.42	2.87
1870, ...	9,052,841 21	3,352,993 39	113,852 00	92,992 49	56,559 85	1.026	1.68

* A count for 1870 shows that the above allowance of 32 per cent. is an under estimate,—the whole number of polls assessed was 56,926;—uncollected, 26,520, or 46 per cent., making the actual percentage of uncollected tax for 1870, upon personal property, 1.17 per cent.

If, in comparing the preceding table, it is borne in mind that the relative amount of personalty, in proportion to real estate, in the total valuation, is much greater in Boston than in New York, the difference is more striking. It is probably safe to conclude that the average result of our system throughout the Commonwealth is, at least, as good as in Boston.

Poll-taxes assessed upon aliens, seem to be the only class of taxes upon which there is a great percentage of loss in the collection. Payment of the tax gives the alien resident no right to participate in the government,—its non-payment is not the cause of his disfranchisement. Hence there is but little inducement for him to pay his own tax and still less for his friend the candidate, or the candidate's committee, to pay it for him. The aggregate of these taxes, compared with the whole sum committed to the collector, is small. The persons assessed are often not to be found when the warrant is received, and the settlement laws have so operated as to make it for the apparent interest of municipalities to abate the tax of the poorer aliens, lest they should become chargeable to them as paupers.

We have no returns of the amounts of uncollected poll-taxes through the state, but approximate figures for the city of Boston are given in the preceding table; it being the opinion of some familiar with the subject, that substantially the whole alien poll-tax is uncollected.

We see, then, that our taxes, so far as they are based on property, real or personal, are collected promptly, and with remarkable completeness. It remains to inquire into the effect of the discounts which towns and cities are authorized to allow for prompt payment.

Origin of the practice.

The original design of this plan seems to have been to keep down the compensation of collectors, by relieving them of the necessity of going after the tax-payers,—it has also been defended as a means of relieving towns from the necessity of borrowing money in anticipation of the revenue of the year.

No trace of it is found in the act of 1785, chapter 46,

"For enforcing the speedy Payment of Rates and Taxes," etc. But in chapter 130 of the acts of 1815, such an abatement or discount is authorized in towns which appoint their treasurer collector of taxes, and by act of 1826, chapter 77, is extended to parishes and precincts. Similar provisions, but extended to all towns, were continued in the revised statutes, chapter 7, §§ 35, 36, and by the general statutes, chapter 11, § 41, were extended to cities.

In our opinion the system is open to very grave abuse, is wholly unnecessary,—not only works an inequality, but an inequality which favors those having money in hand at the expense of those who have not, and puts an increased tax directly upon the polls and estates of the poor and embarrassed, while to the same degree it relieves the forehanded and the rich.

First. The practice is wholly unnecessary. The whole power of the state is behind the tax-gatherer. He can compel payment by arrest, distress, sale, or suit. His demand is just, is for a sum certain, and of which the tax-payer has sufficient notice to enable him to be ready with the means of payment. In addition to all this, a law, first adopted in 1862, and improved in 1873, allows the imposition of interest at rates which render it unprofitable, as a matter of business, to delay payment. For many years the system of discount was not thought of. First introduced in order to make taxes self-collecting in towns which had no collector but the town treasurer, it was long after extended to all towns, and but recently to cities. But though the right of discount is permitted, to how great extent it is availed of, we do not know. It is certain that the taxes of the largest city in the state are collected without its aid, and with wonderful completeness. Some towns have discontinued it after trial, and in many more it would meet the same fate, could the poorer citizens understand its workings.

Objections to the system.

1862, c. 146.
1873, c. 225.

Second. The allowance of the discount works inequality

between the tax-payers who can avail themselves of its provisions, and those who cannot.

We will suppose the valuation of a town to be $100,000, and the amount of money needed for the year, $2,000. If no discount is allowed, the tax voted and laid will be $2,000, and the rate $20 per thousand. But suppose the town has been in the habit of voting a discount of 10 per cent. for prompt payment, and that it is well understood that 80 per cent. of the tax will be paid in season to receive the abatement. The town must vote to raise at least $160 more than the sum needed, and, as in theory every one may avail himself of the discount, cannot safely direct its assessors to levy less than $2,200,—or rather, as the discount is from the gross sum, $2,222.22.

The account of the tax-payer whose estate is included in the valuation at $10,000, and who is able to avail himself of the discount, stands thus:—

Valuation.	Assessed tax.	Discount.	Actual tax.	Actual rate.
$10,000.00	$222.22	$22.22	$200.00	$20.00

While ten poorer citizens, whose aggregate valuations are of the same amount, but who find themselves unable to pay in season to obtain the deduction, stand thus:—

Aggregate valuation.	Assessed tax.	Discount.	Actual tax.	Actual rate.
$10,000.00	$222.22	-	$222.22	$22.22

But if no discount had been allowed, the case would have stood as follows:—

	Valuation.	Rate.	Tax.	
The rich man, . .	$10,000	$20.00	$200.00	An equality.
Ten poor men, . .	$10,000	$20.00	$200.00	

If no allowance is made when the tax is voted, for the amount to be lost in discount, the result must be the same. A greater tax must be assessed the succeeding, or some future year, to make up the deficiency caused by the discount, and of this tax the person unable to pay in season to receive the abatement, must pay more than his share.

It is of the essence of such a discount that it can be availed of by the rich, and cannot by the poor. Whatever its amount, one per cent. or ten, and there is no restriction in the law, it must practically work an inequality at the expense of those who have least.

Third. As a means of relieving the towns from the payment of interest for money borrowed, the plan is most absurd. In one city the tax bills are required to be in the hands of the collector on the 1st of September, and the discount allowed for payment before the 16th of September is such, that the rate of interest paid by the city is equivalent to 120 per cent. per annum,—while, in many towns, the discount calculated in the same way, is equivalent to the payment of interest at 40 per cent. per annum. The bare statement of the fact shows that the practice cannot be defended on the ground of economy in the saving of interest to municipalities.

Fourth. The want of uniformity in the practice, and the various rates of discount in the places which adopt it, render the statistics of rates and amount of taxes unreliable. A place which allows 10 per cent. discount, stands in the list with an apparent rate of $20 per thousand, and an apparent tax of say $80,000, when both rate and tax should be much less.

Fifth. This practice is inconsistent with the attitude which a state ought to maintain toward its subjects. The command, with penalty for disobedience, rather than the reward for that compliance which government, as of course, has a right to expect, is the true policy for a state. The moral effect is bad upon those who are persuaded, with a money reward, to discharge their duty, while those who fail to avail themselves of the discount, find a direct incentive to delay their contributions as long as possible, for only then can they approximate to equality in rates with their more favored neighbors. The longer, without additional expense, they can put off their payments, the nearer does the interest they can make on their money in hand approach that allowed as discount.

Interest upon taxes.

The practice of charging interest upon delinquent taxes, seems of comparatively recent introduction. It is necessary, to preserve an equality of burdens,—for if one man is allowed, without interest, to delay payment of his tax for a year after it has become due, his assessment is, in effect, reduced to a sum equal to the present value only of its amount payable after one year. Its imposition as a penalty for disobedience is entirely consistent with the proper attitude of the state toward the citizen, and it can be so adjusted as to insure prompt payment even by those who are able to realize the highest gains from their investments.

Recommendation for repeal of law.

We accordingly recommend the repeal of the laws authorizing discount for prompt payment.

Collection by suit.

In this connection we will add a suggestion as to the expediency of authorizing—in addition of course to present methods—the collection of all taxes, and assessments in the nature of taxes, by suit, whenever payment has been neglected beyond a fixed or reasonable time.

Quincy, 58. 6 Mass. 40. 8 Met. 393.

The old doctrine was that taxes could not be collected by suit at law, another remedy having been provided (which must be strictly followed), by arrest, distress or sale.

But customs dues have always been collectible by suit, both here and in England, and internal-revenue taxes due the United States may be sued for by the United States, even before they have been assessed.

1842, 34. 1852, 312. 1859, 171. G. S. c. 12, §§ 18–20.

This method has been found so convenient and efficient that, for some years, collectors have been authorized to employ it against delinquent tax-payers for the collection of ordinary taxes.

It is especially valuable in cases where payment is resisted on legal grounds, as it allows all questions to be tried in the ordinary courts, and in the common and usual manner. There are many local taxes, or assessments, for specific purposes, as the building of sidewalks, sewers, etc., the collection of which is commonly intrusted to the boards having charge of the works, and which, if allowed

to become delinquent, should be collectible by suit in all cases. At present, the methods of enforcing their payment must be sought in the special acts or municipal charters by which they are authorized. They are usually levied upon real estate, and a brief reference to the general law is commonly the only rule for their enforcement,—as,
"to be enforced in the same manner as taxes upon real 1867, 132, § 3.
estate"; "such sales to be conducted in like manner as sales for the non-payment of taxes"; and any attempt to levy an assessment of this kind, except by suit, will be found full of technical difficulties, if not impossible.

It may, perhaps, be objected that, as these assessments are usually laid for purposes in the nature of betterments, it is not good policy to allow their collection out of the property of the owner, other than that benefited, as could be done by suit if there were no restrictions,—that for such a tax, if the owner will surrender his estate, the government should demand no more. In some classes of cases this objection might be sound, in others certainly unsound. When valid, it can be met by allowing the owner to bar the suit, by tendering a release of his estate on payment to him of the valuation put upon it, less the amount of the tax,—or upon tender of a release of an interest in it, bearing the same proportion to the whole which the tax bears to the valuation,—or by restricting the levy of execution on the judgment to the assessed estate.

The Tax Commissioner.

At the time of the enactment of the general statutes, G. S. c. 57, §§ 88, 89, 90.
one of the principal sources of revenue was a tax imposed Chap. 11, § 17. 1867, 166.
upon the capital stock of all banks existing by authority G. S. c. 11, § 4. § 12.
of the state, and any deficiency of revenue was met by a 1 Cush. 142.
state tax. In assessing such a tax, the shares in banks and in any corporations, "within or without the state," were assessed to the shareholders after making proper allowance for the real estate or machinery locally assessed where situated. During the war, the national government gave charters to banking institutions. The privi-

leges offered were such, that by the end of the war all state charters had been surrendered. The Commonwealth, deprived of a substantial revenue, endeavored to replace it without resorting to direct taxation.

1863, 236. 11 Allen, 268. The first attempt was an act laying a tax upon shares
1864, 208. 12 Allen, 75, 299. held in Massachusetts corporations by persons without the
13 Allen, 391. 98 Mass. 25. Commonwealth. This was pronounced unconstitutional,
99 Mass. 151. 100 Mass. 184. and was repealed by a law of the subsequent year, which laid a tax of one and one-sixth per cent. upon any excess of value after making a proper allowance for the *fixed* property of the corporations taxable where located.

To secure this tax, it was necessary that assessors should report the value of the real estate and machinery of corporations established in their respective localities, and that corporations should report the amount and value of their capital stock, to some central authority, empowered to aggregate the local assessments of fixed property, to deduct the amount from the value of all the shares, and determine the amount of the tax. As it was not the intention to deprive the cities and towns of the revenue they had received from the assessment of the shares, a
1864, 208, § 8. provision was inserted that the tax collected upon shares taxable by former provisions should be credited and paid over to the cities and towns where the holders of such shares resided. This work could be performed only by some central officer, acting for all the municipalities, who could scan the returns, and make the proper entries, in favor of the cities and towns entitled to the tax. Under
Ib. § 5. the act, the treasurer and auditor of the Commonwealth were made a board of commissioners. The experience of a year, and the scrutiny to which the act had been exposed in the courts, seeming to render a modification of the law
1865, 283. 1866, 192. desirable, the next legislature enacted an amendment, which, with very slight changes, has remained in force. By this act, the treasurer of the state was made tax com-
1865, 183, § 12. missioner. But the operations of the act of the previous year had demonstrated that a very large amount of time and labor must be expended by an officer, who must

annually receive the returns of the assessors of a very §§ 1, 2, 3, 7, 8, 9, 10.
large proportion of the towns of the state; from guar-
dians, administrators, executors, trustees, or copartnerships, who might hold any shares of Massachusetts
corporate stock; from the treasurer of every such organization, and of certain corporations chartered by authority
of other governments than our own, but doing business in
this state. The returns thus received required, for the
proper execution of the law, a careful analysis and com-
parison, that too large a proportion of the whole value of §§ 3, 4, 5, 6, 15, 17.
the stock should not be absorbed by the assessment of the
fixed property, and that the full value of all the shares
should be obtained; and that, when the whole tax for the
year had been determined and adjusted, the municipalities
entitled to share in the amount collected, should receive
their just due. The legislature, recognizing that the
duties here outlined involved a vast amount of detail, and
executive and clerical labor, authorized the tax commissioner (the treasurer) to appoint a deputy, as it was very § 12.
clear that should he attempt personally to discharge the
duties of the new position, he would have but little time
for those of the treasury department.

Some four years since, it having been found that the
very slight supervision which the national bank act permitted to local assessors was insufficient to provide for
the taxation of all the shares, as near an approach to
the methods of the corporation tax act as the limitations 1871, 390. 1873, 315.
of the law of the United States would admit, brought the 14 Allen, 359. 99 Mass. 141.
whole national banking capital of the state, and the adjust-
ment of the tax upon it, under the direction of the tax
commissioner.

Enactments since passed, providing for the better collec- 1867, 52, 188, 299. 1870, 76, 144.
tion of taxes upon corporations, requiring returns by cor- 1871, 297, § 7. 1872, 325, § 8.
porations holding personal property as collateral, by 1873, 141, 321. 1874, 227.
assessors, of municipal debts and assets, steam-boilers,
and of certain property exempt from taxation,—all of
which returns, tabulated by this officer, must be reported
to the legislature, or to the assessors of the cities and

towns of the state,—have imposed duties upon the department which have made the office of his deputy most laborious and important. Of necessity the treasurer, who is the nominal tax commissioner, can give but slight attention to this branch of his office; he must rely on his deputy, with whom his relations are not more closely identified than are those of the town treasurer or collector with the board of assessors. The office and work of the deputy have outgrown the proper dimensions of a bureau, and his office should be recognized as the department where the state taxes are *assessed;* and from it should be transmitted to the state treasurer the "list" of taxes for *collection*, in a manner similar to the practice in use between town assessors and collectors.

When officers of corporations and citizens, assessors and collectors throughout the Commonwealth, and even the legislative department of the government, in referring to the tax commissioner, have reference to the deputy, and not the principal, it is clearly time that his generally received standing should be officially recognized.

1871, 125. As an illustration, we call attention to the fact that when, a few years since, a revaluation of the estates in the Commonwealth was ordered, for the purpose of the state tax, this work—which from our earliest history had always been performed, at great expense, by a large committee of the legislature sitting during the recess—was ordered to be executed by the tax commissioner. The act required the secretary of state to furnish certain returns, the sergeant-at-arms to provide a suitable room; and by the second section of the law "*the treasurer of the Commonwealth*" was directed to prepare for the use of said *tax commissioner* an abstract of returns made to him. In other words, he was ordered to prepare for himself an abstract of returns made to himself. There can be but little doubt that the legislator who drew the act, and the legislature that passed it, knew and intended that this very important work was to be intrusted to the *deputy* tax commissioner. At all events, after the work was enacted into a law, within two years the tax commissioner was again authorized to make a new valuation, to be reported to the legislature of 1876, and there can be no doubt that it was well understood under whose supervision the labor was to be performed.

But it may be asked: Does not the present system work well, and if so, why change the plan?

Expediency of adding to the duties of the department.

While we believe that substantial advantage would follow the change we have suggested, we might not have deemed the subject of sufficient importance to bring to the attention of the legislature had not our views in relation to this department gone beyond the scope of its present duties. We believe that with little or possibly no expense to the Commonwealth, this department might be made the head of the executive officers appointed to carry into effect our assessment laws.

By our present methods there is no head. The law is necessarily complicated. Upon the proper construction of its provisions, the members of the legal profession cannot agree, and cases are frequently taken to the courts for determination. Not a year has passed since the enactment of the general statutes, but its chapter "of the assessment of taxes," has been amended or added to, until upward of eighty acts directly or remotely affecting taxation can be found upon the statute books. The Commonwealth has no agency in its execution except that through the tax commissioner she assesses certain corporations. The general revenue law is intrusted to more than three hundred different cities and towns, who elect from their citizens, officers to execute its provisions. Uniformity of construction and administration under such a system would be impossible, even if every local board desired to do its full duty. But valuation acts have recognized the fact that boards so chosen may yield to the temptation that has made boards of equalization a necessity in other states. It is well known that local boards have been found who would give to the law a construction in the supposed interests of their locality, or, if its language was too plain to be misunderstood, ignore the statute altogether.

The state should have its agent upon every board of assessors in the Commonwealth, and in order not to add to the number of officers or to the expense of town government, he should be selected from the local board. Through such an agent, a tax commissioner, representing the whole state, could obtain an intimate knowledge of the methods and valuations in use in any locality, to the advantage of every municipality, except those who were placing their property below the average, transferring a part of their just burden to other places. That this is now done, no intelligent person can doubt. The most effective remedy will be to have an officer, who will know the whole manner of proceeding in the board, but whose position will tend to place him above local influence when that is being exerted in opposition to the law. The town of which he is a citizen, may safely rely on that feeling which every worthy officer has for the municipalty in which he has his home, for every advantage which he can legally give.

When the tax commissioner was engaged preparing for the legislature the apportionment now in force, he discovered municipalities that valued their property as low as two-thirds, or even one-half, of its admitted market value. These places were advanced to their proper proportion. In how many the evil existed, but remained undiscovered, cannot be known. But had there been an agent in each town, there would have been no trouble in obtaining accurate valuations, and the adjustment of the state and county burdens would have been more nearly equal than it now is, or can be made by existing methods.

It has been noticed by the most casual observers that the character of our population is rapidly changing. Our cities and larger towns are increasing in population and wealth, while a strictly farming district is fortunate if it does not recede. The tendency of population to gravitate to the business centres is marked, and the legislature has been compelled to recognize the fact that her state tax cannot be justly laid upon a valuation established only once in ten years, as was the practice previous to the year eighteen hundred and sixty.

With the system we have suggested, there could be no objection to apportioning the state and county taxes, *each year*, by a valuation based upon the returns of the preceding May. The little hillside towns would be relieved at once, to the extent of their decline, and the prosperous places would assume the burden in proportion to their increased ability.

So generally has the office of the deputy tax commissioner been recognized by assessors as the head of the tax system of the state, that his opinion and ruling is often asked in difficult cases. If actually the head, his rulings would be decisive, to be reversed only by the courts.

Under the present methods he declines to rule, and advises with diffidence.

Objections considered.

The only argument that can be urged with force against the system we propose is, that it centralizes power. To some extent this is true. But if efficiency and uniformity cannot be secured without centralization, it is preferable to inefficiency and unequal apportionment of common burdens.

But does our proposal centralize power, to a degree that is dangerous?

G. S. c. 18, § 31.

As the laws now stand, towns and cities *must* elect not less than *three*, and *may* elect as many assessors as they deem expedient. If the state should select one of a local board, the person so selected could exercise no influence prejudicial to the interests of his townsmen, if the official proceedings were in conformity to law. The advantage to the state is found in the right to select and in the power of holding one person, as her agent, responsible for all returns and information required,—an accountability that it is impossible to apply to a board.

In other states, boards of equalization—expensive and cumbersome—have been appointed by central authority, with power to *doom* counties and municipalities as the only method by which to obtain substantial equality of assessment. In Massachusetts the legislature is the dooming power. Both these methods are arbitrary. There could not fail to be a better apportionment if the state had one agent in every board to see that the revenue law made to govern all, should not be so administered as to produce one result in one part of the Commonwealth, and very different results in another. Under the system we propose, the Commonwealth, holding its agents to strict account, can execute any assessment law with equal force and uniformity in all parts of the state. It can have at the head of its tax system, some one charged to see that the assessment laws are impartially executed, whose rulings would assist all executive officers, and guide them all alike; who can watch the introduction and the result of new methods in other states, and whose recommendations and experience could not fail to be of advantage to the law-making power.

Recommendation.

We recommend that the office of tax commissioner be made *a separate department of the state;* that the head of the department be appointed by the governor and council; that the tax commissioner so appointed shall annually select from the assessors of each city and town one member of each board, who shall be responsible to him for all returns required by law, and to whom he may at any time apply for a report upon any special subject that he may deem important.

We also recommend that the commissioner have power at any time to revoke his appointment in favor of another member of the same board, and that the expense of such extra services as may be required, be paid by the towns at the established rate for the payment of assessors.

The Taxation of Mortgages.

Mortgages.

Upon no points have we found more decided differences of opinion than upon the questions connected with the taxation of mortgages. Some assert, with great earnestness, that mortgages ought not to be taxed at all, because they hold that, if the mortgaged property is taxed, a tax upon the mortgage is clearly double taxation. Others maintain that, while the mortgage should be taxed, the mortgagor should be assessed on such a part only, of the value of the land, as exceeds the amount of the mortgage. And yet others claim that, aside from all question of double taxation, it is the better policy for a state to exempt mortgages, in order that the loaning of money to the owners of the soil may be thereby encouraged, and the building of homes, and the growth of agriculture, trade, and manufactures, promoted. Several of the papers printed in the Appendix advocate, with more or less fullness, these views. Many communications, in answer to our inquiries, were received from assessors bearing upon these points.

Hardly a year passes in which petitions are not presented to the legislature asking for exemption either of the mortgage or the mortgaged estate. In other states a similar agitation has been felt, and in some places has wholly or partially accomplished the purpose sought. In some counties of Pennsylvania, mortgages have been exempted from all taxation, except for state purposes. In Connecticut a system of "offsets" obtains, under which the person in possession of mortgaged real estate is allowed an exemption or deduction of the amount of the mortgage, upon making it certain that the mortgagee shall be taxed in the state for the amount deducted. In New Jersey, all mortgages upon estates, chattels or personal property, taxable by law, in certain of the counties and cities of that state lying contiguous to New York, are exempt from all taxation when in the hands of any inhabitant, corporation or association residing or located in the specified territory.

Laws of New Jersey, Ch. DXI., 1869, p. 1225.

For the proper discussion of the subject, the nature of the property with which we are dealing, the true theory and purpose of our scheme of taxation, and the constitutional limitations governing us, must all be kept in view.

Limitations to be kept in view.

Constitution of Mass. c. 1, § 1, Art. IV.

The clause of the state constitution, so often cited, empowering the general court "to impose and levy proportionable and reasonable assessments, rates and taxes, upon all the inhabitants of and persons resident, and estates lying within the said Commonwealth," would seem by implication, at least, to forbid the exemption of mortgaged real estate, and most likely also of mortgages themselves; while the authority elsewhere given by the same instrument to create immunities or exemptions for certain purposes, can hardly be claimed to authorize the exemption of the mortgage or the mortgaged property, irrespective of the purposes for which they are held or the persons by whom they are owned. But we need not dwell long upon this branch of the inquiry. If the constitution, as it is, stands in the way of a better system, the people have the power and know the method of removing the obstruction.

Ch. 5, §§ 1, 2.

The more important question then is, whether the taxation of mortgages and of mortgaged property is required by the true theory of our scheme of taxation. That theory is, that all persons bound to contribute to the public charges shall do so in proportion to their respective abilities. The persons so bound are the owners of all real estate which lies within the Commonwealth and the owners of certain kinds of personal estate which is within our jurisdiction, whether residents or non-residents, and all inhabitants of and persons resident within the state.

It follows from the statement of this proposition that there is an ability in respect of all real estate proportionate to its full value, however it may be owned or encumbered. This full ability must be reached and be made to contribute. It can be reached by an assessment upon its full value, and in that way only. If deductions are allowed for incumbrances or mortgages, innumerable difficulties occur. Besides the fraud and deception to which the door is thus opened, a practical trouble arises, when the land lies in one town and the mortgage is held in another. Which of the two different rates of taxation liable to prevail in the two towns shall be adopted? If the land lies in Monroe, where the rate of taxation is $41 per thousand, and the mortgage is owned in Nahant, where the rate is $5, at which rate shall the value of the land, offset by the mortgage, be assessed, and in which town? And if the land lies in one state and the mortgage is held in another, what, then, shall be done? There can be but one answer,—the tax must rest upon the full value of the land in the town where it is located. But shall the holder of the mortgage thereby escape taxation? Why should he? He is as surely able to pay as is the occupier of the land; why should he not, also, be taxed?

The claim of double taxation and bad policy considered.

But while the difficulties in the way of making a deduction for incumbrances or mortgages, are so great that most of the opponents of the present system agree that it cannot be done, yet many still claim that the holder of the mortgage ought to be exempt from taxation on it, because the mortgagor, they affirm, really pays both his own tax and that of the mortgagee,—the former to the collector directly, the latter, indirectly, in the increased rate of interest; and because, also, if the tax should be remitted to the mortgagee, the mortgagor would receive the actual relief, in a rate of interest diminished by an amount equal to the tax.

These positions are sufficiently sound to make it important to remember them, if any plan of exemption should be adopted in the future. If any relief is to be given, it should take the form of an exemption of the mortgage rather than of mortgaged estates, and should apply only to future mortgages, or to those whose holders should remit an amount of interest equal to the tax. But it is a mistake to suppose that, were the mortgage exempted in the hands of its holder, the owner of the land would thereby be relieved by a corresponding diminution of interest. The rate of interest upon mortgages depends upon many other things more closely than upon the rate of taxation. The law of supply and demand respecting money at a given time; the security with which investments can be made; the general conditions of business and state of affairs in the country; these, and not the rate of taxation, will determine the rate of interest. Rates of taxation vary largely in different portions of the state. In some towns they are permanently very low, and in others high. In many towns which have permanently low taxes, capitalists are resident, who make loans upon mortgages. There is no reasonable probability that higher taxes will prevail in these places, and yet there is no evidence that mortgagees residing in such towns make loans upon less interest than is obtained by capitalists residing in places where the taxes are high and likely to remain so. Nor have any instances been pointed out in which mortgagees, upon removing from a place in which they have been compelled to pay high taxes, to some more favored town, have called to them their debtors and bade them write down a lesser rate of interest for the future. Neither do savings banks, which are taxed only three-fourths of one per cent. on deposits invested in mortgages, lend at less rates than individuals who pay over one and one-half, nor mutual insurance companies, who pay no tax whatever, demand less than savings banks. On the other hand, the interest paid upon mortgages is substantially the same throughout the state, depending more upon the kind of security and the demand for money, than upon the rate of taxation. In Connecticut, the system of offsets does not give the borrower a lower rate than we enjoy. Her corporations and capitalists are tempted by the extravagant interest paid at the West, to invest in mortgages beyond her borders. It is not shown that in the counties of Pennsylvania, in which mortgages are untaxed, the rates of interest are lower than elsewhere. Undoubtedly the holder of the mortgage finds the exemption comfortable and profitable, but that he should thereby be induced to pay his debtor's tax if he can avoid it, is a step too far. Unless the exemption actually benefits the party who, by reason of want of ability, stands in need of favor, there is no possible ground on which it can be maintained.

Nature of the mortgage important.

The nature of the mortgage, as before stated, must also be kept in mind. It is not every mortgage which is taxable under our law, nor is a mortgage once taxable always taxable until discharged. The usual Massachusetts mortgage also differs from that of other states, in that it is more than a conditional deed of the mortgaged property. This subject is usually treated as though the mortgages under discussion were always mortgages of real estate made to secure the repayment of sums of money or debts, and of no absolute value aside from the land on which they are secured. This is far from being true. Many mortgages are of personal property only, and some of both personal and real. Many are made to secure the performance of duties and obligations other than the repayment of loans of money or debts,—as to save the mortgagee harmless for having signed a note, become surety, or incurred some other conditional obligation for the benefit of the mortgagor, or at his request, and on such there is no money due, and very likely none will ever become due.

Again, most mortgages given for loans of money, or to secure the payment of debts, are drawn with promissory notes in the usual form, negotiable, and signed by the mortgagor. Such notes are parts of the mortgages, but are usually upon separate paper, and may be sued and collected separately. They have, aside from the security of the mortgaged land, an independent value, equal to that of the maker's ordinary note for the same amount. The holder of the mortgage-note may collect it out of the other property of the mortgagor, without attempting to resort to the land, and even after the mortgagor has conveyed all his right in the land to a third person. The security of the mortgage may have become perfectly worthless, by reason of the destruction of buildings or depreciation in value of land, and yet the value of the mortgage, as property—the promise of a solvent debtor—be unimpaired. A land owner of abundant means may choose to mortgage, and actually be able to mortgage land again and again, until the security afforded by it would be utterly worthless, and yet all the mortgages, by reason of his abundant ability to pay them, be worth as much as any property which a capitalist can purchase.

Not only do mortgages differ in these respects, but also in the rights which they confer upon their holders. Of some, the holders are in actual occupation of the mortgaged estates, while the holders of others are not only not in occupation, but have no present right of occupation, and, unless there shall be breach of condition, will never have such a right.

Credits, not mortgages, taxed.

With all the differences here pointed out, if our system treated them all alike, and taxed mortgages as mortgages, it would, no doubt, be open to criticism. So far is it from doing this, that it never taxes mortgages as such; what it does tax is the credit due to the holder of the mortgage, the evidence of which is the mortgage, and the value at which it is assessed is the value of the credit. Nor is the credit always taxed under our system, but only while, by the act of the parties, it is kept distinct from the value of the mortgaged estate; that is, until the holder of the credit comes also into possession of the property which his mortgage covers, for the purpose of foreclosure. Mortgages given, to secure against contingent liabilities, are never taxed to the holders, until, by some breach of the condition, there becomes an obligation or credit due to the holder of the mortgage. Then this credit, or the value of this obligation, is taxed, and, upon any system which taxes credits, it should always be taxed. The circumstance that it is secured, makes it only the more valuable, and increases, rather than takes away, the ability of its owner to pay taxes in respect of it. Nor is the ability of the owner of the mortgaged property to pay taxes diminished by the circumstance that his debt, or obligation to the mortgagee, is secured by mortgage,—it is the debt or obligation which cripples him, not the fact that he has given security that he will discharge it. Not until we are able to establish a system, under which the basis of taxation shall be the balance which each contributor is worth after deducting all his debts—whatever the amount or nature of property in his possession—will debt be allowed to exempt real estate, and then, whether or not the debt is secured by mortgage will be immaterial.

Whether secured or not, immaterial.

An example or two may serve to make more clear the working of our system and its reasonableness. A and B make up a community. A is the landowner, his land being worth $1,000. B is a capitalist, and has, in money, $1,000. It is plain that they should contribute equal amounts to the public charges. Before the next assessment day, B has loaned A his money, receiving only his verbal promise of repayment. A has the money in hand on the assessment day, and is ready to repay it if asked. It is yet plain that B has the same ability to pay taxes, in respect of his money, that he had the year before, and A the same ability, in respect of his land. There is no more reason for exemption to either than before. By the next assessment day the situation has been changed merely in this: A has given to B his note for the money. B's ability, in respect of his money, and A's, in respect of his land, are still unchanged. Each should be taxed as at first on these articles. Another year passes, and, although A is yet abundantly able to pay the note to B, they have quarreled, and he will not do it. As a consequence, B has sued him, and attached his real estate on the writ. They have still the same abilities as before, and should be taxed,—A, in respect of his real estate, B, of his money. Before the next year the suit has been settled, and A, although able to pay as before, has given to B a mortgage to secure the note. There has been no breach of condition, and no interference of B with the use of the land. B surely has no less ability by reason of his security, and A no less by reason thus far of the mortgage. Tax them as before. The next assessment day, however, finds A insolvent, and B in possession of the land, under his mortgage. A has no longer any ability in respect of his land. It is out of his possession, and, although his right to redeem it has not been extinguished, he has no means of regaining its possession. He can no longer be taxed in respect of his land. B still has his mortgage and note against A. The credit is due to him, but, as a credit, it is worthless. In respect of it as a credit, and aside from the land, he no longer has ability. He is no longer assessed upon it, as a mortgage or credit, but only upon the land of which he is in possession, and in respect of which he now has ability. Should A, by good fortune, redeem the land before the next assessment, the assessor will again tax him for it, and B for the money which he again has in hand.

This is an example of the taxation of mortgages, or rather of credits by mortgage, under the Massachusetts system.

In the instance given, has any injustice been done? Has any property been twice taxed, or any person assessed in respect of an ability which he did not possess? If either A or B had been exempted when taxed, would not the other have been compelled to pay more than his fair proportion?

"But," it is said, "the instance given supposes that the borrower is able to repay the loan without having recourse to the mortgaged property, while the common case differs in that, what the mortgagor owns, is usually only a small interest in the mortgaged property." And, again, it is objected that in the example nothing is said about taxing A on the money which he has in possession, either in cash or its proceeds, and for which he owes B.

The money, or its proceeds, in A's hands, may have been taxable, or not, according to circumstances. Whether taxable or not, does not in the least depend upon how the repayment of the money due to B was secured; that is, upon the fact that his real estate was, or was not, mortgaged. In like manner, the fact that the mortgagor, in one sense, owns but an equity, and has no means of discharging the mortgage debt, except out of the land,—in other words, the fact of the existence of the mortgage makes no difference with his ability to pay taxes in respect of the land. He has the same ability which he would have with the same debt and no mortgage,—the debt, not the mortgage, takes away his ability.

Without stopping to discuss whether, in theory, that system of taxation would be most just, which allows a debt to offset property of whatever kind, the circumstance that the debt, in some cases, is secured by mortgage, is plainly immaterial in determining for how much either the debtor or creditor should be taxed.

Practice in other states.

The laws in force in New Jersey, from 1851 to 1868, allowed a deduction to be made from the value of all estate, real or personal, for all debts due to persons in the state. The effect of the system, in that state, is described, and a change recommended, in the report of a commission, of which Chancellor Ogden was chairman, appointed to revise their tax laws, in 1867, and from whose report we make the following extract:—

Report of Hon. Chas. S. Ogden and others to the legislature of New Jersey, in 1868, pp. 11, 12, 13, 14.

"The other principal matter to which the attention of the commissioners has been turned, and to which the communications they have received have been largely directed, is the general subject of deduction for debts.

"The present laws permit a deduction to be made, from the value of the real and personal estate of each individual assessed, for all debts owing from such individual to creditors residing in the state. For debts owing to creditors out of the state, no deductions are allowed. Except, therefore, as to indebtedness to non-resident creditors, the individual is taxed for his property,—not on its amount, but on the difference between that amount and his debts,—in other words, not upon the property he holds, but on the sum he is worth. The property held by him may be extensive, complex and valuable; and yet, while secured and protected to the holder by the government of the state, he may pay nothing toward the expenses of the state in return for the protection received. Lands and goods situated in one part of the state may in this way be exclusively taxed in another; correctly speaking, they are not taxed at all,—the taxes imposed in such cases being not on the land or the tangible goods, but on the credits or claims belonging to the creditor in the place where he lives. The inequalities and inconveniences thus caused are the subject of very general dissatisfaction and complaint. By some it is urged that no deduction should be made but for debts due to creditors in the same township or city; by others, for debts due to creditors in the county; by nearly all it is strenuously urged that such deductions should be allowed only from personal estate. Upon the latter point the judgment of officials, and others from whom communications have been received by the commissioners, or with whom they have personally conferred, has been nearly unanimous.

"The workings of the present laws have caused a general conviction that their provisions should be changed, so far, at least, as to allow no deduction from lands, and to require them to be assessed to the holder, without reference to indebtedness or liens.

"On the other side, many who concur in the necessity of denying such deductions from lands, go further, and urge, with more consistency of reasoning, that the inequalities and inconveniences complained of can be corrected only by allowing no deductions at all,—by assuming, as the basis of taxation in each individual case, the value of the property held, whether personal or real.

"Upon the best consideration they have been able to give, the commissioners are of the opinion that the last-mentioned principle is the true one, and have accordingly made it the principle of the accompanying bill.

"If deductions be allowed from one kind of property, they can discover no satisfactory reasons why they should not be equally allowed from another.

"If the man holding only his farm, and earning by his labor a support for his family, be not allowed to lighten his taxes by deducting his debts from his taxable estate, why allow such deductions to the wealthy holder of notes, mortgages and bonds? The difficulties necessarily encountered in carrying out the principle on which the present laws are in this behalf based, form, in the judgment of the commissioners, a weighty argument against the principle itself. It is found, upon experiment, to be attended with so many and serious evils as to forbid its impartial application. The effort to alleviate these evils, by restricting its application to the holders only of personal estate, is an admission of the unsoundness or impracticable nature of the principle, and will necessarily impose an increased and disproportionate burden of taxation on the agricultural and landed interest of the state.

"Personal property in New Jersey, as in all prosperous communities, consists largely of rights and credits,—termed in the law, incorporal things. They are evidenced and secured by notes, bonds, mortgages, book-accounts, certificates of stock and other contracts, express or implied. They constitute a most important and considerable part of the wealth of the state. They are, to their holders, property of the most productive and available kind. More than all others, they occasion the litigation that occupies our courts and brings into play the expensive machinery and agencies of the law. Why should the holders of this species of property enjoy immunities or be entitled to deductions not allowed to the holders of lands?

"But the principle on which the revised bill is in this respect framed does not derive its support merely from the obvious and acknowledged difficulties of carrying into practice the principle on which the existing tax-laws are formed. The principle of the bill has been adopted because believed to be in itself a sound and equitable one. Taxes on property are defined to be the tribute which that property owes to the state for the protection, security and consequent value it receives from the government of the state. The protection so received is commensurate with the property held, and not with the sum or balance the holder may be found to be worth. If the owner of land be indebted to his creditors for the value of the land, and this indebtedness be represented by note or bond, the land is one property and the note or bond another. Each is protected by the law, and each one owes its tribute to the law. They are in no sense the same,—different in their natures, their titles, and the uses to which they may be put. Each may be sold and transferred by the holder without regard to the other. Nor does the note necessarily represent or depend for its value on the land. It may be paid by other means and other property,—by the industry, the labor, or the future services of the maker. For all other purposes, the note and the land are regarded by the law, and are treated in fact, as distinct and valuable things. Why should they not be treated as such in the laying of taxes? The credit is made, and the note or bond or mortgage is given, because the convenience and advantage, both of buyer and seller, are thereby subserved. The buyer prefers the one property and the seller the other. Taxing each property is not double taxation. The same is true in the transfer or sale of other things as well as of land. In every case when a sale is made upon credit, the credit is the property in the hands of its holder.

"These credits due from solvent debtors are to be included in the aggregate of each individual's taxable estate. The difficulty, if any exists, of deciding in each case what debtors are solvent and what credits are good, is a difficulty that exists equally, whether deductions be or be not allowed. The value of a credit is dependent not alone on the tangible things the debtor may own when the credit is made. It may be, and in fact usually is, dependent on his property of other descriptions, as well as on his honesty, industry and skill. The wealth of a civilized community does not consist merely of what can be seen and touched.

"Prior to 1851, taxes were laid in New Jersey, with the exception of those on polls, on things of the latter description,—that is, upon lands and certainties ratable by law. With the increase of the public expenses, it was conceded that they ought to be laid on a different basis,—on one comprehending all property alike. This was attempted to be done by the law of 1851. That law authorized deductions for debts within certain limits, or between certain persons. The frequent changes since made in the law, as to how and when deductions ought to be made, sufficiently evince that, so long as allowed to any extent, the law must be a constant subject of dispute and change, occasioning the evils not only of an erroneous system, but the perhaps greater evils of an unsettled and changeable one.

"The commissioners are aware how impracticable it is to carry out with exactness, in actual affairs, any theory or principle, however sound in itself; and how difficult it is to devise any system of taxes which shall lay its burdens with entire equality and fairness,—still more, that shall be admitted to do so by all on whom its burdens are laid. They believe, however, that the plan proposed, of taxing property according to its value in the hands of its holder, with no deductions for his debts, is more just and equal than any heretofore tried. They believe that the more carefully it is considered, the more clearly it will appear to be so. While there is, in fact, under this plan, no taxing of the *same property* twice, the taxable property will be largely increased, the work of assessing simplified and lightened, and no encouragement offered to the creation of fictitious debts."

Nor has the system of offsets met with better success in Connecticut. The commissioners appointed in 1867 to consider the subject of taxation, quote in their report a part of the above extract from the New Jersey report, and characterize their own system of offsets as "not only pernicious in its operation, but unsound and unjust in principle."

Report of Commonwealth commissioners, 1868, p. 7.

The Vermont law also allows a deduction from the list of the personal property of each person, of the amount of all debts due from him over and above the sums due him from solvent debtors, with a proviso that any person claiming a deduction on account of debts shall answer the interrogations of the listers or assessors. But we have been informed that the people of that state are yearly becoming more dissatisfied with the working of this system, and may abandon it for what seems the only one practicable; viz., to assume as the basis of taxation the value of property held.

G. S. of Vt. p. 524, § 50.

Evasion of Taxation upon Credits.

Mortgages as well as other debts often escape taxation. Our laws tax "money at interest and other debts due the persons to be taxed more than they are indebted or pay interest for." Our system will not admit tangible property to be offset by debts of any kind, but permits a debt due to any person to be diminished to the extent that such person is himself indebted. This provision, since United States bonds have become an important class of property, has been used to exempt, not only the bonds which the national government have declared shall be free from all state or municipal taxation, but credit property which our system requires shall be assessed, and which the general government has neither the right nor the desire to exempt from assessment.

Evasion of taxation upon credits. G. S. c. 11, § 4.

An illustration will, perhaps, be the best explanation of the manner in which this is accomplished. A merchant has $100,000 in merchandise. As assessment-day draws near, his stock is reduced to $25,000, while $80,000, representing the balance of the $100,000 and his profits, are in his assets as bills receivable. Under our law he should be assessed $105,000. But just previous to the day of assessment he goes to a broker and purchases $80,000 worth of United States bonds. He gives his note and leaves them as collateral security for its payment. He is now ready to make his return for the annual tax. He offers his schedule of $25,000 stock in trade. The assessor reminds him that it is generally understood that he is doing business on $100,000 capital. He does not deny the fact, but answers that the remainder of his capital is invested in United States bonds. But he is asked, Have you no bills receivable for merchandise sold? He admits that he has, but informs the representative of the government that he has no "money at interest or debts due him more than he is indebted or pays interest for." The assessor is compelled to take the $25,000 valuation, and the rest of the community is assessed for the balance. The merchant walks to the broker's office, sells the bonds at a price which is not a matter of much controversy, and with the money he discharges his note, and retires to his counting-room satisfied with the $1,200 gained in the transaction.

This device is available to the holders of mortgages, and used to a very considerable extent. As a remedy, we do not propose that mortgages and other solvent debts should be taxed specifically, without deduction of debts due, for there are obvious objections to such a plan. But we conceive that the owners of United States bonds, whether they are held as an investment or for a temporary purpose, should be content with the exemption accorded to them, and that, under no circumstances, should they be permitted to extend their exempting power to other descriptions of property.

Another device by which credit property, in the nature of and with all the security of a mortgage, evades assessment, may be thus described:

An owner of land cuts the same into building lots and

sells it to purchasers upon these terms: he gives them a bond agreeing to convey the land upon the payment of the agreed price within a certain term of years. He permits the purchaser to take possession of the estate and build his house; it being covenanted that all taxes and assessments on the land and interest upon the principal sum shall be met by the buyer until the purchase-money is fully paid. Whether or not the papers are so drawn as to create a debt due from the purchaser to the seller, we see no reason why the amount upon which interest is paid should not be considered a debt due.

We, therefore, recommend that all sums of money upon which interest is paid, which are secured to the person who receives such interest by any agreement or bond for the sale of real estate, shall be deemed, for the purpose of taxation, money at interest; and that no money at interest or debt due a person to be taxed, shall be offset or lessened by any debts due from such person, except by that amount only which such person may owe in excess of all property held by him, which is legally exempt from taxation.

Recommendation.

The Taxation of "Goods, Chattels, Money, and Effects, wherever they are."

For many years personal estate, for the purpose of taxation, has, under our Massachusetts law, included "goods, chattels, money, and effects, *wherever they are*, ships and vessels *at home or abroad*," "public stocks and securities, stocks in turnpikes, bridges, and moneyed corporations, *within* or *without* the state."

The taxation of goods, chattels, etc.
G. S. c. 11, § 4.

The assessment of our citizens in respect to merchandise located in other states, of ships in distant lands or on the high seas, and of shares and bonds in corporations chartered by other states, with property permanently beyond our borders, has often been characterized as illegal and unjust.

The only communication received by us, in the form of a petition, requested us to recommend to the next general court of the Commonwealth, the repeal of the laws which require a resident of the state to pay a tax upon capital employed without the Commonwealth, where the same is taxed and protected. The petitioners believe that this law constitutes an anomaly in the system of taxation; "that it imposes a double infliction, thereby proscribing a portion of the business community, and that the real interests of the Commonwealth would be enhanced by the repeal of the law." The signers to the petition are business men of Bóston,—among them would be recognized names well known throughout the Commonwealth. The capital represented by the one hundred and twenty signatures amounts to many millions of dollars,—a larger sum, probably, than the entire valuation of the four smaller counties of the state. We have given to the request the thoughtful care due to the importance of the subject and the source from which it came, but are unable to recommend such action as the petitioners desire.

Wishing, however, that their views upon this subject might be fully submitted to the legislature, we invited them to designate some person who should prepare a paper upon the topic, to accompany our report. Failing to receive such a communication, we requested Professor A. L. Perry, of Williams College, a gentleman of acknowledged ability, whose opinions on this subject are well known, to discuss, for this purpose, the question of extra-territorial taxation. The paper which he placed at our disposal will be found in the Appendix.

Paper from Prof. A. L. Perry, of Williams College. See Appendix, p. 419.

The petitioners base their request upon grounds of equity and public policy. They do not claim that legal obstacles exist to the execution of the law. But as it is often urged that the decisions of the United States supreme court prevent the taxation of tangible personal estate, bonds, and other written instruments of credit property, placed beyond the limits of the state imposing the tax, we will consider this point at the outset.

Railroad Co. *v.* Pennsylvania. 15 Wallace, 324.

It is sometimes claimed that, in a recent case, the supreme court of the United States indicated that state and municipal bonds, and the notes of national banks, have a *situs* given them by general custom, and that the fact of the actual presence in a state other than that of the residence of the owner, of such securities, *may, in many cases*, determine the state where the property is taxable. The court did not say that such would be the result, or that the taxation of the securities in the state where found would render invalid an assessment upon the owner in the state of his residence. In this case they distinctly declare, in relation to railroad bonds, that, "all the property there can be in the nature of things in debts of corporations, belongs to the creditors, to whom it is payable, *and follows their domicile, wherever that may be;* their debts can have no locality separate from the parties to whom they are due." And also, that "other personal property, consisting of deeds, mortgages, and debts generally, *has no situs independent of the domicile of the owner*." This case also finds that, "the power of taxation, however vast in its character and searching in its extent, is necessarily limited to subjects within the jurisdiction of the state. These subjects are *persons*, *property*, and *business*." "Unless restrained by provisions of the Federal constitution, the power of the state as to *mode*, *form*, and *extent* of taxation, is unlimited, when the subjects to which it applies are within her jurisdiction."

R. R. Co. *v.* Penn. 15 Wallace, 320.

Ib. p. 324.

Ib. p. 319.

No decision of the United States supreme court can be found restraining this Commonwealth from the assessment of any personal property that has ever had a place upon her tax-list, excepting only United States securities and imported merchandise in the hands of the original importer. The highest court of our own state held that the shares in a turnpike situated wholly without the Commonwealth, and in a manufacturing corporation whose real estate and machinery were located in the State of Maine, were taxable to the holder in the place of his residence, on their full market value. They also decided that ships belonging to members of a copartnership may, by law, be taxed in the place of the firm domicile; and

Low *v.* Austin. 13 Wallace, 29.

Gt. Barrington *v.* Berkshire. 16 Pick. 572.

Dwight *v.* Boston. 12 Allen, 316.

Peabody *v.* Essex. 10 Gray, 97.

Bemis *et al.* v. Boston. 14 Allen, 366.

that personal property in the form of merchandise, of a resident of the state, was taxable here, notwithstanding that the "stock in trade" was situated in St. Louis.

Report of commissioners, Dec. 1834, ch. 7, § 4, p. 25.

The commissioners on the revision of the laws of Massachusetts, recommended for the consideration of the legislature that "personal estate shall, for the purposes of taxation, be construed to include the value of *all lands without this state*, estimated in money." There can be no question as to the *situs* of this class of property, and yet the distinguished lawyers who composed the commission entertained no doubt as to the power of the state to assess the *persons* resident within her limits, in respect to such property. We have felt compelled to discuss this question in its legal aspect, because the power of the Commonwealth to require that personal property without the state should be taxed is often questioned, and because the distinguished gentleman whom we invited to express the views of those who think it should not be assessed, has assumed that the question has already been decided adversely to the methods that have been in use in this Commonwealth from a very early date. If his conclusion is correct, that "Massachusetts cannot, simply because the owner is under her jurisdiction, legally tax personal effects, 'wherever they are,'" it is singular that she continues to tax them year after year, and, with the doors of our courts wide open to all comers, receives the revenue from such assessment.*

Professor A. L. Perry, Appendix, p. 419.

We not only entertain no doubt as to the power of the state to assess her citizens in respect to any personal property,—excepting only United States securities and imported goods,—but we also believe that the real interests

* Since the above was prepared for the printer, we have had an opportunity to examine the latest published decision of the United States supreme court, in a case brought to restrain the execution of state assessment laws by Federal authority. In the case of Tappan v. Merchants' National Bank, 19 Wallace, 499, Chief Justice Waite says, "Personal property, in the absence of any law to the contrary, follows the person of the owner, and has its *situs* at his domicile." "If the state has actual jurisdiction of the person of the owner, it operates directly upon him. If he is absent, and it has jurisdiction of the property, it operates upon him through his property."—October term, 1873, U. S. S. Court.

of the Commonwealth would not be enhanced by the repeal of the present law. The petitioners who requested us to recommend its repeal, base their request mainly upon the supposed inequity of the double taxation which follows our law. But this inequity we fail to see. Our laws have recognized that each subject of the state should contribute to its needs, in proportion to his ability. If this is a just principle of taxation, why should our citizens be released from its application to the foreign investments into which they have chosen to enter? No man makes such investment until he has counted the cost and satisfied himself, that, after paying all expenses, *taxes included*, the profit remaining to him will be equal to the average return of investments in property retained, wholly, in the Commonwealth. If his taxes in this state upon foreign investments were remitted, to precisely their amount would his profits be increased above the average return of property in his own state.

But, the most common argument against this so-called extra-territorial taxation, is the claim that "taxation is the correlative of protection," and that, therefore, no state ought to tax property lying beyond its power of protection. We have already expressed our dissent from this view, and noted the fallacies which it contains, but, even if it were true, it might be suggested, in the case of a person a citizen of one state, with all his property in another, that, after he had paid the state that protected his *property*, there might be an amount due to the Commonwealth that protected *him*,—that there are certain advantages and benefits which a man (especially the head of a family) receives from the state that are not compensated for, even upon the doctrine of "protection," by the payment of a poll-tax, or the taxation of the house that shelters his family.

The state owes her subjects protection in their person and property, not because they have contributed to her revenues, or rendered her service, but because they are her subjects. She owes precisely the same protection to her poorest and humblest subject, from whom not the slightest revenue or service ever comes, as to the weathiest and most powerful, who contribute of their abundance to her support. If one will only open his eyes to this plain fact, and follow it out to its legitimate conclusions, he will see that the original relation of a citizen to the state is something very different from that of a contract, and that the rights and duties of the two, respecting each other, rest upon something very different from a law of compensation.

When it is affirmed, as it often is, by those who deny the right of the state to tax her subjects for their property "wherever it is," that the most equitable system of taxation would be that based wholly upon annual income, we think it should be admitted also that the income from property outside the state is, on this ground, just as liable to taxation as any other. The net return of the investment becomes the available income of the owner, and is enjoyed by him, and when the taxes and other charges upon the property reduce that income below the average amount which can be realized for home investments, the foreign property will be disposed of, and the state will have the advantage of the capital at the price which her business can afford to pay.

The policy of assessing personal property without the state.

Neither can we assent to the policy of exempting such property from taxation upon the ground that the best interests of this state demand it. If Massachusetts were a community with little accumulated wealth, but with natural advantages which needed capital for their development, it might be prudent to join with the demand for such exemption, in the hope that some of our wealthier neighbors would adopt such a policy, and our interests be advanced by the inflow of foreign capital. But such is not our position. The Commonwealth, as compared with her sister states, is a capitalist community. Her own resources have not been fully developed, or her capacity for improvement exhausted, yet very large amounts of capital, which it would be for the interests of the state to have invested within her borders, are used by her citizens with a view to their own profit in developing the resources and adding to the material wealth of other states. This transfer of Massachusetts capital has continued, although it has always been subjected to taxation in our own Commonwealth, and generally in some form assessed in the state in which it has been employed. To remit the tax upon it would be to offer a premium upon its removal.

Before the decision of the United States supreme court that removed from our taxation imported goods, in the original packages, the merchandise of this character, being large in amount, yielded a substantial revenue. The assessment was, however, always one of some difficulty. The value of a cargo could not, under some circumstances, be known until a voyage was closed. It was occasionally needed to cure by abatement an assessment levied upon property that had been destroyed by fire, or sunk in the sea, at the time the tax was laid. Under such circumstances, conscientious merchants were sometimes unwilling to list this class of property under oath. Similar difficulties attend the estimating of the remnant of foreign merchandise still liable to assessment.

Low v. Austin. 13 Wallace, 29.

They are not, however, so great as to prevent substantial accuracy in obtaining the amount required. Should the Commonwealth decide, as a matter of public policy, that the proportion of *merchandise* belonging to Massachusetts citizens, doing business in the Commonwealth, which, in the course of their trade, is carried beyond the limits of the state, should not be included in their assessment, the amount of reduction to our valuation would not, in our opinion, add materially to the burden on other property. Such a course would be a concession, not of the principle of assessing personal property, "wherever it is," in the domicile of the owner, but to the policy of encouraging that enterprise which brings wealth to the state, and employment to our inhabitants. But investments in business enterprises, by our citizens, which are not branches of, or outgrowths of a business centred within the state, and all investments in bonds, in mortgages upon property with-

Opinion adverse to exemption.

out the Commonwealth, and shares in foreign corporations, should be held for full assessment as long as any personal estate is subjected to taxation.

The Taxation of Consigned Goods.

Consigned goods.

Under our laws, merchandise, the property of a person, copartnership or corporation, resident without the limits of the state, consigned for sale in Massachusetts, is not taxable in this Commonwealth.

G. S. c. 11, § 12.

It is neither the property of a citizen of the state nor of a non-resident keeping "a store, shop or wharf," or occupying a "manufactory" in any of our cities or towns.

Considerations of policy have probably restrained the legislature from imposing any tax, although the goods thus sold in our markets are often in direct competition with similar classes of merchandise held by our own citizens, upon which a tax is laid. An attempt to raise a revenue for the state by levying a tax upon all sales by auction, had the effect to transfer an important branch of trade—the importation and sale of tea by the cargo—from Boston to New York, where the sales were permitted without assessment. Such an experience, probably, has induced great care in so adjusting our burdens that our efforts to obtain a revenue should result in no injury to the business interests of the state.

A very large amount of merchandise, the property of foreign merchants, is annually imported into this state and consigned for sale in this market. The Commonwealth could better afford to lose the tax upon this property, and all other of a like class, than that we should be deprived of both the trade and the tax by the consignments being made to ports of adjoining states.

That this was a proper and prudent course, will probably be admitted by all, even by those who are obliged to pay taxes upon stocks of goods sold in direct competition with the consigned merchandise. But unless there is some special policy or superior authority to restrain us, it seems equally clear that we should tax all business and property within our jurisdiction. Is there any such policy which makes it inexpedient to assess consigned goods?

It is admitted that their present exemption was justified by certain conditions, which were beyond our control. But these conditions have been essentially modified.

Until a comparatively recent date, there can be little doubt that the law requiring merchandise to be assessed was universally construed to apply to the amount held at the date of assessment. By an important decision of our supreme judicial court, it was held that the *quantities* of merchandise and other personal property were to be listed by the citizens for appraisement by the assessors, and if any *valuation* was placed upon such property by the person to be assessed, it might be disregarded by the officers in making such an assessment as to them seemed just and proportional. With the war of the rebellion, an immense amount of United States bonds, "free from all state and municipal taxation," became incorporated into the personal property of the community. They were held by all classes, and soon their power to exempt, not only themselves, but other property from assessment, became strikingly apparent. Large stocks of goods and bills receivable, would form the bulk of a mercantile property, except for a brief time, just preceding and covering the first day of May, when those assets would disappear and their place be filled by an equal amount of United States bonds.

Newburyport v. Essex. 12 Met. 211,

Such proceedings, and the fact that hardship sometimes resulted to the citizen by the assessment at a fixed date of a stock, which the necessities of trade required to be exceptionally large at that time, caused a practice to be adopted in some of the larger cities of the state, which placed the tax on merchandise and stock in trade, upon a valuation of the *average amount held* during the twelve months preceding the assessment. This practice which permitted the merchant, under oath, to estimate, in one item of money valuation, the fair average value of his stock, was cordially accepted by all honorable merchants; while those who manifested a disposition to evade their share of public burdens, by manipulating national securities, could be met by a requirement to file an entire list of their stock, and to give such information as would enable the assessors to fairly appraise it. On the part of the assessors, it may be said that in the larger cities and towns it would be impossible to make an assessment of merchandise in any other manner than by permitting a money valuation to be given for stock in trade. This is consequently always permitted, except where fraud is suspected. Upon the construction that the average amount is that intended to be assessed, the opportunities for fraud are diminished, and the fairest assessment possible for this class of property is attained. This practice has been adopted in all the larger cities and towns of the state, if not throughout the Commonwealth.

Modification of conditions.

The first important modification, then, which we now find of previous conditions is, that merchandise and stock in trade is not, as formerly, assessed upon the amount held at a given date, but upon the average amount held during the year.

Low v. Austin. 13 Wallace, 29.

A more important modification still has resulted from a recent decision of the United States supreme court. Under the laws of California, the assessors of San Francisco assessed a stock of wines imported into that state and exposed for sale in that market. The tax was sustained by the highest court of the state; but, on appeal to the United States supreme court, that tribunal, following the doctrine, that "the power to tax is the power to destroy," declared that "goods imported from a foreign country" "are not subject to state taxation whilst remaining in the original cases" "in the hands of the importer."

McCulloch v. Maryland. 4 Wheaton, 316. Weston v. Charlestown. 2 Peters, 466.

The second important change affecting consigned goods

may, then, be said to be, that *imported merchandise*, whether the property of one of our own citizens or of a foreign merchant, consigned to this market for sale, cannot be taxed.

Character of goods.

The course of trade in this state appears to have divided consigned goods into three classes:—

First. Imported goods from foreign countries.

Second. The products of manufacturing corporations in adjoining states, principally woollen and cotton mills, which make some of our larger cities, especially Boston, their financial headquarters and centres, from which to distribute their goods.

Third. Merchandise brought here for sale to meet a local demand.

Effect of their taxation.

If this is, as we believe it to be, a correct classification, it will be easy to see how an assessment of the average stock held here for sale will affect each class.

The first class, like United States bonds, is beyond our assessment, and will not be affected at all.

The second class is made up almost exclusively of goods, which are practically samples only, of a great bulk of merchandise, which goes direct from the place of manufacture to the purchaser. The goods in the usual course of trade, sold, say in Boston or New York, by an inspection of sample pieces or cases, may pass through those places on the way to the buyer, but will find no lodgment there or in the states of which they are the commercial centres, unless the purchaser is located within their limits. One mercantile house is often the agent or consignee of several corporations, and the assessment of the average stock held by him at the same rate at which other property is assessed, so far from justifying a removal to New York to avoid the imposition, would not be sufficient provocation to induce such a merchant, if the whole amount of such a tax was placed upon him in the form of added rent, to remove his place of business from one side of the street to the other.

When these conditions do not exist, the goods belong

to the third class, where large stocks of goods are held because there is a local demand and a market for them here. This class should, in our opinion, be taxed. Since they are here in answer to the law of supply and demand, and for the purpose of profit, there is no danger that the assessment will drive from the state the business they bring, while there is a margin of profit over all expenses. Since also the action of the United States courts has enabled us to assess this class of property, justice to our own citizens requires that non-residents should not be allowed to sell in our own markets in competition with residents, and upon more favorable terms.

Tax should be imposed.

Woodruff *v.* Parham, 8 Wallace, 138.

The effect on business.

We concede that the question here involved is very important in its bearings upon the business interests of the state. But if we have not misapprehended the situation, the method we suggest is both just and wise. Merchants of ability have asked our favorable consideration of a proposition to abandon the tax upon merchandise or stock in trade, and substitute in lieu of it a tax upon sales. We have given this question careful consideration. Possibly, by such a method, the state could regain the tax on imported goods, for the court, in deciding against the right of the state to tax this class of merchandise, admitted that it lost its character as an import after it had been sold. But if so used, it probably would have the effect of inducing this important description of property to seek, to a very considerable extent, other ports of entry where this unusual method of assessment would not be practised. When we formerly levied on this property, we did so in common with nearly every one of our sister states. A tax upon sales would, if applied to what we have designated as the second class of consigned goods, inevitably drive them from the state; for, although for reasons which we have already indicated, the average stock of this class of goods is very light, their sales are heavy. This method, or indeed any that would be just to our resident merchants, we agree might be applied to consigned goods seeking this state for a final market. By the system we recommend, imported goods being free of all tax until sold, will seek our ports in common with those of the other states of the union. The corporations and agencies of other states which make our marts distributing centres, will have no temptation to leave our territory, while those who find a market here will find it for their advantage to remain, and a just assessment will not induce them to go.

So largely do consigned goods centre to our largest city, that in considering the probable effect of imposing this assessment, the question may almost be stated in this form: If the tax is laid, will it drive these goods from the Boston to the New York market? We have already expressed the opinion that we could see no reason to apprehend that the class of business, represented by this merchandise, would leave the state because of the assessment we have suggested; but in view of the fact that our greatest danger of loss lies from the business competition of New York, let us see what is the probable burden of taxation for that municipality as compared with our own business centre.

New York.

Population, by census of 1860, ... 805,658.
Population, by census of 1870, ... 922,531.

Year.	Real Estate.	Personal Estate.	Total Valuation.	Rate of Tax per $1,000.
1869, . . .	$684,183,918	$281,142,696	$965,326,614	$22 70
1870, . . .	742,103,075	305,285,374	1,047,388,449	22 50
1871, . . .	769,302,250	306,947,223	1,076,249,473	21 70
1872, . . .	797,148,665	306,949,422	1,104,098,087	29 01
1873, . . .	836,691,980	292,447,643	1,129,139,623	25 00

New York—Continued.

YEAR.	State Tax.	City and County Tax.	Total Tax.
1869, ...	$2,672,820	$19,240,094	$21,912,914
1870, ...	2,834,501	20,731,739	23,556,240
1871, ...	4,769,354	18,593,173	23,362,527
1872, ...	5,745,049	26,291,242	32,036,291
1873, ...	6,117,365	22,111,125	28,228,490

YEAR.	Gross Debt.	Sinking Fund.	Net Debt.
Jan. 1, 1869, . .	$52,205,430	$15,911,501	$36,293,929
1, 1870, . .	66,040,052	18,006,310	48,033,742
1, 1871, . .	91,489,446	18,115,894	73,373,552
Sept. 16, 1871,* . .	116,709,858	19,422,333	97,287,525
Jan. 1, 1873, . .	118,815,229	23,348,074	95,467,155
1, 1874, . .	131,204,571	24,832,617	106,371,954

* At which date the present comptroller took office.

Boston.

Population, by census of 1860, . . . 177,840.
Population, by census of 1870, . . . 250,526.

YEAR.	Real Estate.	Personal Estate.	Total Valuation.	Rate of Tax per $1,000.
1869, ...	$332,051,900	$217,459,700	$549,511,600	$13 70
1870, ...	365,593,100	218,496,300	584,089,400	15 30
1871, ...	395,214,950	217,448,600	612,663,550	13 10
1872, ...	443,283,450	239,440,850	682,724,300	11 70
1873, ...	470,086,200	223,745,200	693,831,400	12 80

YEAR.	State Tax.	City and County Tax.	Total Tax.
1869, ...	$903,925	$6,375,399	$7,279,324
1870, ...	933,775	7,703,087	8,636,862
1871, ...	933,775	6,856,669	7,790,444
1872, ...	736,480	7,023,362	7,759,842
1873, ...	828,540	7,809,552	8,638,092

Boston—Continued.

Year.	Gross Debt.	Sinking Fund.	Net Debt.
Jan. 1, 1869, . .	$18,928,502	$5,618,309	$13,310,193
1, 1870, . .	23,783,938	7,521,814	16,262,124
1, 1871, . .	26,629,911	9,779,442	16,850,468
1, 1872, . .	29,383,390	11,770,162	17,613,228
1, 1873, . .	33,739,459	13,552,249	20,187,209
1, 1874, . .	39,488,672	14,350,895	25,137,777

These statistics, all taken from official documents, were not brought below the time given, for the reason that the debt of New York for a later date was not attainable, and because the valuations and amount of tax-levies in both cities, in 1874, were disturbed by recent annexations of suburban localities. It was not possible, with the time at our disposal, to get the data which would enable us to show all the items of the above tables for the recent addition to the city of New York. But as the tables stand, they show, for both, an increasing population, and that, between their earliest and latest date, New York has added to her amount of taxation 28 per cent., her gross debt 151 per cent., and her net debt 194 per cent. In the same time Boston has increased her taxes 18 per cent., the gross debt 116 per cent., and the net debt 92 per cent. During this period New York has increased in the item of taxable valuation 17 per cent., Boston 26 per cent. The sinking fund of New York has increased 60 per cent., and of Boston 180 per cent.

These figures indicate, that, by whatever methods the assessments of New York are made, the necessity for a very large revenue to be raised by taxation is inevitable; and though the people of the state should adopt some of the schemes recommended to them, and carry the greater part of the burden by a real estate assessment upon their dwelling houses and farms, yet even then the business property of the city must still carry a very heavy load, and the expense of doing business in New York, by reason of the pressure of local taxation, cannot be materially lighter under any system than it is in Boston.

In the annual message of the mayor of New York, addressed to the common council, January 19, 1874, he declares that "both trade and population will be driven from the city unless the greatest vigilance is exercised to defeat all projects for imposing fresh burdens on this over-taxed community."

We are satisfied that the two classes of consigned goods, which it is most important to retain with us, cannot be driven from our markets by reason of the system we recommend. The first, because by the decision of the United States courts it cannot be taxed at all; the second, because although the sales here are very considerable, the stock held is very small. We have given the reasons why this third class should be taxed, and are confident that its assessment will not drive it from our markets. But, as in some degree the taxation should have this effect, and some commission houses should start upon a pilgrimage to find a place where they can sell goods and see no tax-gatherer, no one can doubt that if there is a demand for a given quantity of goods of any kind, in this or any other market, the goods will come; and although we may regret the loss of the foreign house, our own merchants and factors can meet the demand and supply the goods. The right to tax this kind of goods has been expressly conceded by the United States supreme court.

Woodruff v. Parham. 8 Wallace, 138.

Tax recommended.

We therefore recommend that merchandise and stock in trade be assessed at a valuation based upon the average amount held during the year preceding the date of assessment, and that all such goods liable to assessment be uniformly taxed, whether the property of the seller, or consigned to him by others for the purpose of sale.

DOMICILE.

Domicile.

The system of taxation in our Commonwealth secures, without evasion, the tax upon all the real estate assessed.

In theory it is designed to secure the full taxation of all personal estate not legally exempt. For obvious reasons personal estate cannot be compelled to contribute in the full proportion in which it is held. As the law of domicile now exists, it presents peculiar facilities to a class of citizens for evading a just proportion of common burdens. Personal estate (with a few exceptions, where G. S. c. 11, § 12 the property is used in business) is taxable to the owner in the town where he is an inhabitant on the first day of May, and the terms "inhabitant" and "resident" have been construed to mean "the place where a man has his home." The law recognizing the fact that a person could live in more than one place during a given year, either of which places could be his home, made the question as to which of two or more residences was the legal domicile,—an issue mainly of fact for the decision of a jury,— G. S. c. 11, §§ 2, 6. and provided a heavy fine for any person who should propose any definite sum less than his legal liability, with a view "to make any particular place his residence for the purpose of taxation." A similar penalty was likewise provided for any assessor who should agree to any such proposal.

The penalties provided in this section have never, to our knowledge, been enforced, although it is generally believed the crime indicated is not uncommon.

If proceedings were instituted, two persons only being cognizant of the facts, and both equally guilty, neither could, under such circumstances, be compelled to criminate himself by testifying against the other. Under the decision of our highest courts, that an *intent* to establish a domicile must be actually carried into effect by a *residence* in the place selected, that such a residence as would fix a legal habitation must not be of a temporary character, and that a jury must judge the intent of the person by his acts, but little difficulty was experienced in holding each citizen to a full accountability for the assessment of his personal estate in the place of his residence. Unless his acts were consistent with his declared intent,

Effect of party's own testimony on question of domicile.

by his acts he was judged and his case decided. But when the law was changed, so that a party to a civil suit was permitted to offer himself as a witness in his own behalf, the oath of the citizen as to his *intent* rendered his acts of comparatively little weight, for unless the jury were willing to believe the witness guilty of perjury, the question of the intention was concluded by the evidence of the person assessed. Under the new rule, cases were common where a merely nominal residence was deemed sufficient to change the domicile, and bargains between citizens unwilling to be assessed, and assessors willing to violate law, became notorious.

Law of 1866, c. 170.

Under these circumstances a law was passed, designed to prevent a citizen who changed his domicile from being assessed for a less amount of personal estate than taxed for in the place of his last residence, unless he filed with the assessors his "list" of property under oath.

Its effect considered.

As this law requires a correspondence with and a certificate from the assessors of the city or town which loses an important name from its assessment roll, and as this correspondence and certificate of the amount last assessed must be filed in the office of the assessors within whose jurisdiction the wealthy tax-payer establishes himself, its provisions have generally been regarded, although the absence of any penalty for its violation has caused it in some instances to be openly disregarded. The effect of this law upon those who spend their leisure in devising methods to evade the payment of a fair tax, has been to develop what may be called "the club principle" as applied to assessments. A desirable locality being found where the expenses are small, individuals of large personal property agree to become residents, and their full valuation being assessed, the rate of taxation sinks to a degree which reduces their taxes to a nominal amount. The statistics of the town of Nahant, sometimes called "the tax-payer's paradise," is a good illustration.

Year.	Real Estate.	Personal.	Valuation.	Rate per $1,000.	Tax Levy.
1865, ...	$513,225	$12,710	$525,935	$15 00	$8,047
1866, ...	647,600	329,075	976,675	7 80	7,813
1867, ...	780,150	274,167	1,054,317	9 00	9,678
1868, ...	816,045	985,078	1,801,123	5 50	10,081
1869, ...	935,500	1,982,088	2,917,588	4 50	13,347
1870, ...	985,000	4,160,103	5,145,103	2 50	13,091
1871, ...	1,002,900	4,880,283	5,883,183	2 50	14,984
1872, ...	1,104,050	5,507,152	6,611,202	3 50	23,427
1873, ...	1,157,400	5,085,795	6,243,195	4 20	26,822

The steady increase in valuation from the time when the law of 1866 went into effect, clearly indicates the operation of the enactment. The immediate neighborhood of the metropolis, and the fact that the only check in the ascending values in the column of personal estate, is in the assessment year succeeding the great fire in Boston, indicates the place whence this assessable property came, and suggests certain queries so obvious that we will not here propound them.

The provision of law that personal property shall pay its tax in the place within the state where it is employed in business, and that all other assessable personal estate shall be taxed in the town which is the residence of the owner, is undoubtedly the true rule; and if Nahant or any other municipality can combine the important advantages of furnishing a desirable place of residence, with a small tax levy and a low rate of assessment, such a community may be congratulated on its good fortune, and the rule of law be left to adjust itself as well as it may to the remainder of the Commonwealth.

Defect of the present methods.

But if it shall be found that the residence of certain wealthy citizens in a municipality is only of a nominal sort, and obviously for the purpose of evading, under the forms of law, their just proportion of the public burdens, it is clear that the rule that permits such an evasion should give way to a better one, requiring this class of persons to contribute to the public needs in proportion to their abilities, in the place where they are actual, rather than in that where they are nominal residents.

The city of Boston, which has lost from its assessment rolls during the last six years more than seventeen millions of dollars by domiciliary changes, with some other of the larger and one of the smallest towns of the Commonwealth, has called our especial attention to the ease with which actual residents can evade their just responsibilities, and has requested us to devise a remedy for this state of things. A schedule furnished by the assessors of Boston, covering the years 1869 to 1873 (both inclusive), gave the amounts which that city had lost during those years, and the places to which the persons previously assessed had removed their citizenship.

Of the $13,900,000 which formed the total of the list, more than $2,000,000 was the assessable estate of persons "who established a residence" beyond the limits of the state, principally at Newport. Yet, except for a few weeks in summer, these persons could be seen moving about in their accustomed routine in the city of which they are actual residents. Of the $11,000,000 remaining, more than $9,000,000 found a lodgment in only eight towns, where, upon the "club principle," the owners were able to combine the advantages of rural assessment with city privileges. In
1866, c. 170. some of these eight towns, notwithstanding the provisions of the law which the assessors were sworn to obey, more than a difference in the rate of taxation was accorded to the citizens who had so much property that they could not afford to pay their taxes. In the list submitted to us an item of $2,000,000, which was lost from the valuation of Boston in the year 1870, became a part of the assessable personal estate of a town in Worcester county. The return of the assessors of this municipality, under the provisions of the act of 1861, gave as the whole valuation of personal estate for that year, $1,383,915. If it be said that this statement is not inconsistent with a proper administration of the law, it is answered that the valuation

of the personal property had never been questioned in the place where citizenship had been surrendered, and the class of securities held, rendered any material shrinkage in value, at the time, impossible. Another item of $750,000 was transferred in 1872 to a town in Norfolk county, whose increase of personal property in that year, over the preceding, amounted to less than one third of that sum. Such practices, and the constructive removal of domiciles to places without our state, decrease the aggregate valuation of the Commonwealth, and proportionately increase the state and county taxes of every city and town, except those which, by such methods, gain a present doubtful advantage at the expense of other municipalities.

Remedy proposed.

The remedy we propose is, that actual and not nominal residence should govern the question of domicile. Such a rule was proposed by the commissioners who reported the revised statutes, and the reasons that induced them to suggest the method they recommended are still in full force. The residence of every assessable person should be declared to be, for purposes of taxation, in that place which is his substantial abiding place and home. And, that this reasonable doctrine may not be left open to a construction which its statement in general language would render possible, and that a plain rule, easy to be understood by courts, officers, and citizens, should govern its administration,—

Report of commissioners, p. 27, c. 7, § 9; also, p. 34, § 9.

Recommendation in regard to domicile.

We recommend that each assessable person be deemed to be domiciled on the first day of May, in each year, in that city or town, within the Commonwealth, in which he has resided the greater part of the twelve months preceding, with the ordinary members of his household. And that all persons who have resided within the Commonwealth the greater part of the year preceding the date of assessment, and all persons absent from the state, who have gained no new domicile abroad, shall be deemed to be residents of this state.

This rule to be modified only in favor of those persons who, changing their residence, have established themselves in some municipality with the purpose of acquiring a new domicile therein, and with no intention of again residing in the city or town of which they were last residents. For the purpose of determining the taxable place of each person who, during the year, resides in more than one city or town, all such persons should be required to report to the assessors of all the municipalities in which they have resided, or be liable to assessment and taxation in each.

The General Corporation Tax.

General corporation tax.

In early times natural persons owned all the property in the state, except that of the state itself, or of municipal corporations. A tax upon the inhabitants of the state reached, with substantial certainty and equality, all the property within its jurisdiction, which it was desirable to tax.

With progress came the introduction, wonderful growth and multiplication of private corporations. At the outset their property and members were within the Commonwealth. A tax upon shareholders, for the value of their shares, would then reach the whole of the corporate property.

The system extended, as wealth increased, and as intercommunication between distant places became easy and rapid, non-residents acquired shares in our corporations. The companies invested in property, and transacted business outside the Commonwealth. Residents bought stocks representing property and enterprises situated in distant states, the value and existence of which were unknown to the local assessors. So great was the chance of their escaping all taxation, that it added materially to the value of such stocks as investments.

From these and similar causes, notwithstanding efforts to obtain a full assessment of corporate interests, by means of a system of returns and correspondence between assessors, there was great failure to secure the proper revenue from this class of property. Resident holders often escaped taxation upon their stocks, or if taxed, were sometimes assessed at extremely low valuations. But the system in use had no provision for reaching non-resident shareholders, and no revenue was obtained from this source. So ineffective were the methods in use in 1860 and 1861 that in the former year the returns showed the whole amount of stock in corporations and deposits in savings banks to be $225,347,868,—the amount taxed $78,029,435,—the balance $147,318,433 escaping. In 1861 the corresponding figures were,—

Returns of 1861, under Act of 1861, c. 171.

Whole amount of stock and deposits, ...	$232,156,227
Amount taxed, ...	80,263,840
Balance untaxed, ...	$151,892,387

And this out of a total valuation for the state of only $861,547,583.

Inequality of local assessment of corporate property.

But this enormous loss of revenue was not the sole objection to the system. Another, declared by the secretary of the Commonwealth to be the most serious, was the unequal taxation of the stock of the different corporations. In 1861, shares in the Hamilton Manufacturing Company were rated at $1,000 each in Belmont and Carlisle, and at $83 in Peperell. Shares in the Appleton Company at $900 in Medford, and $40 in Brookline. In the Lawrence Manufacturing Company, at $800 in Groton, and $75.45 in Quincy; and in like manner through the state, and to the end of the list.

A system so objectionable and inefficient could not long be retained.

The war of the rebellion brought with it an enormous expenditure and an inflated irredeemable paper currency, and to our largely increased assessments were added the direct taxes of the United States. The holders of personal property, which, from its nature, is always difficult of assessment, were stimulated to extraordinary efforts to evade their share of the common burden, while the banks,

G. S. 57, § 89. which had formerly paid directly to the state, a yearly tax of one per cent. on their capital, in addition to that levied upon their shareholders, without exception, surrendered their state charters and became national banking associations. The state and the municipalities were consequently deprived of resources at a time when they were experiencing a pressing need of revenue.

Taxation of franchise. 12 Mass. 252. 1828, ch. 96, § 21. The constitutional provision allowing the legislature to impose excises had long before been availed of in the tax upon banking companies. In the contest over the validity of the tax, the courts had enunciated principles which were of easy application to all corporations.

Accordingly, the first step for the more effectual assess-
1862, ch. 224. ment of corporate wealth, was the imposition, in 1862, of a tax upon savings banks for their deposits, and upon
1863, ch. 236. insurance companies. Next came, in 1863, a law taxing dividends paid by corporations to non-resident shareholders. This tax, however, was so imposed as not to be in the nature of an excise tax, and was declared uncon-
11 Allen, 268. stitutional. Before this decision was reached, the law imposing it had been repealed, and the act of 1864
1864, ch. 208. adopted. This law aimed to secure a fair, equal, and complete assessment of all corporate property, whether held by residents or non-residents. In the succeeding
1865, ch. 283. year it was thoroughly and ably revised and amended, and the system thus perfected has since been in operation.
6 Wallace, 632. 12 Allen, 298. Its validity as a franchise tax, or excise, has been tested, and sustained by our courts and those of the United States. It differs, however, from other excise taxes laid by the state upon corporations, in its method of determining valuations and rates, and in the distribution of a part of its proceeds among the cities and towns.

This system of corporate taxation had its origin here, and may be fairly claimed as a Massachusetts specialty. We regard it as a most valuable contribution to fiscal science, and other states have already copied its methods. After ten years' trial it receives the approval not only of asssessors, but of stockholders and corporations. It is direct as to the corporations, and hence challenges attention and investigation. It is indirect as to the shareholder, and upon him its pressure is not irritating. Corporate stocks are seldom the property of the poor, hence the burden is borne by those able to contribute. If it be true that, to rest with equality upon all, taxes, however fairly laid, must subsequently be diffused, no tax-payer has better facilities for the diffusion than the corporation, with its officers and shareholders, its creditors, customers, and employés. Its method of assessment and collection is simple, sure and inexpensive.

The scheme may be outlined as follows :—

It is based upon the right of the state to tax the franchise or right of existence of the corporation, and by it neither its property nor shares, as such, are taxed. But the real estate and machinery of all corporations (being in the nature of fixed property) are assessable by local authorities in the same manner and for the same purposes as other real estate. The only exception to this rule being, that railroads are by law exempt upon a belt of land five rods wide, with all the structures within this limit. It will, however, be seen that this exemption, so far as the interests of the shareholders are concerned, is nominal only. Its effect is to transfer to the treasury of the Commonwealth and to the treasuries of the cities and towns where the shareholders reside, a portion of the tax upon this property, which would otherwise remain with the municipalities through which the tracks of the railways are laid.

General plan of corporation tax.

G. S. ch. 63, §§ 17-20, 4 Met. 566.

The treasurers of all Massachusetts corporations having a capital stock, are required to make, under oath, a return to the tax commissioners of the state, as of the first day of May, within the first ten days of that month, of all the stockholders, with their legal residence, and of the par and market value of the shares of the corporations. The assessors of all the cities and towns where any of the real estate or machinery of these corporations is located, are required to report the value of such property in detail

1865, 283.

to the tax commissioner. All assessors being required to return the total valuation of their municipality and the amount of money to be raised by them for state, county and town taxes, the average rate of taxation is easily obtained.

The tax at the average rate in the Commonwealth is assessed upon the valuation of the franchise, ascertained by taking the sum total of all its shares at the market rate on the first day of May, and deducting the value of the real estate and machinery (if any is owned) locally
1865, 283. assessed. The treasurer of the corporation is required to pay the full amount of this franchise tax direct to the treasury of the Commonwealth; and a tax equal in amount upon every share, assessed at an equitable rate, without the possibility of evasion, has been collected. It only remains to distribute that portion of the tax, which the state does not retain, to the cities and towns entitled to it. This is done by crediting the different municipalities with the proportion of the tax represented by the shareholders resident in those places. When the local treasurer appears, to pay the proportion of state tax due from his town, he finds waiting for him the full amount of tax due, in respect to this class of property, by his fellow-townsmen. When all has been distributed, there still remains in the state treasury a substantial revenue (the tax upon the stock of non-residents) for the needs of the Commonwealth.

The law aims to protect all interested from the under-valuation of the shares by the treasurer of the corporation, by permitting the tax commissioner, upon proper evidence, to fix the value of the stock above the return of the treasurer, subject to an appeal to a board composed of the treasurer and auditor of the Commonwealth and one member of the executive council. This board also decides the claims of different municipalities where each demands the credit for the same tax. The protection against too large a valuation of real estate and machinery, by local assessors, is found in the power of the commissioner to refuse to credit the franchise with the full amount of the assessment, which will compel the corporation to secure from either the authorities of the Commonwealth or the local assessors, an abatement, or pay a double tax upon the difference in the amount assessed by the town assessors and that allowed by the tax commissioner.

Difficulties to be met.

But, however well devised and efficient these checks were deemed, it may be doubted whether there is not danger that they will prove insufficient. In the steady increase of the value of corporate real estate and machinery in proportion to the value of their whole property, we see indications which should be carefully watched. The disposition of towns and cities to place a high valuation upon corporation real estate and machinery has attracted the attention of the state authorities. The effort of close corporations, whose stocks are held as family properties or for dividends only, to keep down their apparent value, should also be observed and met. Local agents, if a system embracing their appointment should be adopted, would greatly aid the central department in the remedy for these abuses; and with such a system we believe that the possibility of evading this tax, in either of the methods indicated, would be obviated.

Another danger should be kept in mind. As this franchise tax is based upon the aggregate valuation of the shares, its effect is to permit tangible property to be offset by debts due, a privilege that under our system is enjoyed by corporations only. This immunity is at once apparent when we consider the supposed case of two railroads having an equal amount of property,—the assets of the first being purchased with the capital stock subscribed by its shareholders, that of the other in part by stock subscriptions and the largest amount of bonds that the property could be made to carry. It is true that a portion of these bonds would be found and taxed to the holders by local assessors. But that proportion held without the state, or the debt of the corporation secured by ordinary mortgage, or floating unsecured, would cancel an amount of assessment upon tangible and intangible property that, under our usual plans, would be taxable in other hands. If this method of lightening assessments is found to be availed of to an extent that produces a practical inequality, it would not seem difficult to remedy the want of uniformity without materially changing the system.

Railroad commissioners' report, 1873. An examination of the returns of the street-railway corporations, in connection with the auditor's report of taxes received from them, will show that in 1873 their total cost of road and equipment was returned at $6,787,822.93. The value of their land and buildings, which, of course, were taxed by the local assessors, was $1,880,806.15, leaving a balance of $4,907,016.78 invested in roads, Ib. p. 56. cars, horses and other equipment. The whole tax paid by them to the state was $39,557.61, or $8.06 on a thousand dollars of the reported cost of their roads and equipment, less real estate. In the same year the average tax in the state was $14.49 per thousand.

The department charged with the administration of the law does not allow these inequalities to escape its notice, and should they become sufficiently great, will, no doubt, promptly inform the legislature and suggest a practical remedy.

The Tax on Bank Shares.

Taxation of bank shares. For many years prior to the inauguration of the present system of national banks, Massachusetts had derived a large revenue from a tax upon the capital stock of banks chartered under her laws and doing business in the state. 1828, ch. 96, § 21. R. S. 9, §§ 1–3. G. S. 57, §§ 88–90. This tax was laid originally under a law of 1828, entitled "An Act to regulate banks and banking," and was continued, substantially without change, until the banks themselves became extinct by being changed into national banks in 1864–1866.

Portland Bank v. Apthorp, 12 Mass. 252. 1863, ch. 215, § 2. 1864, ch. 190, § 3. 1865, ch. 163, § 7. The constitutionality of the tax was questioned at the outset, but was sustained, under that portion of the state constitution empowering the general court "to impose and levy reasonable duties and excises," in an opinion now recognized as a leading authority on the subject of corporate taxation. As the national banks, organized under the act of congress of 1864, spread through the state, the banking capital was relieved from the state tax as rapidly as it became the capital of national banks, and the revenue of the state from this source substantially ceased in 1865.

The act of congress, under which the national banks were organized, allowed the taxation of their shares, under certain limitations, by the state authorities. The first attempt to avail of this permission was made by the law of 1865, entitled "An Act relating to returns and taxation of shares in associations for banking, established under the laws of the United States." This law continued in force until it was repealed by the law of 1871. It required the local assessors to include "all shares in such associations held by persons resident and liable to taxation" in their cities or towns, "in the valuation of the personal property of such person, for the assessment of all taxes imposed and levied in such town by authority of law." Under it no attempt was made to tax the shares owned by non-residents; and there was the same liability of evasion by means of the giving of false residences, and of loss from the negligence of assessors, which has proved so fatal an objection to the system of assessment of corporate shares in the several towns.

1st sess. 38th Cong. ch. 106, § 41. U. S. Stats. at Large, vol. 13, p. 112.

1865, ch. 242.

Ib. § 3.

For the purpose of reaching the shares of non-residents, an additional act was adopted in 1868, entitled "An Act concerning the taxing of bank shares." The first section of this act provided that all the shares owned by non-residents should be assessed to the owners thereof in the cities or towns where the banks were located, in the assessment of all taxes imposed in such place by authority of law. The taxes so assessed were to be collected by the local collectors and paid over by the local treasurers to the state treasury on or before the first Monday in December in each year. This law continued in force until

Non-resident stockholders. 1868, ch. 349.

Ib. § 6.

17

1871, and payments received under it by the state treasury were as follows:—

1868, ...	$30,667 49
1869, ...	197,489 10
1870, ...	181,798 41

Causes for change in method.

14 Allen, 359. 99 Mass. 141. 101 Mass. 575.

Objections were urged against the validity of both these laws, and cases arising under them were determined in the supreme judicial court, the taxes laid being in every case sustained.

Although the laws were declared valid, practical difficulties in their operation, the legislation of congress and decisions of United States courts, led to their repeal and the adoption of a new method in 1871. The shares of resident owners were liable to be assessed upon different valuations in their various places of residence, and in many cases escaped altogether, while the shares of non-residents were assessed in the places where the banks were located, at rates often different from those paid by resident holders. The authorities of bank towns were burdened with the assessment and collection of a tax for the benefit of the state only, and in which their own towns had but little interest. The additional act of congress defining the meaning of the phrase "place where the bank is located," had become a law, and decisions of the supreme court of the United States had been promulgated, declaring the powers and limitations of the states under the congressional acts.

U. S. Stats. at Large, v. 15, p. 34.

3 Wallace, 573. 4 Wallace, 459. 9 Wallace, 353. Ib. 468.

Theory of Act of 1871.

In the light of these decisions, and the operation of the former laws, the legislature of 1871 adopted the act of that year, "relating to the taxation of bank shares." The design of this law was to secure a tax upon every share of bank stock, whether held by residents or non-residents, and to ensure that the tax should be assessed upon a valuation equal to the fair market value of the shares. The towns were to receive so much of the tax as was laid upon shares owned by their own residents, while the taxes upon non-resident shares were to be devoted to the state treasury. Its machinery was simple and effectual. The local authorities of the places where banks were established, assessed and collected a tax upon all the shares of the banks, at the same rate at which they taxed other moneyed capital, and upon the fair cash value of the shares after deducting real estate. The tax commissioner determined the proportionate amount of the tax assessed by each place, upon shares which would not have been taxable therein under the general statutes, and this amount was credited to the state treasury. He then determined the proportionate amount which would have been taxable under the same rule, in places other than that where the bank was located, and these amounts were credited by the state treasurer to such towns. The balance remaining after a credit given to the savings banks, for stock held by them, was the amount assessed upon shares of non-residents, and was the property of the Commonwealth. The efficiency of this system will be seen by a comparison of the amounts retained by the state under it, with the amounts realized under the previous and subsequent acts. The figures are as follows :— Effect of act.

Amounts realized by state :—

Treasurer's reports, 1869, p. 20; 1870, p. 26. Tax commissioner's report, H. Doc. 1874, No. 125, p. 12.

1869, . . .	$197,489 10	Act of 1868, chap. 349.
1870, . . .	181,798 41	
1871, . . .	311,312 41	Act of 1871, chap. 390.*
1872, . . .	134,822 98	Act of 1872, chap. 341.

And there is, also, no doubt that the receipts of the towns, under the act of 1871, were much larger than under either the act of 1868 or that of 1872.

The total addition to the public revenue by the operation of this law, as estimated by the tax commissioner in his report for 1871, was $654,571.54. But, notwithstand- H. Doc. 1872, No. 175, p. 11.

* Under the act of 1871, the state received the tax upon bank shares held by stock insurance companies. But under the acts of 1868, 1872, and 1873, the revenue of the state was from one class of stockholders only, viz., the non-residents of the Commonwealth.

ing this great increase of revenue, a vigorous opposition was organized against the law, which, with annoyances produced by the change from former methods, caused it to be repealed in 1872, and another act passed, "to provide for the collection of taxes upon bank shares," which, with some modifications new to our laws, went back to the old plan of assessing the shares of residents in the places where they resided, and non-residents in the places where the banks were located. But no sooner was this system reinstated, than the old difficulties which led to its abandonment reappeared. The state's proportion of the tax fell from $311,312.41, in 1871, to $134,822.98, in 1872, and at least as great a loss of revenue was occasioned to the towns and cities. Nor was the operation of this law without trouble or annoyance to officials or shareholders.

Act of 1872, and its effect.

Tax commissioner's report, 1873, H. Doc. 1874, No. 125, p. 12.

1873, ch. 315.

This loss of revenue led to the enactment, in 1873, of the law under which bank shares are now taxed. The method of assessment is substantially identical with that of the law of 1871, and such additional changes were made with reference to the method of collection, as have induced a very large majority of the banks of the state to assume the payment of the tax as a current expense, thus obviating many of the objections which led to the repeal of the law of 1871. The effect of this act of 1873 upon the revenue was immediate, the net receipts of the state treasury rising from $134,822.98, in 1872, to $207,209.57, in 1873, a result which the tax commissioner says, "is to be attributed simply to the the fact that, where all the shares are assessed in one place, and the tax collected there, there is no opportunity for evasion."

Act of 1873, and its effect. H. Doc. 1874, No. 125, pp. 12, 13.

An effort was made, in 1874, to repeal this law, but it met with no success, and it is probable that it is the best system which can be adopted, unless the provisions of our general law, taxing corporations, can be extended to the national banks. The only valid objection which lies against the present system is, that, under it, residents are compelled to contribute, in respect of their shares in banks,

1865, ch. 283.

Objections to Act of 1873.

to the revenue of the towns where they are inhabitants, at rates greater or less than the rates at which their neighbors, not owning shares in the same bank, are called upon to contribute. When the whole tax is assumed by the bank, and paid as a current expense, the shareholder neither knows of this inequality nor feels its injustice. In such a case, if the rate in the bank town is lower than the average, the bank is more able to increase its surplus, or declare dividends, than its rivals. If the rate is higher than the average, the bank's surplus is drawn upon so rapidly that it must become interested to reduce the rates, either by diminishing the expenditure of the place, or increasing its valuation to a fair sum. But if the bank, established in a place which has a rate of tax above the average, instead of paying the tax as an expense, deducts it from the shareholder's usual dividend, the inequality is at once noticed and felt, and becomes a cause of complaint. We have received several communications from shareholders and bank officers, complaining of this feature of the law. We append a table showing the rate of taxation in 1873 and 1874, in the several places where banks are established, with the gross valuation of the shares assessed in them at the valuations shown. It will be seen that the rate in some bank towns is remarkably high, and the amount of inequality in any given case can easily be calculated; and, by comparing the rate in a given instance with the average rate at which the commissioner assessed corporate franchises in the same years, each shareholder can compute the amount by which his tax differs from the payment which the bank would make on account of it, were the general corporation tax extended to the national banks.

Appendix, p. 548.

Can the state provide a remedy?

This difficulty would be obviated by the adoption, for the taxation of bank shares, of a system substantially like that of our general law for the taxation of corporations. We have, accordingly, somewhat carefully examined the question whether such a system can be legally adopted.

The provisions of the acts of congress upon the subject are as follows:

Proviso of § 41 of Act of Congress, June 3, 1864. 13 U. S. Stats. at Large, 111.

"*Provided*, That nothing in this act shall be construed to prevent all the shares in any of the said associations, held by any person or body corporate, from being included in the valuation of the personal property of such person or corporation in the assessment of taxes, imposed by or under state authority at the place where such bank is located, and not elsewhere, but not at a greater rate than is assessed upon other moneyed capital in the hands of individual citizens of such state. *Provided, further*, that the tax so imposed under the laws of any state upon the shares of any of the associations authorized by this act, shall not exceed the rate imposed upon the shares in any of the banks organized under authority of the state where such association is located. *Provided, also*, that nothing in this act shall exempt the real estate of associations from either state, county or municipal taxes, to the same extent, according to its value, as other real estate is taxed."

Act of Congress of Jan. 10, 1868. 13 U. S. Stats. at Large, 34.

"*Be it enacted by the Senate and House of Representatives of the United States of America in Congress assembled:*—That the words 'place where the bank is located and not elsewhere,' in section forty-nine of the 'act to provide a national currency,' approved June third, eighteen hundred and sixty-four, shall be construed and held to mean the state within which the bank is located; and the legislature of each state may determine and direct the manner and place of taxing all the shares of national banks located within said state, subject to the restriction that the taxation shall not be at a greater rate than is assessed upon other moneyed capital in the hands of individual citizens of such state; and *provided always*, that the shares of any national bank, owned by non-residents of any state, shall be taxed in the city or town where said bank is located and not elsewhere."

From an examination of these statutes, it will be seen that there are some legal difficulties in the way of taxing all the shares in all the national banks of the state, by one officer or bureau, and at the state capital rather than in the several places where the banks are located. The validity of our present system has been well established

13 Wallace, 573.

by the decisions of the supreme court of the United States, in cases from other states. The revenue from it is too important, both to the state and the cities and towns, to be lightly risked. In our opinion, until there shall be a new legislation on the subject by congress, no substantial change should be made in the method now in use, which we conceive to be the best which is possible within the double limitations of our own constitution and the statutes of the United States.

4 Wallace, 459. 9 Wallace, 353, 468. 19 Wallace, 490.

No change should be made.

But we recommend that congress be requested to modify its enactments, so as to permit this important class of property to be taxed by the several states, in the same manner, and to the same extent as the moneyed corporations of their own creation. Without exception, each sovereignty fosters the corporations it has created, and in every state they are strong enough and able to protect their own interests. Under such a rule, hostile and discriminating taxation would be impossible, while each state would gain from this property a just revenue, by methods familiar to its officers and people.

Recommendation.

TRUST COMPANIES.

Within a few years an important class of corporations have been chartered, which have, in some degree, the character of banking institutions and of savings banks, but whose distinctive title, "trust companies," correctly designates their principal function,—that of corporations acting as trustees.

1867, 151. 1869, 182, 296. 1870, 22, 323. 1871, 142. 1873, 270, 285, 347, 369. 1874, 373.

As the different companies were chartered from time to time, the method of their taxation was varied until, as will be seen in our preliminary draft for a codification, it was impossible to make any other arrangement of existing laws, than to incorporate in the draft sections relating to taxation from several of the charters. These institutions have proved their utility, and will permanently hold large amounts of property. As different schemes of taxation applied to institutions doing the same kind of business are not only embarrassing to the officers who must levy

Appendix, p. 312. §§ 140 to 149, inclusive.

the taxes, but are unfair to the public, and to some of the corporations themselves in their competition with others, —without expressing a preference for either of the existing methods,—we recommend that all trust companies be assessed under a general law, by a uniform system.

Recommendation.

Of the Taxation of Certain Deposits, and of Shares in Corporations, for School District, Parish, Fire and other District Purposes.

School, district and parish taxes.

The territorial limits of these municipal corporations are less than those of the town or city. Fire districts are sometimes made up of portions of two towns. Of course, no contribution to their revenue is provided for out of the proceeds of taxes laid by the state upon corporate franchises. Certain corporate property and owners of shares in corporations will, therefore, escape taxation for these purposes, unless reached in some other method.

1864, 208, § 15.

The act of 1864 provided that, "shares in the capital stock of any corporation, company, or association, taxed by it, should be exempt from taxation to the shareholders." The corresponding provision in the act of 1865 is, that no taxes shall be assessed in any city or town for state, county, or town purposes, upon the shares, for any year for which they pay the tax. The doubt whether, under these acts, shares were taxable to the owners for any purpose, led to the passage, in 1866, of an act declaring that, nothing contained in them "shall be construed to exempt the owners of shares, in the capital stock of any corporation, from liability to taxation for school district and parish purposes."

1865, 283, § 15.

1866, 196.

Street lamps, libraries, sidewalks, police, etc.
1870, ch. 332.

We see no good reason why the owners of such shares should not be taxable for them for fire and other district purposes, as well as for those of school districts and parishes. While it may be said that taxes are raised in fire districts, mainly for the care, preservation, and betterment of real estate, and an argument drawn therefrom for their imposition exclusively upon real estate, in the nature of assessments for betterments, there is no reason why this particular kind of personalty should be exempted, while all other is taxable. The resident of a fire district should contribute towards its expenses, in respect of his shares in a railroad or manufacturing company, as well as for his money at interest, or mortgages, or other credits.

We therefore recommend the adoption of an amendment declaring that such shares shall be taxable to the owners thereof for fire and other district purposes. Recommendation.

Inasmuch as the amount collected by the state from savings banks, is applied in such a manner as to lighten state, county, and town taxes only, it seems that the owner of a deposit in them will escape his fair share of taxation for district and parish purposes, unless he may be taxed for it directly. The act of 1862, imposing the tax on savings-bank deposits, provides that all property taxed under its provisions, "shall be otherwise exempt from taxation for the current year in which the tax is paid." 1862, 224, § 12.

We suggest that this provision be so amended that the exemption will be only from taxes laid for town, county and state purposes, and the deposits be taxable to their owners for school, fire and other district, and parish purposes. And also that deposits in the trust companies recently chartered should be treated in the same manner with reference to this class of taxes. Further recommendations.

Revenue from Licenses, Fees, etc.

The whole revenue accruing to the Commonwealth from licenses, fees, and other indirect taxes, is not large when compared with the total receipts, but is sufficient to merit attention. Licenses, fees, etc.

Much the greater part of the fees, fines, and costs, accruing from the courts, called by some writers "law taxes," does not find its way into the state treasury, but is a large source of revenue for the several counties. As the state tax is, in fact, an annual deficiency bill for the supply of the state treasury, so the tax annually assessed for the several counties does not represent, by any means, their whole expenditures, but is the balance remaining, after large receipts from the courts, licenses for various occupations, for the keeping of dogs, etc., etc., have been applied in meeting the county expenses. The state treasury, however, derives some revenue from court fees, and much more from fees of certain state officers, licenses collected by departments of the government, confiscated liquors, and sometimes from taxes on sales.

1823, ch. 87. 1852, ch. 159. Sales at auction were taxed from 1823 to 1852, when this tax seems to have been finally abandoned. By the 1868, 141, §§ 22-24. act of 1868, licensing the sale of intoxicating liquors, taxes were imposed upon the amounts of the sales. These taxes were collected by the several towns, and divided equally between the towns and the Commonwealth. Sales under this act were allowed only from the 23d day of 1869, 191. May, 1868, to the 30th day of April, 1869, when the validity of licenses under it ceased. The amount received by the Commonwealth was $53,722.38. Under the same statute a large amount was received for licenses ($120,-875) while the law was in force. Appendix, p. 552. We append a table showing the receipts of the state treasury, from 1860 to the present time, from the principal sources of indirect taxation now in use by the Commonwealth. The total amount is $830,483.06 for the last fifteen years. The revenue from these sources is increasing, and the state could no doubt make it very considerable, by an extension either of the license system or of taxation on sales. We make no recommendation in the matter, believing that our present systems of raising the great part of the revenue, directly, are preferable. Should, however, an exigency be found for new taxes, the legislature may properly look to the extension of some of these taxes for additional revenue.

Certain Specific Assessments upon Corporations.

Specific assessments upon corporations. Specific assessments upon certain corporations are laid and collected to reimburse the state for expenses incurred in their oversight and regulation by state officials.

The proceeds of these assessments are found in the yearly reports of the treasurer and auditor. While in one sense revenue, they are more properly payments for specific services rendered. Their collection relieves the state from making appropriations of equal amount, but they are, of course, wholly needed to meet the bills for the payment of which they are levied.

These assessments, as shown by the auditor's report for 1873, are as follows:—

Upon gas-light companies for the payment of the salary of the inspector of gasmeters, $2,934.57. 1861, ch. 168.

Upon railroad companies, for copies of the railroad returns and reports, $1,660,—collected through the clerk of the board of railroad commissioners. 1864, ch. 167.

Upon railroad companies, for the expense of the railroad commission, $9,257.91. 1869, ch. 408.

Upon life insurance companies, one cent on every $1,000 insured, as compensation for the state valuation of policies, $19,956.10. G. S. 58. 1868, c. 317.

The Detail and Form of Assessments.

The act of the year 1861, "to secure a uniform description and appraisal of estates in the Commonwealth for the purpose of taxation," was an important enactment, and has done much to secure the end for which it was passed and to equalize valuations throughout the state. This law, which requires the annual assessments to be recorded in a book to be furnished by the secretary of the Commonwealth, compels an exhibit of the assessment of each citizen, the details of which are spread through twenty-seven columns, while the aggregates of the assessment are condensed into twelve columns of a blank to be forwarded, under the oath of the assessors, to that officer. Detail and form of assessments. 1861, ch. 167.

The law was doubtless drawn in the belief that this system would restrain citizens from evading the assessment of property they were known to possess, and the assessors from being parties to such an evasion, by spreading the full details of the assessment to the view of each tax-paying citizen. The experience of more than a decade must have justified the expectations of its originators, and its practical workings have not exposed it to severe criticism. Its essential features will doubtless remain as a part of our methods of assessment. But, in the opinion of the commission, that part of the law which requires the exposure and valuation of the items of personal property, is needless for any public purpose, and is an unwarrantable violation of that privacy to which every citizen is entitled in the conduct of his affairs.

If it is answered that, without the full knowledge of the detail of each person's estate, it is impossible to assess a just tax, the point is conceded. But because it is essential that the officers of the government, who should be persons of *discretion* as well as of integrity, should know the particular items and the value of each item of personal property assessable, it does not follow that, when they shall have made up their schedule, they should publish to the world information which prudent men withhold from members of their families. It is admitted, that for real estate and for that portion of personal estate which is of necessity open to public view, there can be no objection to the record of details. And in the assessment of real estate the practice not only tends to uniformity and equality of taxation, but is a material assistance to the officers. No careful assessor would desire to proceed with his work by any other plan. As the law now stands, many good citizens, willing to bear their full share of public charges, do not return their "list" under oath, but prefer to take the estimation or dooming of the assessors, to the publicity that would follow an exhibition of their investments. Another class, permitting the officers, without their assistance, to itemize as best they may, the property which they believe assessable persons possess, appear, after the work has been finished, to challenge items of personal property recorded against them, of which they have divested themselves without notice to the assessors, and demand abatements when the whole amount of their tax does not exceed their legal liability. In this connection, we would notice that the law does not permit a personal tax, which is invalid by reason of its assessment, in general terms, to be re-assessed to the person who ought to have been assessed for the property, although the want of specification may have been occasioned by the neglect of the person assessed to give the necessary information, and the fee of the property intended to be taxed is in some member of his family, to whom it has been conveyed. It would seem that the government is fully protected when the sworn return of the citizen is in the hands of the government officer. If the assessors, who represent the state, are compelled to estimate the personal property of the person to be assessed, through his failure to comply with the provisions of law, then an assessment against him in one aggregate sum is all that should be required. When such an assessment is made, it should not be cancelled, if in the hands of any member of the household, or of any trustee for their benefit, unless the value of the property assessable is otherwise taxed. But in any case, the total valuation of the personal estate of any citizen designated in the assessment book as the sworn return of the tax-payer or the estimation of the assessors, is all that should be exposed to public inspection. G. S. ch. 11, § 53.

When the assessors are compelled, for want of definite information, to estimate the liability of any person to assessment, they are assisted in their judgment by indications of property that enable them to approximate to a just assessment. But these signs fail when personal estate is held, not by the person who enjoys its income, but by a trustee for his use. All the indications of wealth may exist, and yet no assessable liability. So completely is it in the power of those holding trust estates to divest themselves of legal responsibility for assessment, without any indication of the fact which the assessors can follow, that we do not see why they should Personal property held by a trustee. Ib. § 12.

not be held equally responsible with executors and admin-
G. S. c. 11, § 12. istrators in regard to the notice of change in the property held by them.

Reduction of personal assessments without a list made under oath. 1866, ch. 170.

An enactment in relation to persons who have changed their domiciles will not permit assessors to assess their personal estate at any less amount than taxed for in the place of their last residence, until they bring in to the assessors a sworn return of their property. Such a restriction does not bind the officers in relation to any other class of citizens when estimating their liability to assessment, but, on the contrary, it is indicated that their judgment shall be for what they deem a just amount, whether the same is for a greater or less sum than the last assessment. But when a tax is levied, the assessors are again enjoined to make no abatement to any person, unless he brings to them a list, under oath, of all his estates liable to taxation. When such a return is filed for the purpose of gaining an abatement of a tax assessed on personal property, the officers are obliged to assess not only the amount that ought at first to have been assessed, but also to add a heavy penalty for neglect to render the list before the levy of tax. It would simply be placing all citizens alike before the law, if a personal property tax should not at any time be reduced without the list which, in theory of law, every assessable person carrries in to the assessors. If our recommendation to shield from public inspection the details of personal assessments is adopted, there can be no valid objection to the uniform application of the rule to all, which now, by law, is applied to certain classes of our citizens.

G. S. ch. 11, § 27.

Ch. 11, § 46.

1865, 121.

Taxation of co partnerships.

When the tax acts were a matter of annual enactment, they recited that, "Whereas there are many persons, within this Commonwealth, engaged in trade, who negotiate much business, and hire stores, shops, and wharves in towns, districts, or other places other than where they dwell, and whose property and ability can be better known to the assessors of the several towns wherein

Tax act, 1817, § 5.

such business is transacted, than to the town, district, or other places where they dwell, therefore," it was ordered that such property should be taxed in the place where the business was carried on. By the report of the commission who prepared the revised statutes, this provision was extended to copartnerships, and the recommendation of the commissioners was enacted into law.

Report of commissioners, p. 35, § 14; also, p. 28, ch. 7, § 14. R. S. ch. 7, § 13.

The supreme judicial court settled the principle that a firm, like an individual, has a domicile, and that the joint property is assessable in that place. This rule has been modified, by later decisions, to the effect that the interest of a resident partner in merchandise kept for sale without the state, in the hands of non-resident partners, is taxable in the domicile of the partner, and not in that of the firm.

Peabody v. Essex, 10 Gray, 97. Bemis et al. v. Boston, 14 Allen, 366; Hoardley v. Essex, 105 Mass. 527.

Soon after the decision first referred to, which found that ships and vessels abroad were taxable to a copartnership in its firm domicile, the legislature changed the law, and made this class of property assessable to the partners in the places of their residence. The practical operation of this law exempted from taxation, in Massachusetts, the shipping of a firm doing business here, to the extent of the interest of partners who had established a domicile without the state. This point was covered by a law that declared that the interest of such members, if the vessels were owned by the copartnership, should be taxable to the firm in its place of business. It is our opinion that, for the reasons laid down in the old tax law, and because the municipality where the firm is domiciled is charged with the expense of the protection of the joint property, and the cost of internal improvements which facilitate business operations, the principle is correct that declares all firm property to be taxable, under our laws, in the place of the partnership domicile. The opposite policy has long prevailed in our adjoining state of New York, and is, doubtless, one of the reasons that has caused the personal property of the state to recede to a point that has brought about a discussion of the expedi-

1859, ch. 114. G. S. ch. 11, §§ 15, 16.

1870, ch. 328.

Personal property of copartnerships should be taxed in firm domicile.

ency of discontinuing its taxation altogether, and placing the whole burden of assessment upon real estate. Under the laws of that state, the property of a copartnership is taxed to the members of the firm in the place of their residence. Although it is conceded that the real estate of New York is not assessed so closely to its real value as in this state, yet the very small amount of personal property taxed, and the enormous rates of taxation prevalent, clearly show that large amounts of merchandise and other tangible property of business firms, easy of estimation by local assessors, wholly escape assessment.

If in two or more towns. Report of commissioners, p. 28, c. 7, § 14; also, p. 35, § 14. R. S. ch. 7, § 13. G. S. ch. 11, § 15.

When the commissioners reported the section by which copartnerships were assessed in their firm name, they inserted a provision that "if they have places of business in two or more towns, they shall be taxed in those several towns for the proportions of property employed in such towns respectively."

This proper rule remains the law to the present time, but in practice some difficulty has arisen in the assessment of the personal property where a firm has places of business in two or more towns. The property is being continually interchanged, and it is a difficult matter for assessors, or even the owners themselves, to state under oath "the proportion of property employed" in the several towns.

G. S. c. 11. § 15.

This difficulty is availed of by certain firms who desire to evade their fair share of taxation. They may have $100,000 in their business. In the place of their financial headquarters they report, say $20,000, all the rest in the town where their manufactory is situated. To the assessors of the latter place they report $20,000, all the remainder being in stock and bills receivable at the business centre. The old tax acts recognized this difficulty, and provided, in the case of persons being taxable for business in a place other than their home, that they should be "held to deliver on oath or affirmation, if required, a list of the whole taxable estate to the assessors of the town, district, plantation or other

Tax act, 1817, § 5.

place, where they may dwell on the said first day of May, distinguishing what part thereof is taxable elsewhere, and in default thereof, they may be doomed by the said assessors."

We are of opinion that copartnerships should be required to render a list of their whole taxable personal property to the assessors of each city or town where their business is carried on. Such a course, we think, would tend to uniformity of assessment, would facilitate the work of assessors, and be much more satisfactory to all firms, except those who find the present law to their advantage, in the facility for evasion which it offers. As between the different cities and towns, there could be no temptation to the firm to place the proportions unfairly, except the difference in the rate of taxation in the respective places. The copartnership, after going through their accounts and fixing their proportions, would be saved the trouble of repeating the operation in every town where they had a portion of their business, and could file with each board of assessors an exact duplicate of an original return.

Property held by executors and administrators. G. S. c. 11, § 12.

There appears to us to be a want of harmony between the provisions of the fifth and seventh divisions of the twelfth section of the chapter in relation to the assessment of taxes. The latter division of the section requires that "the personal estate of deceased persons shall be assessed in the place where the deceased last dwelt" until the executor or administrator "gives notice to the assessors that the estate has been distributed and paid over to the parties interested therein." This would seem to give a plain rule, and the supreme court, for want of the notice to the assessors of the place where the deceased last dwelt, has sustained a tax in that place, although the executors had closed their accounts and charged themselves with the fund as trustees, thirteen months before, and their final account as executors had been allowed by the probate court more than eleven months before the date at which a tax elsewhere assessed upon them in their

Hardy v. Yarmouth, 6 Allen, 277.

capacity as trustees was by this decision declared illegal.

G. S. ch. 11, § 12. It seems to us, in view of this interpretation of the law, that the provisions of the fifth division of the section referred to, that "personal property held in trust by an *executor*, *administrator* or trustee, the income of which is payable to another person, shall be assessed to the *executor*, *administrator* or trustee, in the place where such other person resides," cannot in many cases be executed without twice taxing the same property. Under the law as it now stands, estates are held for assessment "in the place where the deceased last dwelt" which have long since become for all practical purposes trust estates. Assessors and representatives of estates are often in doubt as to the liability of the property to assessment, as they apply the words of the law to the facts of a well-understood case. Another difficulty with the seventh clause is the application of the rule of continuing the assessment of the estate. Upon the wording of the clause, it is clear that if an executor or administrator should close his accounts and pay over the estate in full, without notice to the assessors, he must be held to pay the tax upon the whole valuation. It is not so clear that if he pays out nearly all of it and has a small balance in his hands, but that the assessors are bound to make him, or at all events have the power to grant him an abatement on the full tax, upon his filing with them a list of the remnant of the property held. We are of opinion that all persons holding funds in any fiduciary capacity should be held for the tax upon the full amount last assessed, in default of proper notice to the assessors, and that some definite time should be fixed (say three years) in which, without notice to the assessment board, "the personal estate of a deceased person shall be assessed in the place where the deceased last dwelt," and that after that date the funds follow the rule of trust estates as provided in the fifth division of the section regulating the place of assessment of personal property.

Information to assessors. It often happens, especially in the larger cities of the

Commonwealth, that assessors, calling at dwellings in the performance of their duties, find upon the premises none of the persons who, by the theory of the law, are supposed to be always at their home. It needs no argument to show that this class of officers cannot perform their duty efficiently without proper information, promptly furnished by those whose duty it is to impart it. The twenty-first section of the chapter of the assessment of taxes should be amended by adding to the classes there specified, the words "all other persons." G. S. c. 11, § 21.

Assessors to have power to summons witnesses.

In a legal sense, an assessor is a state officer; the law he executes is the state's enactment. The treasurer of the Commonwealth issues his warrant for a state tax to the boards of assessors of the several cities and towns, and their warrant for the collection of a tax runs in the name of the Commonwealth. But when a tax has been assessed, the warrants of the state and the county are first satisfied in full, and the loss by reason of abatements comes wholly upon the municipality which is the limit of the jurisdiction of each board of assessors. A tax which they believe to be just, and decline to abate, can be carried by appeal from them to the county commissioners. G. S. § 17. 1867, ch. 166. G. S. ch. 11, §§ 38, 39. Ib. ch. 12, § 49. Ib. ch. 11, §§ 43, 45.

It having been represented to us that the question of the right to summon witnesses and provide for their compensation has prevented the defence of cases that ought to have been maintained, it seems to us only proper that such a right should exist at the cost of the municipality that receives the benefit of the tax. We do not, however, recommend that boards of assessors should have the right to involve their cities or towns in legal expense beyond the limit indicated, except with such proceedings as are now requisite for such a purpose.

As to assessment records.

By the law of eighteen hundred and sixty-one, the secretary of the Commonwealth is required to furnish to the assessors of each city and town, annually, suitable books for the purpose of assessment, which "shall contain blank columns numbered from one to twenty-seven inclusive." We have already expressed the opinion that some 1861, ch. 167, § 1.

of these columns could with advantage be omitted. But as the book is now ordered to be constructed, or as it would be if reduced as we have recommended, it makes a ponderous volume, well enough adapted for office use, where one a year is all that is required, but utterly impracticable for field-work, where in the larger cities and towns the bulk of the duty of the assessors must be performed, and where using a separate volume for each ward or district, the accumulation of a few years would fill any ordinary office. In many of the cities and towns the book furnished by the state is discarded, and at their own expense a more convenient form is provided that condenses the information required, or places part of it in books to be written in the field, and part in books transcribed in the office, enabling the assessment to proceed with the required dispatch and economy of labor.

The danger of this custom is the evil that the enactment of 1861 was designed to cure. With different methods, we may lose, to a greater extent than now, uniformity of valuation.

In our opinion, the needs of different municipalities may be met, and the interests of the state be amply protected by permitting such form of books only to be used as shall be approved by the tax commissioner. With this restriction, there can be no danger of an undue degree of latitude.

1871, c. 125.
1874, c. 317.

Such a regulation becomes not only important to local officials, but to the Commonwealth, if its officer is to be entrusted with the details of valuation for the purpose of state and county taxation.

Recommendations:

Holding the views above indicated, we would in this connection, recommend—

As to detail of personal property. 1861, c. 167.

First. That the aggregate valuation only of each citizen's personal estate be exposed to public inspection, with such a record as will indicate if the valuation is by a return of the person assessed, or is the estimation of the assessors. The detail, by which the aggregate valuation is obtained, to be retained by the board of asssessment, subject only to the inspection of the tax commissioner or other authorized official, unless by the direction or order of the person assessed.

Second. That no reduction in the amount of valuation of personal estate be made to any citizen, without the return of all the assessable personal property in the manner provided by law; or, if the value assessed is held by any member of his household, or in trust for their benefit.

As to reduction of personal assessment. G. S. c. 11. §§ 22–28 and §46. 1866, 170. 1865, 121.

Third. That all personal property of a copartnership, be assessed in the place where the business is transacted, and if the firm have places of business in two or more towns, that the whole amount assessable be returned to the assessors of every place where any part of the business is carried on, under the oath of some member of the firm as to the proportion of property employed in each of such places.

As to copartnerships. G. S. c. 11, §§ 15, 16. 1870, 328.

Fourth. That executors, administrators, trustees, and all persons holding personal estates in a fiduciary capacity, be held for assessment upon the full amount last assessed, unless notice of change in the estate be given to the assessors, and that all personal property in the hands of executors and administrators be held to follow the rule of taxation of trust estates, after three years from the first proceedings in the probate court.

As to property held in a fiduciary capacity. G. S. c. 11, § 12.

Fifth. That the twenty-first section of the eleventh chapter of the general statutes be amended by adding to the classes therein specified, "all other persons."

As to information to assessors. G. S. c. 11, § 21.

Sixth. That assessors have power to summon witnesses before the county commissioners, at the expense of the town or city within whose jurisdiction they act.

As to witnesses. G. S. c. 11, §§ 43–45.

Seventh. That the tax commissioner have authority to designate the form of assessment book required by law, and to permit the assessors of any city or town to modify the method prescribed: *provided*, that all such modifications are approved by him, and are made without expense to the Commonwealth.

As to assessment books. 1861, 167, § 1.

Of the Appeal in Cases of Abatement refused by the Assessors.

Appeal in cases of abatement refused by assessors. G. S. 11, § 45.

At present, "if the assessors refuse to make an abatement to a person, he may, within one month thereafter, make complaint thereof to the county commissioners by filing the same with their clerk, and if, upon a hearing, it appears that the complainant is overrated, the commissioners shall make such an abatement as they deem reasonable."

There are two objections urged against this remedy: *First.* That it consumes, in many of the counties at least, a great amount of time. *Second.* That because the proceedings of county commissioners are not according to the course of the common law, their rulings on matters of law cannot be revised in the ordinary way, but only by a petition to the supreme judicial court for a writ of *certiorari.* This remedy is expensive, too much out of the common course to be readily availed of, and, under the practice adopted by the supreme court, gives to the town in whose favor the commissioners have decided, an undue advantage, in making the answer of the commissioners conclusive upon the petitioners.

A third objection is, that the complainant can have no relief unless he himself is overrated. If his neighbors are underrated, he is as clearly entitled to relief, but can in no way obtain it. It is probably impossible to avoid this third objection without a radical change in the machinery of assessment. In some states, valuation lists are made up by "listers" for the several towns, and reported to a central officer or board, sitting at the county seat, with power to revise them, by adding to or taking from the valuation of any individual, or by increasing or diminishing the entire list by a percentage. When the several lists have been thus revised, the officer or board assesses, in accordance with them, the taxes of the towns composing the county.

The process of revision affords an opportunity for every

one to appeal from the lister of his town to the central board, and gives him the advantage of a summary remedy before a fresh tribunal. We, however, do not wish to recommend so radical a change in the system of assessment. Should a central bureau be established, with supervisory power over the local assessors, persons feeling aggrieved might be authorized to ask his rulings upon questions of law,—such rulings, when communicated to the local assessors, to be binding upon them until overruled by some court of competent jurisdiction.

The other objection can be removed by such changes in the times of holding the sessions of boards of county commissioners, and in the course of procedure in matters pending before them, as shall ensure the speedy disposition of appeals from assessors, and the certain and easy revision of such questions of law as they may decide adversely to either party.

Whether such changes can be made without the entire remodelling of the present county commissioner system, is a grave question, but outside of our present purpose and limits. The necessity for improvement in the administration of several matters, of which these boards have had exclusive jurisdiction, has led to recent statutes allowing parties to apply either to the superior court, or to county commissioners, for relief in certain cases. It is believed that the operation of this concurrent remedy has been good so far as it has been applied. But there are grave objections to its extension to appeals from assessors, or petitions for the abatement of taxes; and rather than to look for farther relief in that direction, we would, if it were fairly within our province, unhesitatingly recommend a thorough revision of the functions and modes of procedure of the boards of county commissioners.

Exemptions from Taxation.

Exemptions from taxation.

Since, in the resolve requiring our appointment and assigning our duties, "the laws of the state relating to taxation" held the first place, and since these embrace incomparably vaster pecuniary interests, and involve questions of much greater difficulty and importance than the laws relating to the other topic assigned us, we have given to these the chief place in our report. But we have not been unmindful of the laws relating to exemption from taxation, respecting which we submit the following considerations.

G. S. ch. 11, § 5. By existing statutes the following persons and polls are exempt from taxation by this Commonwealth.

First. The property of the United States.

Second. The property of the Commonwealth, except real estate of which the Commonwealth is in possession under a mortgage for condition broken.

Third. The personal property of literary, benevolent, charitable and scientific institutions incorporated within this Commonwealth, and the real estate belonging to such institutions, occupied by them or their officers for the purposes for which they were incorporated.

Fourth. All property belonging to common-school districts, the income of which is appropriated to the purposes of education.

Fifth. The Bunker Hill Monument.

Sixth. The household furniture of every person, not exceeding one thousand dollars in value, his wearing apparel, farming utensils, and mechanics' tools necessary for carrying on his business.

Seventh. Houses of religious worship and the pews and furniture (except for parochial purposes), but portions of such houses appropriated for purposes other than religious worship shall be taxed at the value thereof to the owners of the houses.

Eighth. Cemeteries, tombs and rights of burial, so long as the same shall be dedicated for the burial of the dead.

Ninth. The estate, both real and personal, of incorporated agricultural societies.

Tenth. The property to the amount of five hundred dollars of a widow or unmarried female, and of any female minor whose father is deceased, if her whole estate, real and personal, not otherwise exempted from taxation, does not exceed in value the sum of one thousand dollars.

Eleventh. Mules, horses and neat-cattle less than one year old, and swine and sheep less than six months old.

Twelfth. The polls and any portion of the estates of persons who, by reason of age, infirmity and poverty, are, in the judgment of the assessors, unable to contribute fully towards the public charges.

Thirteenth. Beet-sugar manufactories, for ten years from 1872. 1872, 327.

Fourteenth. So much of the income from a profession, trade or employment as exceeds the sum of two thousand dollars. G. S. ch. 11, § 4. 1873, 354.

The first of the above-enumerated classes, the Commonwealth has neither the power nor the right to tax.

The second class a small number of economists advocate the propriety of taxing, on the ground, as they term it, that there ought not to be any "deadheads" in taxation, and that the Commonwealth ought to keep as clean and as rigorous accounts with herself as with her subjects. But any such doubtful advantage would hardly compensate for the additional cost which the process would involve, and this subject may probably be dismissed as not needing any extended consideration. Rossire et al. v. Boston. 4 Allen, 57.

But, as many persons claim that the third class ought no longer to be exempted, we have given to this question very careful attention, and, as the result, we recommend that the existing laws of the Commonwealth relating thereto remain unchanged. Recommendation in regard to educational and charitable institutions. See opinion of minority p. 181.

Briefly stated, the following positions upon this point seem to us to be sound:

Taxation is a certain requirement which the state makes upon its subjects for the public welfare. Though nominally and technically levied upon property, it is really laid upon persons, and is a lawful demand that they use their property not solely for their own good, but also for the good of others. It is not, indeed, a demand for property as such, but only for a particular species of property, viz., money. As already remarked, taxation is not a payment to society for certain social privileges and immunities, but it is the enforcement of the right, and the fulfilment of the obligation revealed in the very existence of the state and its subjects. Like all the service which the state requires, this involves the righteous surrender or subjection of the individual will to the will of the community. When this self-surrender is free and complete, there is nothing more to be desired, either on the part of the individual or the state. The perfect individual and the perfect state would both be found in the free and full surrender of every individual to the welfare of every other. Whatever favors this most desirable attainment, should receive every encouragement. All gifts, whereby an individual shows any true self-forgetfulness for the public good, will not only be welcomed, but the disposition to make them will be encouraged and fostered by every wise state. As a general rule, all such gifts are in the exact line of what the state seeks to secure by its taxation, and there is really just as great an absurdity in taxing them as there would be in retaxing the taxes themselves. Instead of taxing such gifts, the state might more profitably encourage them by bounties. She should encourage all acts of every sort whereby a man is disposed to render an unselfish service to his fellow-men, always indeed superintending such acts and repressing whatever would be injurious, but also always fostering that self-forgetfulness, in the free and full exercise of which, by every individual, consists the highest well-being, both of himself and the state. Property, which passes out of private hands a free-will offering for public uses, and which loses thereby its entire power of reproducing itself for private gain or emolument, deserves very different treatment, for it must ever stand in a very different relation to the state from that which private parties can still control for private ends.

The only proper question in such a matter is, whether the gifts are really for the public good. An individual may be truly unselfish, and yet not wholly wise, and might generously, but ignorantly, direct his gifts in a way for the public injury. But in such a case the proper course for the state would be, not to tax such gifts, but to refuse or prohibit them.

It is very possible that the property given to our charitable, educational or religious institutions, may, at any time, find itself directed, either by the will of its donors or its managers, into channels not favorable to the public welfare, and it is very clear that over all such matters the state should exercise her wise supervision and just authority. We believe that the machinery for such an exercise is already provided by our courts, but if not, we recommend the enactment of statutes by which, even if individuals or corporations devote property, ostensibly for charitable, educational or religious purposes, but in a way not favorable or even prejudicial to charity, education or religion, such mistakes may be lawfully corrected.

Opinion that present supervision is sufficient.

It would be a singular contradiction, not only to the treatment of education, which has given this Commonwealth such glory in the past, but also to the entire educational system for which Massachusetts has such eminence at the present time, if we should put the slightest bar upon, or fail to give every encouragement to any efforts for the promotion among our people of knowledge in every department of literature, science or art. The original constitution of the state still remains unaltered in its declaration that,—

Efforts for knowledge should be encouraged.

"Wisdom and knowledge, as well as virtue, diffused generally among the body of the people, being necessary for the preservation of their rights and liberties; and as these depend on spreading the opportunities and advantages of education in the various parts of the country, and among the different orders of the people, *it shall be the duty of legislatures and magistrates, in all future periods of this Commonwealth*, to cherish the interests of

Chap. 5, § 2.

literature and science, and all seminaries of them; especially the university at Cambridge, public schools and grammar schools in the towns; *to encourage private societies and public institutions, rewards and immunities, for the promotion of agriculture, arts, sciences, commerce, trades, manufactures*, and a natural history of the country; to countenance and inculcate the principles of humanity and general benevolence, public and private charity, industry and frugality, honesty and punctuality in their dealings; sincerity, good humor, and all social affections and generous sentiments among the people."

This is, to-day, the fundamental rule for the guidance and control of the legislature in its dealings with the subject. Before and since its formal announcement, in 1780, the practice of the state has been uniform and unbroken to obey its commands and encourage religion, science and charity, by giving the property donated to those objects immunity from the burdens of taxation. Were not the donors of such funds justified in believing that our legislatures and magistrates, in all future periods of the Commonwealth, would observe their duty in cherishing and preserving these immunities? Would not their repeal, so far as it would bring under taxation, funds heretofore donated in the belief that the immunity would be permanent, savor of a breach of the public faith?

Report of secretary of board of education, 1873, p. 108.

We now levy an educational tax amounting, for 1873, to $3,889,053.80, for the support of our admirable system of common and normal schools, and whatever any one might think of this sum, whether too much or too little, no one will probably complain of the principle upon which such a tax is laid. Every one acknowledges that the state would be derelict in duty and forgetful of all of her high interests, if making no provision for the education of her people. But the same arguments which require the establishment of common schools, require also, and more emphatically, the establishment of higher seminaries of learning, academies, colleges and professional schools. As a matter of fact, these higher schools have not grown out of the lower, and do not rest upon them, but the higher school is, historically, first, and the lower one is not its precursor, but its product; there is no law of evolution by which the common school grows up into the college, for, as an historical fact, the college is actually first, and gives birth to the common school. No one can trace the history of education in any country in Europe, without noticing that the university is, in every instance, the mother and the foster nurse of common schools. It is not by the lower education of the many that we come to have the higher education of the few, but the exact converse of this is the universal rule. The education of the many is always dependent on the education of the few.

The higher institution of learning the parent of the common school.

It is interesting to note how clear a knowledge of this great fact was entertained by the early founders of this Commonwealth. At the outset of their educational work, and as its foundation, they established Harvard College as early as 1636, and the sight must be very dim which does not see the dependence of the entire system of the common education of the people upon this institution alone, or the strength and sustenance which Harvard and her sister colleges give to the common schools of the Commonwealth to-day.

The first order for the establishment and support of common schools in the colony of Massachusetts Bay, was issued by the general court in 1647, and is as follows:—

"It being one chiefe project of y^{t} ould deluder, Satan, to keepe men from the knowledge of ye Scriptures, as in form^{r} times by keeping y^{m} in an unknowne tongue, so in these latt^{r} times by pswading from ye use of tongues, y^{t} so at least ye true sence & meaning of ye originall might be clouded by false glosses of saint seeming deceivers, y^{t} learning may be not buried in ye grave of o^{r} fath^{rs} in ye church & com̄onwealth, the Lord assisting o^{r} endeavo^{r}s,—

Records of Mass. Bay Col., 1647, vol. 2, p. 203.

"It is therefore ord^{r}ed, y^{t} ev^{r}y towneship in this jurisdiction aft^{r} ye Lord hath increased y^{m} to ye number of 50 household^{rs}, shall then forthwth apoint one wthin their towne to teach all such children as shall resort to him to write & reade, whose wages shall be paid eith^{r} by ye parents or mast^{rs} of such children, or by ye inhabitants in gen^{r}all, by way of supply, as ye maior p^{r}t of those y^{t} ord^{r} ye prudentials of ye towne shall appoint; provided, those y^{t} send their children be not oppressed by paying much more y^{n} they can have y^{m} taught for in oth^{r} townes; & it is furth^{r} ordered, y^{t} where any towne shall increase to ye numb^{r} of 100 families or household^{rs}, they shall set up a gramer schoole, ye m^{r} thereof being able to instruct youth so farr as they may be fited for ye university, provided, y^{t} if any towne neglect ye pformance hereof above one yeare, y^{t} every such towne shall pay 5£ to ye next schoole till they shall p^{r}forme this order."

This seems to have been copied from an order issued three years earlier by the united colonies of Connecticut, and which was there coupled with a provision for the maintenance of poor scholars in Cambridge. The early impulse to all this came not from the uneducated, but in both

Barnard's legislation respecting common schools of Conn. 1636–38.

Massachusetts and Connecticut, "the natural and acknowledged leaders in the enterprise, the men who, by their religious character, wealth, social position and previous experience in conducting large business operations, commanded public confidence in church and Commonwealth, were educated men."

Though Harvard College has received munificent gifts from the state, her largest endowments, as well as those of other colleges, have come from private benefactions. But for these, the colleges would have had no existence, or would have owed their establishment and support wholly to the state, as is the case with the great educational institutions of the Old World. Nowhere has private beneficence more lavishly released the state from the necessity of taxing its subjects for the support of higher institutions of learning than in the United States, and in no one of these has this been more conspicuous than in our own Commonwealth. It will not prove wise economy for the state to repress such beneficence by laying a tax upon its exercise, nor is it a very enlightened or comprehensive view which can only behold the taxes which are not levied upon the property of these institutions, and does not see the much larger taxes which would have to be laid in behalf of education, had not private beneficence relieved the state of so large a part of its work. If a penny saved is as good as a penny earned, a pound saved is surely better to the possessor than the penny he has lost.

It should be remembered that the exemption in question, so far as real estate is concerned, only relates to the premises from which these institutions derive no revenue.

It should be noted, also, that, as a matter of fact, there is no practical inequality in the working of this exemption, calling for its removal, since the average rate of taxation in the towns most largely endowed with this class of exempted property, is less than the average rate through the Commonwealth.

We recommend the continuance also of the fourth class of exemptions in the foregoing list, for the same reasons as apply to the class just considered. Recommendation in regard to common school districts.

We have never heard of any one desiring to tax the property specified in the fifth of the foregoing enumerations. Certain minor exemptions.

The people of the state have always exercised the right, reserved or declared in their constitution, of encouraging agriculture and manufactures by granting, to some extent, immunity from taxation to property employed for these purposes. For many years prior to 1828, the annual tax acts exempted machinery in cotton, woollen and linen manufactories, and also sheep. The present statutes exempt "farming utensils," "mechanics' tools not exceeding three hundred dollars in value, necessary for carrying on his business," "mules, horses and neat-cattle less than one year old; and swine and sheep less than six months old." 1828, c. 143, passed March 4, 1829.

Towns have recently been authorized to exempt, for a limited term, property engaged in the manufacture of beet-sugar, though we are not informed that any town has actually had occasion to avail itself of this authority. The 1872, 327.

aggregate value of all the farming utensils, mules, horses and neat-cattle less than a year old, and swine and sheep less than six months old, and of mechanics' tools, exempted by law, is large. But this value is so widely distributed, that the exemption attracts but little attention, and the inequality resulting from it is unfelt.

With reference to these minor exemptions, we have no recommendation to make, except that when the next census of the state shall be taken, it be so done that an accurate knowledge may be obtained of the amount and distribution of the property covered by them. We believe that the state did wisely in discontinuing the exemption of cotton and woollen manufacturing property, and that it is very questionable whether the manufacture of beet-sugar will be greatly encouraged by relief from taxation. If it will, and the people desire so to encourage it, we believe that the exemption should be by general law, operative throughout the state, rather than under the vote of a town. Farther than these suggestions, we recommend no change in the present treatment of the sixth, eleventh and thirteenth classes in the above list.

No change recommended in certain minor exemptions.

Literary, etc. Common school districts. Houses of religious worship.

The same line of argument which applies to the third and fourth classes in the list, would also continue the present exemption to the seventh.

Appendix, pp. 369–403.

We have received from Messrs. Francis E. Abbot and Charles W. Eliot, valuable contributions to the discussion of the general question relating to the exemption of property devoted to literary, charitable and religious uses, and solicit the attention of the legislature to their papers, given in the Appendix.

Houses of religious worship are public works for the public service. If they ever become used for any other purpose than that of religious worship, while the property thus used becomes taxable under our present laws, it never can be converted to any private emolument. No religious society can sell its house of worship and put its proceeds into the pockets of its members. Having once been consecrated to the public advancement of religion, it can never be alienated from this use. The advantages of having these houses thus employed are, in the eye of the state, somewhat different from the advantages sought by the individuals who thus employ them. To the individual, religion is an end which he seeks for its own sake, but to the state, it is a means to be used for the promotion of its highest interests. The state uses religion and favors its advancement, because it is a means of civilization,—because it helps the state forward in its own line of highest progress. Our own state constitution aptly expresses this when it declares that "the public worship of God, and instruction in piety, religion and morality, promote the happiness and prosperity of a people and the security of a republican government."

Constitution, Art. XI. of Amendments.

Institutions of religion are therefore just as properly objects of state favor and patronage as institutions of learning, or any other institutions wherein private property has been alienated from private ends and has become devoted exclusively to the public welfare. In fact, state favor may more properly be granted to institutions of religion than to any other, since all the prosperity of any state—its culture, its freedom from crime, its social order—will rest ultimately upon the religion of its subjects, and will be perfect in exactly the degree that this religion is perfect and completely prevalent. What religion will do for the next life, or whether there is any future life, or whether religion is anything other than a superstition or delusion,—these are questions which the state properly leaves to the individual judgment and conscience. The state has to do with the present life, and finding here so potent an auxiliary in religion, every state in the history of the world has thus far not only availed itself of religious influences, but has contributed more or less prominently to their support and extension. Our own history offers no exception to this universal rule. The absolute dependence of the state upon Christian influences for the perfect peace, purity and freedom of its subjects, was not only affirmed by our fathers, in the earliest history of Massachusetts, but has been repeated by their children in every generation to our time. The declaration above quoted from the Massachusetts Bill of Rights illustrates this conviction; and the exemption from taxation, which from the beginning has been accorded in this state to houses of religious worship, is one of its practical consequences.

So important were the public worship of God and the preaching of the Bible felt to be to all the interests of the Commonwealth, that at the very first court, held Aug. 23, 1630, it was ordered that ministers should be maintained at the public charge, and this order was repeated and continued as the law of Massachusetts for more than two hundred years.

Mass. Col. Rec. Vol. I. p., 373.

Ib. p. 240.

At a general court held at Boston, Sept. 6, 1638, this matter was discussed, and the action taken was as follows:

"The court taking into consideration the necessity of an equal contribution to all common charges in towns, and observing that the chief occasion of the defect herein ariseth from hence, that many of those who are not freemen, nor members of any church, do take advantage thereby to withdraw their help in such voluntary contributions as are in use,—

"It is therefore hereby declared that every inhabitant in any town is liable to contribute to all charges, both in church and common wealth, whereof he doth or may receive benefit; and withal it is also ordered, that every such inhabitant who shall not voluntarily contribute, proportionably to his ability, with other freemen of the same town, to all common charges, as well for upholding the ordinances in the churches as otherwise, shall be compelled thereto by assessment and distress to be levied by the constable, or other officer of the town, as in other cases."

Ib. Vol. IV., p. 310.

And in 1657 the court answered in the affirmative the question propounded, whether the vote of the town of

Ipswich to pay £100 toward buying or building a house for their minister, bound all or any of the inhabitants, or only such as chose to contribute.

In 1671 the same court ordains, "that the ministers of God's word regularly ordained over any Church of Christ orderly gathered and constituted shall be freed from all rates for the country, county and church, and for the town also, except where, by special contract with the town, they have consented thereto: provided this freedom shall extend only to such estate as is their own proper estate and under their own custody and improvement."

Mass. Col. Rec. Vol. IV., Part II., pp. 485, 486.

So, too, the general court of the Plymouth Colony was not slow to pass laws for the support of preaching at the public charge:

In 1657, "Whereas this general court taking into theire seriouse Consideration the great defect that either is or like to bee in y[e] severall Townshipes in this jurisdiction for want of an Able Godly Teaching Minnestry and the great prejudice to the soules of many like to ensue; and being desirous according to our duties that such defects should not bee for want of due Incurragment to such as either are or shalbee imployed in soe good a worke of the Lord for his honner and the good of soules"

Plymouth Colony Laws, pp. 101, 102.

"And in consideration that in asmuch as the severall Townshipes graunted by the Government: was that such a Companie might bee received as should maintaine the publicke worshipe and service of God there, doe therefore judge that the whole body Church and towne are mutually ingaged to support the same:"

"And therefore order and agree, That in whatsoever Towneship there is or shalbee an able Godly Teaching Minister which is approved by this Government, that there four men be chosen by the Inhabitants or in case of theire neglect chosen by any three or more of the Majestrates to make an equall and just proportion upon the estates of the Inhabitants according to their abilities to make up such a convenient maintainance for his comfortable attendance on his worke as shalbee agreedupon by the Church in each Townshipe where any is with the concurrence of the rest of the Inhabitants if it may be had or by the Majestrates aforesaid in case of their apparent neglect, and that destresse, according as in other just cases provided, be made upon such as refuse to pay such theire proportions which is in justice due. But in case there bee any other way whereby any township doe or shall agree that may effect the end aforesaid this law not to be binding to them."

Plymouth Colony Laws, p. 269.

And in 1670, having again designated who is to collect the minister's salary, they go on to say that: "Whereas it hath been and is the pious care, and true intent of this Court, that all such Plantations and Townships as are by them granted, should maintain the public Sabbath Worship of God, and the preaching of the Word, and to do that end afford them such proportions of land as may accommodate such a society as may be able to maintain the same, and yet through the corruption or sinful negligence of many, or most of the Inhabitants of some Plantations, they do or may content themselves to live without the Ministry of the Word, to the great dishonor of God, and danger of their Souls; and there being great reason to fear that many may be acted therein by worldly and covetous principles," they therefore enact that henceforth in such towns the general court will yearly impose a rate or tax to be kept as a stock for building a meeting-house and settling a minister.

Anc. Laws and Ch. of Mass. Bay, p. 25.

The Province Charter, granted in 1691 by William and Mary, and consolidating the Colonies into the Province of Massachusetts Bay, recognizes "the ends for which the said plantations were at first encouraged," and gives great powers to the inhabitants, "whereby our subjects, inhabitants of our said province, may be religiously, peaceably and civilly governed, protected and defended; so as their good life and orderly conversation may win the Indians, natives of the country, to the Knowledge and obedience of the only true God and Saviour of mankind, and the Christian faith, which his royal majesty our royal grandfather King Charles the first, in his said Letters-patent declared was his royal intention, and the adventurers free profession to be the principal end of the said plantation."

Obedient to the professions of their fathers and the wishes of their royal master, the general court of the new province, in 1692, enacted "An Act for the settlement and support of ministers and schoolmasters," which continued the support of religious teaching and worship at the common charge. Occasional additional acts in the same line were passed during the remainder of the provincial period, and we find our ancestors throwing off their allegiance to Great Britain and adopting the constitution of 1783, with no thought but that the support of religion was as legitimate a common charge as any expense of government. From this review we see that the original exemption of church property in Massachusetts was a necessary deduction from the principle that the property used solely for public purposes of state should not be taxed, as its taxation simply amounted to taking from one purse to fill another, making the aggregate of the country's funds no greater, and entailing useless expense and risk in the assessment and collection,—apparently a sound principle and one which marks out a list of exemptions about the propriety of which there can be but little question.

Anc. Laws and Ch. of Mass. Bay, pp. 243–245.

Province Laws, pp. 256, 435.

The charges for the support of religious teaching and maintaining the worship of God and religious observances were considered by the founders of our state to be common charges, as much as the ordinary expenses of the town government, and very much as the expenses of maintaining common schools is by us considered a common charge to be paid from the public treasury.

That upon careful and independent consideration the men who framed our State Bill of Rights and Constitution, and the people who adopted them, understood and approved this policy of the state and desired to continue it, is shown by the articles of those instruments touching the subject. They were adopted in 1780, the question of a new constitution having been before the people for more than three years, during which one constitution, framed by the legislature, had been rejected by the people. These articles are given in full in the Appendix, and continued to be a part of our fundamental law until 1833, when the third was replaced by the XIth Amendment, the effect of which was to relieve those not belonging to a parish from compulsory contributions for the support of religion.

Appendix, p. 211.

Religion the foundation of national prosperity.

The foundation which religion furnishes for national prosperity may be seen from the relation which it has always borne to education and public virtue. The course of education among any people will have its direction and character ultimately determined by that people's religious life. The university, which is the mother of the common school, is herself the daughter of the church. The motto upon the seal of Harvard College, "*Christo et Ecclesia*" (for Christ and the Church), not only indicates the lofty and sacred purpose of its founders, but points us also to the source whence have issued all the streams of modern education. A religious quickening always precedes and gives birth to the intellectual quickening of any people; and where the religious impulse grows weak the intellectual impulse also begins to decline. Judging from the whole history of modern education, we should expect both our common schools and our colleges to decay, if the same religious impulse by which they were undoubtedly produced should not remain to preserve them. "I have always despaired," said the superintendent of schools in Ohio, "of establishing even a good common school, where there was not a working church to sustain it." Not only will the education of any people always be shaped in the long run by their religion, but their practical morality also will never rise higher than their religious faith requires. It is very easy to overlook the actual facts which demonstrate this. Many think that because there is a natural light of reason which reveals virtue, men need only open their eyes to this light in order to shape their conduct accordingly. That this ought to be the case, no one will deny; but the lamentable fact remains otherwise. Men do not do their duty simply because they know what it is. It is only by the love of virtue that men become virtuous; but the sad fact shows itself to every open eye, that the knowledge of virtue does not awaken a love for it in the actual human nature. No matter how pure or lofty it may be, no instruction in morality, if it went no farther than this, has ever sunk deeply into society, nor been able to change widely the action of men. It has never had any power to mould society internally and from the centre. The great forces which move men, by which, when we go to the bottom of it, all changes in individual character, and all revolutions in society are ultimately controlled, are religious forces; and to suppose that these are to be any less potent in the future than they have been, or any less necessary to the state, is not only to close the eye to all the lessons of history, but to be blind to the most obvious truths of human nature itself. Any treatment of Christian churches by a Christian state which would curb their influence, would be just as disastrous to the state as to the church. "If these churches," said Dr. South, "were not used as preaching places, we should soon need them as prisons."

The only question, therefore, which accords with the spirit prevailing through our whole history, and, we do not doubt, equally so with the temper of our times, is whether the exemption from taxation now granted to houses of religious worship is really favorable to the churches and to the healthiest Christian influence. This question, we think, may be safely left to the churches themselves.

That the system of exemption should be exchanged for a system of bounties, will not be long argued; for why be at the expense and the loss of levying and assessing a tax, only to pay it out again to the same parties from

Exemptions preferable to bounties.

whom it is taken? The advantage of having every appropriation made by the legislature annually scanned by the public, which it is thought this method would secure, does not seem to us very noteworthy, when we consider the small proportion of these exemptions as compared with the taxable property of the state, and the fact that their actual amount is at any time easily ascertainable. From the returns which we have carefully collected, and which will be found in the Appendix, it appears that the property thus exempted is only about one and a half per cent. of the total taxable valuation of the Commonwealth.

Appendix, Table I., p. 470.

Partial taxation not desirable.

That the system of entire, should be exchanged for one of partial, exemptions, by which a religious society should be allowed to hold (in its house of worship) a certain valuation and be taxed for the remainder, is not, in the opinion of the Commission, advisable. From this view one of our number dissents, for reasons given at the close of the report. In the opinion of the Commission this method would be attended with too many practical difficulties to permit its success, even if its success were desirable. Houses and lands have such different values at different places, that to exempt the same sum in all would be neither reasonable nor proportional; while to exempt different sums, on whatever principle these differences should be determined, would lead, in our judgment, to disputes difficult to adjust and impossible to terminate.

Opinion of minority, p. 181.

The objection that costly churches are not favorable to religion, and that the property which their construction has consumed is thus permitted to escape taxation without any compensating benefit, easily admits of two answers. Without discussing the question of their religious bearing, costly and beautiful temples, as works of art, may have ends of education to subserve sufficiently important and desirable to warrant the expenditure of all that they have cost. It would be a strange utility, even in this age, which should grudge the place which a structure like the Milan

Cathedral holds in the midst of a busy city, or which should undertake to estimate in money the worth of the sentiments which its presence is calculated to inspire. In the second place, it is quite an unwarranted assumption to claim that the property put into these costly churches escapes the tax-gatherer without furnishing him any return in kind. The taxable property of the neighborhood is augmented thereby to a degree often much greater than the amount which the churches have cost, and if it be a question of exact equivalence, the builders of these churches, instead of being called upon to relieve taxpayers of a part of their burden, might much more justly claim from them a compensation beyond the exemption.

Exemption need not trouble conscience.

It is not easy to see the force of the difficulty which some persons feel respecting these exemptions on grounds pertaining to conscience. I am conscientiously opposed, one says, to an exemption which goes to the support of any religion; while another objects on the same ground to the exemption which favors some views of religion foreign to his own. But till those who urge these objections are directly and solely responsible for this procedure of the state, we are unable to see how their conscience should be troubled about it. If they disapprove of this procedure, their conscience may constrain them to all proper steps to change it, but here their responsibility ends. If their efforts fail, they will, of course, regret the fact, but the action of the state, still continuing in this direction, will hardly give them any remorse. A man pays his taxes because the state compels him to do so. If the state is wrong in its exactions, she will assuredly, in the long run, suffer for them; but right or wrong, the man pays them without hesitation, unless he chooses to try titles of strength with her. He may feel that he is unjustly oppressed, but as long as this is not his fault, and as long as he has not come to the solemn point where "resistance to tyrants is obedience to God," his conscience ought not to ruffle him because he pays his taxes. For the use to which the state appropriates his taxes, he is not responsible. The state uses the taxes it collects, in many expenditures which one may think unwise and wrong; but the conscience of a man which allows itself to be put, on this account, as a screen against the payment of taxes, is as different, to say the least, from ordinary consciences, as is the intellect which puts it there different from that of ordinary men. We, at least, fail to understand it.

Present limit of exemption.

It should be clearly understood that the only church property now exempted from taxation by our state is

1865, c. 206, § 1.

"only such houses of religious worship as are owned by a religious society, or held in trust for the use of religious organizations."

If there are any houses of religious worship in the Commonwealth not owned by a religious society, and not held in trust for the use of religious organizations, but owned in a way which would permit them to be legally alienated, so that neither they nor their proceeds could be used for places of religious worship, these houses are clearly taxable by the laws of the Commonwealth existing to-day, and clearly ought to be. There is a broad and clear distinction, quite independent of any question of religious freedom or toleration, between the claims for exemption of the property which is consecrated forever, by our own statutes and courts, to religious uses within our own borders, and that property which might at any time be sold, and the proceeds either be devoted here to other uses than those of worship, or even transported entirely beyond the dominion of the state.

Cemeteries.

We recommend no change in the present treatment of the eighth of the classes named in the list.

Agricultural societies.

There has been some complaint that the property mentioned in the ninth class exceeds, in some cases, an amount needed for the ends for which agricultural societies were established. The amount of property thus held in the whole state, as will be seen by the Appendix to this report, is less than a half million of dollars, and, we think, does not call as yet for any legislative action.

Appendix, Table 6, p. 526.

There has been some claim for the repeal of the tenth class in the above enumeration, partly because it has been thought unnecessary on account of the provision named in the twelfth class, and partly because in some instances an undivided estate largely exceeding in value the sum exempted, has had claimants enough to bring the undivided portions within the exempted sum. On this latter ground, there is undoubted liability to wrong, and actual cases of injustice in this respect have been brought to our notice, but the reasons do not yet seem sufficient to demand that the present statute relating thereto be repealed. Unmarried females. Persons unable to contribute.

No change would probably be wished in the provision for the twelfth class in these exemptions. The question relating to the fourteenth class we have elsewhere discussed. Ib. Income.

In addition to the aforenamed classes exempted by statute, the following property is also exempted from taxation in this state by universal usage and by judicial decision: bridges, turnpikes and highways and their appurtenances, court-houses, jails, municipal property held for public purposes, the real estate location of railroads five rods in width, and the assets, other than real estate and national bank stock, of mutual insurance companies. Of these, the only topics which seem to call for any special remark, are the real estate location of railroads and the assets of mutual insurance companies. Property exempted by usage and judicial decision.

Upon the ground that the "railroad is a public work, established by public authority, intended for the public benefit, the use of which is secured to the whole community and constitutes a public easement," Chief Justice Shaw founded a decision, rendered in 1842 in the case of the Western Railroad Corporation, exempting from taxation such land as it had power to take by right of eminent domain and the structures thereon "reasonably incident to the support of the railroad, or to its proper and convenient use for the carriage of passengers and the transportation of commodities." A strip not exceeding five rods in width was at that time all which a railroad Railroads. 4 Met. 564 and 569.

corporation was authorized to take without the consent
G. S. 63, § 20. of the owner; and subsequent statutes have confined the exemption within that limit.

Mutual Ins. Cos. The assets of mutual insurance companies were declared exempt on different grounds. The fire companies were originally associations of individuals who, without actually raising a common fund, agreed to contribute in case of the burning of the property of a member. It is not probable that for many years after their introduction they held any considerable accumulations of personal property. An attempt to tax such an accumulation belonging to the Worcester company, was the occasion of a decision by the supreme court, in 1851, that such companies were "not liable to taxation for personal estate invested in their corporate names and held by them for
7 Cush. 601. the purposes of their incorporation." This decision went upon the ground that it had never been the policy of the state to assess the personal property of corporations, except the machinery of manufacturing companies. As an element of weight in determining their decision, the court says: "These institutions have now been established within this Commonwealth upwards of half a century, without any attempt hitherto to render them liable to taxation in this mode."

10 Mass. 517. 17 Mass. 460. 4 Met. 181. 9 Met. 199. 7 Gray, 277. 8 Allen, 330. This doctrine that corporations were not taxable on personal property had been enunciated in other cases, and has been since adhered to by the court. These decisions, no doubt, restrained assessors from any attempt to tax mutual life insurance companies upon their assets. Upon the enactment of the corporation tax laws of 1864 and 1865, an attempt was made to collect under them a franchise tax from such of the mutual life companies as had a guaranty capital. But the court, in the case of the Berkshire company, decided that those statutes were not intended to apply to mutual life insurance companies, making, in their discussion of
98 Mass. 25. the cause, this statement: "The business of mutual life insurance has never been treated by the legislature as an

appropriate object of taxation. A tax upon it is, in effect, a tax upon prudence; and for this reason, probably, has never been resorted to unless in the case now under consideration."

In the case both of the railroad and insurance company, if the question of the exemption was new, and uncomplicated by other matters, the ground on which it ought to be decided would, in our opinion, be clear. Other things being equal, we see no good reason why, as business corporations, they should not be taxed on the full value of their estates,—a million dollars employed in the business of transportation or of mutual insurance should contribute to the public charge equally with the same sum employed in manufactures or commerce. But the discontinuance of a specific exemption is a different matter. It is necessary to inquire whether by means of other taxes the same ability would not be reached and made to contribute to the proper extent,—whether such adjustments have not been made as to practically counterbalance the immunity,—what difference the repeal would make in the distribution of the public revenue, and, in view of competition with like capital subject to other sovereignties, what effect would the imposition of a fresh tax upon our corporations have on the business of their rivals.

Effect of exemption in case of railroads.

As compared with other property, how much tax does th railroad pay?

When the decision of 1842 was made, the shares were assessed to the holders. When the present system of corporate taxation was introduced, the shares were no longer a subject of assessment. The whole contribution to the public charges made by railroad property is now found in the sum of the assessments made by the local authorities upon their real estate outside the exempted five rods, and of the franchise tax.

The railroad commissioners' report, for 1873, gives the total cost of the tangible property of the seventy-eight railroads of the state, classified as road, equipment, and other property, as $157,609,820.33. A number of them are located partly outside the Commonwealth. The proportion for Massachusetts is $99,485,251.09, and there can be little doubt that their property in the state, if valued by the local assessors, would equal that sum. The amount paid by them under the law taxing franchises was $622,831.18. The rate for 1873 being $14.49 per thousand, the valuation to which it was applied was $42,982,-132. This sum represented the net value of the proportion for Massachusetts of all the property and franchises of her railroad corporations, after deducting the assessed value of their real estate in this state, outside the five-rod location. The assessed value so deducted was $22,127,981, and it is fair to presume that this amount was taxed locally at rates equal, on the average, to that used in assessing the franchise tax. Assuming this, the whole tax, both local and franchise, paid by railroad property, was $943,366, while the rate of tax, assuming the actual value of this property to be $100,000,000, was $9.43 per thousand.

But it must be remembered that the stock of some roads stands much higher in the market than the par which is presumed to represent the cost of its property, while that of others, although representing actual expenditure for track and other tangible property, is depreciated or worthless.

It is plain, therefore, that much railroad property is not fully taxed, and that the poorer corporations derive an advantage from this exemption. Should it be taken away by statute, we should expect that one practical effect would be to raise the assessed value of railroad real estate to such a sum as would leave no excess on which to lay a franchise tax under the present system. In other words, the repeal of the exemption would abolish the tax in its present form.

The appreciated value of the lands and buildings in towns and cities built up by the corporations, could not but produce such a result. The whole contribution of these corporations to the common charges would then be absorbed by the places in which their roads are located, leaving to the state no revenue from the shares of non-residents, and to other towns in which shareholders reside, no part of the tax.

We cannot, therefore, recommend its repeal, but would rather suggest that the means of compelling railroad property to contribute its full share, be sought in some better method of valuing the corporate franchise for assessment by the tax commissioner.

Valuation of corporate franchise of railroads.

As to the mutual insurance companies, the case seems to stand thus: the gross assets of the mutual fire insurance companies, by the commissioner's report for 1873, were $4,459,626. Of this they had invested in real estate $261,596, and in United States bonds $465,373, leaving a balance of over $3,700,000. The only tax paid by them to the state was upon premiums received, and amounted, in 1873, to only $11,044.83,—a very small percentage upon their assets, which, if in the hands of an individual, would have been taxable at ordinary rates. The risks of these companies are mostly written on property in Massachusetts, and there is but little competition between them and foreign companies. In the same year the assets of our mutual life insurance companies were $24,334,523.40. They held real estate to the value of $1,010,776.62, and government bonds to the value of $1,686,018.50, leaving a balance of $21,-637,728.28. If owned by individuals, it would have been assessed at usual rates; or, if deposited in savings banks, would have been taxed directly by the state.

Mutual insurance companies.

Auditor's report for 1873, pp. 66-67.

No tax is assessed upon these companies by the state except a specific imposition intended to cover the expense of the state valuation of their policies. The only taxes to which they are subjected are those upon their real estate and national bank stock, and incidentally upon their investments in Massachusetts corporations; and these, as compared with the total value of their assets, are of inconsiderable amount.

Should the state at any time wish to take away the exemption, the best method of assessing them would be by some form of the franchise tax. But we are not prepared to recommend any such measure at present. Their contracts with policy-holders have been made on the basis of exemption; and a state tax on the whole fund out of which all these contracts are to be met, while it would not impair their obligation, might make their performance impossible. Again, the companies are in competition for home and foreign business with companies chartered elsewhere, and with whose taxes on foreign business we cannot interfere, although we may regulate their competition in our own state. In our opinion, the question how far it would be wise to disturb, by the imposition of fresh taxes, the adjustment which has been arrived at under the long-continued policy of the state, is one which should be thoroughly considered by the insurance department before its decision by the legislature. Should, therefore, at any time, there be an apparent necessity for revenue from this source, we should advise that the expediency and method of obtaining it be considered as a question of insurance, full as much as of taxation.

Reservoirs. A few words seem in place here on the law concerning the taxation of reservoirs, which, if executed, would work a practical exemption respecting this class of property.

For several years past, the assessment of reservoirs has been a matter of disagreement and litigation between mill-owners and the authorities of towns where structures have been built for the storage of water. The manufacturer has complained that, being assessed on the cost of the reservoir in the town where it is situated, he is again taxed upon the same value in the town where his mill is located; the water-power being assessed as one of the elements of value in the appraisement of the real estate in the place
1872, 306. where it is used. A recent enactment requires that all reservoirs with connecting dams and the land flowed shall be assessed at a value "not exceeding a fair valuation of land of like quality in the immediate vicinity." This law, we are informed, has not been obeyed in some towns where

reservoirs are located, the authorities deeming the act to be unconstitutional; the position of the officers who refuse to obey the law being, that the legislature cannot enact that the estate of A shall be valued at the same price as the estate of B, when the market value of the first estate is ten times greater than the latter. We are unable to see why a given amount invested in the construction of a reservoir which has cost and will sell for all that has been expended on the work, should not be assessed at the same rate as a like amount of property in any other form. But in view of the fact that the question of the constitutionality of the law is to be tested in the courts, and that proceedings for that purpose have already been commenced, we make no recommendation upon this subject.

Returns of Exempt Property.

By a law passed at the last session of the legislature, the assessors of cities and towns were required to return to the tax commissioner the valuation of all property exempt from taxation, held by charitable, literary, and agricultural societies, and in houses of religious worship. The returns made in compliance with the law, with such additional information as has been obtained by correspondence with assessors and from other sources, are compiled in tabular form in the Appendix.

Returns of exempt property. 1874, 227. G. S. 11, § 5.

Appendix, pp. 470–533.

We cannot claim that they are more than approximately correct, and since they were put in such a form as to prevent any further amendment, without considerable trouble and expense, important omissions have been brought to our notice. One of the colleges in the western part of the state that has been in operation nearly ten years, the valuation of whose property amounts to nearly half a million dollars, is not included, while another, situated within a few hundred feet of the State House, would, had its value been returned by the assessors of Boston, have increased the aggregate of exempt property some sixty thousand dollars.

Agricultural College.

Boston College.

It is undoubtedly true, that but a very small per cent. of

the personal property of these corporations has been re-
1874, ch. 227. turned. These omissions are undoubtedly due to the fact that the law requiring returns was enacted when the assessors had partially finished their annual labors, and not brought to the attention of many of them until their work was concluded.

We can see no objection, but, on the contrary, many advantages, in an annual return that shall cover every description of exempt property specified in the general statutes. The details of the property covered by the first five divisions, and also by the seventh of section five of the eleventh chapter, should be given, and the *aggregate* valuation upon the best knowledge and belief of each local board should be returned for the other divisions. With the assessors' books, could be forwarded the proper blanks, and in a few years a class of statistics, substantially accurate, showing the whole valuation of the state, could be compiled, from which important deductions could be made for many purposes.

Recommendation.

We recommend that chapter 227 of the acts of the year 1874 be amended so as to require the return of all property exempt from local taxation.

Necessity of a Frequent Apportionment of the State Tax.

Necessity of a frequent apportionment of the state tax.

In any action looking to the revision of the tax laws, it should not be forgotten that, although the polls and taxable property of the whole Commonwealth are steadily increasing, a considerable number of its towns are diminishing in respect of population and wealth.

Appendix, p. 551.

There will be found in the Appendix three tables bearing on the subject. The first is compiled from the aggregates returned by the local assessors, showing the polls and valuations of the whole state from 1861 to 1874.

Ib. p. 557.

The second gives the amount of the whole taxable property of the Commonwealth, including not only that locally assessed, but also the deposits in savings banks, the excess of the value of corporate property over real estate and machinery, and that portion of the national bank shares not included in local valuations. And the third gives the names, with polls and valuations in 1861 and every fourth year thereafter, of those towns whose valuations were less in 1873 than in 1861. An obvious deduction from the inspection of these tables is, that the state tax ought frequently to be reapportioned so as to bear equally, in proportion to ability. The present apportionment was made in 1872. A copy of the act will be found in the Appendix.

Appendix, p. 558.

Ib. p. 355.

Present State of the Statutes—A Codification Desirable.

Present state of statutes—a codification desirable.

From the preceding pages, it is evident that many acts concerning the subject of taxation have been passed since the last revision of the statutes in 1860. In order to be certain how much of this legislation is now in force, we found it expedient to make a preliminary draft for a codification of these laws, and of the eleventh and twelfth chapters of the general statutes. This draft is given in the Appendix, not in order that it may be enacted, but as affording an easy means of obtaining a substantially accurate view of our existing legislation on the subject, and as an aid in some future revision.

Appendix, p. 225.

In the same connection, we give a list of the chapters and titles of the acts passed since the general statutes, which contain provisions with reference to the assessment or collection of taxes. These are arranged in chronological order, and many of them have been wholly or partially repealed.

Ib. p. 220.

In order to complete this part of the subject, we have also appended a compilation of those portions of the state and Federal constitutions bearing upon the question which we have discussed.

Appendix, p. 211.

From an examination of this portion of our work, it will be evident that a revision of the laws relating to taxation, even if no important changes are to be made, will soon be advisable, in order that they may be readily found and understood. Besides the tables already referred to, there will be found in the Appendix additional discussions, prepared at our request, by gentlemen who have given special attention to the respective topics of which they treat, and whose papers we deem worthy of the careful attention of the legislature.

With the thanks due these gentlemen, we would also express our acknowledgments to the executive departments of the Commonwealth for the facilities they have so generously and readily furnished us for gaining the information we have sought.

Respectfully submitted,

THOMAS HILLS.
JULIUS H. SEELYE.
JAMES M. BARKER.

JANUARY, 1875.

REPORT OF THE MINORITY

UPON

THE EXEMPTION FROM TAXATION OF LITERARY AND CHARITABLE INSTITUTIONS AND HOUSES OF RELIGIOUS WORSHIP.

Unable to agree with the conclusions of my colleagues in regard to an important class of property now wholly exempt from assessment, the reasons that influence me can probably be better stated if the whole question of the exemption from taxation of literary and charitable organizations and churches is considered from the stand-point from which the minority of the commission views the subject.

In a question of exemption, the practical side of the subject, the amount of property shielded from the common burden, and the inquiry as to the rapidity with which it is accumulating, naturally precede the consideration of the more important question of the justice or expediency of the exemption. The apparent great increase in this property which the statistics disclose, is no doubt due in part to a more careful appraisement, under the provisions of the recent law, than that made four years since under a legislative order, summarily executed.

Property exempt in 1870—churches, $22,862,697; literary and charitable, $14,231,294. Ho. Doc. 216, 1870. 1874—churches, $30,242,800; lit. and charitable, $23,221,000. Appendix, pp. 470–533.

1874, 227.

But, on the other hand, an inspection of the tables in the Appendix leaves no doubt that the total of $53,463,800 is much below the real value of the property held by the organizations there classified. The small amount of personal property returned is conclusive upon this point. The Commonwealth endeavored, some years since, to

1864, 239. 1865, 271.

ascertain the amount of personal estate held in trust by this description of property-holders. The success of the effort can be measured by an inspection of a volume of some two hundred and fifty pages, which indicates that the personal property held at that time would aggregate to a large amount, and that this class of investors, as little desired, as any other in the community, to make a public exhibit of their accumulations.

Report of sec. of Commonwealth, 1866.

But it may be said, Do you object to the prosperity of these institutions? In proportion to their resources, are their means for doing good. To complain of their having too much property is as unreasonable as to complain of having too much virtue, knowledge and charity.

The answer would seem to be: We do not object to the success of these organizations; on the contrary, we rejoice at it. But when the state requires a revenue, and orders that the property of the community shall be assessed to supply it, valuable property should not be left out of the assessment because the holders are using it to promote religion, education and benevolence.

Upon a different view, it would be difficult to say why a good corporation should be exempt and a benevolent citizen taxed.

Theory upon which exemption can be justified.

Upon one ground, and one alone, can exemption from assessments, which ought to be common burdens, be justified. If these religious, charitable and educational associations are agents or instrumentalities of the state, doing the work which but for them the Commonwealth herself must do, and doing it as well and at as little cost as the officers or agents of the government would do it; or if an organization whose sphere is beyond the duty of the state, but so important to her best interests that it must be sustained at any cost, and cannot sustain itself and do its work if its property is taxed,—if these conditions exist, the state is justified in increasing the assessments of all others that these institutions may be exempt. Few will be found who are not ready to admit that it is the duty of the state to provide for the sick in body or in mind, the poor, and all others whose necessities demand that relief which we call "charity,"—and few who will not agree that among the highest obligations which the Commonwealth owes to her children, is an education limited only by the capacity, the ambition, and the opportunities of each seeker after knowledge. These duties and obligations belong to the state, not to any individual or association. It follows that the state has a right to select her agents, and may select organizations which she has called into being, or permits to exist. But the agent is entitled to no exemption, except as the representative of the state which has the right to say—if, in her judgment, the required duty is not being done well or economically—that she prefers different agents.

Limitation of extent of exemption.

If the hospital, or college, is doing the work of the state, it follows that the property necessarily used in such service should be exempt; but this exemption should not be allowed to extend to real property beyond that needed for actual accommodation and use. Judicial decisions have declared that, as the laws now stand, there is practically no limit to the amount of land a literary or charitable organization can withdraw from assessment, except the ability of the corporation to purchase, and the discretion of its managers. A corporation receiving exemption from taxation because it is doing the work of the state, should be permitted to hold no dead property; certainly no unproductive or unused real estate. Its exemption can be maintained only upon the theory that its real estate is reasonably necessary for the proper performance of its duties, and that its other property is actively employed in the work it is doing as the representative of the Commonwealth. The state gives immunity from taxation to property used in her service, and it should not be granted in advance of that use.

Wesleyan Academy v. Wilbraham. 99 Mass. 599. Mass. Gen. Hos. v. Somerville. 101 Mass. 319.

The Commonwealth, in granting a charter to a literary or charitable corporation, limits the amount of property it may hold. The right to ascertain at any time the amount of property held, must be as undoubted as the right to establish a limitation.

Legislative limit can be largely exceeded.

Probably the principal reason that applications to the legislature for power to hold additional property are not more numerous from corporations holding exempt estates, may be found in the fact that the limitation can be largely and legally exceeded. An organization is permitted to hold one hundred thousand dollars by its act of incorporation; it expends that amount in the purchase of land and the erection of buildings. Its location being well chosen, its real estate advances in value, and in time is worth double its cost. By existing laws, this excess of one hundred per cent. over the amount it was authorized to hold cannot be taxed. If it is properly used in the service of the state, there is no reason why the whole amount should not be exempt for the same reasons which justified the original exemption; but of the justice or expediency of this additional immunity, the state should be the judge. The exemption granted by the legislature should always be deducted from the present value of the property, and any excess above the legal limitation taxed. Upon an application for an additional exemption, the question as to the amount of property necessary for the duties to be performed, the efficiency and economy manifested in the work, and the nature and character of the investments, would all be open to legislative inquiry and discretion.

Limitation based on income of property.

Some corporations, exempt from taxation, have charters in which the limitation is based upon the annual income of their investments. It is difficult to see how such a provision can be termed a limitation, as applied to real estate occupied by the corporation. The discretion of the officers, and the wealth of the organization, is the measure of the restraint as to the area to be acquired. If used by the corporation for the purposes for which it was created, or in the form of vacant land not used at all, no income would accrue, and the limitation would be absolutely without force. Such a form of exemption is unnecessary for any proper purpose. All charters of this character should be

99 Mass. 599.
101 Mass. 319.

amended, and the discretion of the legislature as to the amount of property to be held free from taxation by its literary and charitable organizations should be expressed in uniform terms. It would be a safe rule to refuse all charters to petitioners who were unwilling to either state unequivocally the amount of property they desired to hold, or to trust future legislatures with the question of the expediency of increasing their exemption.

Exemption of personal property of literary and charitable institutions. 1857, c. 154. G. S. c. 11, § 5, clause 7. Ib. c. 11, § 13.

For many years the state, it is believed, with only a single exception, has refused to permit portions of houses of religious worship to be used for secular purposes, without subjecting the proportion of the edifice so used, to taxation. All property, both real and personal, held by a religious society as a ministerial fund, is assessed at the full value. The income of the stores under the church, or of the fund left by some benevolent parishioner, may be sacredly devoted to the maintenance of that worship, for the benefit of which the church itself is relieved from assessment. But the law refuses to look beyond the fact that the property is used for the purpose of producing an income, and orders its taxation.

Ib. c. 11, § 5, clause 3.

A similar rule applies to the real estate of literary and charitable institutions, but not to their personal property,— that, whatever may be its character or use, is wholly exempt. It is not easy to perceive why this discrimination should be made, unless it is claimed that these corporations are of more benefit to the state than the church, or need, to a greater extent, its support and assistance. The rule of exemption for the religious society would seem to be the correct one, and should be applied to every corporation that occupies or uses property exempt from taxation.

If it is claimed that the assessment of the personal property of these corporations would impair their usefulness by diminishing their resources, and consequently their power to do the work they were chartered to perform, the correctness of the position must be conceded. By precisely the amount assessed, are the means of every person and corporation paying a tax

1828, c. 143, § 2. diminished for all other purposes. When the state discontinued the exemption of the polls and estates of clergymen, of the presidents and professors of our colleges, and other public teachers,* the income of the institutions, with which they were connected, was reduced to the extent that the salaries of these officers were raised to meet their additional expense.

But because such an effect was produced, and will be repeated if the income-paying personal property of literary and charitable corporations shall be assessed, it does not follow that the repeal of the exemption was not then and would not now be right. If the contrary is claimed, by what reasoning can that action of the state be justified which exempts the income-paying personal estate of the academy or benevolent society and taxes that of the church,—which increases the usefulness of the college and hospital by the remission of a tax upon mortgages and bank stock, and decreases it by an assessment of the real estate from which an income is derived?

Proposed taxation in England of government and other exempt property.

The pressure and discontent caused by the increased rates of local taxation in England, have caused the government of that country recently to give special attention to the subject. In a bill which was introduced as a reformatory measure, it was proposed to do away with all exemptions previously accorded to literary and charitable corporations, and tax for local purposes even the property of the government. Speaking for the ministry, the Hon. Geo. J. Goschen said: "We propose to take one intelligible and uniform system, and to render every hereditament, corporeal or incorporeal, liable to those burdens." "The effect of these proposals will be that government property will be rated; but the rule must be universal. We believe that the claims of government property to exemption are very considerable; and if claims are set

Report of speech in House of Commons on local taxation, April 3, 1871, p. 200.

* Previous to 1821 the exemption of the polls and estates of these classes was for their full amount. By chap. 107 of the Acts of 1821, the exemption was not allowed to exceed eight thousand dollars, and in 1828 was removed altogether.

up on behalf of municipal buildings, charities and the like, it must clearly be understood that it may be necessary for us to reconsider our decision on this point."

Total exemption not justified by partial service.

It is conceded, that so far as these corporations are doing the work of the state, their exemption from assessment is a proper exercise of power for the good of all. But it cannot be admitted, and will hardly be claimed, that any partial service entitles the organization, by which it is rendered, to total exemption; or, in other words, if one-half of the real estate of a corporation is used in the service of the public, and therefore exempt, that the other half, though used for other purposes, should be relieved from assessment as a payment for the services rendered by the first half. Remission from assessment can be granted only because the state does not intend to tax its own agencies. The Commonwealth pays its indebtedness by other methods than exemption from taxation.

Need of state supervision.

By no existing law can the state, or its officers, know the character or extent of the literary or charitable work of corporations receiving by exemption, an annual grant equal to the tax upon the property held by them. The state, consequently, does not know if the only condition that will justify exemption has been complied with. She cannot tell whether an organization, which confines its operations solely to the members of a single sect, is not protecting from assessment an ecclesiastical property largely exceeding in value the houses of religious worship, to which, for denominational purposes, her exemption was intended to be limited. Neither can the state know whether what purports to be a charity is not exercising a harmful, rather than a beneficial, influence on the community; or, if the work be of a character that would meet with approval, whether it is not being done at such a cost as to render a change of agencies needful.

By existing methods, a charter having been obtained, or an organization effected under general laws, no state supervision of any kind is ever exercised or expected.

Such diversity of practice has grown up under our exemption laws, that estates claimed to be occupied for charitable purposes will, under precisely similar circumstances, be held for assessment in some localities, and relieved from all taxation in others. The state has the undoubted right to know how all who claim to represent her are doing the work they assume to perform. She has an equal right to accept services, and to reject or discontinue them. Existing for the good of the whole community, and seeking that end, she makes no contract by implication, and can be accused of no breach of faith when she holds her agents to strict account, or, discharging them from any position of trust or employment, withholds the compensation previously granted. But the power of the state should be exercised understandingly. She should know, by her proper officers, the nature and extent of the services rendered to the public by all who receive exemption as the agents of the Commonwealth, and the full amount and character of the property they hold.

Recommendation of minority for returns and taxation in certain cases.

It is therefore recommended that all literary and scientific institutions be required to annually report to the board of education, in such form as that body shall designate; that all benevolent and charitable corporations be required to make like returns to the board of state charities; that all these organizations make such returns of all property held by them as the tax commissioner may require; that all income-paying personal property held by these corporations be taxed; and in any year, when the returns are not made by any corporation, or when the exemption of the property of any corporation has ceased, that the tax commissioner notify the local authorities to assess the real estate of such corporation. It is also recommended that all charters heretofore granted to literary or charitable corporations, where the limitation as to the amount of property is based upon the income of the estate, be amended in such a manner that the limitation shall state the amount of property that may be held. And, also, that all excess above the amount legally exempted, as determined

for amendment of certain charters—for taxation in certain cases.

by the market value of the property at the date of assessment, be taxed at the same rate as other property.

Taxation of churches.

The reasons that render the remission of taxation to literary and charitable institutions a proper exercise of power, will not justify the exemption of houses of religious worship. The church is not the servant, the agent or the representative of the state. Beyond the power to preserve peace and order in the community, and to prevent religious rites or ceremonies from becoming a public nuisance, the state has no right to control, direct, or even inspect, the work of the religious organizations. Her active interference in the affairs of any church can be sustained only by that law of self-preservation, inherent in every sovereignty, that repels any attack upon its life, and justifies the exercise of its utmost powers to crush any conspiracy that attempts to undermine its foundations. Until that necessity shall arise which will require the Commonwealth to assert that the state, and not the church, is the supreme power in the land, she must stand outside the door of the house of religious worship. It is no part of her work to furnish religion, and in no sense can ecclesiastical organizations be her agents or representatives.

Church not agent of state. Mass. Cons., Part I., Art. II. Appendix, p. 211.

When our puritan state adopted the constitution of Massachusetts, the experience of more than a century induced her to modify the close connection which was at first instituted between the church and state. Though it was still ordered that direct taxation should be imposed, for parish purposes, upon those who did not attend public worship, the state did not attempt to legislate a creed, but provided that moneys, paid for the support of religious organizations, should be applied to the benefit of the denomination of which the rate-payer was a member. A half century later, the state yielded the principle of involuntary taxation for the support of public worship, and again declared, in the words of her earlier enactments, that "all religious sects and denominations . . . shall be equally under the protection of the

Connection of church and state in Mass. Octo. 1780, Mass. Cons., Part I., Art. III. Appendix, p. 211.

Nov., 1833. Amendments to Cons., Art XI. Appendix, p. 212.

law, and no subordination of any one sect or denomination to another shall ever be established by law."

Whatever claim the state may have asserted in her earlier history, to provide religion for the people, or to levy direct assessments for the support of any special creed, or for the maintenance of the public worship of all denominations, has long since been conceded. The last vestige of the direct connection between church and state exists among us, to this extent,—by the laws of the Commonwealth a tax may be assessed by methods similar to those in use for ordinary taxes, compelling a citizen to pay his proportion of an assessment voted by an organization of which he is a voluntary member.

G. S. c. 30, §§ 20, 21.

It is clear that the exemption of ecclesiastical property cannot be maintained on the ground that the church is an agency for doing a work that the state must either do herself or provide for.

Influence of church, justification for exemption.

But it is claimed, that although it is no part of the duty of the state to provide religion, or to see to the maintenance of religious institutions, yet, that their influence upon the community is so great and beneficial, as to justify indirect taxation (for which exemption is only another name), or even direct assessment for their preservation and support.

In this view of the matter, if the church was planted when the state was founded, and it was a necessity to the new Commonwealth, taxation for its support may have been right. Certainly, if all the citizens of the state were members of the church, it was as equitable a way of meeting necessary expenses as could have been devised. It may be conceded that if the state, which has no duty to fulfil in that field where the church finds its appropriate labor, considers the influence of the organization upon the community important for her own good, she is justified in imposing taxation for the value of this benefit, if it would be lost to her without such action.

Cost of exemption compared with service to state.

The property held by the religious societies and churches in the United States, and in this Commonwealth, has become so valuable, has increased, and is increasing, so rapidly, that the question, whether in some cases the cost of the exemption is an economical expenditure of the public revenue, is frequently joined to that which doubts the necessity of any remission where great wealth is clearly indicated; and upon the view that the state is interested only to the extent of enabling religious teaching to be maintained, the questions, in such a case, would seem to be difficult to answer, especially at a time when the assessments, of which they are relieved, are pressing with unusual severity upon the community.

Take the case of a religious society of say one hundred members. They erect a church of moderate cost upon an ample building lot. The influence of the organization may be worth all it costs the community by indirect taxation. In a generation the lot, which has been held without assessment, and consequently without cost, becomes valuable. It is then sold, and the proceeds, ten times the cost, are invested in a house and lot, which is the religious home of a membership no larger, and of no greater influence in the Commonwealth, than that which established the church. It is hard to see upon what theory of benefit to the state the exemption and consequent tax upon the public has increased tenfold, while the service rendered by the church remains the same, and will be no greater when, a generation or two later, the process is repeated.

Considerations affecting questions of exemption.

Before considering the duty and interest of the state upon the question of continuing an exemption so long enjoyed, it is admitted that the following considerations must influence the conclusion: *First*, the absolute non-interference of the state in the affairs of the church. *Second*, the good which it is conceded the state receives from the church. *Third*, that the property of the church has become very valuable, and is rapidly increasing. *Fourth*, that exemption from taxation renders it profitable to hold property, and is a perpetual temptation to undue accumulation.

With this statement of the question, what, if any, change should be made?

State should not interfere in church affairs.

The first position would appear to be conclusive against the right of exemption, where the ability to contribute exists. The state acts only on material things. She cannot touch religion; it is intangible. She has no right to interfere with, or even to attempt to influence that public worship which is the outward observance of religion. She only knows the church, to protect it in the unmolested enjoyment of its faith, and must require it to contribute, in proportion to its ability, to the needs of the one supreme power in the Commonwealth.

Character of obligation of state to church.

The second consideration, while it admits the good that the state receives from the church, does not concede that the Commonwealth is indebted to it in a sense that requires a payment, or gift of money, to discharge the obligation. The church, like the citizen, cannot help serving the state, for each, working faithfully for the ends which they deem important, are advancing her interests. Both church and citizen should stand alike in the favor and regard of the state.

Property of church.

The third and fourth points may be considered together. They both relate to that tangible property which the state protects by her power, and which she taxes for her revenue.

U. S. census, 1870, Vol. I., p. 506.

The statistics show that in the United States, in twenty years, the number of churches increased from 38,061 to 63,082, an advance of 66 per cent., while the property held by them showed an increase in the same time of 306 per cent., rising from $87,328,801 in 1850 to $354,483,581 in 1870. Between these dates our own state increased her houses of worship from 1,475 to 1,764, and their valuation from $10,206,184 to $24,488,285, an advance of 20 per cent. of the number of churches, and 139 per cent. of their property. The substantial accuracy of the valuation of 1870 was tested by the estimation of the property in that year by the assessors of the state. They found the value to be $22,862,697. The same

Ho. Doc. 216, 1870.

officers again valued this class of property, in connection with their duties, in May, 1874, and in four years the increase was 32 per cent. The value of church property in Massachusetts now stands at $30,242,800. Appendix, p. 512.

These statistics show plainly that the property of the churches is increasing much faster than the churches themselves,—that is, the religious organizations that have been and are exempt from taxation upon their property are growing wealthy.

Is it desirable that this great amount of property should increase in the ratio in which it has been advancing, without taxation to check the tendency to lock up a vast amount of wealth in a single edifice?—not to the end that such buildings should not be erected, but that the community may have more of them at less cost.

Expense of modern church-building.

It requires neither statistics nor argument to prove the extravagance of some of our modern church-buildings,—the fact must be noticed by the most casual observer. But when, within ten years, seven churches are placed within a circle not exceeding a half-mile in diameter, the valuation of which is reckoned by millions, the question is forced home upon us, whether the legislators of past generations, who framed the exemption law, contemplated its application to such edifices as these, and if the people of to-day who pay in increased taxes the deficiency caused by the remission of assessments upon these splendid churches are willing that the exemption should continue.

A correspondent of a New York religious paper describes the buildings and their use as follows :—

"Christian Union," N. Y., Dec. 23, 1874.

"The new churches present a somewhat new feature in Protestant church-building. They are to be more like church institutions or church homes than mere houses of public worship. The new Old South, for example, was begun with its parsonage; to this was added the chapel, with its beautiful glass apartments, so arranged as to adapt itself to all possible requirements of the social meeting and the Sunday-school. Connected with these are parlors for church-gatherings, rooms for benevolent work, and even a kitchen, well supplied with furniture, for use on festival occasions. Last of all comes the church proper, a stately sanctuary, beautiful in design and rich in the embellishment of religious architectural art. The new Second Church largely follows the same plan. The new Trinity is to combine, in its large design, rooms or chapels for its social, business and benevolent work. This follows the plan and practice of the European Catholic churches,—an innovation worthy of considertion, and one which, perhaps, may be wisely extended.

"These seven churches on the Back Bay, four of which are Unitarian and three Trinitarian, are all built of stone, and when the last one is completed will represent at least $2,000,000. It is hard to prophecy whether they are to be made centres of public religious hospitality, life and energy, or are to stand as the monument of the religious heroism, genius and vital piety of a generation gone. It is a somewhat significant fact that, while all of the public halls are crowded on the Sabbath, and Tremont Temple and Music Hall frequently turn away hundreds from their doors, the Back Bay churches are restricted to special congregations, which are usually small and thin. Park-street Church, which is hospitable and central, is always crowded, as Trinity used to be when on Summer Street. But the Back Bay churches seem to stand apart and aloof from the people, and to be as far removed from their hearts as they are separated from them by geographical position."

Effect of beautiful church edifices.

But, it will be said, does not the public enjoy the beauty of these stately monuments,—do they not stand, not only as a fitting tribute from man, offering his best work to the praise of his Maker, but as public educators, appealing to man's better nature, and offering to all a refining and elevating spectacle?

The correctness of this position may be admitted, but the answer seems plain. The church was exempted from taxation because of its moral effect upon the community, not that it might become a teacher of the fine arts. Exemption may be justified by the former of these considerations, not by the latter.

But it will probably be objected, that the community is asking a double contribution. The money the church paid for this splendid building made the neighborhood desirable, and men not only wished to visit the locality, but to live where beautiful objects would always be near them. Competition for land in the immediate vicinity of the church advanced the price, valuable buildings placed upon it added still more to the worth of the estates. And now the public comes, and asks that after the church has created this value, that she submit herself to be taxed. True, in part. But, as a rule, the dwellings precede the church, and the effect here noticed follows the erection of every fine building, whether built for public uses or business, or as a home for a family.

Exemption being justified on the ground that religion and virtue may flourish, it is not difficult to determine which of two exemptions of a half-million dollars is of the greatest good to the public,—fifty churches worth ten thousand each, or one house of religious worship that in its splendid appointments absorbs the entire sum.

If the taxation of the churches would tend to lower the architectural style of our ecclesiastical edifices, the public would content itself with the knowledge that the money thus saved from the church-building was probably actively employed in the real work of the organization, and would receive with deeper gratitude than they can now feel, the gift of a beautiful public building from the hands of men willing to contribute to the advancement and adornment of the religion of their faith, and willing to meet the expense without aid from the public in the form of an involuntary assessment.

Taxation not an act of bad faith.

But, it is said, good men of our own time, and of former generations, have given of their wealth and built these beautiful temples, and, relying upon the fact that as they had been exempt from taxation from our earliest history, they had a right to expect that the property consecrated to religious uses would remain untaxed to the end of time, and that its assessment would be an act of bad faith on the part of the Commonwealth.

To this position, it may be answered, that the state has never made such a contract, and the nature of the case

1828, c. 143. will not allow one to be implied. Less than fifty years ago the tax acts annually exempted from assessment the machinery used in cotton, woollen and linen factories, as an encouragement to manufactures. From the settlement of the country, the state has exempted churches as an encouragement to religion. Certainly those who invested their property in manufactures, and built up the material prosperity of the state, could complain of the bad faith which now subjects such property to assessment, if the claim in behalf of the church can be sustained. Neither can the position be maintained, if it is admitted that the state exempted them only because their moral force in the community was a necessity to her existence. But if the exemption was granted for the selfish reason that the church performed the work of many policemen, by rendering their services unnecessary, it would certainly be consistent with the original motive, to withdraw the exemption when the state provides for police service in another way. The state makes no contract with her citizens with regard to their taxes, and certainly she has made none with any class, promising them immunity from taxation.

Review of connection of church and state in Mass.

Mass. Records, 1631, vol. 1, p. 87. Ib. 1634, vol. 1, p. 354. Ib. 1660, vol. 4, part 1, p. 420. Ib. 1664, vol. 4, part 2, p. 117.

The history of the connection of the church and the Commonwealth may be stated to be: that the first settlers were members of one denominational faith, and that all persons and estates were taxed for the support of that branch of the Christian church whose members alone were the freemen or citizens of the state. Religious toleration was after a time accorded to this extent: that membership in the puritan church was not a necessary qualification for enfranchisement. Then the tax for the benefit of that church was remitted, provided it was paid for the support of Christian worship of some denomination. Then followed the taxation of the polls and estates of the clergy, which had been wholly or partially exempt, and the remission of the involuntary tax which had compelled churched and unchurched to be taxed for the maintenance of public worship. Now the power of the state, under

Mass. Cons., Part I., Art. III. Appendix, p. 211.

1821, c. 107, § 6. 1828, c. 143, § 2. 1833, Amend. to Cons., Art. XI. Appendix, p. 212.

the forms of law, assesses and collects a tax voted by a society of which a citizen is a voluntary member, and compels its payment before he can dissolve his connection with the parish. G. S. c. 30, §§ 20, 21.

Very few can be found in the community who would retrace any of the steps by which we have arrived at our present position. It is now time for the next forward step. Policy of state in relation to church exemption.

The church, feeble in its infancy, has been nourished into a mature strength; it is of age, and can stand alone. The necessity of government support being removed, its maintenance should be a perfectly voluntary act on the part of those immediately connected with it. The presence of the tax-gatherer, demanding a parish tax in the name of the Commonwealth, can be justified only when it is a necessity for the existence of the church, and the church a necessity for the state. But it may be said, that although the church, as a whole, is strong, it is composed of many different societies and associations, some of whom have large possessions, while many others find it no easy task to raise the means to meet current expenses.

Would you place an assessment upon these poorer churches which might compel them to break up their organization and close their doors?

This question reveals the practical difficulty of the subject. If the churches were all wealthy, they would all have the ability to pay, and should be taxed and compelled to pay the assessment. If they were poor, and without ability to pay, they ought to be relieved from assessments which would crush them; and none but those who desire their extinction would object to the exemption.

Among the citizens of the Commonwealth, we find individuals so poor that food, clothing and shelter is provided for them at the public charge, and others so prosperous that the valuation of counties do not equal their wealth. Among the churches will be found some with structures so modest and inexpensive, that many of them could be annually built with the amount that would be the just tax upon the ecclesiastical property of a single congregation.

The theory that there should be no connection between the church and the state, would seem to require no exemption; the position that the church is a necessity to the state, requires that there should be no taxation. The adoption of the first would reduce the number of the churches; the other withdraws from productive employment a large amount of capital, and places upon the community from which it is drawn an annual tax upon its value. Neither of these results can be beneficial to the state. Is there, then, a middle course, which can be maintained upon a theory consistent with our republican methods, that avoids on the one side the extinction of institutions which the Commonwealth has fostered for more than two centuries, and on the other, the accumulation of a vast untaxed ecclesiastical property?

Citizen and church alike the care of state.

The state has no higher duty than to protect and care for her citizens; for their rights and interests she is bound to watchful vigilance. In our past history, the church has been placed above the citizen; the one has been exempted, the other taxed. The church certainly has no right to complain if it is placed on the same level with the citizen. The state recognizes the fact that for her subject a certain amount of income and of household goods are necessary for the decent maintenance and comfort of a family. The first two thousand dollars of income, and the first one thousand dollars' worth of furniture, are exempt for each citizen; his income and property above these amounts are taxed. Why should not the state, acknowledging the fact that a certain amount of property is necessary to the proper and decent maintenance of a religious organization, assess all above such amount?*

* An indication of public opinion on this subject may be found in the communications of assessors, in answer to our circular of August 15, which did not invite special attention to this subject (see Appendix, page 205). Returns were received from forty-three municipalities outside the state capital. One city and

Objections to limited exemption.

Two principal objections will be urged against such a course. Those who desire full taxation and no exemption, say that it is not so much the amount of the indirect tax imposed upon them that they complain of, as the principle involved in the assessment. They object to being compelled, by indirect taxation, to contribute to the support of creeds and modes of worship, to which they are conscientiously opposed, however small may be the contribution. Such an objection is entitled to respectful and careful consideration. But the answer to their position would seem to be, that the state knows nothing, and should know nothing, of creeds, denominations, or even of religion itself. But she recognizes this truth, that any religion which a civilized state permits to exist within her limits, makes life and property more secure, and promotes peace, order and prosperity in the community; and if, to attain these ends, she exempts from assessment, houses of religious worship, or, in other words, indirectly taxes her citizens that Jews and Gentiles, Catholics and Protestants, may be enabled to continue their public observance of worship, it is not that religion may increase, or that creeds may flourish, but that the state may be benefited.

The other objection to a limited exemption comes from those who look with disfavor upon any taxation of religious property. They say that equality of assessment will not and cannot result from it; that a given amount exempted in one locality, which would be sufficient for the release

thirteen towns favored taxing the property without any exemption; four cities and seventeen towns favored taxing the property with limited exemption; eight towns favored total exemption.

Assuming that these officers were representatives of the communities in which they lived,—

The first class represented	19,694	polls,	$54,834,444	valuation.
second "	"	35,280	"	124,458,308	"
third "	"	7,898	"	45,238,481	"

The assessors of Boston favored limited exemption,—adding their statistics, the second class represents 118,634 polls, $890,276,521 valuation.

The above figures are based on the local assessors' valuation of 1873, which gave for the state 408,131 polls and $1,763,429,990 valuation.

from assessment of the entire estate, would be wholly inadequate in another locality. The point must be conceded. Any exemption that might be made of a fixed amount would produce this effect, not only in the exemption of church, but of other property. The law exempts two thousand dollars of professional income. A citizen lives in the city, where rents and the cost of living are high, and the whole is consumed in necessary expenses. Another of equal ability lives in the country; he is exempt upon the same sum, but the purchasing power of his income is such in a locality of lower prices, that he saves one-half the amount. A similar illustration could be made with the exemption of one thousand dollars on household furniture. The answer to this objection is, that in every limited exemption there is an inherent inequality.

Shall we, therefore, retain total exemption and still greater inequality?

Take the case of a little country church worth one thousand dollars, and a city church with a valuation of three hundred thousand. There can be no doubt which congregation needs most the government aid, if any is to be rendered. With a tax-rate of one and one-half per cent., the inequality of total exemption is manifest. The poorer society saves fifteen dollars, which may buy the fuel that will warm their vestry, while the richer organization saves four thousand five hundred dollars,—enough for the minister's salary.

Total exemption not needed for advancement of religion.

To claim that the assessment in excess of an exemption large enough to provide a proper and convenient house of religious worship, in any part of the state, would injure the cause of true religion, appears to be identical with the position that the possession of a large amount of property is essential to its advancement. The history of the world will show that the power of the church has increased in proportion to its property, not that its religious life has been quickened as its prosperity has been indicated by earthly possessions.

No one will deny the great influence which the church exerts in our Commonwealth. Its ministers and leaders, well educated and intelligent, are our foremost citizens. The power of the religious organizations has been exerted with great effect in behalf of the state upon extraordinary occasions; and it will be no small advantage to the community, if the church, compelled, in common with all others, to bear the burdens of the state, shall, in ordinary and peaceful times, exert its influence in the cause of good government, economically administered.

Influence of church for good government.

It is recommended that all laws that provide for the assessment and collection of parish taxes be repealed, and that exemption from taxation for any house of religious worship be limited to twenty-five thousand dollars.

Recommendation of minority in relation to parish taxes and houses of religious worship.

Respectfully submitted,

THOMAS HILLS.

APPENDIX.

CIRCULAR ISSUED BY THE COMMISSIONERS.

COMMONWEALTH OF MASSACHUSETTS.

OFFICE OF THE COMMISSIONERS ON TAXATION,
STATE HOUSE, BOSTON, August 15, 1874.

To the Assessors and Collectors of Taxes of

GENTLEMEN:—We have been appointed, by authority of chapter seventy of the Resolves of the current year, Commissioners to consider and report upon "the expediency of revising and amending the laws of the State relating to taxation, and the exemptions therefrom." A law of the Commonwealth (chap. 227 of the Acts of 1874) will require of assessors, on or before the first day of October next, a return of all property of certain classes exempt from taxation. But we desire not only the statistics from your assessment books, but the opinion of gentlemen who, as officers, have had experience in the administration of the law we are called upon to consider. While the Resolve under which the Commission was appointed will require a report upon the question of exemption, our authority is clear to consider and report upon any changes that may be deemed needful. We, therefore, invite you to give us the benefit of your knowledge upon any point in relation to the subject of taxation, to assist us in judging if any better system of taxation than that now existing can be devised; or in what manner our present system can be made more effective. The subject naturally divides into three general divisions: the taxation of polls, real estate and personal property. In regard to the poll-tax, we are aware only of discussions relating to its abolishment, and as to its being rated as equal to a certain valuation, in order that the amount raised upon polls shall bear a similar relation to the amount needed for revenue to that obtained from property. The taxation of real estate, when the same is mortgaged, is claimed by many persons to result in oppressive double taxation, and relief is sought by the assessment of the estates to the mortgagors and mortgagees respectively in the proportion of their several interests, or by the exemption of the mortgagee from taxation, in order that the mortgagor may find his relief in the abatement of his interest account. In assessing personal property the following classes are now taxed, and the question of remitting the assessment upon some or all of this description of property is often urged: mortgages, money at interest and debts due over and above the debts of the person assessed; cash or money; goods, wares and merchandise; machinery and tools; ships and other vessels; horses, other animals and vehicles; household furniture exceeding one thousand dollars in value; shares in all corporations; bonds of all kinds, except those of the United States; income from an annuity; income from a profession, trade or employment exceeding two thousand dollars. This last-mentioned item, its taxation being an assessment on the ability to earn money, has, especially within the past few years, been the subject of much discussion. The system of assessing and collecting taxes, as shown in the eleventh and twelfth chapters of the General Statutes, has remained substantially the same in Massachusetts for many years. But the method of applying that system has given rise to much legislation. The laws supposed to be in force in whole or in part at this time, which have been passed since the publication of the General Statutes, are as follows: 1860, chapters 72, 85, 123; 1861, chapters 167, 171, 215; 1862, chapters 158, 174, 183, 224; 1863, chapters 119, 164, 236; 1864, chapters 172, 201, 208, 294; 1865, chapters 68, 121, 206, 234, 242, 267, 283; 1866, chapters 48, 170, 174 (section 6), 196, 291; 1867, chapters 42, 52, 101, 160, 166, 188, 299; 1868, chapters 165, 211 (section 1), 276, 283, 315, 320, 349; 1869, chapters 110, 169, 190, 423, 428, 443; 1870, chapters 144, 328, 394; 1871, chapter 298; 1872, chapters 245, 306, 310, 325; 1873, chapters 141, 156, 225, 272, 315, 354; 1874, chapters 28, 227, 238, 317. It has been intended to give reference to laws under which the State, by its own officers, assesses and collects taxes, as well as to those that call for the performance of duties by local assessors. If you are aware of any enactment now in force not included in the above enumeration, we would thank you to communicate the information. If no other result should follow the action of the legislature in instituting this inquiry than that this mass of law should be reduced to one enactment, such a codification would not be without value. As we desire communications from every assessor and collector in the Commonwealth, as well as from all citizens who have anything which they deem of importance upon the subject of taxation to bring to our attention, allow us to suggest, in order that your views upon any topic may be considered with those of others under the same head, when the subject is under consideration, that you *use only one side* of paper, and if you write upon more than one subdivision of the subject, that you date and sign each of such divisions, as if the same were a single communication, adding to your signature your official designation. Leave a line or two between each sub-head, in order that if you write upon the exemption of churches, literary, charitable and other institutions; polls, real estate, income, mortgages, merchandise, domicile or taxable residence, or any other head of the subject as found in the General Statutes or any of the laws recently enacted, your opinion upon any subdivision may be cut off and arranged with those of other officers upon the same subject. We should be glad to hear from you, even if you have no changes to suggest. It is important information to know that in the opinion of administrative officers the law as it stands produces good results. But it is especially important that if your experience has led you to form opinions as to how our system of taxation can be changed for the better, or our present methods be made more effective, that we should be put in possession of your views.

Very respectfully,

THOMAS HILLS,
JULIUS H. SEELYE,
JAMES M. BARKER,
Commissioners.

A COMPILATION

OF THOSE

ARTICLES OF THE MASSACHUSETTS BILL OF RIGHTS AND CONSTITUTION,

AND OF THE AMENDMENTS THERETO,

RELATING TO

Taxation and the Exemptions Therefrom,

AND OF THOSE

PARTS OF THE CONSTITUTION OF THE UNITED STATES LIMITING THE POWER OF THE STATES WITH REGARD TO TAXATION.

COMPILATION.

ART. II. It is the right as well as the duty of all men in society, publicly, and at stated seasons, to worship the SUPREME BEING, the great Creator and Preserver of the universe. And no subject shall be hurt, molested or restrained, in his person, liberty or estate, for worshipping GOD in the manner and season most agreeable to the dictates of his own conscience; or for his religious profession or sentiments; provided he doth not disturb the public peace, or obstruct others in their religious worship.

Massachusetts Bill of Rights, Article II.

ART. III. As the happiness of a people, and the good order and preservation of civil government, essentially depend upon piety, religion and morality; and as these cannot be generally diffused through a community, but by the institution of the public worship of GOD, and of public instructions in piety, religion and morality: therefore, to promote their happiness, and to secure the good order and preservation of their government, the people of this Commonwealth have a right to invest their legislature with power to authorize and require, and the legislature shall, from time to time, authorize and require, the several towns, parishes, precincts and other bodies politic, or religious societies to make suitable provision, at their own expense, for the institution of the public worship of GOD, and for the support and maintenance of public Protestant teachers of piety, religion and morality, in all cases where such provision shall not be made voluntarily.

Same, Article III. as originally adopted, and in force until 1833.

And the people of this Commonwealth have also a right to, and do, invest their legislature with authority to enjoin upon all the subjects an attendance upon the instructions of the public teachers aforesaid, at stated times and seasons, if there be any on whose instructions they can conscientiously and conveniently attend.

Provided notwithstanding, that the several towns, parishes, precincts, and other bodies politic, or religious societies, shall, at all times, have the exclusive right of electing their public teachers, and of contracting with them for their support and maintenance.

And all moneys paid by the subject to the support of public worship, and of the public teachers aforesaid, shall, if he require it, be uniformly applied to the support of the public teacher or teachers of his own religious sect or denomination, provided there be any on whose instructions he attends; otherwise it may be paid towards the support of the teacher or teachers of the parish or precinct in which the said moneys are raised.

And every denomination of Christians, demeaning themselves peaceably, and as good subjects of the Commonwealth, shall be equally under the protection of the law; and no subordination of any one sect or denomination to another shall ever be established by law.

Same, Amendment XI., adopted 1833 as a substitute for Article III.

ART. XI. Instead of the third article of the bill of rights, the following modification and amendment thereof is substituted:—

As the public worship of God, and instructions in piety, religion and morality, promote the happiness and prosperity of a people, and the security of a republican government; therefore, the several religious societies of this Commonwealth, whether corporate or unincorporate, at any meeting legally warned and holden for that purpose, shall ever have the right to elect their pastors or religious teachers, to contract with them for their support, to raise money for erecting and repairing houses for public worship, for the maintenance of religious instruction, and for the payment of necessary expenses: and all persons belonging to any religious society shall be taken and held to be members, until they shall file with the clerk of said society a written notice declaring the dissolution of their membership, and thenceforth shall not be liable for any grant or contract which may be thereafter made or entered into by such society: and all religious sects and denominations, demeaning themselves peaceably, and as good citizens of the Commonwealth, shall be equally under the protection of the law; and no subordination of any one sect or denomination to another shall ever be established by law.

Massachusetts Bill of Rights, Article X.

ART. X. Each individual of the society has a right to be protected by it in the enjoyment of his life, liberty and property, according to standing laws. He is obliged, consequently, to contribute his share to the expense of this protection; to give his personal service, or an equivalent, when necessary: but no part of the property of any individual, can, with justice, be taken from him, or applied to public uses, without his own consent, or that of the representative body of the people. In fine, the people of this Commonwealth are not controllable by any other laws than those to which their constitutional representative body have given their consent. And whenever the public exigencies require that the property of any individual should be appropriated to public uses, he shall receive a reasonable compensation therefor.

ART. XXIII. No subsidy, charge, tax, impost, or duties, ought to be established, fixed, laid, or levied, under any pretext whatsoever, without the consent of the people, or their representatives in the legislature. Same, Article XXIII.

The next provision is found in that part of the first chapter of the constitution, which gives the general court power to impose taxes and define the principles which are to govern it in so doing. This is the latter half of Art. IV., section I., chapter I., and after granting to the general court certain other powers, continues as follows:—

And to impose and levy proportional and reasonable assessments, rates and taxes, upon all the inhabitants of, and persons resident, and estates lying within the said Commonwealth; and also to impose and levy reasonable duties and excises upon any produce, goods, wares, merchandise, and commodities whatsoever, brought into, produced, manufactured, or being within the same; to be issued and disposed of by warrant, under the hand of the governor of this Commonwealth for the time being, with the advice and consent of the council, for the public service, in the necessary defence and support of the government of the said Commonwealth, and the protection and preservation of the subjects thereof, according to such acts as are, or shall be in force within the same. Extract from Massachusetts Constitution, Article IV., § 1, ch. 1.

And while the public charges of government, or any part thereof, shall be assessed on polls and estates, in the manner that has hitherto been practised, in order that such assessments may be made with equality, there shall be a valuation of estates within the Commonwealth, taken anew, once in every ten years at least, and as much oftener as the general court shall order.

CHAPTER V.

THE UNIVERSITY AT CAMBRIDGE, AND ENCOURAGEMENT OF LITERATURE, &C.

SECTION I.

The University.

Massachusetts Constitution, ch. 5, § 1.

ARTICLE I. Whereas our wise and pious ancestors, so early as the year one thousand six hundred and thirty-six, laid the foundation of Harvard College, in which university many persons of great eminence have, by the blessing of GOD, been initiated in those arts and sciences which qualified them for public employments, both in church and state; and whereas the encouragement of arts and sciences, and all good literature, tends to the honor of GOD, the advantage of the Christian religion, and the great benefit of this, and the other United States of America,—it is declared, that the PRESIDENT AND FELLOWS OF HARVARD COLLEGE, in their corporate capacity, and their successors in that capacity, their officers and servants, shall have, hold, use, exercise and enjoy, all the powers, authorities, rights, liberties, privileges, immunities and franchises, which they now have, or are entitled to have, hold, use, exercise and enjoy; and the same are hereby ratified and confirmed unto them, the said president and fellows of Harvard College, and to their successors, and to their officers, and servants, respectively, forever.

Article II.

ART. II. And whereas there have been, at sundry times, by divers persons, gifts, grants, devises of houses, lands, tenements, goods, chattels, legacies and conveyances, heretofore made, either to Harvard College in Cambridge, in New England, or to the president and fellows of Harvard College, or to the said college, by some other description, under several charters successively; it is declared, that all the said gifts, grants, devises, legacies and conveyances, are hereby forever confirmed unto the president and fellows of Harvard College, and to their successors, in the capacity aforesaid, according to the true intent and meaning of the donor or donors, grantor or grantors, devisor or devisors.

Art. III. And whereas by an act of the general court of the Colony of Massachusetts Bay, passed in the year one thousand six hundred and forty-two, the governor and deputy-governor, for the time being, and all the magistrates of that jurisdiction, were, with the president, and a number of the clergy in the said act described, constituted the overseers of Harvard College; and it being necessary, in this new constitution of government, to ascertain who shall be deemed successors to the said governor, deputy-governor, and magistrates; it is declared, that the governor, lieutenant-governor, council and senate of this Commonwealth, are, and shall be deemed, their successors; who, with the president of Harvard College, for the time being, together with the ministers of the congregational churches in the towns of Cambridge, Watertown, Charlestown, Boston, Roxbury and Dorchester, mentioned in the said act, shall be, and hereby are, vested with all the powers and authority belonging, or in any way appertaining, to the overseers of Harvard College; provided, that nothing herein shall be construed to prevent the legislature of this Commonwealth from making such alterations in the government of the said university, as shall be conducive to its advantage, and the interest of the republic of letters, in as full a manner as might have been done by the legislature of the late Province of the Massachusetts Bay. Article III.

CHAPTER V.

SECTION II.

The Encouragement of Literature, &c.

Wisdom and knowledge, as well as virtue, diffused generally among the body of the people, being necessary for the preservation of their rights and liberties; and as these depend on spreading the opportunities and advantages of education in the Section II.

various parts of the country, and among the different orders of the people, it shall be the duty of legislatures and magistrates, in all future periods of this Commonwealth, to cherish the interests of literature and the sciences, and all seminaries of them; especially the university at Cambridge, public schools, and grammar schools in the towns; to encourage private societies, and public institutions, rewards and immunities, for the promotion of agriculture, arts, sciences, commerce, trades, manufactures, and a natural history of the country; to countenance and inculcate the principles of humanity and general benevolence, public and private charity, industry and frugality, honesty and punctuality in their dealings; sincerity, good humor, and all social affections and generous sentiments among the people.

Amendment of 1855, Article XVIII.

ART. XVIII. All moneys raised by taxation in the towns and cities for the support of public schools, and all moneys which may be appropriated by the state for the support of common schools, shall be applied to, and expended in, no other schools than those which are conducted according to law, under the order and superintendence of the authorities of the town or city in which the money is to be expended; and such moneys shall never be appropriated to any religious sect for the maintenance, exclusively, of its own schools.

The direct limitations upon the power of the state in matters of taxation, contained in the constitution of the United States, are found in the first part of section 8, and in section 10 of Article I., which are as follows:—

Constitution of United States, Article I., § 8.

SECT. 8. The congress shall have power:—To lay and collect taxes, duties, imposts and excises, to pay the debts and provide for the common defence and general welfare of the United States; but all duties, imposts and excises shall be uniform throughout the United States:—To borrow money on the credit of the United States:—To regulate commerce with foreign nations and among the several states, and with the Indian tribes:— * * * * * * * * *

Section 10.

SECT. 10. No state shall enter into any treaty, alliance, or confederation; grant letters of marque and reprisal; coin money; emit bills of credit; make anything but gold and silver coin a tender in payment of debts; pass any bill of attainder, *ex post facto* law, or law impairing the obligation of contracts; or grant any title of nobility. No state shall, without the consent of the congress, lay any imposts, or duties on imports or exports, except what may be absolutely necessary for executing its inspection laws; and the net produce of all duties and imposts, laid by any state on imports, or exports, shall be for the use of the treasury of the United States; and all such laws shall be subject to the revision and control of the congress. No state shall, without the consent of congress, lay any duty of tonnage, keep troops, or ships of war, in time of peace, enter any agreement or compact with another state, or with a foreign power, or engage in war, unless actually invaded, or in such imminent danger as will not admit of delay.

NOTE.—In addition to the express prohibitions, is the implied one, enforced in judicial decisions, which forbids a state by taxation or otherwise to interfere with or hinder the free exercise of all the powers granted to the general government, and hence will not allow it to tax the officers, or means or instruments of the United States or its property within the state.

SCHEDULE OF ACTS

CONTAINING

PROVISIONS WITH REFERENCE TO THE ASSESSMENT AND COLLECTION OF TAXES.

SCHEDULE OF ACTS

PASSED SINCE THE GENERAL STATUTES, CONTAINING PROVISIONS WITH REFERENCE TO THE ASSESSMENT AND COLLECTION OF TAXES.

Acts of the year One Thousand Eight Hundred and Sixty.

Chapter 85. An act to ascertain the ratable estate within this Commonwealth.
Chapter 123. An act concerning the valuation of the property of this Commonwealth.

Resolves of the year One Thousand Eight Hundred and Sixty.

Chapter 72. Resolves relating to corporations and the assessment of taxes upon the shares thereof.

Acts of the year One Thousand Eight Hundred and Sixty-one.

Chapter 167. An act to secure a uniform description and appraisal of estates in the Commonwealth for the purposes of taxation.
Chapter 171. An act relating to corporations and the assessment of taxes upon the shares thereof.
Chapter 215. [Extra Session.] An act to amend section third of the act to secure a uniform description and appraisal of estates in the Commonwealth for the purpose of taxation.

One Thousand Eight Hundred and Sixty-two.

Chapter 26. An act requiring the return of amount paid for assessing and collecting taxes in the Commonwealth in the year one thousand eight hundred and sixty-one.
Chapter 146. An act to authorize interest on taxes.
Chapter 158. An act concerning taxes upon polls.
Chapter 174. An act for the more equal assessment of taxes.
Chapter 183. An act in relation to the collection of taxes.
Chapter 224. An act to levy taxes on certain insurance companies and on depositors in savings banks.

One Thousand Eight Hundred and Sixty-three.

Chapter 119. An act to secure more equal taxation.
Chapter 164. An act in addition to an act to levy taxes on certain insurance companies and on depositors in savings banks.
Chapter 218. An act to provide for the reimbursement of bounties paid to volunteers, and to apportion and assess a tax therefor.
Chapter 236. An act to levy a tax on the stock of corporations held by persons whose residence is out of the Commonwealth.

One Thousand Eight Hundred and Sixty-four.

Chapter 144. An act to preserve the right of suffrage to soldiers and sailors.
Chapter 172. An act to prevent fraudulent evasions of taxation.
Chapter 201. An act concerning the records of corporations and returns to assessors.
Chapter 208. An act levying a tax upon certain corporations.
Chapter 210. An act to provide for the valuation of the property of the Commonwealth.
Chapter 294. An act relating to the assessment of taxes for the current year.

One Thousand Eight Hundred and Sixty-five.

Chapter 68. An act to preserve the right of suffrage to soldiers and sailors.
Chapter 121. An act relating to the abatement of taxes.
Chapter 206. An act in relation to the assessment of taxes.
Chapter 242. An act relating to returns and taxation of shares in associations for banking, established under the laws of the United States.
Chapter 267. An act concerning the tax on depositors in savings banks.
Chapter 283. An act to amend and revise chapter two hundred and eight of the acts of the year one thousand eight hundred and sixty-four, entitled "An act levying tax upon certain corporations."

One Thousand Eight Hundred and Sixty-six.

Chapter 48. An act concerning the taxation of incomes.
Chapter 170. An act concerning the assessment of taxes.
Chapter 196. An act in relation to the tax on shares in corporations for school district and parish purposes.
Chapter 291. An act in relation to returns to be made by corporations to the tax commissioner.

One Thousand Eight Hundred and Sixty-seven.

Chapter 42. An act to provide for refunding certain taxes illegally assessed.
Chapter 52. An act concerning the collection of State taxes upon corporations.
Chapter 101. An act in relation to the taxation of lands sold by the Commonwealth.
Chapter 151. An act to incorporate the Boston Safe Deposit Company.
Chapter 160. An act in relation to taxation of the Mercantile Savings Institution in the city of Boston.
Chapter 166. An act in relation to warrants for a State tax.
Chapter 188. An act in relation to the returns by assessors, of shares in banking institutions.
Chapter 299. An act in relation to the collection of taxes upon corporations.

One Thousand Eight Hundred and Sixty-eight.

Chapter 77. An act to incorporate the Worcester Safe Deposit Company.
Chapter 165. An act explanatory to an act to levy taxes on certain insurance companies.
Chapter 211. An act in relation to the assessment of taxes.
Chapter 283. An act in relation to the taxation of insurance companies.
Chapter 315. An act in relation to the taxation of deposits in savings banks.
Chapter 320. An act relating to the assessment of taxes upon estates omitted in the annual taxation.
Chapter 349. An act concerning the taxing of bank shares.

One Thousand Eight Hundred and Sixty-nine.

Chapter 182. An act to incorporate the New England Trust Company.
Chapter 190. An act concerning the return of false and fraudulent lists of property to assessors of taxes.

Chapter 296. An act to amend an act to incorporate the Worcester Safe Deposit Company.

Chapter 428. An act to amend the charter of the Pawners' Bank of Boston.

Chapter 443. An act to repeal section one of chapter two hundred and eleven of the acts of the year one thousand eight hundred and sixty-eight, concerning the assessment of taxes.

Chapter 444. An act in relation to the returns of assessors.

One Thousand Eight Hundred and Seventy.

Chapter 22. An act to amend the act incorporating the Worcester Safe Deposit and Trust Company.

Chapter 76. An act in relation to returns from assessors of cities and towns.

Chapter 144. An act in relation to the returns of certain corporations to the tax commissioner.

Chapter 323. An act to incorporate the Northampton Loan and Trust Company.

Chapter 328. An act concerning the taxation of ships or vessels.

Chapter 394. An act in relation to the collection of re-assessed taxes.

One Thousand Eight Hundred and Seventy-one.

Chapter 112. An act to require a return of the amounts paid for assessing and collecting taxes in the year one thousand eight hundred and seventy.

Chapter 125. An act to secure a more equal apportionment of the State and county taxes upon the several cities and towns.

Chapter 142. An act in addition to an act to incorporate the New England Trust Company.

Chapter 297. An act relating to insurance companies.

Chapter 298. An act to abolish the highway tax.

Chapter 332. An act to fix the salary of the deputy tax commissioner.

Chapter 390. An act relating to the taxation of bank shares.

One Thousand Eight Hundred and Seventy-two.

Chapter 227. An act to establish the salary of the first clerk in the tax commissioner's department.

Chapter 245. An act in addition to an act to levy taxes on certain insurance companies and on deposits in savings banks.

Chapter 259. An act to establish the polls and estates of the several cities and towns in the Commonwealth.

Chapter 306. An act to make uniform the taxation of reservoirs.

Chapter 310. An act in relation to the assessment of taxes in fire districts.

Chapter 321. An act to provide for the collection of taxes upon bank shares.

Chapter 325. An act in relation to certain matters of insurance.

Chapter 327. An act to encourage the manufacture of beet sugar.

Resolves of the year One Thousand Eight Hundred and Seventy-two.

Chapter 46. Resolve in favor of certain literary, charitable and scientific institutions.

Acts of the year One Thousand Eight Hundred and Seventy-three.

Chapter 141. An act in relation to the taxation of insurance companies.

Chapter 156. An act to increase the compensation of assessors of taxes.

Chapter 225. An act to authorize cities and towns to charge interest on certain taxes.

Chapter 270. An act to incorporate the Boston Mortgage Company.

Chapter 272. An act amending an act relating to the assessment of taxes upon estates omitted in the annual taxation.

Chapter 285. An act to incorporate the Chapin Banking and Trust Company, of Springfield.
Chapter 315. An act relating to the taxation of bank shares.
Chapter 347. An act to incorporate the Fall River Banking and Trust Company.
Chapter 354. An act relating to the taxation of incomes.
Chapter 369. An act to incorporate the Springfield Banking and Trust Company.

One Thousand Eight Hundred and Seventy-four.

Chapter 28. An act in relation to treasurers and collectors of taxes in cities.
Chapter 227. An act providing for a valuation and return of property and estates exempted from taxation.
Chapter 238. An act relating to the collection of taxes.
Chapter 317. An act to secure a more equal apportionment of the State and county taxes upon the several cities and towns.
Chapter 373. An act to amend an act to incorporate the Boston Safe Deposit Company.
Chapter 375. An act concerning associations for religious, charitable, educational, and other purposes.

Resolves of the year One Thousand Eight Hundred and Seventy-four.

Chapter 70. Resolve authorizing the appointment of a commission to inquire into the expediency of revising and amending the laws of the State relating to taxation and the exemptions therefrom.

PRELIMINARY DRAFT

FOR A CODIFICATION OF THAT PORTION OF CHAPTERS ELEVEN AND TWELVE OF THE GENERAL STATUTES OF THE COMMONWEALTH, AND OF THE SUBSEQUENT ENACTMENTS RELATING TO TAXATION, WHICH WERE IN FORCE JANUARY 1, 1875.

[EXPLANATORY NOTE.—The sections of existing statutes from which each section is drawn are printed at the top of the sections. The marginal references are to statutes, etc., bearing on the subject-matter, whether now in force or repealed.

As the codification was prepared for the use of the Commissioners, simply to give a substantially accurate view of the existing law, verbal alterations have not been noted.]

OF TAXATION.

CHAPTER I.

OF THE ASSESSMENT OF TAXES.

[INDEX.]

Be it enacted, &c., as follows:

PERSONS AND PROPERTY SUBJECT TO TAXATION.

[G. S. 11, § 1.]

Poll tax. R. S. 7, § 1. 1843, 87. 1844, 145.

1 SECT. 1. A poll tax shall be assessed in the
2 manner hereinafter provided, on every male in-

habitant of the Commonwealth above the age of twenty years, whether a citizen of the United States or an alien.

G. S. 11, § 1. 7 Mass. 523. 4 Met. 181. 5 Met. 594.

[G. S. 11, § 2.]

SECT. 2. All property, real and personal, of the inhabitants of this state, not expressly exempted by law, shall be subject to taxation as hereinafter provided.

Property tax. R. S. 7, § 2. G. S. 11, § 2. 4 Met. 564. 4 Cush. 12. 8 Cush. 237. 4 Gray, 500. 106 Mass. 540. 16 Gray, 293. 101 Mass. 317. 1867, 101.

[G. S. 11, § 3. 1872, 306.]

SECT. 3. Real estate, for the purpose of taxation, shall include all lands within this state, and all buildings and other things erected on or affixed to the same.

Real Estate. R. S. 7, § 3. G. S. 11, § 3. 10 Cush. 514. 101 Mass. 328. 102 Mass. 79. 1862, 224, § 12.

But all reservoirs of water, with the dams connected therewith and the lands under the same, used to maintain a uniform supply of water for mill-power, shall be assessed for the purposes of taxation in the town or towns where located, at a valuation not exceeding a fair valuation of land of like quality in the immediate vicinity.

Reservoirs of water, how taxed. 1872, 306.

[G. S. 11, § 4. 1865, 283, § 15; 1866, 196; 1873, 354.]

SECT. 4. Personal estate shall, for the purposes of taxation, include goods, chattels, money and effects, wherever they are, ships and vessels at home or abroad, money at interest, and other debts due the persons to be taxed more than they are indebted or pay interest for, public

Personal Estate. R. S. 7, § 4. G. S. 11, § 4. 1839, 139, § 2. 1849, 149. 16 Pet. 435. 6 Pick. 98. 16 Pick. 572. 9 Met. 73, 199. 7 Cush. 600. 10 Cush. 128. 1866, 48. 1867, 160. 1873, 354. 10 Allen, 100.

12 Allen, 309, 598. 101 Mass. 333. 105 Mass. 526. 106 Mass. 540.

stocks and securities, stocks in turnpikes, bridges and moneyed corporations, within or without the state, the income from an annuity, and so much of the income from a profession, trade or employment, as exceeds the sum of two thousand dollars a year; and which has accrued to any person during the year ending on the first day of May of the year in which the tax is assessed, but no income shall be taxed which is derived from property subject to taxation: *provided*, that no taxes shall be assessed in any city or town for state, county or town purposes upon the shares in the capital stock of corporations paying a tax on their corporate franchises under the provisions of this chapter for any year in which they pay the tax thereunder: but such shares shall be taxable to the owners thereof for school district and parish purposes.

Proviso. 1865, 283, § 15.

1866, 196.

NOTE.—This section embraces the provisions of § 4 of G. S. 11, as modified by the acts regulating the income tax and by the corporation tax-laws. Whether the phrase, "corporations paying a tax on their corporate franchises under the provisions of this chapter," is precisely equivalent in effect to the words, "said corporations," in § 15 of cap. 283 of 1865, query?

PROPERTY AND PERSONS EXEMPTED FROM TAXATION.

[G. S. 11, § 5. 1865, 206, § 1; 1867, 101.]

Exempted Property. R. S. 7, § 5. G. S. 11, § 5. G. S. 13, § 75. 1862, 224, § 12. Property of the United States.

SECT. 5. The following property and polls shall be exempted from taxation:—

First. The property of the United States.

Second. The property of the Commonwealth, except real estate of which the Commonwealth is in possession under a mortgage for condition broken. But in all cases where lands belonging to the Commonwealth are or have been sold by the commissioners of public lands, and agreements for deeds are or have been given by said commissioners, the land shall be free from taxation for the space of three years, unless previously built upon or otherwise improved by the purchasers or their assigns; and upon the expiration of three years from the date of such sale, such lands shall be taxable to the purchasers thereof or their assigns, in the same manner and to the same extent as if deeds of the same had been executed and delivered.

Property of the state. 1853, 122. 4 Met. 564. 8 Cush. 237. 4 Gray, 500. 1867, 101.

Third. The personal property of literary, benevolent, charitable and scientific institutions incorporated within this Commonwealth, and the real estate belonging to such institutions, occupied by them or their officers for the purposes for which they were incorporated.

See 1867, 101. certain institutions. 2 Cush. 611. 12 Cush. 54. 11 Allen, 470. 99 Mass. 599. 101 Mass. 319.

Fourth. All property belonging to common school districts, the income of which is appropriated to the purposes of education.

school districts. 1843, 85.

Fifth. The Bunker Hill Monument.

Bunker Hill Monument.

Sixth. The household furniture of every person, not exceeding one thousand dollars in value, his wearing apparel, farming utensils,

Household furniture, etc. 1865, 206, § 1.

and mechanic's tools, not exceeding three hundred dollars in value, necessary for carrying on his business.

Churches. 1841, 127. 1 Met. 538. 1865, 206, § 1.

Seventh. Houses of religious worship, and the pews and furniture (except for parochial purposes); but portions of such houses appropriated for purposes other than religious worship, shall be taxed at the value thereof to the owners of the houses; and only such houses of religious worship are exempted from taxation as are owned by a religious society, or held in trust for the use of religious organizations.

Cemeteries, etc. 1841, 114, § 7.

Eighth. Cemeteries, tombs and rights of burial, so long as the same shall be dedicated for the burial of the dead.

Estate of agricultural societies. 1851, 215.

Ninth. The estate, both real and personal, of incorporated agricultural societies.

of certain females to amount of five hundred dollars. 1858, 43. 1873, 315, § 14.

Tenth. The property, to the amount of five hundred dollars, of a widow or unmarried female, and of any female minor whose father is deceased, if her whole estate, real and personal, not otherwise exempted from taxation, does not exceed in value the sum of one thousand dollars.

Cattle, etc.

Eleventh. Mules, horses and neat cattle, less than one year old; and swine and sheep less than six months old.

Polls and estates of persons unable to pay. 1873, 315, § 14.

Twelfth. The polls and any portion of the estates of persons who by reason of age, infirmity and poverty, are, in the judgment of the assessors, unable to contribute fully towards the public charges.

NOTE.—The twelfth clause of G. S. 11, § 5, exempted the polls and estates of Indians. It was repealed by 1869, ch. 463. The twelfth clause of the above section corresponds to the thirteenth of § 5, G. S. 11.

[1872, 327, § 1.]

Property used in the manufacture of beet sugar may be exempted by town. 1872, 327.

SECT. 6. Any city or town, for the term of ten years next after the fourth day of May, 1872, may exempt from taxation for any purpose whatsoever, all the machinery, buildings, real estate, and all other property owned by any individual or individuals, corporation or corporations, organized under any law of this state, and used exclusively in the business of manufacturing beet sugar: *provided*, that this exemption from taxation shall not apply to lands upon which beets are raised for the purpose of manufacture.

WHERE POLLS AND PROPERTY SHALL BE ASSESSED.

[G. S. 11, § 6.]

Poll tax, where assessed.

R. S. 7, § 6. G. S. 11, § 6. 1 Met. 242, 250. 4 Met. 181. 11 Cush. 362. 2 Gray, 484. 12 Cush. 44, 52, 54. 12 Allen, 111.

SECT. 7. The poll tax shall be assessed upon each taxable person, in the place where he is an inhabitant on the first day of May in each year, except in cases otherwise provided for by law. The poll tax of minors liable to taxation shall be assessed to, and in the places of the residence of, the parents, masters or guardians, having control of the persons of such minors; but if a minor has no parent, master or guardian, within this state, he shall be personally taxed for his poll, as if he were of full age. The poll tax of every other person under guardianship, shall be assessed to his guardian in the place where the guardian is taxed for his own poll.

[G. S. 11, § 7.]

Person to be taxed where he designates his place of residence to be. 1850, 276. G. S. 11, § 7.

SECT. 8. A taxable person in a city or town, on the first day of May, who, when inquired of by the assessors thereof, refuses to state where he considers his legal residence to be, shall, for the purpose of taxation, be deemed an inhabitant of such place. If, when so inquired of, he designates another place as his legal residence, said assessors shall notify the assessors of such place, who, upon receiving the notice, shall tax such person as an inhabitant of their city or town. But such person shall not be exempt from the payment of a tax legally assessed upon him in the city or town of his legal domicile.

[1866, 170, § 1.]

Assessors to furnish information as to personal property of persons changing their domicil. 1866, 170, § 1.

SECT. 9. When any person liable to be taxed for personal property, shall have changed his domicile, it shall be the duty of the assessors of the city or town where he resides, to require forthwith of the assessors of the city or town where such person was last taxed as an inhabitant, such written statement of any facts within their knowledge as will assist in determining the value of the personal estate of such person, and also the amount he was last assessed in such city or town; and such information shall be furnished by the assessors of the city or town where he was last taxed or assessed.

[1874, 172, §§ 1, 2.]

Penalty for fraudulently evading taxation.

1864, 172, § 1.

SECT. 10. Any inhabitant of this Commonwealth who shall escape taxation by wilfully and designedly changing or concealing his residence, or by any other act, with the intent so to escape, shall be liable, upon conviction therefor, to pay a fine of twice the amount of the last tax paid by such person; or if he shall have paid no tax in this Commonwealth, a fine of not less than one hundred, nor more than five thousand dollars.

1864, 172, § 2.

Any person offending against the provisions of this section may be indicted and tried in any county where any of the acts or things made criminal by this section are done, or in the county where such person is liable to taxation.

[G. S. 11, § 8.]

Real estate, where taxed.

R. S. 7, § 7. G. S. 11, § 8. 1 Cush. 142. 4 Cush. 260.

SECT. 11. Taxes on real estate shall be assessed in the city or town where the estate lies, to the person who is either the owner or in

2 Gray, 185. 7 Gray, 127, 277. 16 Gray, 583. 4 Allen, 57. 101 Mass. 310.

possession thereof on the first day of May. Mortgagors of real estate shall, for the purposes of taxation, be deemed owners until the mortgagee takes possession, after which the mortgagee shall be deemed the owner.

[G. S. 11, § 9.]

Tenant may recover of land lord, taxes paid, unless, etc. R. S. 7, § 8. G. S. 11, § 9.

SECT. 12. When a tenant paying rent for real estate is taxed therefor, he may retain out of his rent the taxes paid by him, or may recover the same in an action against his landlord, unless there is an agreement to the contrary.

[G. S. 11, § 10.]

Real estate of person deceased may be assessed to heirs, etc. One liable for whole, with right to contribution. R. S. 7, § 12. G. S. 11, § 10.

SECT. 13. The undivided real estate of a deceased person may be assessed to his heirs or devisees without designating any of them by name, until they have given notice to the assessors of the division of the estate and the names of the several heirs or devisees; and each heir or devisee shall be liable for the whole of such tax, and when paid by him he may recover of the other heirs or devisees their respective portions thereof.

[G. S. 11, § 11.]

Real estate of deceased person may be assessed to estate of deceased where title is in dispute. 1847, 226. G. S. 11, § 11. 9 Gray, 433. 16 Gray, 292, 337. 97 Mass. 321.

SECT. 14. The real estate of a person deceased, the right or title to which is doubtful or unascertained by reason of litigation concerning the will of the deceased, or the validity thereof, may be assessed in general terms to the estate of the deceased; and said tax shall constitute a lien upon the land so assessed, and may be enforced by the sale of the same or a part thereof, as provided for enforcing other liens for taxes on real estate.

[G. S. 11, § 12.]

Personal estate taxed where owner resides. R. S. 7, §§ 9, 10. 1839, 139, § 2. G. S. 11, § 12. 6 Pick. 98. 1 Met. 242, 250. 4 Cush. 546. 11 Cush. 362. 3 Gray, 494. 7 Gray, 277. 14 Allen, 366. 101 Mass. 329. 103 Mass. 279. 104 Mass. 587. 1865, 283. 1873, 315.

SECT. 15. All personal estate within or without this state, shall be assessed to the owner in the city or town where he is an inhabitant on the first day of May, except as follows:—

except stock in trade, etc. employed in other towns. 1839, 139, § 1. 1859, 114. 4 Met. 186. 4 Cush. 543. 10 Cush. 65. 6 Gray, 579. 13 Gray, 491.

First. All goods, wares, merchandise and other stock in trade (except ships or vessels owned by a copartnership), including stock employed in the business of manufacturing or of the mechanic arts, in cities or towns within the state, other than where the owners reside, whether such owners reside within or without this state, shall be taxed in those places where the owners hire or occupy manufactories, stores, shops or wharves, whether such property is within said places or elsewhere on the first day of May of the year when the tax is made.

Machinery, where taxed, etc. 1837, 86. 12 Allen, 316. 100 Mass. 183. 12 Allen, 316.

Second. All machinery employed in any branch of manufactures, and belonging to a person or corporation, shall be assessed where such machinery is situated or employed; and, in assessing the stockholders for their shares in any manufacturing corporation, there shall first be deducted from the value thereof, the value of the machinery and real estate belonging to such corporation.

Horses, etc. 1857, 301, § 1. 8 Allen, 330.

Third. Horses, mules, neat cattle, sheep and swine, kept throughout the year in places other than those where the owners reside, whether such owners reside within or without this state, and horses employed in stages or other vehicles for the transportation of passengers for hire, shall be assessed to the owners in the places where they are kept.

Property of persons under guardianship. 1855, 106. 1859, 258. 2 Gray, 494. See 1864, 208, § 8. 4 Allen, 462. 105 Mass. 528.

Fourth. Personal property belonging to persons under guardianship, shall be assessed to the guardian in the place where the ward is an inhabitant, unless the ward resides and has his home without the state, in which case it shall be taxed to the guardian in the place where he is an inhabitant.

Trust property, etc. 5 Cush. 93. 6 Gray, 132. 105 Mass. 528. 1865, 283, § 2. 1873, 315, § 15.

Fifth. Personal property held in trust by an executor, administrator or trustee, the income of which is payable to another person, shall be assessed to the executor, administrator or trustee, in the place where such other person resides, if within the state, and if he resides out of the state it shall be assessed in the place where the executor, administrator or trustee resides, and if there are two or more executors, administrators or trustees residing in different places, the property shall be assessed to them in equal portions in such places, and the tax thereon shall be paid out of said income. If the executor, administrator or trustee is not an inhabitant of this state, it shall be assessed to the person to whom the income is payable, in the place where he resides.

Property deposited to accumulate. 13 Allen, 267.

Sixth. Personal property placed in the hands of a corporation or individual, as an accumulating fund for the future benefit of heirs or other persons, shall be assessed to such heirs or persons, if within the state, otherwise to the person so placing it, or his executors or administrators, until a trustee is appointed to take charge of such property, or the income thereof.

of deceased persons. 1848, 235. 1852, 234. 5 Pick. 236. 4 Cush. 1. 6 Allen, 277. 102 Mass. 348. 97 Mass. 322.

Seventh. The personal estate of deceased persons shall be assessed in the place where the deceased last dwelt. After the appointment of an executor or administrator, it shall be assessed to such executor or administrator until he gives notice to the assessors that the estate has been distributed and paid over to the parties interested therein. Before such appointment it shall be assessed in general terms to the estate of the deceased, and the executor or administrator subsequently appointed shall be liable for the tax so assessed in like manner as though assessed to him.

[G. S. 11, § 13.]

Property held as a ministerial fund. R. S. 7, § 10. G. S. 11, § 13. 19 Pick. 542.

SECT. 16. Property held by a religious society as a ministerial fund shall be assessed to the treasurer of the society. If such property consists of real estate, it shall be taxed in the town where it lies; if it consists of personal property, it shall be taxed in the town where such society usually hold their meetings.

[G. S. 11, § 14.]

Personal property mortgaged, etc.
R. S. 7, § 11.
G. S. 11, § 14.
10 Met. 334.

SECT. 17. Personal property mortgaged or pledged shall, for the purposes of taxation, be deemed the property of the party who has the possession.

[G. S. 11, § 15.]

Partners may be jointly taxed for stock in trade.
R. S. 7, § 13.
1859, 114.
G. S. 11, § 15.
9 Cush. 298.
7 Gray, 132.
105 Mass. 526.

SECT. 18. Partners in mercantile or other business, whether residing in the same or different places, may be jointly taxed under their partnership name in the place where their business is carried on, for all the personal property employed in such business, except ships or vessels. If they have places of business in two or more towns, they shall be taxed in each of such places for the proportion of property employed therein. When so jointly taxed each partner shall be liable for the whole tax.

[G. S. 11, § 16. 1870, 328.]

Ships or vessels owned by a copartnership,—when and how to be taxed.
G. S. 11, § 16.
1870, 328.

SECT. 19. Ships or vessels owned by a copartnership shall be assessed to the several partners in their places of residence, proportionally to their interests therein, if they reside within the Commonwealth. But the interests of the several partners who reside without the Commonwealth shall be assessed to the copartnership in the place where their business is carried on.

[1867, 166.]

Treasurer,—how to send warrant for state tax. G. S. 11, § 17. 1867, 166, §§ 1, 2.

SECT. 20. When a state tax is to be assessed, the treasurer shall send his warrants for the assessing thereof by mail to the assessors of the several cities and towns in the Commonwealth.

[G. S. 11, § 18.]

By what rules all taxes to be assessed. R. S. 7, § 16. G. S. 11, § 18. 12 Met. 178.

SECT. 21. The assessors shall assess state taxes for which they receive warrants from the treasurer, according to the rules prescribed in this chapter. They shall in like manner assess all county taxes which are duly certified to them, all city or town taxes voted by their places, and all taxes duly voted and certified by school and other districts therein.

G. S. 24, § 44. G. S. 39, § 26. 1870, 333, § 2.

[G. S. 11, § 19.]

Penalty if assessors refuse obey warrant. In such case commissioners to appoint. R. S. 7, §§ 17, G. S. 11, § 19.

SECT. 22. If the assessors of a city or town neglect to obey a warrant so received from the treasurer, or to assess such a county, town or district tax, each assessor so neglecting shall forfeit a sum not exceeding two hundred dollars; and the commissioners in the respective counties shall forthwith appoint other suitable persons to assess such tax, according to the warrant of the treasurer. The persons so appointed shall take the same oath, perform the same duties, and be liable to the same penalties, as are provided in the case of assessors of towns.

[G. S. 11, § 20.]

Town, etc., liable for state or county tax not assessed. R. S. 8, § 37. 1852, 312. G. S. 11, § 20.

SECT. 23. If within five months after the receipt of a warrant from the state treasurer, or a certificate from the county commissioners requiring the assessment of a tax, the same is not assessed and certified as the law requires, the amount of the tax may be recovered of the city or town where the neglect occurs, in an action of contract by the treasurer of the state or county respectively.

[G. S. 11, § 21.]

Keepers of taverns, etc., to give names of persons taxable. Penalty. 1837, 176. 1839, 135. G. S. 11, § 21.

SECT. 24. Keepers of taverns and boarding-houses, and masters and mistresses of dwelling-houses, shall, upon application of an assessor in the place where their house is situated, give information of the names of all persons residing therein and liable to be assessed for taxes. Every such keeper, master or mistress, refusing to give such information or knowingly giving false information, shall forfeit twenty dollars for each offence.

[G. S. 11, § 22.]

Assessors to give notice to bring in lists of polls and property.

SECT. 25. Before proceeding to make an assessment, the assessors shall give seasonable notice thereof to the inhabitants of their respective places, at any of their meetings, or by posting up in their city or town one or more notifications in some public place or places, or by some other sufficient manner. Such notice shall require the inhabitants to bring in to the assessors, within a time therein specified, true lists of all their polls and estates, both real and personal, not exempted from taxation.

R. S. 7, § 19. G. S. 11, § 22. 12 Met. 211. 5 Cush. 97. 8 Cush. 55. See 1865, 121. 1869, 190. 8 Gray, 511. 101 Mass. 89.

[G. S. 11, § 23.]

SECT. 26. The assessors shall in all cases require a person bringing in such a list, to make oath that the same is true; which oath may be administered by either of the assessors.

shall verify lists by oath of the party. R. S. 7, § 20. G. S. 11, § 23.

[G. S. 11, § 24.]

SECT. 27. The assessors of each place shall at the time appointed make a fair cash valuation of all the estate, real and personal, subject to taxation therein, except as provided in section three.

to make cash valuation. R. S. 7, § 21. 1853, 319, § 1. G. S. 11, § 24. 4 Gray, 254. 1872, 306.

[G. S. 11, § 25.]

SECT. 28. They shall receive as true the list brought in by each individual according to the provisions of this chapter, unless on being thereto required by the assessors, he refuses to answer on oath all necessary inquiries as to the nature and amount of his property.

to receive lists as true, unless, etc. R. S. 7, § 22. G. S. 11, § 25. 12 Met. 211. 8 Cush. 64. 10 Allen, 100. 112 Mass.

[1869, 190.]

Penalty for making false return to assessors. 1869, 190.

SECT. 29. Whoever shall deliver or disclose to any assessor or assistant assessor of taxes, elected or appointed in pursuance of the laws of this Commonwealth, any false or fraudulent list, return or schedule of property, as and for a true list of his estates, real and personal, not exempted from taxation, with intent thereby to avoid the lawful assessment or payment of any tax, or with intent thereby to defeat or evade the provisions of law in relation to the assessment or payment of taxes, shall be punished by a fine not exceeding one thousand dollars or imprisonment in jail not exceeding one year.

[G. S. 11, § 26.]

Penalty for agreeing to assessment on limited amount, etc., with view to residence, etc. 12 Allen, 599. G. S. 11, § 26.

SECT. 30. Any person who in any way, directly or indirectly, proposes or agrees to an assessment on any specific or limited amount less than he is liable by law to be taxed for, with a view or as an inducement to make any particular place his residence for the purpose of taxation, shall be punished by a fine of one thousand dollars; and any assessor guilty of making or assenting to any such proposal shall be subject to a like penalty.

[G. S. 11, § 27.]

Assessors shall make an estimate, when lists are not brought in.

SECT. 31. They [the assessors] shall ascertain as nearly as possible the particulars of the personal estate, and of the real estate in possession or occupation, as owner or otherwise, of any person who has not brought in such list, and make an estimate thereof at its just value, according to their best information and belief.

R. S. 7, § 23. G. S. 11, § 27. 8 Cush. 63.

[G. S. 11, § 28.]

SECT. 32. Such estimate shall be entered in the valuation, and shall be conclusive upon all persons who have not seasonably brought in lists of their estates, unless they can show a reasonable excuse for the omission.

Estimate of assessors to be conclusive, unless, etc. R. S. 7, § 24. G. S. 11, § 28. 5 Cush. 97. 8 Cush. 63.

[1866, 170, § 2.]

SECT. 33. When the assessors of any city or town shall have received notice from the assessors of any other city or town within the Commonwealth, of the amount at which a person having been an inhabitant thereof was last taxed on personal property, such notice shall be filed in their office, subject to public inspection; and they shall not assess such person upon any less amount of personal estate than he was last assessed, until he shall have brought in to such assessors a list of his personal estate in accordance with the provisions of sections twenty-five and twenty-six.

Assessors to file information received, subject to public inspection, and not to tax less, etc. 1866, 170, § 2. 1869, 190.

[G. S. 11, § 33.]

SECT. 34. They shall make a list of the valu-

Assessors to deposit a copy of valuation in office.

R. S. 7, § 29. G. S. 11, § 33. 2 Gray, 298. 1 Pick. 482. 14 Mass. 177.

ation and the assessment thereon, and, before the taxes assessed are committed for collection, shall deposit the same, or an attested copy thereof, in their office, or if there is no office, with their chairman, for public inspection.

[G. S. 11, § 34.]

What shall be contained in valuation. R. S. 7, § 30. G. S. 11, § 34. See 1861, 167. 16 Gray, 293. 2 Allen, 594. 102 Mass. 151.

SECT. 35. The first part of the list shall exhibit the valuation and assessment of the polls and estates of the inhabitants assessed; and shall contain in separate columns the following particulars, to wit:—

estates of inhabitants. 21 Pick. 64. 7 Gray, 128.

The names of the inhabitants assessed; and opposite to their names—

The number of polls.
The amount of their poll tax.
The description of their real estate.
The true value of their real estate.
The tax assessed on such real estate.
The description of their personal property.
The true value of their personal property.
The tax on their personal property.
The sum-total of each person's tax.

estates of non-residents.

The second part shall exhibit the valuation and assessment of the estates of non-resident owners; and shall contain in separate columns the following particulars, to wit:—

The names of the non-resident owners of property assessed, or such description of them as can be given.

Their places of abode, if known.
The description of their estate.
The true value of such estate.
The tax thereon.

NOTE.—The section from which this is taken seems to be in force, although the lists actually in use are those furnished by the Secretary under 1861, ch. 167.

[1861, 167, § 1.]

SECT. 36. The secretary of the Commonwealth shall furnish to each of the cities and towns in the state on or before the first day of May in each year, suitable blank books for the use of the assessors of said cities and towns in the assessment of taxes, which books shall contain blank columns numbered from one to twenty-seven, inclusive, with uniform headings for a valuation list, and blank tables for aggregates, in the following form :—

Secretary to furnish assessment books with uniform tables. 1861, 167, § 1. 101 Mass. 327. G. S. 11, §§ 33, 34.

Valuation List for the of May 1, 18

NAMES OF PERSONS ASSESSED.	Number of polls.	Total cash tax on polls.	Value of each person's whole stock in trade.	Description of taxable cash assets.	Value of cash assets.	Value of machinery used in manufacturing establishments.	Number of live stock, each kind specified separately.	Value of each kind of live stock.	Description of all other ratable personal estate not before named.	Value of same.	Aggregate of each person's ratable personal estate.	Total tax on personal estate.
Column No. 1.	2	3	4	5	6	7	8	9	10	11	12	13

Buildings of all kinds, described by naming their uses.	Value of buildings, exclusive of land.	Description by name or otherwise, of each and every lot of land, owned by each person.	Number of acres or feet in each lot of land.		Value of same.	Superficial feet of wharf.	Value of same.	Aggregate value of real estate.	Total tax on real estate.	Total cash tax on polls, personal and real estate.	Highway Tax.			
			Acres.	Feet.							Tax on polls.	Tax on personal estate.	Tax on real estate.	Aggregate highway tax.
14	15	16	17		18	19	20	21	22	23	24	25	26	27

TABLE OF AGGREGATES

for the of of Polls, Property, Taxes, etc., as assessed May 1, 18 .

Total number of polls.	Total tax on polls.	Total value of personal estate.	Total value of real estate.	Total tax for State, county, city and town purposes, including highway tax.	Rate per cent. of total tax.	Total valuation, May 1, 18 .	Total number of dwelling-houses.	Total number of horses.	Total number of cows.	Total number of sheep.	Total number of acres of land taxed in the city or town.
1	2	3	4	5	6	7	8	9	10	11	12

[1861, 167, § 2.]

Assessors how to enter valuation and assessments in the books. 1861, 167, § 2. 102 Mass. 79.

SECT. 37. The assessors in each of the several cities and towns shall enter in the books furnished, in accordance with the provisions of the preceding section the valuation and assessments of the polls and estate of the inhabitants assessed, in the following order:—

In column number one.—The names of the inhabitants or parties assessed for polls or estate.

In column number two.—The number of polls for which any person named in the preceding column is taxable.

In column number three.—Total amount of cash tax on polls.

In column number four.—The amount of each person's whole stock in trade, including all goods, wares and merchandise, at home or abroad, of ratable estate, whether paid for or otherwise.

In column number five.—A description of all ratable cash assets, viz.: amount of money at interest more than the person assessed pays interest for, including public securities; the amount of money on hand, including deposits in any bank, or in any savings bank which is not exempted by law from taxation; the number of shares of stock which are taxable, with the name of the corporation, in any bank, railroad, insurance, manufacturing or other incorporated company.

In column number six.—The true ratable value of the several items enumerated in the preceding column, placed opposite the description of said property or shares.

In column number seven.—The true value of machinery used in all kinds of manufacturing establishments, including steam-engines, etc., the value of such machinery to be entered opposite the description of the building in which it is used.

In columns numbers eight and nine.—The whole number of taxable live stock, including horses, mules, asses, oxen, cows, steers, heifers, sheep and swine, each kind to be stated separately, with the value affixed to each.

In columns numbers ten and eleven.—Description of all other ratable personal estate not before enumerated, such as carriages, income, plate, furniture, tons of vessels, etc., with the true value of the same.

In column number twelve.—The aggregate of each person's ratable personal estate.

In column number thirteen.—The total tax on each person's personal estate.

In column number fourteen.—Buildings of all kinds shall be described in the following order:—

Dwelling-houses; barns; shops of all kinds, naming their use; stores; warehouses; distil-houses; breweries; tanneries and other manufactories of leather; rope-walks; grist-mills; saw-mills; steam and other mills not above enumerated; cotton factories, with the number of spindles and looms used in the same; woollen factories, with the number of sets of cards used in the same; linen factories, with the number of spindles and looms; print works; bleacheries; gas-works; paper mills; card factories; boot and shoe factories; India rubber factories; carriage and car factories; pianoforte and musical instrument factories; sewing-machine factories; chair, pail, tub and other wooden-ware factories; oil factories; glass factories; all kinds of iron and brass works; and all other buildings not above named.

In column number fifteen.—True value of buildings enumerated in the preceding column placed opposite the description of the same, including water-wheels, such value to be exclusive of land and water-power, and of the machinery used in said buildings.

In columns numbers sixteen, seventeen and eighteen.—A description, by name or otherwise, of each 99 Mass. 29. and every lot of land assessed, the same placed opposite the name of the person or party to whom it is taxable, with the number of acres or feet in each lot; the number of quartz sand-beds, of stone-quarries and ore-beds; and the true value thereof.

In columns numbers nineteen and twenty.—The

number of superficial feet of wharf, and the total value of the same.

In column number twenty-one.—The aggregate value of each person's taxable real estate.

In column number twenty-two.—The total tax on real estate.

In column number twenty-three.—The aggregate cash tax assessed to each person on polls, personal and real estate.

1871, 298.

In columns numbers twenty-four, twenty-five, twenty-six and twenty-seven.—The amount assessed for highway tax; on polls; on personal estate; on real estate, and the aggregate of the same.

[1861, 167, § 3; 215, § 1.]

Assessors how to fill up tables of aggregates. 1861, 167, § 3.

SECT. 38. The assessors shall fill up the table of aggregates by an enumeration of the necessary items included in the lists of valuation and assessments required by the preceding section, and shall, on or before the first day of October, in each of the first four years of each decade, deposit in the office of the secretary of the Commonwealth an attested copy of the same, containing:—

First.—The total number of polls.

Second.—The total tax on polls.

1861, 215, § 1.

Third.—The total value of personal estate.

1871, 298.

Fourth.—The total value of real estate.

Fifth.—The total tax for state, county and town purposes, including highway tax.

Sixth.—The rate per cent. of total tax.

Seventh.—The total valuation of the city or town.

Eighth.—Total number of dwelling-houses assessed.

Ninth.—Total number of horses assessed.

Tenth.—Total number of cows assessed.

Eleventh.—Total number of sheep assessed.

Twelfth—The total number of acres of land assessed in the city or town.

The assessors shall make similar returns in the first four years of the last half of each decade; and in every fifth and tenth year of each decade, they shall deposit in the office of the secretary of the Commonwealth, on or before the first day of October, a certified copy, under oath, of the assessors' books of those years, and said books, thus deposited, shall contain an aggregate sheet properly filled in accordance with the foregoing provisions, which shall be in like manner certified by the assessors; and in every fifth and tenth year of each decade, the secretary shall furnish duplicate copies of blank books to the cities and towns for the foregoing purpose: *provided, however,* that in the case of the city of Boston, the returns required by this section to be deposited in the office of the secretary, may be deposited on or before the first day of November, in the several years respectively.

[1861, 167, § 4.]

Secretary to cause copy of preceding sections to be printed with assessors' books. 1861, 167, § 4. G. S. 11, § 36.

SECT. 39. The secretary of the Commonwealth shall cause to be printed and bound in the books to be furnished for the use of the assessors a copy of sections thirty-six, thirty-seven and thirty-eight, and such certificates as are required by the same, and by the General Statutes, to be signed by the assessors, together with such explanatory notes as may by him be deemed expedient, for the purpose of securing uniformity of returns under the several headings; and he shall compile and cause to be printed annually for the use of the legislature the aggregate returns from the cities and towns in the Commonwealth, arranged by counties, so as to exhibit the total valuation of the towns, cities, counties, and state.

[1861, 167, § 5.]

Penalty for neglect on part of assessors. 1861, 167, § 5.

SECT. 40. If the assessors of any town or city shall neglect to comply with the requirements of sections thirty-seven and thirty-eight, each assessor so neglecting shall forfeit a sum not exceeding two hundred dollars.

[1861, 171, §§ 1, 2.]

Assessors to make return to secretary every three years concerning certain corporations. 1861, 171, § 1.

SECT. 41. The assessors of the several cities and towns shall, on or before the first day of September in every third year after eighteen hundred and sixty-one, return to the secretary of the Commonwealth the number and names of the several industrial corporations, and the number and names of the banks and insurance companies established in their respective cities and towns, with the amount of capital stock owned by each, reckoned at the par value thereof, the number of shares issued, and the amount for which the real estate and machinery of manufacturing corporations are taxed in such cities and towns; also, the number and names of savings banks in such cities and towns, and the whole amount of deposits in each; also, the number of shares in industrial corporations, railroads, banks, insurance companies and steamship companies, specifying the number of shares in each company which are taxed in such cities and towns, and the value of such shares as they stand upon the assessors' books; also, the amount of deposits in any savings banks, specifying the name thereof, taxed in their respective cities and towns. They shall also, at the same time, return to the secretary the name of any other association or corporation organized for loaning money, and established in their respective cities and towns, with the amount of their capital stock and deposits, if known, and the amount for which they are taxed, for the year eighteen hundred and sixty-one, and for every third year thereafter.

And of certain other corporations and associations.
1861, 171, § 2.

[1861, 171, §§ 3, 4.]

Secretary to transmit to towns blanks. 1861, 171, § 3.

SECT. 42. The secretary of the Commonwealth shall, on or before the first day of June of every third year after eighteen hundred and sixty-one, transmit to the several cities and towns suitable blank forms, to enable the several assessors to make the returns prescribed in the preceding section, and shall make a digest of the returns of the assessors, made to him in conformity with the foregoing provisions of this act, in convenient form, for the use of the legislature, and shall cause the same to be printed on or before the first day of January of every third year after eighteen hundred and sixty-two, and, in addition to the number provided for the legislature, shall cause one copy of the same to be sent to the clerk of each city and town in this Commonwealth.

to digest and print returns for use of legislature. 1861, 171, § 4.

[1861, 171, § 5.]

Penalty on agents, assessors, for refusal. 1861, 171, § 5.

SECT. 43. If any agent or assessor wilfully refuses or neglects to perform any duty required of him by section forty-one, he shall forfeit a sum not exceeding three hundred dollars.

NOTE.—This and the two preceding sections were the substance of ch. 171 of 1861. The returns required under subsequent acts relating to the assessment of corporations, seem to have superseded those required by the act of 1861, and it has fallen wholly into disuse. We cannot find that it has been repealed.

[1864, 210, § 3.]

Assessors to return under oath opinion as to cause of diminution of aggregate values. 1864, 210, § 3.

SECT. 44. Whenever it shall have been ascertained by the assessors of any city or town that the aggregate values of their city or town, respectively, have been diminished since the first day of May of the preceding year, they shall return with the table of aggregates, or books, which they are required by section thirty-eight to deposit in the office of the secretary of the Commonwealth, a statement in writing, under oath, of the causes which, in their opinion, have produced such diminution.

NOTE.—This provision, being a part of the act of 1864, to provide for the valuation of the property of the Commonwealth, in order to reapportion the state tax, seems to have been considered as temporary. No returns have for many years been received under it.

[1864, 210, §§ 4, 6.]

Penalty for neglect. 1864, 210, § 4.

How recovered. 1864, 210, § 6.

SECT. 45. If the assessors of any city or town shall neglect to comply with the requirements of the preceding section, each assessor so neglecting shall forfeit a sum not exceeding two hundred dollars, which may be recovered in the supreme judicial court of this Commonwealth, by information filed in said court by the attorney-general.

[1874, 227, § 1.]

Assessors to enter certain exempted property on valuation,

SECT. 46. It shall be the duty of the assessors of each city and town in each year to and prepare statement. 1874, 227, § 1.

enter upon the valuation list of their respective city or town, in the appropriate columns, after the enumeration of the taxable persons and estates therein contained, a statement and description of all the property and estate, and the fair ratable value thereof, situate in such city or town, or which would be taxable there but for the provisions of the third, seventh and ninth divisions of section five, with the names of the persons or corporations owning the same, and the purpose for which it is used, which are exempted from taxation by the foregoing provisions of law, with a reference to the law by which such exemption is allowed.

[1874, 227, § 2.]

To forward statement thereof to tax commissioner. 1874, 227, § 2.

SECT. 47. The assessors of each city or town shall, on or before the first day of October in each year, make and forward to the tax commissioner a statement showing the whole amount of property enumerated in the preceding section, and the amount in each class, and stating separately the aggregate amount belonging to each of the four classes embraced in the third division of section five.

[1865, 283, § 1.]

Shall also return to tax commissioner names of, and detailed statement concerning, certain corporations.

SECT. 48. The assessors of the several cities and towns shall annually, on or before the first Monday of August, return to the tax commissioner hereinafter named, the names of all corporations, except banks of issue and deposit, having a capital stock divided into shares, chartered by this Commonwealth or organized under the general laws, for the purposes of business or profit, and established in their respective cities and towns, or owning real estate therein, and a statement in detail of the works, structures, real estate, and machinery owned by each of said corporations, and situated in such city or town, with the value thereof, on the first day of May preceding, and the amount at which the same is assessed in said city or town for the then current year.

1865, 283, § 1. G. S. 18, §§ 51-53. 1864, 208, § 1. 98 Mass. 25. 99 Mass. 146. 104 Mass. 586. 105 Mass. 526.

They shall also, at the same time, return to said tax commissioner, the amount of taxes laid, or voted to be laid, within said city or town, for the then current year, for state, county and town purposes, including highway taxes.

Also, of the amount of taxes laid or voted for current year.

[1865, 283, § 14.]

SECT. 49. If the assessors of any city or town shall neglect to comply with the requirements of the preceding section, each assessor so neglecting shall forfeit the sum of one hundred dollars.

Penalty for neglect. 1865, 283, § 14. 99 Mass. 148.

[1870, 76, § 1.]

SECT. 50. The assessors of each city and town in the Commonwealth, shall, on or before

Assessors to return to tax commissioner, town indebtedness and assets.

1870, 76, § 1.

the first Monday of August, return to the tax commissioner the aggregate amount of the assets of their respective cities or towns, and the amount of indebtedness of such cities or towns, for which notes, bonds or other similar evidences of debt, the payment of which is not provided for by the taxation of the then current year, were outstanding on the first of May then next preceding, with a concise statement of the various purposes for which such indebtedness was incurred, and the amount incurred for each purpose.

[1873, 321, § 1.]

Also, number, etc., of steam-boilers. 1873, 321, § 1.

SECT. 51. The assessors of each city and town shall, in each year, on or before the first Monday in August, return to the tax commissioner a statement showing the whole number of steam-boilers located in their respective cities and towns on the first day of May then next preceding, by whom and when built, and the aggregate estimated amount of horse-power which such boilers are capable of furnishing. Such return shall also state the number of accidents causing permanent injuries to persons, which have arisen from the use of such boilers during the year, with the causes thereof, as far as may be ascertained by the assessors.

[1873, 321, § 2.]

SECT. 52. The tax commissioner shall in due season forward to the assessors, blanks suitable for making the returns required by the preceding section, and shall include in his annual report to the legislature a tabular statement of statistics derived from such returns.

Tax commissioner to forward blanks and report to legislature. 1873, 321, § 2.

[G. S. 11, § 29.]

SECT. 53. The assessors, when they think it convenient, may include in the same assessment their state, county, and town taxes, or any two of them.

State, county and town taxes in one assessment. R. S. 7, § 25. G. S. 11, § 29.

[G. S. 11, § 30.]

SECT. 54. In the city of Boston, all taxes assessed for city or county purposes may be assessed separately, as county taxes and as city taxes, or under the denomination of city taxes only, as the city council from time to time directs. Chelsea, North Chelsea and Winthrop shall not be taxed for county purposes.

County and city taxes in Boston, how assessed. Chelsea, etc., exempt. R. S. 7, § 26. R. S. 14, § 34. G. S. 11, § 30. 21 Pick. 64.

[G. S. 11, § 31.]

SECT. 55. The assessors shall assess upon the polls, as nearly as may be, one-sixth part of the whole sum to be raised; but the whole poll tax assessed in one year upon an individual for town, county and state purposes, except highway taxes separately assessed, shall not exceed two dollars; and the residue of such whole sum

Proportions to be assessed on polls and property. R. S. 7, § 27. G. S. 11, § 31. 1859, 157. See 1862, 158. 9 Gray, 38. 15 Gray, 42. 1 Allen, 319.

shall be apportioned upon property, as provided in this chapter.

[1871, 298, § 2.]

Highway taxes to be assessed and collected as other town taxes.
1871, 298, § 2.
G. S. 18, § 10.
G. S. 44, §§ 3, 4.

SECT. 56. Towns shall vote to raise such sums of money as are necessary for making and repairing highways and town ways, and order that the same shall be assessed upon the polls and estates of the inhabitants, residents and non-residents, as other town charges are assessed, and the same shall be collected as other town taxes are collected.

[G. S. 11, § 32.]

Assessors may add five per cent. for convenience of apportionment.
R. S. 7, § 28.
G. S. 11, § 32.
15 Mass. 144.
8 Pick. 408.

SECT. 57. Assessors may add to the amount of a tax to be assessed, such sum, not exceeding five per cent. thereof, as any fractional divisions of the amount may render convenient in the apportionment.

[G. S. 11, § 35.]

Form of tax list for collectors.
R. S. 7, § 31.
G. S. 11, § 35.
9 Pick. 97.
2 Gray, 298.
See 1868, 211, § 2.

SECT. 58. The tax list committed to the collectors shall be in substance as follows:—

NAMES.	Number of Polls.	Poll Tax.	Tax on Real Estate.	Tax on Personal Property.	Total.	Time when paid.

NON-RESIDENTS.

NAMES.	Places of abode, if known.	Tax.	

[G. S. 11, § 36.]

SECT. 59. The assessors, or other persons empowered to assess the taxes in a city or town shall, at the close of said valuation list, subscribe and take the following oath:—

Valuation list to be sworn to by assessors. 1853, 319, § 2. G. S. 11, § 36. 1861, 167, § 4.

"We (the assessors, or mayor and aldermen, as the case may be, of) do hereby solemnly swear that the foregoing list is a full and true list of the names of all persons known to us, who are liable to taxation in (here insert the name of the city or town) during the present year, and that the real and personal estate contained in said list, and assessed upon each individual in said list, is a full and accurate assessment upon all the property of each individual, liable to taxation, at its full and fair cash value, according to our best knowledge and belief."

[G. S. 11, § 37.]

SECT. 60. Any assessor or other person assessing taxes in a city or town, who omits to take and subscribe the oath prescribed in the preceding section, shall be punished by a fine of ten dollars; but the omission to take and subscribe said oath shall not prevent the collection of a tax otherwise legally assessed.

Penalty on assessors omitting to take oath. 1857, 306, §§ 1, 2. G. S. 11, § 37.

[G. S. 11, § 38.]

SECT. 61. The assessors shall, within a reasonable time, commit said tax list with their warrant to the collector, or if no collector is chosen, to a constable, or if there is no constable, to the sheriff or his deputy, for collection.

Assessors to commit lists to collectors, etc. R. S. 7, §§ 32, 34. R. S. 8, § 33. R. S. 15, § 33. G. S. 11, § 38. 13 Met. 85. 6 Gray, 387, 502. 99 Mass. 472.

[G. S. 11, § 39.]

Contents and form of warrant. R. S. 7, § 33. G. S. 11, § 39. 1 Met. 328. 6 Met. 345.

SECT. 62. The warrant shall specify the duties of the collector as prescribed by law in the collection of taxes, the times when and the persons to whom he shall pay them in, shall be substantially in the form heretofore used, and need not be under seal.

[G. S. 11, § 40.]

If warrant is lost, etc., new one may issue. R. S. 8, § 51. R. S. act of amend. § 1. G. S. 11, § 40.

SECT. 63. When a warrant issued for the collection of taxes is lost or destroyed, the assessors may issue a new warrant therefor, which shall have the same force and effect as the original warrant.

[G. S. 11, § 41.]

Discounts. R. S. 7, § 35. G. S. 11, § 41. 13 Gray, 476. 2 Allen, 594.

SECT. 64. Towns, at their annual meeting, and city councils of cities, may allow a discount of such sums as they think expedient to persons making voluntary payment of their taxes within such periods of time as they prescribe. In such case the collectors shall make such discount accordingly.

[G. S. 11, § 42.]

Rates to be posted up. R. S. 7, § 36. G. S. 11, § 42.

SECT. 65. When such discount is allowed, the assessors, at the time of committing their warrant to the collector, shall post up in one or more public places within the city or town, notice of the rates of discount.

[1873, 225, § 1.]

Cities and towns may charge in-

SECT. 66. Whenever a city or town has

fixed a time within which taxes assessed therein shall be paid, such city by its city council, and such town, at the meeting when money is appropriated or raised, may vote that on all taxes remaining unpaid after a certain time, interest shall be paid at a specified rate, not exceeding one per centum per month; and may also vote that on all taxes remaining unpaid after another certain time, interest shall be paid at another specified rate, not exceeding one per centum per month; and the interest accruing under such vote or votes shall be added to, and be a part of such taxes.

terest on unpaid taxes, and at what rate. 1862, 146. 1873, 225, § 1.

[G. S. 11, § 43.]

SECT. 67. A person aggrieved by the taxes assessed upon him, may apply to the assessors for an abatement thereof; and, if he makes it appear that he is taxed at more than his just proportion, they shall make a reasonable abatement.

Abatements. R. S. 7, § 37. G. S. 11, § 43. 9 Met. 205. 5 Cush. 93. 7 Cush. 273. 8 Cush, 55, 66. 1865, 121. 8 Gray, 509. 13 Gray, 321. 12 Allen, 612.

[G. S. 11, § 44.]

SECT. 68. If legal costs have accrued before making such abatement, the person applying for the abatement shall pay the same.

Costs before abatement, etc. R. S. 7, § 38. G. S. 11, § 44. See § 73.

[G. S. 11, § 45.]

SECT. 69. If the assessors refuse to make an abatement to a person, he may, within one month thereafter, make complaint thereof to the county commissioners, by filing the same with

If assessors refuse to abate, etc. R. S. 7, § 39. G. S. 11, § 45. 6 Pick. 98. 7 Cush. 273. 8 Cush. 55. 6 Allen, 131.

their clerk, and if, upon a hearing, it appears that the complainant is overrated, the commissioners shall make such an abatement as they deem reasonable.

[G. S. 11, § 46.]

No abatement unless, etc.
R. S. 7, § 40.
1853, 319, § 3.
1857, 306, § 3.
G. S. 11, § 46.
4 Pick. 399.
5 Pick. 451, 498.
7 Pick. 106.
21 Pick. 382.
4 Met. 599.
11 Met. 339.
5 Cush. 97.
6 Cush. 477.
8 Cush. 63.
5 Gray, 365.
8 Gray, 509.
1 Allen, 199.
3 Allen, 546.
101 Mass. 87.

SECT. 70. No person shall have an abatement unless he has filed with the assessors a list, subscribed by him, of his estate liable to taxation, and made oath that it is full and accurate, according to his best knowledge and belief. When such list is not filed within the time specified by the assessors for bringing it in, no complaint from the judgment of the assessors shall be sustained by the county commissioners, unless they are satisfied that there was good cause why such list was not seasonably brought in.

[1865, 121.]

Abatements not to be made if no list is brought in, except in certain cases.
1865, 121.
1868, 211, § 2.
1869, 443.
101 Mass. 87.

SECT. 71. When the assessors of a city or town have given notice to the inhabitants thereof to bring in true lists of all their polls and estates not exempt from taxation, in accordance with the provisions of section twenty-five, they shall not afterwards abate any part of the tax assessed on personal estate to any person who did not bring in such list within the time specified therefor in such notice, unless such tax exceeds, by more than fifty *per centum*, the amount which would have been assessed to that person on personal estate if he had seasonably brought in said list; and if said tax exceeds by more than fifty *per centum* the said amount, the abatement shall be only of the excess above said fifty *per centum: provided, however,* that this act shall not affect any person who can show a reasonable excuse for not seasonably bringing in said list.

[G. S. 11, § 47.]

Abatement to be applied for within six months. R. S. 7, § 41. G. S. 11, § 47.

SECT. 72. No abatement shall be allowed to a person unless he makes application therefor within six months after the date of his tax bill.

[G. S. 11, § 48.]

If tax is paid, amount of abatement to be paid out of town treasury. R. S. 7, § 42. G. S. 11, § 48. 13 Gray, 223. 3 Allen, 546, 550.

SECT. 73. A person having an abatement made shall, if his tax has been paid, be reimbursed out of the treasury of the city or town to the amount of the abatement allowed, together with all charges, except the legal costs provided for in section sixty-eight.

[G. S. 11, § 49.]

Party entitled to certificate. R. S. 7, § 43. G. S. 11, § 49.

SECT. 74. Every person whose tax is abated shall be entitled to a certificate thereof from the assessors, or clerk of the commissioners, or other proper officer.

[1868, 211, § 2; 1869, 443.]

Persons liable and omitted, how assessed. 1868, 211, § 2.

SECT. 75. When any person, on or before the fifteenth day of September, in any year,

G. S. 11, § 50.
1865, 206, § 2.
1869, 443.
1865, 68.

gives notice in writing, accompanied by satisfactory evidence, to the assessors of a city or town, that he was on the first day of May of that year, an inhabitant thereof, and liable to pay a poll tax, and furnishes under oath a *true* list of his polls and estate, both real and personal, not exempt from taxation, the assessors shall assess him for his polls and estate ; but such assessment shall be subject to the provisions of section seventy-one ; and the assessors shall on or before the first day of October, deposit with the clerk of the city or town a list of the persons so assessed. The taxes so assessed shall be entered in the tax list of the collector of the city or town, and he shall collect and pay over the same in the manner specified in his warrant.

[1865, 68, § 1.]

Soldiers, etc., to be assessed and entitled to vote.
1864, 144.
1865, 68.

SECT. 76. Whenever any person shall make application to the assessors of any city or town of this Commonwealth to be assessed a poll tax for the then current year, and it shall appear that such applicant was, on the first day of May preceding, a resident of said city or town and liable to pay a poll tax therein, but was not assessed therefor, and that such applicant is or has been during any portion of the two years preceding such application engaged in the military or naval service of the United States, it shall be the duty of such assessors forthwith to assess such tax and notify the treasurer of such city or town of the same, and the person so assessed shall, upon payment of said tax, be entitled to the right to vote in said city or town, to the same extent as if his taxes had been assessed and paid in the manner provided by law before the sixth day of March, eighteen hundred and sixty-five.

[1868, 320, §§ 1, 2; 1873, 272.]

Omitted estates, how taxed. 1868, 320, § 1. 1873, 272. G. S. 11, § 50, repealed by 1865, 206, § 2.

SECT. 77. When the assessors of any city or town, after the time when their warrant has been committed to the collector of taxes, shall discover that the real or personal estate of any person to an amount not less than one hundred dollars, and liable to taxation, has been omitted from the last annual assessment of taxes in such city or town, said assessors shall proceed forthwith to assess such person for such estate in like manner as he should have been assessed in such last annual assessment. The taxes so assessed, shall be entered in the tax list of the collector of the city or town, and he shall collect and pay over the same in the manner specified in his warrant: *provided*, that such tax shall not be assessed after the fifteenth day of September for any such omission.

1868, 320, § 2. 1873, 315, § 4.

No tax of any city or town shall be invalidated by reason that, in consequence of the provisions of this section, the whole amount of the taxes assessed in such city or town shall exceed the amount authorized by law to be raised.

[G. S. 11, § 51.]

Assessors to be responsible only for fidelity, etc.
R. S. 7, § 44.
G. S. 11, § 51.
4 Pick. 399.
5 Pick. 451, 498.
7 Pick. 106.
21 Pick. 382.
4 Met. 599.
11 Met. 339.
4 Gray, 42.
1872, 310.
3 Allen, 410.
4 Allen, 382.
97 Mass. 424.
98 Mass. 469.
99 Mass. 208.

SECT. 78. The assessors shall not be responsible for the assessment of a tax in a city, town, parish, religious society, fire district or school district, for which they are assessors, when such tax is assessed by them in pursuance of a vote for that purpose, certified to them by the clerk or other proper officer, of such city, town, parish, religious society, fire district or school district, except for the want of integrity and fidelity on their own part.

[G. S. 11, § 52; 1873, 156.]

Pay of assessors.
R. S. 7, § 45.
G. S. 11, § 52.
1855, 224.
3 Met. 431.
1873, 156.

SECT. 79. Each assessor shall be paid by his city or town, two dollars and fifty cents a day, for every whole day that he is employed in that service, with such other compensation as the city or town shall allow.

[G. S. 11, § 53.]

Taxes, invalid, etc., except poll taxes, may be reassessed.
1859, 118, § 1.
G. S. 11, § 53.
1870, 394.
13 Allen, 269.
97 Mass. 322.
99 Mass. 32, 208.
102 Mass. 73.

SECT. 80. Every tax, except a poll tax, which is invalid by reason of any error or irregularity in the assessment, and which has not been paid, or which has been recovered back, may be reassessed by the assessors for the time being, to the just amount to which, and upon the estate or to the person to whom, such tax ought at first to have been assessed, whether such person has continued an inhabitant of the same city or town or not.

[1870, 394, § 1.]

Reassessed taxes, how entered upon warrant. G. S. 11, § 53. 1870, 394, § 1.

SECT. 81. Taxes reassessed under the provisions of the preceding section, shall be committed to, and collected and paid over by, the collector of taxes for the time being, in the same manner as other taxes, except that the name of the person to whom the taxes were originally assessed shall be stated in the warrant; and the bond of such collector shall apply to such reassessed taxes.

[G. S. 11, § 54.]

Tax to be void to extent of illegal excess. 1859, 118, § 4. G. S. 11, § 54. See G. S. 12, § 56. 99 Mass. 208.

SECT. 82. If, through any erroneous or illegal assessment or apportionment of taxes, a party is assessed more or less than his due proportion, the tax and assessment shall be void only to the extent of the illegal excess.

[1865, 283, § 12; 1871, 332.]

Treasurer of the Commonwealth to be tax commissioner, etc. 1864, 208, § 5. 1865, 283, § 12. 1871, 332. 1866, 298, § 4. 1867, 167, § 6. and 188, § 2. 1870, 224, § 61.

SECT. 83. The treasurer of the Commonwealth shall be tax commissioner, with all the powers and duties conferred and imposed by this chapter upon that office. He may appoint a deputy, who shall, under his direction, exercise and perform said powers and duties, subject to appeal as provided in section one hundred and thirty-three, and who shall receive a salary at the rate of twenty-five hundred dollars per year;

and may also appoint such clerks as may be necessary for the performance of the duties required by law.

[1870, 144 § 1.]

Corporations holding stock, etc., as collateral, to make returns to tax commissioner. G. S. 68, § 13, and ch. 57, §§ 150, 152. 1865, 283. 1869, 444. 1870, 144, § 1.

SECT. 84. Every corporation established within this Commonwealth by special charter, or organized under the general laws thereof, which holds on the first day of May, in any year, shares of stock in corporations other than those subject to taxation on their corporate franchises under the provisions of this chapter, or bonds of any description, as collateral security for borrowed money, or other liability, shall annually, between the first and tenth days of May, return to the tax commissioner the whole number of such shares and bonds so held, the names and residences of the persons pledging the same, and the number, denomination and the par value and cash market value, if known, of the shares and bonds pledged by each; and the tax commissioner shall, on or before the twentieth day of June in each year, transmit to the assessors of the several cities and towns of the Commonwealth, a true copy of the list furnished by such corporations.

Tax commissioner to transmit list to assessors.

NOTE.—The phrase, "subject to taxation on their corporate franchise under the provisions of this chapter," is used as the equivalent of the words, "subject to taxation under the provisions of chapter two hundred and eighty-three, of the acts of the year one thousand eight hundred and sixty-five, and acts in amendment thereof," in § 1, ch. 144, of 1870. Whether this use is precisely accurate, query?

[1870, 144, § 2.]

Penalty for neglect. 1870, 144, § 2.

SECT. 85. Any corporation neglecting or refusing to make the returns required by the preceding section, or wilfully making a return which is materially false or defective, shall forfeit for each offence a sum of not less than fifty, nor more than one thousand dollars, to be recovered by an action of tort to the use of the city or town in which the person pledging such stock or bonds resides.

[1867, 188 § 2.]

Tax commissioner to furnish lists and information to assessors. 1865, 283. 1867, 188, § 2.

SECT. 86. The tax commissioner shall annually, on or before the twentieth day of June in each year, cause to be forwarded to the assessors of every city and town in this Commonwealth, a list of all Massachusetts corporations known to him to be taxable on the first day of May next preceding said twentieth day of June, on their corporate franchises, under the provisions of this chapter, and such other information in his possession, as in his judgment will assist the assessors of the cities and towns in the assessment of taxes.

See note to §§ 4 and 84.

[1873, 315 § 1.]

OF THE TAXATION OF BANK SHARES.

Tax upon bank shares to be assessed to owners in town where bank is located. 99 Mass. 141. 14 Allen, 359. 104 Mass. 586.

SECT. 87. All the shares of stock in banks, whether of issue or not, existing by authority of the United States or of this Commonwealth, and located within this Common-

3 Wallace, 585. G. S. 57, §§ 88-90; ch. 11. 1864, 208. 1865, 242. 1867, 188. 1868, 349. 1871, 390. 1872, 321. 1873, 315, § 1.

wealth, including shares in the capital stock of the Mercantile Savings Institution in the city of Boston, shall be assessed to the owners thereof in the cities or towns where such banks are located, and not elsewhere, in the assessment of all state, county and town taxes imposed and levied in such place by the authority of law, whether such owner is a resident of said city or town or not, at the fair cash value of such shares on the first day of May of the year in which the tax shall be assessed, first deducting therefrom the proportionate part of the value of the real estate belonging to the bank, at the same rate, and no greater, than that at which other moneyed capital in the hands of citizens and subject to taxation is by law assessed. And the persons or corporations who appear from the records of the banks to be the owners of shares at the close of the business day next preceding the first day of May in each year, shall be taken and deemed to be the owners thereof for the purposes of this section.

[1873, 315, § 2.]

Bank to pay taxes to collector of town where located. 1873, 315, § 2.

SECT. 88. It shall be the duty of every such bank, or other corporation, to pay to the collector, or other person authorized to collect the taxes of the city or town in which such bank or other corporation is located, at the time in each year when other taxes assessed in the said city or town become due, the amount of the tax so assessed in such year upon the shares in such bank or other corporation. If such tax shall not be so paid, the said bank or other corporation shall be liable for the same; and the said tax, with interest thereon at the rate of twelve per centum per annum from the day when the tax became due, may be recovered in an action of contract brought by the treasurer of such city or town.

[1873, 315, § 3.]

Corporation to have lien upon shares for taxes paid. 1873, 315, § 3.

SECT. 89. The shares of such banks or other corporations shall be subject to the tax paid thereon by the corporation or the officers thereof, and the corporation and the officers thereof shall have a lien on all the shares in such bank or other corporation, and on all the rights and property of the shareholders in the corporate property for the payment of said taxes.

[1873, 315, § 4.]

Rate of taxation in places where banks are located. 1873, 315, § 4. 101 Mass. 575.

SECT. 90. Assessors of cities and towns in which any national bank or banking association is located, for the purpose of ascertaining the rate at which taxes shall be assessed, shall omit from the valuation upon which the rate is to be based, the value of all shares held by non-residents of said cities and towns, and no tax of any city or town shall be invalidated by reason of any excess of the amount thereof over the amount to be raised in consequence of the provisions of this section.

[1873, 315, § 5.]

Cashier to make sworn statement to assessors, of names, etc., of shareholders. 1873, 315, § 5.

SECT. 91. It shall be the duty of the cashier of every such bank to make and deliver to the assessors of the city or town in which such bank is located, on or before the tenth day of May in each year, a statement verified by the oath of such cashier showing the name of each shareholder, with his residence and the number of shares belonging to him at the close of the business day next preceding the first day of May, as the same then appeared on the books of said bank. In case the cashier shall fail to make such statement, the assessors of the city or town in which the bank is located shall forthwith, upon such failure, proceed to obtain a list of shareholders, with the residence of and number of shares belonging to each.

Assessors to obtain lists of shareholders if cashier neglects.

To transmit return.

In either case the assessors of each city and town shall, immediately upon obtaining such list, or statement, transmit to the tax commissioner a true copy of the same, and shall further, by notice in writing, inform said commissioner of the rate per centum upon the valuation of the city or town of the total tax in such city or town for the year, immediately upon the ascertainment thereof, and also of the amount assessed by them upon the shares of each bank located therein.

[1865, 242 §§ 1, 2; 1867, 188, § 1.]

Assessors to return par and market value, etc., to tax commissioner. 1865, 242, §§ 1, 2. 1867, 188, § 1.

SECT. 92. The assessors of every city and town in which any association for the purposes of banking is or shall be established by authority of the United States, shall annually, between the first and tenth day of May, ascertain the amount of the capital stock of such association, the par value and the fair market value of each share, and the amount and value of real estate held and owned by such association, and where the same is located, and shall, on or before the fifteenth day of May, in each year, return the same to the tax commissioner of the Commonwealth.

[1873, 315, § 6.]

Commissioner to determine amount of offset against payments to be made to the town, etc. 1873, 315, § 6.

SECT. 93. Said commissioner shall thereupon, as soon as may be, determine from the returns provided for by section ninety-one, and otherwise, the proportionate amount of the tax so assessed upon the shares in each of said banks which has been assessed upon shares which, according to the provisions of sections fifteen, sixteen, seventeen and eighteen of this chapter, would not be taxable in said city or town, which amounts, as finally determined under the provisions of this act, shall be a charge to said city or town as an offset against any payments to be made from the treasury of the Commonwealth to said city or town.

[1873, 315, § 7.]

To determine amount which shall become a credit to town. 1873, 315, § 7.

SECT. 94. Said commissioner shall, in like manner, determine the proportionate amount of tax so assessed upon shares in each of said banks, which, according to the provisions of sections fifteen, sixteen, seventeen and eighteen, would be taxable in each city or town in this Commonwealth other than that in which the bank is located, which amounts, as finally determined under the provisions of this chapter, shall become a credit to such city or town.

[1873, 315, § 8.]

To inform assessors of the aggregate amount of charges and credits. 1873, 315, § 8.

Right of appeal.

SECT. 95. Said commissioner shall, by written or printed notice, delivered at the assessors' office or sent by mail, inform the assessors of each city or town affected thereby, of the aggregate amount of charges and credits against and in favor of such city or town under the two preceding sections, as determined by him, forthwith, upon the determination thereof. From this determination an appeal may be made by said assessors, within ten days from the date of said notice, to the board of appeal provided for in section one hundred and thirty-three, which board shall hear such appeal, decide the matter in question, and notify said commissioner and the party appealing thereof, and their decision shall be final.

[1873, 315, § 9.]

Commissioner to certify to state treasurer aggregate amount of charges and credits. 1873, 315, § 9.

SECT. 96. Said commissioner shall, at the expiration of ten days after notice given, as provided in the preceding section, or upon being informed of the decision of the board of appeal, if an appeal is made, certify to the treasurer and receiver-general the aggregate amount of charges mentioned in section ninety-three against each city and town in the Commonwealth, and also the aggregate of credits mentioned in section ninety-four in favor of each city or town, as finally determined under sections ninety-three, ninety-four and ninety-five, and the treasurer shall thereupon withhold, out of any sums of money which are or may become payable out of the state treasury to any city or town against which a charge is certified, the amount so certified; and shall allow or pay over to each city or town in favor of which a credit is certified, the amount so certified.

[1873, 315, §§ 10, 11.]

Allowance of one per centum for expense of assessing and collecting tax. 1873, 315, § 10.

SECT. 97. In the adjustment and determination of amounts due under the provisions of this chapter in relation to the taxation of bank shares, an allowance of one per centum upon the amount so assessed and collected shall be made for the expenses of assessing and collecting the same, and no city or town shall be entitled to any allowance of credits or payments under the provisions of this chapter in relation to the taxation of bank shares or of corporations having a capital stock divided into shares, for the purpose of business and profit, in any year, until the assessors thereof shall have complied with the requirements of the said provisions of this chapter in relation to the taxation of bank shares.

Saving clause. 1873, 315, § 11.

No bank, the shares in which are made taxable by section eighty-four, shall be subject to taxation under the provisions of section one hundred and twenty-six, nor shall the shareholders be taxable for state, county or town purposes, except under the provisions of this chapter in respect to their shares therein.

[1873, 315, § 12.]

Amount paid into treasury by savings banks and insurance companies, to be deducted, etc. 1873, 315, § 12.

SECT. 98. The amount actually paid into the treasury of the Commonwealth in each year, under the provisions of this chapter, on account of shares in banks or banking associations, which on the first day of May are the absolute property of any savings bank or institution for savings subject to taxation under the provisions of section one hundred and four, or of any insurance corporation which is subject to taxation under the provisions of section one hundred and twenty-six shall be deducted from the tax payable under the provisions of said sections by such savings bank, institution for savings or insurance corporation at the next payment to the Commonwealth after the assessment of bank shares as herein provided. The tax commissioner may require a statement of all such shares so owned by any such savings bank, institution for savings or insurance corporation, to be made in a form approved by him, and signed and sworn to by the treasurer or like financial officer thereof. He shall, from such statement and other evidence, and subject to appeal by such corporation, as herein provided in similar cases, determine the amounts to be deducted, and certify the same to the treasurer of the Commonwealth upon the final determination thereof.

Commissioner to determine amount to be deducted.

[1873, 315, § 13.]

SECT. 99. The tax commissioner shall, as soon as may be after the first Monday in December in each year, certify to the treasurer the amount assessed and collected for that year in respect of shares in such banks or other corporations owned absolutely by any society, district or institution of any of the classes specified in the third, fourth and ninth divisions of section five, and the treasurer shall thereupon pay

Commissioner to certify to treasurer amount assessed and collected. 1873, 315, § 13.

over such amounts to the corporations owning such shares.

[1873, 315, § 14.]

Owner of shares in certain cases to be furnished with certificate of exemption from taxation. 1873, 315, § 14.

SECT. 100. It shall be the duty of the assessors of each city or town, upon request of any person resident in such city or town, who is the owner of any shares in such banks or other corporations which, under the provisions of the tenth and twelfth divisions of section five would be entitled to exemption from taxation, to give such owner a certificate setting forth such fact, and it shall be the duty of the treasurer of such city or town, upon request therefor and the deposit with him of such certificate, to pay over to such owner the amount so collected in respect of such shares, immediately upon the allowance of the amount which shall be made to such city or town under the provisions of this chapter in relation to the taxation of bank shares.

[1873, 315, § 15.]

Executors, administrators, and guardians to make return. 1865, 283, § 2. 1873, 315, § 15.

SECT. 101. Shares in such banks and other corporations shall be included in the returns required to be made by the provisions of section one hundred and twenty-four.

[1873, 315, § 16.]

Tax to be refunded in certain cases. 1873, 315, § 16.

SECT. 102. Whenever it shall be made to appear to the tax commissioner by certificate of the assessors or a majority of them or other satisfactory evidence, that any tax assessed in accordance with the provisions of the seventh section of chapter three hundred and twenty-one of the acts of the year eighteen hundred and seventy-two, which has been paid over or accounted for to the state treasury in conformity with said act, has been assessed in respect to shares in banks upon which the owners have also been specifically taxed for the said year, in the city or town in which such owner resides, for state, county and town purposes, the tax commissioner shall, within a reasonable time thereafter, certify to the treasurer and receiver-general, the name of the person who appears to be the owner of such shares, and the amount so paid or credited in each case, and the treasurer shall thereupon pay over to said person such amount.

NOTE.—This section is retained because of the possibility that some claims covered by it are yet unadjusted.

[1873, 315, § 18.]

Assessors to give certificate in such cases. 1873, 315, § 18.

SECT. 103. It shall be the duty of the assessors, for the time being, of the several cities and towns, upon the request of any person or persons, who shall appear from their records to have been assessed under the provisions of the seventh section of chapter three hundred and twenty-one of the acts of the year eighteen hundred and seventy-two, or any other section of said act, to give such person or persons a certificate, setting forth the fact of such assessment, with the name of the bank, the number of shares in respect to which such assessment was made, and the amount of tax so assessed. Such certificate shall be competent evidence of facts to authorize refunding under the preceding section.

Of the Taxation of Savings Banks.

[1862, 224, § 5; 1868, 315.]

Savings banks and institutions to pay three-fourths per cent. on deposits. G. S. 57, §§ 135, [illegible]55. 1862, 224, § 4. 1863, 164. 1864, 208, § 7. 1865, 267. 1868, 315. 5 Allen, 428. 12 Allen, 312. 6 Wallace, 594. 6 Wallace, 611.

Sect. 104. Every savings bank and institution for savings, incorporated under the laws of this Commonwealth, including the Mercantile Savings Institution in the city of Boston, shall pay to the treasurer of the Commonwealth a tax, on account of its depositors, of three-fourths of one per cent. per annum on the amount of its deposits, to be assessed, one-half of said annual tax on the average amount of its deposits for the six months preceding the first day of May, and the other on the average amount of its deposits for the six months preceding the first day of November, and such tax shall be paid semi-annually within ten days after the first Mondays of June and December, each payment to be an assessment, by the treasurer, of one-half the annual percentage.

Such taxes to be paid in June and December. 1862, 224, § 5.

[1862, 224, §§ 8, 9.]

Savings banks and institutions for savings shall make semi-annual return of deposits. G. S. 57. 1862, 224, §§ 8, 9.

SECT. 105. Every savings bank and institution for savings incorporated under the laws of this state, including the Mercantile Savings Institution in the city of Boston, shall semi-annually on or before the second Mondays of May and November, make to the treasurer of the Commonwealth a return, signed and sworn to by its president and treasurer, of the amount of its deposits on the first days of May and November of each year, and of the average amount of its deposits for the six months next preceding each of said days. Every such corporation neglecting to make such return shall forfeit fifty dollars for each day of such neglect; and any such corporation that wilfully makes false statements in any such return, shall be liable to pay a fine of not less than five hundred nor more than five thousand dollars.

Penalty for neglect.

[1862, 224, § 11.]

Penalties on such corporations, etc., for neglecting to pay taxes. 1862, 224, § 11. 1867, 52. 100 Mass. 531.

SECT. 106. Every corporation or association of persons neglecting to pay the taxes imposed by section one hundred and four shall be liable for the same with costs and interest, in an action of contract, in the name of the Commonwealth at the suit of the treasurer; and shall be further liable, on the application of the treasurer of the Commonwealth therefor, to any one of the justices of the supreme judicial court, to injunction restraining said corporation or association, and the agents thereof, from any further prosecution of its business, until all such taxes with costs and interest shall be fully paid.

[1862, 224, § 12.]

Deposits so taxed, to be exempt from further taxation. G. S. 11, §§ 4, 5.

Returns of deposits to assessors not required. G. S. 57, §§ 150-152. 1862, 224, § 12. 1869, 444. 1870, 144.

SECT. 107. All deposits taxed under section one hundred and four shall be otherwise exempt from taxation for the current year in which the tax is paid; and no savings bank shall be required to make any return of deposits in accordance with the provisions of the one hundred and fiftieth and one hundred and fifty-second sections of chapter fifty-seven of the General Statutes, so long as this tax is imposed by law.

OF THE TAXATION OF INSURANCE COMPANIES.

[1873, 141, § 1.]

Tax of one per cent. upon premiums received by insurance companies, except life companies. G. S. 58. 1862, 224. 1871, 297. 1872, 325. 1873, 141, § 1.

SECT. 108. Every fire, marine, fire and marine, and other insurance company, incorporated under the laws of this Commonwealth, except life insurance companies, and except such companies as are subject to taxation on their corporate franchise under the provision of this chapter, shall, as hereinafter provided, annually pay a tax or excise of one per centum on all premiums received during the year for insurance, whether in cash or in notes absolutely payable, and one per centum on all assessments made upon policy-holders by such company: *provided, however,* that in the assessment of such tax, premiums received in other states where they are subject to a like tax, shall not be included.

NOTE.—"Taxation on their corporate franchise," etc., used as equivalent to "the provisions of chapter two hundred and eighty-three," etc., in the original section.

[1873, 141, § 2.]

Of two per cent. on companies incorporated in other States. 1873, 141, § 2.

SECT. 109. Every fire, marine, fire and marine, and other insurance company, corporation, association or partnership, which is incorporated or associated by authority of any other state of the United States, shall, as hereinafter provided, annually pay a tax or excise upon all premiums charged or received on contracts made in this Commonwealth for the insurance of property or interests therein, or received or collected by agents in this Commonwealth, at the rate of two per centum, and at such greater rate, if any, as shall be equal to the highest rate imposed during the year by the laws of such other state upon insurance companies incorporated by authority of this Commonwealth, or upon their agents, when doing business in such state.

[1873, 141, § 3.]

Upon life insurance companies incorporated in other States. 1873, 141, § 3.

SECT. 110. Every life insurance company, corporation, association or partnership, incorporated or associated by authority of any other state of the United States, by the laws of which state a tax is imposed upon the premium receipts of life insurance companies chartered by this Commonwealth, doing business in such state, or upon their agents, shall annually, so long as such laws continue in force, pay a tax or excise upon all premiums charged or received upon contracts made in this Commonwealth, at a rate equal to the highest rate imposed during the year upon life insurance companies chartered by this Commonwealth, or their agents, doing business in such other state.

[1873, 141, § 4.]

Of four per cent. upon companies incorporated in other countries, or two per cent. where there is a guarantee fund. 1873, 141, § 4.

SECT. 111. Every fire, marine, fire and marine, and other insurance company, corporation, association or partnership, incorporated or associated under the laws of any government or state other than one of the United States, shall, as hereinafter provided, annually pay a tax of four per centum upon all premiums charged or received on contracts made in this Commonwealth for insurance, or received or collected by agents in this Commonwealth: *provided, however*, that whenever it is made to appear to the satisfaction of the tax commissioner that any such company, corporation, association or partnership, has, during the whole term for which the tax is to be assessed, kept deposited with the insurance or other departments of any state of the United States, or in the hands of trustees, resident in and citizens of such states, for the general benefit and security of all policy-holders residing in the United States, securities approved by the insurance commissioner, of the value of two hundred thousand dollars, which have been at all times available for the payment of losses in this Commonwealth, the tax upon the premiums of such company, under this section, shall be assessed at the rate of two per centum. The certificate of the insurance commissioner may be received by the tax commissioner as sufficient evidence that such securities have been so deposited.

[1873, 141, § 5.]

Allowance for return premium, etc. 1873, 141, § 5.

SECT. 112. In determining the amount of tax due under the four preceding sections there shall be deducted in each case, from the full amount of premiums and assessments, unused balances on notes taken for premiums on open policies, all sums paid for return premiums on cancelled policies, and all sums actually paid to other insurance companies incorporated under the laws of this Commonwealth, or to the agents of foreign companies, for re-insurance on risks, for which a tax on the premium would be due, had no re-insurance been effected: *provided*, that nothing in this section shall be so construed as to allow dividends in scrip or otherwise, in stock, mutual or mixed companies, to be considered return premiums.

[1873, 141, § 6.]

Fees and penalties, etc., imposed in other States to be imposed here. 1873, 141, § 6.

SECT. 113. Like fines, fees, penalties, deposits, obligations and prohibitions (not being less in amount than those required by other provisions of law of this Commonwealth in similar cases) are imposed upon and required of all insurance companies, corporations, associations and partnerships, incorporated or associated by authority of any other state of the United States doing insurance business in this state, and their agents doing business for or with them, as are or shall hereafter be, by law of such state, imposed upon companies incorporated by this state, or upon their agents, doing insurance business in such state. Compliance with the requirements of the provisions of this section as to deposits, obligations and prohibitions, may be enforced, and all such fines, fees and penalties may be collected by information brought in the supreme judicial court by the attorney-general at the relation of the insurance commissioner, and upon such information, and upon a request therefor, the court shall issue an injunction restraining the further prosecution of the business of such company, corporation, association, partnership, or agent named therein, until such requirements are complied with, and until such fines, fees, and penalties are paid, with costs and interest.

[1873, 141, § 7.]

Companies and agents to make returns of premiums received, to tax commissioner. 1873, 141, § 7.

SECT. 114. Every company, which, by the provisions of section one hundred and eight is required to pay a tax, shall, between the first and fifteenth days of November, in each year, cause to be made to the tax commissioner a return, signed and sworn to by its secretary, or other officer cognizant of the facts, which shall set forth the amount insured by said company, the premiums received and assessments collected during the year ending with the thirty-first day of October then next preceding. Every agent of any company, corporation, association or partnership, which is incorporated or associated by authority of any government other than this Commonwealth, doing or authorized to do insurance business in this Commonwealth, shall, between the first and fifteenth days of November, in each year, make to the tax commissioner a return, signed and sworn to by him, containing the names of every such company, corporation, association or partnership, for which he has acted as agent during any part of the year ending with the thirty-first day of October then next preceding, with the amount insured by him, the premiums received, and assessments collected by him, or by his authority, for each such company, corporation, association or partnership, during such year; but such agents only of life-insurance companies are required to make return as are not accountable to any other agent in this Commonwealth for premiums received.

Such returns shall contain a statement of the whole amount of premiums charged or received by, or in behalf of, each company, corporation, association or partnership, either in cash or notes absolutely payable, and the amount claimed as a deduction therefrom, under any of the provisions of this chapter specifying the whole amount so claimed, and also the classes of deductions and amount of each class.

[1873, 141, § 8.]

Assessment to be made and notice given. 1873, 141, § 8.

SECT. 115. The tax commissioner shall, thereupon, upon such statements, and on such other evidence as he may obtain, proceed to assess upon such companies, corporations, associations and partnerships, and their agents, the taxes prescribed by the provisions of the sections of this chapter from one hundred and eight to one hundred and twenty-one, both inclusive, and shall forthwith, upon making such assessment, forward written or printed notices to such companies, or their agents, in this Commonwealth, stating the amounts so determined by him to be payable by each company, corporation, association, partnership or agent, as the case may be. Such taxes shall be paid to the treasurer and receiver-general on the tenth day of December next succeeding the time fixed in the preceding section for making the statement therein required.

Taxes, when to be paid.

The tax commissioner shall, on or before such tenth day of December, deliver to the treasurer and receiver-general a certificate setting forth the names of every such company, corporation, association, partnership and agent, upon whom such tax has then been assessed; and shall, in like manner, make certificate of any further assessments, if any, as may be made after that date. All such taxes, whether assessed before or after the tenth day of December, shall bear interest from that date until they are paid, at the rate of twelve per centum per annum.

Unpaid taxes to bear interest.

[1873, 141, § 9.]

SECT. 116. Every company, corporation, association, partnership and agent, failing to make the return required by the provisions of the sections of this chapter from one hundred and eight to one hundred and twenty-one, both inclusive, shall forfeit twenty-five dollars for such default; and continuing in such failure for the space of ten days after a written

Penalties for failure to make return.
1873, 141, § 9.

or printed notice thereof, authorized by the tax commissioner, has been deposited in the post-office, postage paid, and addressed to such company, corporation, association, partnership or agent, shall be subject to a further penalty of five hundred dollars; and in addition, the company, corporation, association, or agent, so failing, shall be liable, upon information by the attorney-general, at the relation of the tax commissioner, to injunction, restraining it or him, as the case may be, from transacting the business of such company, corporation, association or partnership in this Commonwealth, until such returns are made.

For making false return.

If any such return contains statements which are false, and are known, or which by the exercise of reasonable care might have been known to the agent making it, or to the officers making it, to be so, such agent or corporation shall be liable for the amount of tax thereby lost to the Commonwealth, and, in addition, to a penalty of not less than five hundred or more than five thousand dollars.

How enforced.

Such penalties may be recovered by an action of tort, brought at the instance of the treasurer against the company, corporation, association, partnership or agent in default; and no such company, corporation, association, partnership or agent shall be liable to the money penalties imposed by this section, if it is made to appear that the return was duly made and deposited by said agent in the post-office, postage paid, and properly directed to the tax commissioner, and that there was no neglect on his part.

[1873, 141, § 10.]

Companies and agents liable for taxes. 1873, 141, § 10.

SECT. 117. Every insurance company incorporated by authority of this Commonwealth, and every such company, corporation, association or partnership, incorporated or associated by authority of any other state or government, shall be liable for the full amount of all taxes so assessed upon the premiums or assessments received by such company, corporation, association or partnership, or by its agents; and each agent of any such company, corporation, association or partnership, incorporated or associated by authority of any state or government other than this Commonwealth, shall also be liable for the amount assessed upon premiums and assessments received by him, which, with interest at the rate of twelve per centum per annum, may be recovered in an action of contract brought in the name of the Commonwealth. Such corporation, company, association or partnership, shall be further liable, upon information by the attorney-general at the relation of the treasurer and receiver-general, to injunction restraining said company, corporation, association or partnership, and the agents thereof, from the further prosecution of its business, until all taxes due as aforesaid, with costs and interest, are fully paid. Any return made, or tax paid by an agent, shall be a discharge to that extent, of the company, corporation, association or partnership, from its liability to make a return or pay a tax under the provisions of this chapter contained in the sections from one hundred and eight to one hundred and twenty-one, both inclusive.

[1873, 141, § 11.]

Agents not to make or procure insurance until bond is filed. 1873, 141, § 11.

SECT. 118. No person shall, as agent of any insurance company, corporation, association or partnership, not incorporated or associated under the laws of this Commonwealth, make or procure to be made, any insurance in this Commonwealth, until he has given a bond to the treasurer and receiver-general of the Commonwealth, with sufficient sureties, to be approved by said treasurer, in the sum of two thousand dollars, with condition that he will make all the returns, and pay all taxes, fines and penalties, which, by the provisions of any law of this Commonwealth, he is or shall hereafter be required to make and pay, according to the requirements of such laws. Any person mak-

Penalty.

ing insurance, or causing or procuring insurance to be made, in violation of the provisions of this section, shall be liable to pay a fine of not exceeding one thousand dollars: *provided, however*, as to agents in this Commonwealth, of life-insurance companies incorporated or associated by authority of any state or government other than this Commonwealth, that such agent or agents, only, of such life-insurance companies, shall give the bond required by this section, as are not accountable to any agent in this state for premiums received.

Proviso as to sub-agents of certain life insurance companies.

[1873, 141, § 12.]

Treasurer may require new bond. 1873, 141, § 12.

SECT. 119. If at any time the treasurer and receiver-general shall become satisfied that any bond already filed with him under the provisions of any law of this Commonwealth, by any agent or general agent of any insurance company, corporation, association or partnership, has become insufficient as a security, whether from death, removal from the state, or pecuniary insufficiency of the sureties, he shall require such agent to file a new bond with another surety or sureties, with like conditions. The same penalties and prohibitions shall apply to any agent, general agent and company, corporation, association or partnership failing, for the space of ten days after notice, to file such

Penalty for not filing new bond.

new bond, as are or shall be provided by law, for failure or neglect to file the original bond.

[1873, 141, § 13.]

Duties of tax commissioner may be performed by his deputy. 1865, 283, § 12. 1873, 141, § 13.

SECT. 120. The duties required by the twelve preceding sections to be performed by the tax commissioner may be performed by his deputy, appointed under the provisions of section eighty-three.

[1873, 141, § 14.]

Laws relative to insurance companies to apply to all companies, partnerships and individuals doing any kind of insurance business in this State. G. S. 58. 1873, 141, § 14.

SECT. 121. All general laws relating to the duties, obligations, prohibitions and penalties appertaining to insurance companies incorporated by authority of this Commonwealth, and all laws defining the powers and duties of the insurance commissioner in relation thereto, shall, except as provided in the thirteen preceding sections, apply to any company, corporation, association, partnership or individual, doing any kind of insurance business in this Commonwealth, by whatever authority incorporated, formed or associated.

OF THE TAXATION OF CERTAIN OTHER CORPORATIONS.

[1865, 283, § 3.]

Corporations, except banks, to return annually names of stockholders, etc.

SECT. 122. Every corporation chartered by this Commonwealth, or organized under the general laws, for purposes of business or profit,

G. S. 68.
1864, 208, §§ 2, 3.
1865, 283, § 3.
1866, 291.
1867, 127.
98 Mass. 25.

having a capital stock divided into shares, excepting banks of issue and deposit, and except those specified in section one hundred and twenty-nine, shall annually, between the first and the tenth day of May, return to said commissioner, under the oath of its treasurer, a complete list of its shareholders, with their places of residence, the number of shares belonging to each on the first day of May, the amount of the capital stock of the corporation, its place of business, the par value and the market value of the shares on said first day of May. Such return shall, in the case of stock held as collateral security, state not only the name of the person holding the same, but also the name of the pledger and his residence. The returns shall also contain a statement in detail of the works, structures, real estate and machinery owned by said corporation, and subject to local taxation within the Commonwealth, and the location and value thereof. Railroad and telegraph companies shall return the whole length of their lines, and the length of so much of their lines as is without the Commonwealth. Other corporations, except those embraced in section one hundred and twenty-nine, shall also return the amount, value and location of all works, structures, real estate and machinery owned by them and subject to local taxation without the Commonwealth.

[1866, 291, § 1.]

Penalties on corporations for not making returns. 1866, 291, § 1. 1865, 283.

SECT. 123. Any corporation which shall fail to make any of the returns required by the provisions of [sections one hundred and twenty-two, one hundred and twenty-eight, one hundred and twenty-nine, and one hundred and thirty of this chapter,] shall be liable, on application of the tax commissioner therefor to any of the justices of the supreme judicial court, to injunction restaining said corporation and the agents thereof, from the further prosecution of its business, until the returns required by law shall be made.

NOTE.—The words included in brackets are used as equivalent to the words, "chapter two hundred and eighty-three of the acts of the year eighteen hundred and sixty-five," in the original section.

[1865, 283, § 2.]

Guardians, etc., to make annual returns of stock owned, etc. 1864, 208, § 4. 1865, 283, § 2.

SECT. 124. Every guardian who holds, or whose ward holds stock in any corporation, and every executor, administrator or other person, who holds in trust any such stock, shall, between the first and the tenth day of May in each year, return under oath to said commissioner, the names and residences on the first day of that month, of themselves and all such wards or other persons to whom any portion of the income from such stock is payable, the number of shares of stock so held, and the name and location of the corporation in which they are held.

Partners to make like returns.

Every copartnership shall, between the first and the tenth day of May in each year, make a like return, stating the amount of such stock owned by the firm, and the names and residences of all the partners, and the proportional interest or ownership of each partner in said stock.

[1865, 283, § 4.]

Cash value of stock to be determined by tax commissioner, etc. 1864, 208, § 5. 1865, 283, § 4.

SECT. 125. The tax commissioner shall ascertain, from the returns or otherwise, the true market value of the shares of each corporation included in the provisions of section one hundred and twenty-two, and shall estimate therefrom the fair cash valuation of all of said shares constituting the capital stock of such corporation on the first day of May next preceding, which shall be taken as the true value of its corporate franchise for the purposes of this chapter.

He shall also ascertain and determine the value and amount of all real estate and machinery owned by each corporation, and subject to local taxation, and to the deductions hereinafter provided; and for this purpose he may take the amount or value at which such real estate and machinery are assessed at the place where the same are located as the true amount or value; but such local assessment shall not be conclusive of the true amount or value thereof.

[1865, 283, § 5.]

Tax to be paid by corporations. 1861, 167. 1864, 208, § 5.

SECT. 126. Every corporation embraced in section one hundred and twenty-two, shall

1865, 283, § 5.
99 Mass. 151.
6 Wallace, 632.

annually pay a tax upon its corporate franchise at a valuation thereof, equal to the aggregate value of the shares in its capital stock, as determined in the preceding section, after making the deductions provided for in this section, at a rate determined by an apportionment of the whole amount of money to be raised by taxation upon property in the Commonwealth during the same current year, as returned by the assessors of the several cities and towns under section forty-eight, upon the aggregate valuation of all the cities and towns in the Commonwealth for the preceding year, as returned under section thirty-eight: *provided*, that in case the return from any city or town shall not be received prior to the twentieth day of August, the amount raised by taxation in said city or town the preceding year, as certified to the secretary of the Commonwealth, may be adopted for the purpose of this determination; and *provided, further*, that the amount of tax assessed upon polls the preceding year, as certified to the secretary of the Commonwealth, may be taken as the amount of poll-tax to be deducted from the whole amount to be raised by taxation, for the purpose of ascertaining the amount to be raised by taxation upon property. From the valuation, ascertained and determined as aforesaid, there shall be deducted,—*First*, in case of railroad and telegraph companies, whose lines extend beyond the limits of the Commonwealth, such portion of the whole valuation of their capital stock, ascertained as aforesaid, as is proportional to the length of that part of their line lying without the Commonwealth; and also an amount equal to the value, as determined by the tax commissioner, of their real estate and machinery located and subject to local taxation within the Commonwealth: *Second*, in case of other corporations, included in section one hundred and twenty-two, an amount equal to the value, as determined by the tax commissioner, of their real estate and machinery, subject to local taxation, wherever situated.

[1865, 283, § 6.]

Remedy of corporation when tax commissioner fixes value of real estate, etc., at less than the assessors fix the same. 1865, 283, § 6.

SECT. 127. In case the value of the real estate and machinery located within the Commonwealth, of any corporation, as determined by the commissioner, shall be less than the value as determined by the assessors of the city or town where such real estate or machinery is taxable, said commissioner shall notify the corporation of such determination, and if said corporation shall not, within one month from the date of such notice, make application to said assessors for an abatement, and shall not, in case of the refusal of said assessors to grant an abatement, forthwith prosecute an appeal in accordance with the provisions of section sixty-nine, and give notice thereof to the tax commissioner, such determination shall be conclusive upon said corporation. The tax commissioner may appear before the county commissioners and be heard upon any appeal made to them, and the decision of the county commissioners shall be conclusive as to the value.

[1865, 283, § 7.]

Foreign telegraph companies using lines in this State to make returns and pay tax. 1864, 208, § 9. 1865, 283, § 7. 1866, 291. 99 Mass. 151.

SECT. 128. Every corporation or association chartered or organized elsewhere, which shall own, or control and use, under lease or otherwise, any line of telegraph within this Commonwealth, shall be required to make all the returns prescribed in section one hundred and twenty-two to be made by telegraph companies within the Commonwealth, excepting the list of its shareholders; and shall annually pay a tax at the same rate, and to be ascertained and determined in the same manner as is provided in section one hundred and twenty-six; and all telegraph lines controlled and used by such corporation or association within this Commonwealth, shall, for the purposes of this act, be taken and considered as part of its own lines.

[1865, 298, § 8.]

Mining companies, etc., doing business out of the State or

SECT. 129. Every corporation chartered by this Commonwealth, or organized under the general laws, for the purpose of engaging, without the limits of the Commonwealth, in the business of coal mining or other mining, quarrying or extracting carbonaceous oils from the earth, or for the purpose of purchasing, selling or holding mines or lands without the Commonwealth; and every such company or association, incorporated elsewhere, and having an office or place of business within the Commonwealth, for the direction of its affairs or transfer of shares, shall, semi-annually, between the first and the tenth day of June and December, make a return, under the oath of its treasurer or president, to the tax commissioner, of the whole amount of its capital stock, as fixed by the corporation, on the first day respectively of May and November next preceding, and pay to the treasurer of the Commonwealth a tax of one-twentieth of one per cent. upon said capital stock at the par thereof. All officers of such corporation, and other persons assuming to represent such corporation within the Commonwealth, by having charge of its affairs, or of books for the transfer of its shares, shall severally be personally liable for the amount of the tax imposed under this section upon said corporation, if the same shall not be paid by the corporation. The capital stock of any corporation established in this Commonwealth, subject to taxation under this section, shall not be reduced except upon

chartered elsewhere, to make returns, etc. 1864, 208, § 10. 1865, 283, § 8. 99 Mass. 148. 1867, 299.

application to the supreme judicial court sitting in any county. In case of such application, written notice shall be given to the tax commissioner and attorney-general of the Commonwealth, ten days at least before the hearing.

[1865, 283, § 9; 1866, 291, § 2.]

Mining companies to make report of business to tax commissioner.
1864, 208, § 10.
1865, 283, § 9.
1866, 291, § 2.

SECT. 130. Every corporation mentioned in the preceding section, except those incorporated under the authority of states other than this Commonwealth, shall annually on or before the tenth day of June, submit to the tax commissioner a report of the business of the corporation for the year ending on the first day of March next preceding, which report shall be signed and sworn to by its treasurer and a majority of its directors, and shall contain a full and accurate statement of the property held by such corporation, and of all the receipts and expenditures during said year in or on account of its business, and of all products thereof. Said report shall contain such details as shall be prescribed by the tax commissioner, who shall furnish to each corporation blank forms therefor.

[1865, 283, § 10.]

Tax on profits, how assessed.
1865, 283, § 10.
1866, 291, § 2.

SECT. 131. The tax commissioner shall, from such report or otherwise, ascertain and determine the net profits or gains of each corporation, from whom a report is required under the preceding section, during the year aforesaid, from its property and business; and shall assess a tax of four per cent. upon the amount thereof.

[1865, 283, § 11.]

SECT. 132. The tax commissioner shall, as soon as may be after the first Monday in August, notify the treasurer of each corporation liable thereto, of the amount of its tax under sections one hundred and twenty-six, one hundred and twenty-eight and one hundred and thirty-one, to become due and payable to the treasurer of the Commonwealth within thirty days from the date of such notice: *provided*, that it shall not be due and payable earlier than the first day of November. Such notice shall also state that within ten days after the date thereof, the said corporation may apply for a correction of said tax, and be heard thereon before the board of appeal hereinafter established.

Treasurers to be notified of tax assessed, etc. 1865, 283, § 11. 1866, 291, § 2.

[1865, 283, § 13.]

SECT. 133. The treasurer and auditor, together with one member of the council to be named by the governor, shall constitute a board of appeal, to which board any party aggrieved by the decision of said tax commissioner upon any matter arising under this chapter may apply within ten days after notice of such

Board of appeal from tax commissioner established. 1865, 283, § 13.

decision. Upon such appeal said board shall, as soon as may be, give a hearing to such party, and shall thereupon decide the matter in question, which decision shall be final.

NOTE.—It may be doubtful whether the words, "matter arising under this chapter," are not broader than the words "matter arising under this act," in the original section.

[1865, 283, § 14.]

Penalties. 1865, 283, § 14. 99 Mass. 148.

SECT. 134. Any guardian, executor, administrator, trustee or copartnership neglecting to comply with the requirements of section one hundred and twenty-four, shall forfeit the sum of one hundred dollars; and any corporation neglecting to make returns according to the provisions of sections one hundred and twenty-two, one hundred and twenty-five, one hundred and twenty-six and one hundred and twenty-seven, or refusing or neglecting, when required thereto, to submit to the examinations provided for in section one hundred and thirty-seven, shall forfeit two per cent. upon the par value of its capital stock; all which penalties may be recovered by an action of tort, brought in the name of the Commonwealth, either in the county of Suffolk or in the county where the corporation is located. If any corporation fails to pay the taxes required to be paid to the treasurer of the Commonwealth under the provisions of this chapter, contained in sections from one hundred and twenty-two to one hundred and fifty-four, both inclusive, he may forthwith commence an action of contract in his own name, as treasurer, for the recovery of the same, with interest. All penalties under the same may also be enforced, and all taxes under the same may also be collected by information brought in the supreme judicial court at the relation of the treasurer of the Commonwealth, and upon such information the court may issue an injunction restraining the further prosecution of the business of the corporation named therein, until all such taxes due or penalties incurred shall be paid, with interest and costs. In any proceeding under this section the certificate of the tax commissioner or his deputy shall be competent evidence of all determinations made and notices given by him, and of all values, amounts and other facts, required to be fixed or ascertained by him, under the said sections.

1866, 291, § 2. 1867, 52.

NOTE.—The sections from 122 to 154, both inclusive, containing the provisions of chap. 283, of 1865, the reference to them is substituted somewhat inaccurately, perhaps, for the reference in the original section to that act.

[1865, 283, § 15.]

SECT. 135. No taxes shall be assessed in any city or town for state, county or town purposes, upon the shares in the capital stock of said corporations, except those incorporated

Taxes not to be assessed to shareholders on certain shares, and to be distributed to towns, etc.

1864, 208, §§ 8, 15.
1865, 283, § 15.
1866, 291, § 2.
1866, 196.

under the authority of states other than this Commonwealth, for any year for which they pay to the treasurer the tax on their corporate franchises under this chapter ; but such proportion of the tax collected of each corporation under section one hundred and twenty-six as corresponds to the proportion of the stock of such corporation owned by persons residing in this Commonwealth, shall be credited and paid to the several cities and towns where it appears from the returns or other evidence that such shareholders resided on the first day of May next preceding, according to the number of shares so held in such cities and towns respectively: *provided*, that in case stock is held by copartners, guardians, executors, administrators or trustees, the proportion of tax corresponding to the amount of stock so held, shall be credited and paid to the towns where the stock would have been taxed, under the provisions of the fourth and fifth clauses of section fifteen and of section eighteen of this chapter; and *provided, further*, that when a town owns stock in any corporation taxed upon its corporate franchise under this chapter, a return to said town shall be made in like manner as is provided in the case of stock held by individuals residing in said town.

Said commissioner shall ascertain and determine the amount due to each city and town, under this section, subject to appeal as herein before provided, and shall notify the treasurer of each city and town thereof, and certify the amount, as finally determined, to the treasurer of the Commonwealth, who shall thereupon pay over the same.

[1865, 283, § 16.]

Lessee as well as lessor liable for tax. 1865, 283, § 16.

SECT. 136. The lessee of the works, structures, real estate or machinery of any corporation taxed under sections one hundred and twenty-six, one hundred and twenty-eight, one hundred and twenty-nine, one hundred and thirty-nine, and one hundred and thirty-one, shall be liable as well as the lessor, to pay the amount of said tax, and upon such payment, may, in the absence of any agreement to the contrary, retain the same out of the rent of the property, or recover the same in an action against the lessor.

[1865, 283, § 17.]

Corporations taxable, to submit books, etc., to examination. 1864, 208, § 16. 1865, 283, § 17.

SECT. 137. Every corporation taxable under the sections of this chapter, from one hundred and nineteen to one hundred and fifty, both inclusive, shall, when required, submit its books to the inspection of the tax commissioner, and its treasurer and directors to examination on oath in regard to all matters affecting the determinations which are to be made by said commissioner.

[1865, 283, § 18.]

Taxes on franchise imposed by other laws not affected, except, etc. 1862, 224, §§ 1, 3. 1865, 283, § 18.

SECT. 138. The tax herein imposed upon any corporation, shall not affect nor prevent the imposition and collection of any other tax now authorized, or that may hereafter be authorized, upon any especial privilege, franchise or business, enjoyed or exercised by such corporation.

[1865, 283, § 19.]

Other returns need not be made. 1864, 201 and 208, §§ 6, 9. 1865, 283, § 19.

SECT. 139. Corporations making the returns, and paying the tax imposed by sections from one hundred and nineteen to one hundred and fifty, both inclusive, shall be relieved from making the returns required by chapter two hundred and one of the acts of the year eighteen hundred and sixty-four.

OF THE TAXATION OF CERTAIN TRUST AND BANKING COMPANIES.

[1865, 283, § 18.]

Massachusetts Hospital Life Insurance Co. 1862, 224, § 3. 1865, 283, § 18.

SECT. 140. The Massachusetts Hospital Life Insurance Company shall pay upon all moneys and property in the possession or charge of said company, as deposits, trust funds, or for purposes of investment, the same rate of tax as shall be imposed upon or paid by savings banks or institutions for savings on account of deposits.

[1867, 151; 1869, 182, § 8; 296, § 6; 1870, 22; 323, § 4; 1871, 142, § 3; 270, § 10; 1873, 270, § 10; 285, § 6; 347, § 6; 369, § 6; 1874, 373, § 8.]

SECT. 141. The Worcester Safe Deposit and Trust Company, the Northampton Loan and Trust Company, the New England Trust Company, the Boston Safe Deposit and Trust Company, the Chapin Banking and Trust Company, the Fall River Banking and Trust Company, the Springfield Banking and Trust Company, and the Boston Mortgage Company, shall be subject to the provisions of those sections of this chapter which apply to the corporations mentioned in section one hundred and twenty-two, and any laws which may hereafter be passed in amendment or lieu thereof.

Worcester Safe Deposit and Trust Company. 1869, 296, § 6. 1870, 22. Northampton Loan and Trust Company. 1870, 323, § 4. New England Trust Company. 1869, 182, § 8. 1871, 142, § 3. Boston Safe Deposit and Trust Company. 1867, 151. 1874, 373, § 8. Chapin Banking and Trust Co. 1873, 285, § 6. Fall River Banking and Trust Company. 1873, 347, § 6. Springfield Banking and Trust Company. 1873, 369, § 6. Boston Mortgage Company. 1873, 270, § 10.

NOTE.—The charters of these corporations subject them to chap. 283 of 1865, and any laws in amendment or lieu thereof.

The provisions of this and the nine following sections are found in private charters. They should find place here, since without them no assessor can be sure of doing his duty according to law.

[1869, 296, § 6.]

SECT. 142. The taxes upon all personal property absolutely committed in trust to the management of the Worcester Safe Deposit and Trust Company shall be assessed to said corporation in the manner prescribed for personal property held in trust or belonging to persons under guardianship, in section fifteen of this chapter, or in any acts which may hereafter be passed in lieu or amendment thereof.

Worcester Safe Deposit and Trust Co., how assessed on property in trust, taxable by cities and towns. 1869, 296, § 6.

G. S. 11, § 12.

To make returns.

Said corporation shall annually, between the first and tenth days of May, return to the tax commissioner a true statement, attested by the oath of some officer of the corporation, of all money and property in detail so held in trust, on deposit and for safe keeping, with the names and residences of the beneficiaries or owners, and the interest of each beneficiary or owner therein, on the first day of May of that year, under the penalties and provisions for the enforcement thereof provided in sections one hundred and twenty-three and one hundred and thirty-four. Said commissioner shall, on or before the twentieth day of June in each year, cause to be printed and sent to the assessors of each town and city in the Commonwealth a true copy of said return.

1865, 283, § 14. 1866, 291, § 1.

[1870, 323, §§ 4, 5.]

Northampton Loan and Trust Company, how assessed on property held in trust, etc., taxable by cities and towns. 1870, 323, §§ 4, 5.

SECT. 143. The taxes upon all property intrusted to the charge of or deposited with the Northampton Loan and Trust Company, shall be assessed to said corporation in the manner prescribed for personal property held in trust or belonging to persons under guardianship, in section fifteen, or in any acts which may hereafter be passed in lieu or amendment thereof; and said corporation shall, annually, between the first and tenth days of May, return to the tax commissioner a true statement,

G. S. 11, § 12.

To make returns, etc.

attested by the oath of some officer of the corporation, of all such personal property so held, with the names and residences of the beneficiaries, and the interest of each beneficiary therein, on the first day of May of that year, under the penalties and provisions for the enforcement thereof provided in sections one hundred and twenty-three and one hundred and thirty-four, for corporations failing to make returns. Said commissioner shall, on or before the twentieth day of June in each year, cause to be printed and sent to the assessors of each city and town in the Commonwealth a true copy of said return.

1865, 283, § 14. 1866, 291, § 1.

[1871, 142, § 3.]

New England Trust Company to make return and pay tax to treasurer on trust funds. 1871, 142, § 3.

SECT. 144. The New England Trust Company shall also, annually, between the first and tenth days of May, return to the tax commissioner a true statement, attested by the oath of some officer of the corporation, of all personal property held upon any trust on the first day of May, which would be taxable if held by any individual trustee residing in this Commonwealth, and the name of every city or town in this Commonwealth where any beneficiary resided on said day, and the aggregate amount of such property then held for all beneficiaries resident in each of such cities and towns, and also the aggregate amount held for beneficiaries not resident in this Commonwealth, under the

Penalties. 1865, 283, § 14. 1866, 291, § 1. 1865, 283, § 5. 1865, 283, §§ 11, 12, 13, 15, 17.

pains and penalties provided in sections one hundred and twenty-three and one hundred and thirty-four, for corporations failing to make returns. Said corporation shall, annually, pay to the treasurer of the Commonwealth a sum to be ascertained by assessment upon an amount equal to the total value of such property, at a rate to be ascertained and determined by the tax commissioner, under section one hundred and twenty-six and acts in amendment thereof. No taxes shall be assessed in any city or town for state, county or town purposes upon or in respect of any property held in trust as aforesaid, but such proportion of the sum so paid by said corporation as corresponds to the amount of such property held for beneficiaries resident in this Commonwealth, shall be credited and paid to the several cities and towns where it appears from the returns or other evidence that such beneficiaries resided on the first day of May next preceding, according to the aggregate amount so held in trust for beneficiaries residing in such cities and towns respectively; and in regard to such tax so to be assessed and paid, as aforesaid, said corporation shall be subject to sections eighty-three, one hundred and thirty-two and one hundred and thirty-three, and the last paragraph of section one hundred and thirty-five and section one hundred and thirty-seven and the acts in amendment and lieu thereof, so far as the same may be applicable thereto.

[1873, 285, § 7; 347, § 7; 369, § 7; 1874, 373, § 9.]

Boston Safe Deposit and Trust Company, and the Chapin, Fall River, and Springfield Banking and Trust Companies to make return and pay certain tax to treasurer. 1873, 285, § 7. 1873, 347, § 7. 1873, 369, § 7. 1874, 373, § 9.

SECT. 145. The Boston Safe Deposit and Trust Company, the Chapin Banking and Trust Company, the Fall River Banking and Trust Company, and the Springfield Banking and Trust Company, severally, shall annually, between the first and tenth days of May, return to the tax commissioner a true statement, attested by the oath of some officer of the corporation, which in the case of the first named of said companies shall be the oath of the president, treasurer or actuary of the corporation, of all personal property held upon any trust on the first day of May, which would be taxable if held by an individual trustee, residing in this Commonwealth, and the name of every city or town in this Commonwealth where any beneficiary resided on said day, and the aggregate amount of such property then held for all beneficiaries resident in each of such cities and towns, and also the aggregate amount held for beneficiaries not resident in this Commonwealth, under the pains and penalties provided in sections one hundred and twenty-three and one hundred and thirty-four, for corporations failing to make returns. Said corporation shall annually pay to the treasurer of the Commonwealth a sum

1865, 283, § 14. 1866, 291, § 1.

to be ascertained by assessment by the tax commissioner, upon an amount equal to the total value of such property, at the rate ascertained and determined by him, under section one hundred and twenty-six and any acts in amendment or lieu thereof.

[1873, 285, § 8; 347, § 8; 369, § 8; 1874, 373, § 10.]

Also to make returns and pay taxes on other trusts, etc., to treasurer.
1873, 285, § 8.
1873, 347, § 8,
1873, 369, § 8.
1874, 373, § 10.

SECT. 146. Said corporations respectively, shall also, annually, between the first and tenth days of May, return to the tax commissioner a true statement, verified in the manner required in the preceding section, of the amount of all sums deposited with it on interest or for investment, other than those specified in sections one hundred and forty-five and one hundred and forty-eight, together with the name of every city and town in this Commonwealth where any beneficial owner resided on said first day of May, and the aggregate amount of such deposits then held for the benefit of persons residing in each of such cities and towns under a like penalty. Said corporation shall, annually, pay to the treasurer of the Commonwealth a sum to be ascertained by assessment, by the tax commissioner, upon an amount equal to the total value of such deposits at three-fourths the rate ascertained and determined by him, under section one hundred and twenty-six, and any acts in amendment or lieu thereof.

[1873, 285, § 9; 347, § 9; 369, § 9; 1874, 373, § 11.]

SECT. 147. No taxes shall be assessed in any city or town for state, county or town purposes, upon or in respect of any such property held in trust, or any such amounts deposited on interest, or for investment, as are specified in the two preceding sections, but such proportions of the sums so paid by said corporations as correspond to the amount of such property held for beneficiaries or payable to persons resident in this Commonwealth, shall be credited and paid to the several cities and towns where it appears from the returns or other evidence that such beneficiaries resided on the first day of May next preceding, according to the aggregate amounts so held for beneficiaries and persons residing in such cities and towns respectively; and in regard to such sums so to be assessed and paid, as aforesaid, said corporations shall be subject to sections eighty-three, one hundred and thirty-two, one hundred and thirty-three, the last paragraph of section one hundred and thirty-five, and section one hundred and thirty-seven and acts in amendment or lieu thereof, so far as the same are applicable thereto.

No taxes to be assessed in any city, etc., on same.
1873, 285, § 9.
1873, 347, § 9.
1873, 369, § 9.
1874, 373, § 11.

1865, 283, §§ 11, 12, 13, 15, 17.

[1873, 285, § 10; 347, § 10; 369, § 10; 1874, 373, § 12.]

Other deposits on demand, etc., to be taxed to person to whom same is payable. 1873, 285, § 10. 1873, 347, § 10. 1873, 369, § 10. 1874, 373, § 12.

SECT. 148. Deposits with said Boston Safe Deposit and Trust Company, which can be withdrawn on demand or within ten days, and deposits with the other companies mentioned in the three preceding sections, which can be withdrawn on demand, shall, for purposes of taxation, be deemed money in possession of the person to whom the same is payable.

[1869, 428, § 5.]

Collateral Loan Company of Boston exempt until 1875. 1869, 428, § 5.

SECT. 149. No tax shall be levied upon the Collateral Loan Company, of Boston, for any year prior to the year eighteen hundred and seventy-five.

NOTE.—This section governed assessments at the time the codification was commenced. We therefore retain it as of force for certain purposes.

General Provisions.

[1867, 52, § 11.]

State taxes due from corporations, how collected by warrant, when corporation neglects to pay. 1862, 224. 1864, 208. 1865, 283. 1866, 291. 1867, 52, § 1.

SECT. 150. When any tax remains due from any corporation, except municipal corporations, to the Commonwealth, for the term of ten days after notice given through the mail by the treasurer of the Commonwealth to the treasurer or other financial agent of such corporation that such tax is due and unpaid, the treasurer of the Commonwealth may issue his warrant, directed to the sheriff, or his deputies, of the county in which such corporation has its place of business, commanding the collection of such tax. Such warrant may be substantially in the form of those now issued by the assessors of towns, except as is hereinafter provided; and the officer to whom the same may be delivered for service, shall proceed in the manner in which collectors and others serving such warrants are authorized to proceed. Such warrants shall not run against the body of any person, nor shall any property of such delinquent corporation be exempt from seizure and sale thereon. The officer having such warrant shall collect such tax, and interest upon the same, at the rate of twelve per centum per annum, from the time when such tax became due, and shall be entitled to collect and receive for his fees the sum which an officer would be entitled by law to receive upon an execution for a like amount. He shall also collect one dollar for the warrant, which shall be paid over to the treasurer of the Commonwealth.

NOTE.—In a final codification this section might better be included in the chapter relating to the collection of taxes.

[1867, 52, § 2.]

Corporation aggrieved may try legality of tax by petition to S. J. C. 1867, 52, § 2. 99 Mass. 146.

SECT. 151. Any corporation feeling aggrieved by the exaction of said tax, or of any portion thereof, may, within six months from the date of the payment of the same, whether such payment be after or before the issue of the warrant herein provided for, file a petition to the supreme judicial court, in the nature of a petition of right, setting forth the amount of the tax, and costs thereon so paid, the general legal grounds, if any, upon which it is claimed such tax should not have been exacted, and specifically the grounds in fact, if any, upon which it is so claimed. Said petition shall be entered and heard in said court in the county of Suffolk. Service of the same shall be made upon the treasurer and the attorney-general of the Commonwealth, in the same manner as a writ of original summons is now served upon an individual. The proceedings upon such petition shall conform, as near as may be, to the proceedings in equity causes in said court. No such petition shall be brought in order to procure the abatement of any tax, except where it is claimed that such tax is in part assessed upon property not legally subject to taxation.

[1867, 52, § 3.]

Tax to be repaid if adjudged illegal. 1867, 52, § 3.

SECT. 152. If the court, upon a hearing or trial, shall adjudge that said tax, and the costs thereon, have been illegally exacted, a copy of the judgment or decree in the cause shall be transmitted by the clerk of the court to the governor of the Commonwealth, and the governor shall thereupon draw his warrant upon the treasurer of the Commonwealth for the amount adjudged to have been unjustly exacted, with interest, and costs to be taxed by the clerk of the court, as in equity causes; and the treasurer shall pay the same, without any further act or resolve making appropriation therefor. And so much thereof as may have been paid out of the treasury of the Commonwealth to any city or town may be deducted and set off from and against any sum afterwards due and payable to such city or town.

Amount paid to towns to be set off.

[1867, 52, § 4.]

SECT. 153. The manner of collection herein provided for, shall be in addition to those now provided by law. The remedy herein provided, by petition, shall take the place of any and all actions which might otherwise be maintained by such corporation on account of the assessment and collection of such tax, and shall be the exclusive remedy.

These remedies exclusive for corporation, but in addition to others for State. 1867, 52, § 4.

N. B.—The concluding paragraph of § 4, chap. 52, of 1867, from which this section is taken, viz.: "This act shall apply to all taxes now due, as well as to those which may hereafter become due," is omitted, because it is supposed that the taxes due at the date of its passage, March 2, 1867, have been collected.

[1867, 299, § 1.]

SECT. 154. When it is made to appear to the satisfaction of the tax commissioner that any corporation assessed under section one hundred and twenty-nine is doing no business and has taken actual measures, in good faith, to procure a

Taxes due from certain mining corporations taking measures to dissolve, may be abated in part. 1865, 283, § 8. 1867, 299, § 1.

legal dissolution of the corporation, or reduction of its capital stock, upon a sworn statement by the treasurer or other officer of said corporation setting forth the facts and that there is no money in the treasury of said corporation, and if it is made to appear to the satisfaction of said commissioner that there is not sufficient property and assets belonging to any corporation so assessed to satisfy the claim of the Commonwealth for taxes assessed as aforesaid with the costs of collection, said commissioner may in his discretion, accept for the Commonwealth a sum in satisfaction and composition of all such assessments due and the interest thereon, not less than ten per cent. of the amount of said assessments due from said corporation; and upon said commissioner certifying to the treasurer of the Commonwealth the facts of said composition and the amount to be paid thereunder, and upon payment thereof by said corporation, its officers and stockholders shall be absolved and freed from any and all liability to the Commonwealth for the amount of the assessments included in such composition.

CHAPTER II.

OF THE COLLECTION OF TAXES.

INDEX.

[G. S. 12, § 1.]

Collectors to collect taxes.
R. S. 7, § 34.
R. S. 8, §§ 1, 33.
G. S. 12, § 1.

SECT. 1. Every collector of taxes, constable, sheriff, or deputy sheriff, receiving a tax list and warrant from the assessors, shall proceed to collect the taxes therein mentioned, according to the warrant.

[G. S. 12, § 2.]

to complete collections, though term expire.
R. S. 8, § 2.
G. S. 12, § 2.
102 Mass. 75.

SECT. 2. The collector shall, unless removed from office as hereinafter provided, complete the collection of taxes committed to him, although his term of office expires before such completion.

[G. S. 12, § 3.]

Demand to be made.
R. S. 8. § 3.
G. S. 12, § 3.
1 Met. 328.

SECT. 3. Collectors shall, before distraining the goods of a person for his tax, demand payment thereof from such person, either personally or at his usual place of abode, if to be found within their precincts.

[G. S. 12, § 4. 1874, 238.]

When credit doubtful, taxes may be collected forthwith.

SECT. 4. When the credit of a person taxed is considered doubtful by the assessors, they may, by a special warrant, order the collector forthwith to compel payment by distress or imprisonment, whether the tax is made payable immediately, at a future day, by instalments or otherwise.

R. S. 8, § 12. G. S. 12, § 4. 1874, 238.

[G. S. 12, § 5.]

SECT. 5. If a person claims the benefit of an abatement, he shall exhibit to the collector demanding his taxes, a certificate of such abatement, from the assessors or other proper officer, as provided in the preceding chapter; and shall be liable to pay all costs and officers' fees incurred before exhibiting such certificate.

Persons claiming abatement must produce certificate. Liable to costs. R. S. 8, § 4. G. S. 12, § 5. 9 Met. 504.

[G. S. 12, § 6.]

SECT. 6. If, in the assessors' lists or in their warrant and list committed to the collectors, there is an error in the name of a person taxed, the tax assessed to him may be collected of the person intended to be taxed, if he is taxable and can be identified by the assessors.

Errors in names not to defeat collection. R. S. 8, § 5. G. S. 12, § 6. 6 Met. 474. 7 Gray, 127. 12 Cush. 56. 97 Mass. 321.

[G. S. 12, § 7.]

SECT. 7. If a person refuses or neglects to pay his tax, the collector shall levy the same by distress or seizure and sale of his goods, including any share or interest he may have as a stockholder in a corporation

Distress and sale to pay taxes: except, etc. R. S. 8, § 7. G. S. 12, § 7. 1846, 195, § 1. 9 Met. 504. 11 Cush. 338. 7 Gray, 133.

incorporated under authority of this Commonwealth, and excepting the following goods:

The tools or implements necessary for his trade or occupation; beasts of the plough necessary for the cultivation of his improved lands; military arms, utensils for housekeeping necessary for upholding life, and bedding and apparel necessary for himself and family.

[G. S. 12, § 8.]

Distress, how long kept, how advertised and sold
R. S. 8, § 8.
G. S. 12, § 8.
1 Met. 328.
13 Met. 85.
11 Cush. 338.

SECT. 8. The collector shall keep the goods distrained, at the expense of the owner, for four days at least, and shall, within seven days after the seizure, sell the same by public auction, for payment of the tax and charges of keeping and sale, having given notice of the sale by posting up a notification thereof in some public place in the city or town, forty-eight hours at least before the sale.

[G. S. 12, § 9.]

Sale may be adjourned once.
R. S. 8, § 9.
G. S. 12, § 9.

SECT. 9. The collector may once adjourn such sale for a time not exceeding three days: he shall forthwith give notice of such adjournment, by posting a notification at the place of sale.

[G. S. 12, § 10.]

Seizure of shares, how made.
1846, 195 § 2.
G. S. 12, § 10.

SECT. 10. The seizure of a share or other interest in a corporation may be made by leaving with any officer of the corporation, with whom a copy of the writ may by law be left when the share of a stockholder is attached on mesne process, an attested copy of the warrant, with the certificate thereon, under the hand of the collector, setting forth the tax which the stockholder is to pay, and that, upon his neglect or refusal to pay, the collector has seized such share or interest.

[G. S. 12, § 11.]

SECT. 11. The sale of such share or interest shall be made in the manner prescribed by law for the sale of goods by collectors of taxes in like cases, and also subject to the provisions of sections forty-six and forty-seven of chapter one hundred and thirty-three of the General Statutes, respecting sales on executions.

Sales of shares seized, how made.
1846, 195, §§ 3, 4.
G. S. 12, § 11.
4 Cush. 10.
11 Cush. 338.

[G. S. 12, § 12.]

SECT. 12. If the distress or seizure is sold for more than the tax and charges of keeping and sale, the collector shall return the surplus to the owner, upon demand, with an account in writing of the sale and charges.

Surplus to be returned to owner.
R. S. 8, § 10.
G. S. 12, § 12.
5 Gray, 530.

[G. S. 12, § 13.]

SECT. 13. If a person refuses or neglects for fourteen days after demand to pay his tax, and the collector cannot find sufficient goods upon which it may be levied, he may take

After fourteen days, party may be imprisoned.
R. S. 8, § 11.
G. S. 12, § 13.
13 Met. 85.
2 Gray, 298.
7 Gray, 133.
13 Gray, 93.
9 Gray, 190.
3 Allen, 5.

the body of such person and commit him to prison, there to remain until he pays the tax and charges of commitment and imprisonment, or is discharged by order of law.

[G. S. 12, § 14.]

Copy of warrant, etc., to be left with jailer. R. S. 8, § 13. G. S. 12, § 14.

SECT. 14. When the collector commits a person to prison, he shall give the keeper thereof an attested copy of the warrant, with a certificate thereon, under the hand of the collector, setting forth the sum which such person is to pay as his tax, with the cost of taking and committing him, and that upon his having neglected payment for fourteen days, or otherwise, as the case may be, and for want of goods whereof to make distress, he has taken his body.

[G. S. 12, § 15. 1862, 183, § 9.]

Persons imprisoned for non-payment of taxes, how discharged. 1857, 141, § 24. G. S. 12, § 15. See ch. 124. 1862, 183, § 9.

SECT. 15. When a person committed to prison for non-payment of taxes, desires to take the oath for relief of poor debtors, he may represent the same to the jailer; and the jailer shall make the same known to some magistrate named in section one, chapter one hundred and twenty-four of the General Statutes; and the magistrate shall thereupon appoint a time and place for the examination of the debtor, and shall direct the jailer to cause the debtor to be present at the same. The notice required in such case to be given to the creditor, may be given to either of the assessors or the collector by whom the party was committed. And the assessors and collector, or any of them, may appear and do all things which a creditor might do in case of arrest on execution. And if the person so committed to prison for the non-payment of taxes is unable to pay the same, he shall be entitled to his discharge in like manner as persons committed on execution.

[G. S. 12, § 16.]

Collectors, when liable to pay, etc. R. S. 8, § 50. G. S. 12, § 16. 3 Met. 152.

SECT. 16. If such person is discharged, the collector shall be liable to pay the tax, with the charges of imprisonment, unless he arrested and committed the party within one year after the tax was committed to him to collect, or unless he is exonerated therefrom by the city, town or parish to which the tax is due.

[G. S. 12, § 17.]

Collectors may demand aid. Penalty. R. S. 8, § 6. G. S. 12, § 17.

SECT. 17. A collector, when resisted or impeded in the exercise of his office, may require any suitable person to aid him therein; and if such person refuses to render such aid, he shall forfeit a sum not exceeding ten dollars

[G. S. 12, § 18.]

Persons removing from collector's precinct, without paying.

SECT. 18. When a person, after the assessment of a tax upon him, removes out of the

R. S. 8, § 14. G. S. 12, § 18. 1842, 34. 5 Allen, 563.

precinct of the collector without paying his tax, the collector may demand payment thereof wherever such person is found; and in default of payment the collector may forthwith proceed to collect the tax by making a distress, or by commitment of such person to the prison of the county where he is found; or the collector may issue his warrant to the sheriff of the county or his deputy, or to any constable of the place where such person is found, directing them to distrain the property or take the body of such person, and to proceed therein in like manner as required of collectors in like cases.

[G. S. 12, § 19.]

Remedy if persons remove, etc., without paying. R. S. 8, § 15. G. S. 12, § 19. 1852, 312. 1859, 171. 6 Mass. 44. 23 Pick. 235. 8 Met. 393. 6 Allen, 558.

SECT. 19. When a person taxed removes as aforesaid, or dies, or neglects to pay his tax for one year after it is committed to the collector, or, being an unmarried woman, marries before payment of the tax, the collector may, in his own name, maintain an action of contract therefor in like manner as for his own debt, and he may for that purpose in like manner have a process of foreign attachment against any trustee of such person.

[G. S. 12, § 20.]

against executors and administrators. 1848, 235. 1852, 234. 1852, 312. G. S. 12, § 20. 97 Mass. 321.

SECT. 20. When a tax is assessed upon the personal estate of a deceased person, the collector may maintain an action of contract therefor in his own name, as for his own debt, against the executor or administrator; and if a tax is so assessed before the appointment of an executor or administrator, he may enforce it against the estate and its representative after such appointment, in like manner as if the assessment had been made subsequently thereto.

[G. S. 12, § 21.]

against persons who are not owners of the real estate taxed to them. R. S. 8, §§ 16, 17. G. S. 12, § 21.

SECT. 21. When a person is taxed for real estate in his occupation, but of which he is not the owner, the collector, after demand of payment, may levy the tax by distress and sale of the cattle, sheep, horses, swine or other stock or produce of such estate, belonging to the owner thereof, which, within nine months after such assessment is committed to him, shall be found upon the premises, in the same manner as if such stock or produce were the property of the person so taxed; but such demand need not be made if the person on whom the tax is assessed resided within the precinct of the collector at the time of the assessment, and subsequently removes therefrom and remains absent three months.

[G. S. 12, § 22.]

Taxes to be lien on real estate for two years, etc. R. S. 8, § 18. G. S. 12, § 22.

SECT. 22. Taxes assessed on real estate shall constitute a lien thereon for two years after they are committed to the collector; and

1856, 239, § 1. 7 Pick. 15. 2 Gray, 185. 6 Allen, 576. 99 Mass. 31. 106 Mass. 29.

may, with all incidental costs and expenses, be levied by sale thereof, if the tax is not paid within fourteen days after a demand of payment made either upon the person taxed or upon any person occupying the estate; but the collector may sell real estate for taxes after two years have elapsed, unless the estate has been alienated in the meantime.

[G. S. 12, § 23.]

reassessed, to be a lien, unless, etc. 1859, 118, § 1, 2. G. S. 12, § 23. 99 Mass. 32. 1870, 394.

SECT. 23. Taxes reassessed on real estate shall constitute a lien thereon from the time they are committed to the collector, unless the estate has been alienated between the first and second assessments; and may be levied as provided in the preceding section.

[G. S. 12, § 24.]

Resident mortgagee of real estate, when to be called upon for taxes. 1848, 166, § 1. G. S. 12, § 24.

SECT. 24. If a mortgagee of real estate situated in the place of his residence, previously to the assessment of a tax, gives written notice to the clerk of such place that he holds a mortgage thereon, with a description of the estate, the collector, before proceeding to sell it for non-payment of taxes, shall demand payment of said taxes of the mortgagee, as provided in section twenty-two.

[G. S. 12, § 25.]

When non-resident appoints attorney, demand how made.

R. S. 8, § 20. 1848, 166, § 2. G. S. 12, § 25.

SECT. 25. If a mortgagee or non-resident owner of real estate, previously to the assessment of a tax, gives a written authority to some inhabitant of the place as his attorney, to pay the taxes imposed on such estate, and the authority is filed with, or recorded by, the clerk of the place, the demand of payment shall be made upon such attorney before the estate is sold; otherwise, no demand need be made of payment of taxes assessed on the real estate of non-resident owners.

[G. S. 12, § 26.]

When made, collector to wait two months.

R. S. 8, § 21. G. S. 12, § 26.

SECT. 26. When a demand is made upon the attorney, under the preceding section, the collector shall not advertise the sale of the lands until two months from the time of such demand.

[G. S. 12, § 27.]

Affidavit of collector, etc., evidence of demand on attorney.

R. S. 8, § 22. G. S. 12, § 27.

SECT. 27. The affidavit of a disinterested person, or the collector who makes the sale of land for the payment of taxes, taken before a justice of the peace, and recorded by the clerk of the place where the land lies, before a sale is made, and stating the demand of payment of the tax, the person of whom, and the time and manner in which, it was made, shall be competent evidence of the demand.

[G. S. 12, § 28.]

Sales of real estate, how advertised. R. S. 8, § 24. G. S. 12, § 28. 13 Gray, 77.

SECT. 28. The collector shall give notice of the time and place of sale of real estate taken for taxes, by an advertisement thereof, three weeks successively, in some newspaper of the county where the real estate lies, if there is such newspaper, and if not, then in a newspaper printed in an adjacent county; the last publication to be at least one week before the time of sale.

[G. S. 12, § 29.]

Contents of advertisement. R. S. 8, § 25. 1848, 106, § 3. G. S. 12, § 29. 4 Cush. 265. 7 Cush. 503.

SECT. 29. The advertisement shall contain a substantially accurate description of the several rights, lots or divisions of the estate to be sold, the amount of the tax assessed on each, the names of all owners known to the collector, and the taxes assessed on their respective lands.

[G. S. 12, § 30.]

Notices, how posted. R. S. 8. § 27. 1848, 166, § 4. G. S. 12, § 30.

SECT. 30. The collector shall, three weeks before the sale, post a notice, similar to that required by the two preceding sections, in some convenient and public place in his precinct, and a like notice on the premises by him advertised to be sold, if any part thereof is bounded by a street, lane, court or highway.

[G. S. 12, § 31.]

When name of place has been changed.
R. S. 8, § 26.
G. S. 12, § 31.

SECT. 31. When real estate to be sold under the provisions of this chapter is situated in a place the name of which has been changed by law within three years next preceding the sale, the collector shall, in his advertisement and notices of the sale, designate such place by its former and present name.

[G. S. 12, § 32.]

Affidavit of posting and publishing to be evidence, if recorded.
R. S. 8, § 23.
G. S. 12, § 32.

SECT. 32. The affidavit of a disinterested person, taken before a justice of the peace, of the posting and publishing notifications of the sale of real estate by a collector or other officer, for payment of taxes, made upon one of the original advertisements, or a copy thereof, and filed and recorded in the registry of deeds for the county or district where the land lies, within six months after the sale, shall be competent evidence of such notice.

[G. S. 12, § 33.]

Sale by auction of sufficient, etc.
R. S. 8, §§ 28, 29.
G. S. 12, § 33.
13 Gray, 77.
See 1862, 183; §§ 1, 10.
3 Allen, 535.

SECT. 33. If the taxes are not paid, the collector, at the time and place appointed for the sale, shall sell by public auction so much of the real estate, or the rents and profits of the whole estate, for such term of time as shall be sufficient to discharge the taxes and necessary intervening charges; or he may, at his option, sell the whole or any part of the land;

and, after satisfying the taxes and charges, he shall, upon demand, pay the residue of the proceeds of the sale, if any, to the owner of the estate.

[1862, 183, § 10.]

Fees and charges allowed. G. S. 12, § 33. 1862, 183, § 10.

SECT. 34. The following charges and fees, and no other, shall be allowed to the collector, and shall be added to the amount of the tax, as provided in the preceding section:

For making a written demand, twenty cents;

For preparing advertisement, fifty cents;

For advertisement in newspaper, the actual cost of the same;

For posting up notices on each piece of real estate, twenty cents;

For copy of notice, and the publication thereof, and obtaining affidavit of disinterested persons, fifty cents;

For recording affidavit at registry of deeds, the fees of the register;

For preparing deed, two dollars;

For poundage, four per cent. on the first hundred dollars, two per cent. on the second hundred dollars, and one per cent. on the balance of the tax.

And in the event that any delinquent taxpayer offers to pay the tax before the day of sale, such charges shall be added to the tax as have intervened at the time of said offer to pay.

[G. S. 12, § 34.]

SECT. 35. The collector may adjourn his sale from day to day, not exceeding seven days in the whole; and he shall give notice of every such adjournment by a public declaration thereof, at the time and place previously appointed for the sale.

Collector may adjourn sale, etc. R. S. 8, § 30. G. S. 12, § 34. See 1862, 183, § 1.

[1862, 183, §§ 1, 5.]

SECT. 36. If at the time and place of sale no person shall appear and bid for the estate, or the rents and profits thereof, or for the whole or any part of the land, an amount equal to the tax and charges, and the sale shall have been adjourned from day to day, as provided in the thirty-fifth section, a public declaration of the fact shall then and there be made by the collector; immediately after which, provided no bid shall be made equal to the tax and charges, the collector shall give public notice that he shall, and that he then and there does, purchase on behalf of the town or city by which the tax is assessed, the said estate, in one of the forms set forth in the thirty-third section: *provided, however,* that no sum exceeding the amount of the tax and the incidental costs and expenses of levy and sale shall be offered by him therefor, and the

Collectors may purchase for town if no other sufficient bid is made. 1862, 183, § 1. 6 Allen, 576.

1862, 183, § 5.

same shall be allowed him in his settlement with such town or city.

NOTE.—This section is intended to embrace the provisions of §§ 1 and 5, of chap. 183, of 1862.

[1862, 183, § 3.]

When purchasers fail to pay and take deed within ten days, conveyance to be made to town, etc. 1862, 183, § 3.

SECT. 37. If within ten days after the sale of real estate for the payment of taxes, any purchaser thereof shall fail to pay the collector the sum offered by him, and receive his deed, the sale shall be null and void, and the town or city shall be deemed to be the purchaser of the estate according to the provisions of the preceding section. And the deed to be given to the collector in such case shall, in addition to the statements now required by law, set forth the fact of the preceding sale, and the failure of the purchaser to pay the sum offered as aforesaid.

[G. S. 12, § 35.]

Deed to be given to purchaser, subject, etc. G. S. 12, § 35. See 1862, 183, §§ 2, 6. 6 Allen, 576.

SECT. 38. The collector shall execute and deliver to the purchaser a deed of the real estate, or rents and profits sold; which deed shall state the cause of sale, the price for which the estate or rents and profits were sold, the name of the person on whom the demand for the tax was made, the places in the city or town where the notices were posted, the newspaper in which the advertisement of such sale was published, and the place of residence of the grantee; and if the real estate has been sold, shall convey, subject to the right of redemption provided for in the forty-fourth section, all the right and interest which the owner had therein at the time when the same was taken for his taxes. Such deed, to be valid, shall be recorded within thirty days from the day of sale.

When deed to be recorded. R. S. 8, § 31. 1848, 166, § 5. 2 Gray, 185.

[1862, 183, § 6.]

Collector's deed to include special warranty, and town to refund in case of error, etc. 1862, 183, § 6. 10 Allen, 49.

SECT. 39. In the deed which the collector shall execute and deliver to a purchaser other than the city or town by which the tax is assessed, there shall also be inserted a special warranty that the sale has in all particulars been conducted according to the provisions of law; and if it should subsequently appear that, by reason of any error, omission or informality in any of the proceedings of assessment or sale, the purchaser has no claim upon the property sold, there shall be paid to said purchaser, upon his surrender and discharge of the deed so given, by the town or city whose collector executed said deed, the amount paid by him, together with ten per cent. interest per annum on the same, which shall be in full satisfaction of all claims for damages for any defects in the proceedings.

[1862, 183, § 2.]

Deeds to towns, etc., to include additional statements; their rights thereunder.

SECT. 40. Whenever the town or city by which the tax is assessed becomes the pur-

1862, 183, § 2.
6 Allen, 576.

chaser, the deed to be given by the collector shall, in addition to the statements above required, set forth the fact of the non-appearance of a purchaser at the sale advertised by him, and shall confer upon such town or city the same rights as belong to an individual to whom such a deed may be given. And the several towns and cities of this Commonwealth, in their corporate capacity, are hereby authorized as holders of said deeds, to exercise the same rights and perform the same duties as any individual purchaser of real estate taken for taxes.

[1862, 183, § 4.]

Custody of such deeds to be in hands of treasurers.
1862, 183, § 4.

Towns, etc., may make regulations for custody and sale of estates so held.

SECT. 41. Such deeds shall be placed in the custody of the treasurer of the city or town, to whom all applications for the redemption of the estate so sold shall be made. And the several towns and cities of the Commonwealth may make such regulations for the custody, management and sale of such estates, and the assignment of the tax titles thus obtained, not inconsistent with the laws of the Commonwealth, as they may deem expedient. But nothing herein contained shall take from the owner of said real estate, or his heirs or assigns, the right to redeem the same, as hereinafter provided.

[1862, 183, § 8.]

Such estates to be taxed. 1862, 183, § 8.

SECT. 42. If any estate shall be purchased by any city or town, according to the provisions of this chapter, taxes shall be assessed upon the same in the same manner as though the same were not so purchased; and said taxes shall be deducted from the proceeds of the final sale, as provided in the previous section.

[1862, 183, § 7.]

How sold if not redeemed. 1862, 183, § 7.

SECT. 43. If the owner does not redeem the property so purchased by the city or town, within the time prescribed by the following section, said town or city may at any time proceed to sell the said real estate at public auction, after having given the same notice as is required in section twenty-eight of this chapter, executing and delivering to the highest bidder thereof a quitclaim deed; and from the money arising from said sale shall be deducted the expenses of making the sale, together with the amount paid at the first sale for tax and charges, with ten per cent. interest per annum thereon, and all intervening taxes and necessary charges; and the balance, if any, shall be deposited in the city or town treasury, to be paid to the party legally entitled to the estate, if the same had not been sold for taxes, if the

Application of proceeds.

same shall be called for within five years, and if not demanded within that time, the same shall inure to the benefit of said city or town.

[G. S. 12, § 36.]

Owner may redeem within two years, etc. R. S. 8, § 32. 1850, 98, §§ 1, 2. G. S. 12, § 36. See 1862, 183.

SECT. 44. The owner of real estate sold for payment of taxes, or his heirs or assigns, may within two years from the day of sale redeem the estate sold, by paying or tendering to the purchaser, or his heirs or assigns, the sum paid by him, with ten per cent. interest, and all necessary intervening charges; and when the rents and profits are sold for payment of taxes, the same may be redeemed at any time within two years, in the manner provided for the redemption of rents and profits taken on execution. And in the following cases, real estate so sold may be redeemed, by any person having such title thereto that he might have recovered the same if no such sale had been made, at any time within two years after he has actual notice of the sale:—

First. When no person is named in the tax list as the owner or occupant of the premises, they being taxed as belonging to persons unknown;

Second. When the person who is named in said list is merely a tenant or occupant of the premises, and not the rightful owner thereof;

Third. When there is any error in the name of the person intended to be taxed;

Fourth. Mortgagees of record.

98 Mass. 44.

[G. S. 12, § 37.]

Estates, how redeemed when purchaser cannot be found, etc. 1848, 166, §§ 6, 8. G. S. 12, § 37.

SECT. 45. If, upon reasonable search, the purchaser of real estate sold for non-payment of taxes cannot be found in the place of which he is described in the collector's deed as resident, the owner of the estate may redeem it as provided in the preceding section, on paying to the treasurer of the place in which it is situated the amount which he would be required to pay to the purchaser; and the affidavit of any disinterested person of the making such search, taken before a justice of the peace, and filed in the registry of deeds for the district or county in which the land is situated, within ninety days from the completion of the search, shall be competent evidence of the facts therein stated.

[G. S. 12, § 38.]

Duty of treasurer. 1848, 166, § 7. G. S. 12, § 38.

SECT. 46. Such treasurer shall receive the money and give to the person paying it a certificate of such payment, specifying the estate on which the tax was originally assessed. The certificate may be recorded in the registry of deeds, with a note of reference from such record to the collector's deed; and, when so recorded, shall have the effect to release and discharge all right and title acquired under the collector's deed. The treasurer shall hold all money received by him under the preceding section, for the use and benefit of the persons entitled thereto; and shall pay it over on reasonable demand.

[G. S. 12, § 39.]

Mortgagee may pay taxes on real estate in certain cases. 1856, 239, §§ 1-3. See § 44. G. S. 12, § 39.

SECT. 47. After proceedings have been commenced for the sale of real estate for a tax assessed thereon, and before the sale is made, the holder of any mortgage thereon may pay such tax, with all intervening charges and expenses; and when the owner of real estate for three months after demand has neglected to pay such a tax, and the collector has made demand therefor upon a holder of a mortgage thereon, such holder may in like manner pay such tax, charges and expenses.

[G. S. 12, § 40.]

shall pay such taxes upon taking possession. Entitled to deed on tender. G. S. 12, § 40. 1856, 239, §§ 1-3. 5 Allen, 65.

SECT. 48. The holder of a mortgage, upon taking possession of real estate thereunder, shall be liable to pay all taxes due thereon, and the expenses of any sale for taxes that has been commenced or taken place; to be recovered of him in an action of contract by the collector, or, when a sale has taken place, by the purchaser; and upon tender by the mortgagee to the purchaser, within the time provided for owners of real estate to make tender in section forty-four, of the sum paid by him, with ten per cent. interest, and all necessary intervening charges, such purchaser shall, at the expense of the mortgagee, execute and deliver to him a valid deed of assignment of all interest acquired by virtue of the tax sale.

[G. S. 12, § 41.]

Mortgagee entitled to receipt for such taxes paid to collector. May tack same to mortgage. 1856, 239, §§ 1-3. G. S. 12, § 41.

SECT. 49. For all sums paid to a collector by the holder of a mortgage under either of the two preceding sections, the collector shall, upon demand, give him a receipt therefor, duly acknowledged; and such sum shall be added to and constitute part of the principal sum of the mortgage; and the mortgage shall not be redeemed, without the consent in writing of the holder, until such sums and interest thereon, are paid; and such receipt recorded in the registry of deeds for the district or county where the land lies, within thirty days from its date, shall be notice to all persons of the payment of such sums and the lien upon the estate therefor.

[G. S. 12, § 42.]

S. J. Court to have equity powers. 1856, 239, § 4. G. S. 12, § 42. 10 Met. 101. 11 Gray, 410. 98 Mass. 44.

SECT. 50. In all cases of sale of real estate for the payment of taxes assessed thereon, the supreme judicial court shall have equity powers, if relief is sought within five years from the sale.

[G. S. 12, § 43.]

When tax list, etc., is committed to sheriff, etc.
R. S. 8, § 34.
G. S. 12, § 43.

SECT. 51. When the tax list and warrant of the assessors is committed to the sheriff, or his deputy, he shall forthwith post in some public place in the city or town assessed, an attested copy of said list and warrant; and shall make no distress for a tax, till after thirty days from the time of such posting.

[G. S. 12, § 44.]

Sheriff's fees for collecting.
R. S. 8, § 35.
G. S. 12, § 44.

SECT. 52. If a person pays his tax on such list within said thirty days, the officer shall receive for his fees five per cent. on the sum assessed; but if a tax remains unpaid after said thirty days, the officer shall proceed to collect the same by distress or imprisonment, in the manner collectors are required to proceed in like cases. The officer may also levy his fees for service and travel, in the collection of each person's tax, as in other cases of distress and commitment.

[G. S. 12, § 45.]

When treasurers are made collectors, how to proceed.
R. S. 8, § 36.
R. S. 15, § 61.
G. S. 12, § 45.
8 Allen, 330.

SECT. 53. When the city council of a city or the inhabitants of a town vote to appoint their treasurer a collector he may issue his warrants to the sheriff of the county, or his deputy, or any of the constables of the city or town, returnable in thirty days, requiring them to collect any or all taxes due; and such warrants shall be in substance the same and confer like powers as warrants issued by assessors to collectors.

[1874, 28, §§ 1, 2.]

City treasurers may appoint deputy collectors and issue warrants for collectors. 1874, 28, §§ 1, 2.

SECT. 54. City treasurers as collectors of taxes may appoint, subject to the approval of the board of aldermen, such deputy collectors of taxes as they may from time to time deem expedient and may issue their warrants to them as provided in the preceding section, and such deputy collectors shall give bonds for the faithful discharge of their duties in such sums as the board of aldermen may from time to time prescribe, and such deputies shall have the same powers as collectors of taxes in towns.

NOTE.—This section has the same force with sections one and two, of chap. 28, acts of 1874, if the second section of that act was intended to confer any powers in addition to those given by sect. 45, of chap. 12, G. S., although it is not easy to understand the meaning or purpose of chap. 28, of 1874.

[G. S. 12, § 46.]

Collectors to exhibit accounts every two months, if required. R. S. 8, § 45. G. S. 12, § 46.

SECT. 55. Every collector shall, once in two months, if required, exhibit to the mayor and aldermen, or selectmen, and where there are no such officers, to the assessors, a true account of all moneys received on the taxes committed to him, and produce the treasurer's receipts for all money paid into the treasury by him.

[G. S. 12, § 47.]

Penalty.
R. S. 8, § 46.
G. S. 12, § 47.

SECT. 56. If a collector neglects to so exhibit his accounts, he shall forfeit the sum of two and a half per cent. on the sums committed to him for collection.

[G. S. 12, § 48.]

Collectors to be credited with abatements, etc.
R. S. 8, § 43.
G. S. 12, § 48.
9 Met. 503.
13 Gray, 324.

SECT. 57. The collector shall be credited with all sums abated according to law, and with the amount of taxes assessed upon any person committed to prison within one year from the receipt of the tax list by the collector, and before paying his tax, and also with any sums which the city or town may see fit to abate him, due from persons committed after the expiration of a year.

[G. S. 12, § 49.]

Deficiency in state or county tax, how supplied.
R. S. 8, § 42.
G. S. 12, § 49.

SECT. 58. If the collector fails to collect a tax, without his own default, and there is a deficiency of the amount due on a state or a county tax, such deficiency shall be supplied by him from the proceeds of the collection of city or town taxes, if any in his hands; and, if he have none, by the city or town treasurer, on the written requisition of the collector.

[G. S. 12, § 50.]

Same, when collectors neglect to pay.
R. S. 8, § 38.
G. S. 12, § 50.

SECT. 59. If a collector of taxes neglects to pay, within the time required by law, such sums of money as ought by him to be paid to the state or county treasurer, the city or town by which such collector was appointed, shall be liable for such sums, to be recovered in an action of contract by such state or county treasurer respectively.

[G. S. 12, § 51.]

Remedy for collector's neglect. R. S. 8, § 44. 1852, 312. G. S. 12, § 51.

SECT. 60. If a collector neglects seasonably to pay a state or county tax committed to him, whereby the city or town is compelled to pay the same, or neglects seasonably to account for and pay in a city or town tax committed to him, the city or town may recover the amount thereof, with all damages sustained through such neglect, and interest, by an action of contract, declaring on his official bond if any had been given.

[G. S. 12, § 52.]

If collector becomes insane, etc., selectmen may remove him. R. S. 8, § 40. G. S. 12, § 52. 7 Gray, 130.

SECT. 61. If a collector becomes insane, or in the judgment of the selectmen otherwise unable to discharge his duty, or absconds, removes, or, in the judgment of the selectmen, is about to remove, from the place, or refuses on demand to exhibit to the mayor and aldermen, or selectmen, or assessors, his accounts of collections, as herein provided, the selectmen may remove him from office, and appoint another collector, as in the case of the death of the collector.

[G. S. 12, § 53.]

Tax list of deceased collector, how completed. G. S. 12, § 53.

Temporary collector. R. S. 8, § 39. 1838, 43. 1 Met. 524. 4 Gray, 253.

SECT. 62. If a collector dies before completing the collection of a tax committed to him, the selectmen may appoint some suitable person to complete the collection, who shall receive a reasonable compensation, to be paid by the town, and they may commit the same tax list to him, with their warrant, accordingly; and when a temporary collector is appointed by the selectmen, the assessors shall commit the tax list to him, with their warrant, and he shall have the same powers and be subject to the same duties and liabilities as other collectors.

[G. S. 12, § 54.]

If collector dies, etc., list to be delivered to selectmen. R. S. 8, § 41. G. S. 12, § 54. 1 Met. 525.

SECT. 63. In the case of death or removal from office of a collector, his executors or administrators, and all other persons, into whose hands any of his unsettled tax lists may come, shall forthwith deliver the same to the selectmen.

[G. S. 12, § 55.]

Compensation of collectors. R. S. 8, § 47. G. S. 12, § 55.

SECT. 64. Collectors shall be paid such compensation for their services as their cities or towns shall determine.

[1862, 183, § 11.]

Taxes to have priority in insolvent estates.

SECT. 65. In the order for a dividend, under section ninety-five of chapter one hundred and eighteen of the General Statutes, taxes assessed by the state, or any county, city, or town therein, shall have priority or preference next after debts due to the United States and to the state.

G. S. 118, §§ 95, 96.
1862, 183, § 11.

NOTE.—This section is not properly a part of an act for the collection of taxes, but of the acts regulating the courts of insolvency. As the section from which it is taken was part of an act in relation to the collection of taxes, it is here inserted.

[G. S. 12, § 56.]

Recovery of Taxes Collected.

SECT. 66. No tax paid to a collector shall be recovered back by suit, unless it appears that it was paid after an arrest of the person paying it, a levy upon his goods, a notice of sale of his real estate, or a protest by him in writing, and the damages awarded in a suit or process based upon any error or illegality in the assessment or apportionment of a tax, shall not be greater than the excess above the amount for which the plaintiff was liable to be taxed. And no sale, contract or levy shall be avoided by reason of any such error or irregularity.

Taxes paid to collector, when recovered back.
1859, 118, §§ 3, 4.
See ch. 11, § 54.
G. S. 12, § 56.
1873, 315, §§ 12, 13, 14.
9 Gray, 38.
13 Gray, 476.
1 Allen, 319.
10 Allen, 48.
99 Mass. 208.
102 Mass. 348.

POLLS AND ESTATES.

[Chapter 259 of the Acts of the year 1872.]

AN ACT TO ESTABLISH THE POLLS AND ESTATES OF THE SEVERAL CITIES AND TOWNS IN THE COMMONWEALTH.

Be it enacted, &c., as follows:

SECT. 1. The number of polls, the amount of property, and the tax of one thousand dollars, including polls at half a mill each, for each city and town in the several counties of the Commonwealth, as contained in the schedule hereto annexed, are hereby established, and shall constitute a basis of apportionment for state and county taxes during the decade ending in the year eighteen hundred and eighty-two, unless otherwise provided by the legislature, to wit:—

BARNSTABLE COUNTY.

TOWNS.	Polls.	Property.	Tax of $1,000, including Polls at half a mill each.
Barnstable,	1,138	$2,880,361 14	$2 09
Brewster,	295	800,893 33	57
Chatham,	613	1,025,358 39	85
Dennis,	829	1,521,982 74	1 22
Eastham,	178	233,874 22	21
Falmouth,	650	1,293,695 74	1 01
Harwich,	827	1,083,774 41	99
Mashpee,	69	94,845 87	08
Orleans,	404	568,979 20	50
Provincetown,	1,056	2,102,071 83	1 64
Sandwich,	810	1,444,517 43	1 17
Truro,	347	298,893 69	33
Wellfleet,	583	855,929 09	74
Yarmouth,	579	1,610,171 50	1 14
Total,	8,378	$15,815,348 58	$12 54

BERKSHIRE COUNTY.

TOWNS.	Polls.	Property.	Tax of $1,000, including Polls at half a mill each.
Adams,	2,900	$6,679,320 34	$4 98
Alford,	120	311,989 33	22
Becket,	357	490,644 00	44
Cheshire,	445	881,121 33	69

BERKSHIRE COUNTY—CONTINUED.

TOWNS.	Polls.	Property.	Tax of $1,000, including Polls at half a mill each.
Clarksburg,	153	$247,442 66	$0 21
Dalton,	307	1,113,828 70	74
Egremont,	248	579,198 41	43
Florida,	330	206,957 00	27
Great Barrington,	1,102	4,963,402 75	3 17
Hancock,	178	495,515 29	35
Hinsdale,	458	883,906 68	70
Lanesborough,	366	765,788 33	59
Lee,	920	1,725,051 50	1 37
Lenox,	504	1,492,673 83	1 04
Monterey,	186	308,160 16	26
Mount Washington,	62	99,381 00	08
New Ashford,	48	109,439 00	08
New Marlborough,	504	919,417 25	74
Otis,	252	325,529 00	30
Peru,	118	197,715 16	16
Pittsfield,	2,484	8,856,082 51	5 92
Richmond,	295	546,406 82	44
Sandisfield,	342	546,026 32	46
Savoy,	209	279,228 66	25
Sheffield,	538	1,367,702 91	99
Stockbridge,	462	2,659,644 32	1 64
Tyringham,	130	305,898 00	23
Washington,	156	290,378 50	23
West Stockbridge,	523	928,665 41	75
Williamstown,	689	1,718,937 65	1 25
Windsor,	193	314,619 66	26
Total,	15,579	$40,610,072 48	$29 24

BRISTOL COUNTY.

TOWNS.	Polls.	Property.	Tax of $1,000, including Polls at half a mill each.
Acushnet,	281	$682,324 06	$0 50
Attleborough,	1,285	2,987,311 91	2 22
Berkley,	196	327,809 65	27
Dartmouth,	793	2,340,476 23	1 63
Dighton,	458	867,692 24	69
Easton,	974	2,903,498 20	2 02
Fairhaven,	661	1,676,529 57	1 22
Fall River,	7,070	27,513,445 21	18 08
Freetown,	326	841,317 93	61
Mansfield,	587	884,314 40	76
New Bedford,	5,333	25,483,267 65	16 14
Norton,	429	827,559 67	65
Raynham,	444	1,177,491 29	84
Rehoboth,	441	803,565 74	65
Seekonk,	246	606,265 33	44

BRISTOL COUNTY—Continued.

TOWNS.	Polls.	Property.	Tax of $1,000, including Polls at half a mill each.
Somerset,	475	$979,392 73	$0 76
Swanzey,	323	669,337 78	52
Taunton,	4,855	15,273,009 41	10 50
Westport,	662	1,526,683 63	1 14
Total,	25,839	$88,371,292 63	$59 64

COUNTY OF DUKES COUNTY.

TOWNS.	Polls.	Property.	Tax of $1,000, including Polls at half a mill each.
Chilmark,	152	$327,835 56	$0 25
Edgartown,	480	1,205,113 77	88
Gay Head,	38	11,014 00	02
Gosnold,	26	162,514 00	10
Tisbury,	428	706,958 84	59
Total,	1,124	$2,413,436 17	$1 84

ESSEX COUNTY.

TOWNS.	Polls.	Property.	Tax of $1,000, including Polls at half a mill each.
Amesbury,	1,793	$2,331,694 62	$2 13
Andover,	1,019	3,406,297 79	2 31
Beverly,	1,872	5,849,009 38	4 03
Boxford,	235	817,822 79	55
Bradford,	530	1,103,752 84	85
Danvers,	1,298	2,927,161 52	2 20
Essex,	420	943,770 71	71
Georgetown,	582	868,536 58	75
Gloucester,	3,496	7,709,462 73	5 82
Groveland,	520	774,183 26	67
Hamilton,	198	536,020 22	38
Haverhill,	3,967	9,342,712 44	6 92
Ipswich,	815	1,762,137 86	1 34
Lawrence,	6,625	18,570,198 36	13 13
Lynn,	7,558	21,787,103 36	15 29
Lynnfield,	211	711,866 84	48
Manchester,	429	1,219,013 64	86
Marblehead,	2,152	3,388,539 78	2 87
Methuen,	904	1,987,472 13	1 50
Middleton,	235	445,943 46	35
Nahant,	138	5,565,328 53	3 01
Newbury,	290	882,549 55	61
Newburyport,	3,218	8,269,884 02	5 98
North Andover,	729	2,196,427 34	1 53
Peabody,	2,100	5,427,619 59	3 92
Rockport,	941	1,688,770 59	1 36
Rowley,	303	546,301 01	44

ESSEX COUNTY—CONTINUED.

TOWNS.	Polls.	Property.	Tax of $1,000, including Polls at half a mill each.
Salem,	5,558	25,382,251 19	16 19
Salisbury,	966	1,903,012 04	1 49
Saugus,	512	1,488,852 07	1 04
Swampscott,	541	2,104,515 38	1 38
Topsfield,	321	755,450 34	56
Wenham,	240	504,944 95	39
West Newbury,	518	1,129,092 87	86
Total,	51,234	$144,327,699 78	$101 90

FRANKLIN COUNTY.

Ashfield,	332	$558,337 62	$0 46
Bernardston,	238	478,234 80	37
Buckland,	523	602,238 16	58
Charlemont,	251	397,298 44	34
Colrain,	366	729,502 68	57
Conway,	377	869,061 87	65
Deerfield,	837	1,464,055 28	1 19
Erving,	211	260,911 42	24
Gill,	194	481,482 11	35
Greenfield,	888	2,475,857 02	1 75
Hawley,	172	171,115 66	18
Heath,	155	312,175 72	24
Leverett,	235	370,054 70	31
Leyden,	109	251,343 33	19
Monroe,	49	63,609 96	06
Montague,	698	1,007,781 91	88
New Salem,	268	349,997 66	32
Northfield,	456	789,612 10	65
Orange,	785	1,122,926 29	99
Rowe,	158	184,585 28	18
Shelburne,	374	1,066,305 18	75
Shutesbury,	160	209,984 00	19
Sunderland,	206	465,132 06	35
Warwick,	232	258,329 35	25
Wendell,	145	206,909 42	18
Whately,	310	802,511 69	58
Total,	8,729	$15,949,353 71	$12 80

HAMPDEN COUNTY.

Agawam,	483	$965,323 95	$0 75
Blandford,	278	536,872 12	42

HAMPDEN COUNTY—CONTINUED.

TOWNS.	Polls.	Property.	Tax of $1,000, including Polls at half a mill each.
Brimfield,	313	$717,093 08	$0 54
Chester,	350	496,540 46	44
Chicopee,	2,387	4,379,262 85	3 51
Granville,	338	480,283 41	42
Holland,	94	146,605 88	12
Holyoke,	2,811	6,261,712 49	4 72
Longmeadow,	356	1,209,609 84	82
Ludlow,	258	485,955 30	39
Monson,	672	1,393,765 94	1 07
Montgomery,	93	158,231 00	13
Palmer,	818	1,412,195 71	1 16
Russell,	163	283,149 66	23
Southwick,	292	729,392 87	53
Springfield,	7,140	29,500,151 56	19 16
Tolland,	134	302,583 66	23
Wales,	222	373,372 12	31
Westfield,	1,997	5,163,347 03	3 73
West Springfield,	688	2,161,000 48	1 49
Wilbraham,	554	883,278 57	74
Total,	20,441	$58,039,727 97	$40 91

HAMPSHIRE COUNTY.

TOWNS.	Polls.	Property.	Tax of $1,000, including Polls at half a mill each.
Amherst,	935	$3,324,202 76	$2 22
Belchertown,	584	1,132,103 19	89
Chesterfield,	233	405,371 16	33
Cummington,	255	391,155 65	33
Easthampton,	773	2,955,277 21	1 95
Enfield,	310	716,497 09	53
Goshen,	96	150,824 50	13
Granby,	236	546,724 41	41
Greenwich,	193	306,966 73	26
Hadley,	616	1,480,119 87	1 09
Hatfield,	426	1,617,664 78	1 07
Huntington,	278	562,987 01	44
Middlefield,	180	425,139 66	31
Northampton,	2,403	7,349,272 04	5 09
Pelham,	167	203,607 00	19
Plainfield,	158	278,990 75	23
Prescott,	139	217,396 88	18
South Hadley,	665	1,960,330 07	1 37
Southampton,	296	588,242 98	46
Ware,	892	1,759,527 89	1 38
Westhampton,	127	443,460 82	30
Williamsburg,	604	1,535,881 73	1 11
Worthington,	240	373,670 88	32
Total,	10,806	$28,725,415 06	$20 59

MIDDLESEX COUNTY.

TOWNS.	Polls.	Property.	Tax of $1,000, including Polls at half a mill each.
Acton,	486	$1,037,827 04	$0 79
Arlington,	869	3,968,954 00	2 53
Ashby,	298	538,289 02	43
Ashland,	685	1,149,051 92	95
Ayer,	492	897,098 96	72
Bedford,	228	555,862 26	41
Belmont,	436	2,617,009 39	1 60
Billerica,	485	1,565,065 74	1 07
Boxborough,	105	267,586 66	19
Brighton,	1,331	7,137,224 78	4 44
Burlington,	201	474,776 95	35
Cambridge,	10,323	45,646,076 22	29 29
Carlisle,	154	373,391 29	27
Charlestown,	8,271	28,314,873 65	19 10
Chelmsford,	600	1,764,033 18	1 23
Concord,	645	2,364,666 82	1 57
Dracut,	523	1,391,920 72	1 00
Dunstable,	137	326,185 22	24
Everett,	654	2,107,796 48	1 44
Framingham,	1,244	3,897,847 34	2 68
Groton,	465	1,743,460 03	1 15
Holliston,	856	1,857,291 57	1 41
Hopkinton,	1,099	2,079,868 55	1 65
Hudson,	915	1,296,966 72	1 14
Lexington,	625	2,249,651 27	1 50
Lincoln,	239	700,779 78	49
Littleton,	248	755,331 16	52
Lowell,	9,186	27,811,128 12	19 29
Malden,	1,945	6,372,237 44	4 34
Marlborough,	2,320	2,699,682 30	2 59
Maynard,	522	916,118 50	75
Medford,	1,530	6,263,456 43	4 08
Melrose,	881	2,627,733 75	1 83
Natick,	1,863	2,932,489 58	2 48
Newton,	3,199	19,244,632 61	11 77
North Reading,	263	531,633 64	41
Pepperell,	526	1,171,801 73	88
Reading,	759	1,702,763 48	1 28
Sherborn,	267	984,136 41	65
Shirley,	341	927,209 84	66
Somerville,	3,832	13,372,478 79	8 98
Stoneham,	1,390	2,104,304 51	1 81
Stow,	296	777,846 50	56
Sudbury,	330	1,035,945 50	71
Tewksbury,	317	984,172 58	68
Townsend,	611	766,804 31	71
Tyngsborough,	175	316,817 86	25
Wakefield,	1,438	2,969,802 34	2 29
Waltham,	2,368	8,021,324 14	5 42

MIDDLESEX COUNTY—CONTINUED.

TOWNS.	Polls.	Property.	Tax of $1,000, including Polls at half a mill each.
Watertown,	1,150	$4,907,134 30	$3 17
Wayland,	360	703,298 23	55
Westford,	534	1,063,516 64	83
Weston,	342	1,327,178 64	87
Wilmington,	231	513,090 74	39
Winchester,	772	3,398,370 13	2 18
Woburn,	2,527	7,564,366 26	5 26
Total,	72,889	$241,090,362 02	$163 83

NANTUCKET COUNTY.

TOWNS.	Polls.	Property.	Tax of $1,000, including Polls at half a mill each.
Nantucket,	923	$2,357,831 09	$1 71
Total,	923	$2,357,831 09	$1 71

NORFOLK COUNTY.

TOWNS.	Polls.	Property.	Tax of $1,000, including Polls at half a mill each.
Bellingham,	344	$515,725 93	$0 44
Braintree,	1,092	2,186,788 92	1 70
Brookline,	1,522	21,501,469 85	12 13
Canton,	947	2,786,565 18	1 95
Cohasset,	558	1,937,175 89	1 30
Dedham,	1,355	4,829,464 96	3 23
Dover,	167	409,896 21	30
Foxborough,	708	1,505,935 49	1 15
Franklin,	620	1,582,983 09	1 15
Holbrook,	425	1,216,276 87	86
Hyde Park,	1,507	4,898,294 61	3 34
Medfield,	296	848,688 81	60
Medway,	905	1,666,371 47	1 33
Milton,	657	5,452,958 68	3 21
Needham,	976	3,031,378 55	2 09
Norfolk,	270	474,490 49	39
Norwood,	466	1,188,850 41	86
Quincy,	1,847	4,929,735 34	3 53
Randolph,	1,102	1,929,429 19	1 57
Sharon,	371	822,389 80	62
Stoughton,	1,191	2,434,962 24	1 88
Walpole,	532	1,352,977 46	98
West Roxbury,	2,310	15,368,478 81	9 28
Weymouth,	2,510	5,173,496 62	3 99
Wrentham,	546	1,166,231 78	89
Total,	23,224	$89,211,016 65	$58 77

PLYMOUTH COUNTY.

TOWNS.	Polls.	Property.	Tax of $1,000, including Polls at half a mill each.
Abington,	2,619	$4,220,356 81	$3 54
Bridgewater,	852	2,391,899 09	1 69
Carver,	279	602,417 89	46
Duxbury,	680	1,180,932 56	96
East Bridgewater,	827	1,245,410 31	1 07
Halifax,	184	337,558 21	27
Hanover,	440	1,002,267 23	75
Hanson,	367	502,514 51	45
Hingham,	1,208	3,246,673 86	2 32
Hull,	73	258,880 98	17
Kingston,	425	1,428,795 16	97
Lakeville,	318	572,712 25	46
Marion,	237	485,308 23	37
Marshfield,	480	827,907 29	68
Mattapoisett,	358	602,126 13	50
Middleborough,	1,322	2,382,045 41	1 92
North Bridgewater,	2,294	3,516,509 83	3 01
Pembroke,	395	621,066 78	53
Plymouth,	1,443	3,828,322 31	2 74
Plympton,	215	310,922 34	27
Rochester,	301	508,534 97	42
Scituate,	663	1,093,852 80	91
South Scituate,	458	1,004,412 33	76
Wareham,	726	1,163,960 63	98
W. Bridgewater,	440	850,497 97	67
Total,	17,604	$34,185,885 88	$26 87

SUFFOLK COUNTY.

TOWNS.	Polls.	Property.	Tax of $1,000, including Polls at half a mill each.
Boston,	61,148	$638,870,531 46	$368 24
Chelsea,	4,452	12,405,134 86	8 78
Revere,	343	1,016,113 29	71
Winthrop,	133	533,628 41	35
Total,	66,076	$652,825,408 02	$378 08

WORCESTER COUNTY.

TOWNS.	Polls.	Property.	Tax of $1,000, including Polls at half a mill each.
Ashburnham,	598	$970,764 72	$0 81
Athol,	1,045	2,093,389 54	1 63
Auburn,	257	532,348 99	41
Barre,	654	1,916,326 66	1 34
Berlin,	273	436,751 70	37
Blackstone,	1,112	2,301,719 56	1 77

WORCESTER COUNTY—CONTINUED.

TOWNS.	Polls.	Property.	Tax of $1,000, including Polls at half a mill each.
Bolton,	286	$578,263 34	$0 45
Boylston,	198	556,767 68	39
Brookfield,	727	1,210,255 71	1 00
Charlton,	525	1,022,738 26	80
Clinton,	1,251	3,021,080 13	2 22
Dana,	202	273,117 33	25
Douglas,	598	972,710 86	81
Dudley,	601	996,905 48	83
Fitchburg,	3,317	11,283,337 05	7 62
Gardner,	968	1,753,531 67	1 41
Grafton,	1,006	1,903,027 53	1 51
Hardwick,	522	1,168,036 78	88
Harvard,	376	1,036,539 10	74
Holden,	482	934,992 56	74
Hubbardston,	439	881,670 88	69
Lancaster,	425	2,328,167 05	1 44
Leicester,	708	2,122,772 00	1 48
Leominster,	1,232	2,961,363 92	2 18
Lunenburg,	315	765,487 66	56
Mendon,	306	712,574 42	53
Milford,	2,662	4,932,915 45	3 94
Millbury,	1,050	1,958,885 07	1 56
New Braintree,	164	592,433 93	40
Northborough,	378	1,327,854 03	89
Northbridge,	817	1,936,368 26	1 43
North Brookfield,	1,109	1,620,848 18	1 41
Oakham,	231	370,521 56	31
Oxford,	718	1,310,451 73	1 05
Paxton,	198	326,809 33	27
Petersham,	310	770,893 62	56
Phillipston,	177	298,445 00	25
Princeton,	308	957,602 93	66
Royalston,	343	859,138 08	63
Rutland,	268	520,180 30	41
Shrewsbury,	452	1,104,404 99	81
Southborough,	513	1,391,240 48	99
Southbridge,	1,250	2,312,315 49	1 85
Spencer,	1,101	2,060,940 58	1 64
Sterling,	445	1,237,743 84	88
Sturbridge,	546	964,681 65	78
Sutton,	622	1,195,893 65	94
Templeton,	736	1,161,246 67	98
Upton,	529	841,077 61	71
Uxbridge,	707	1,862,082 21	1 34
Warren,	714	1,479,329 54	1 14
Webster,	1,201	2,216,306 08	1 77
Westborough,	968	1,981,057 26	1 53
West Boylston,	697	1,021,478 74	89
West Brookfield,	454	831,177 83	67

WORCESTER COUNTY—CONCLUDED.

TOWNS.	Polls.	Property.	Tax of $1,000, including Polls at half a mill each.
Westminster,	484	$876,810 69	$0 71
Winchendon,	1,027	1,892,527 00	1 51
Worcester,	11,638	37,263,867 13	25 51
Total,	51,240	$124,212,169 49	$91 28

SECT. 2. This act shall take effect upon its passage. [*Approved April 25, 1872.*

AN ACT

TO SECURE A MORE EQUAL APPORTIONMENT OF THE STATE AND COUNTY TAXES, UPON THE SEVERAL CITIES AND TOWNS.

[Chapter 317 of the Acts of the year 1874.]

Be it enacted, &c., as follows:

SECT. 1. The tax commissioner shall be furnished, by the secretary of the Commonwealth, with the returns of the assessors of the several cities and towns, required by chapter one hundred and sixty-seven of the acts of eighteen hundred and sixty-one, for the four years preceding the year eighteen hundred and seventy-six.

SECT. 2. The tax commissioner shall cause to be prepared an abstract from the returns made to him under an act entitled "An Act levying a tax upon certain corporations," and under chapter three hundred and fifteen of the acts of the year eighteen hundred and seventy-three, for the three years next preceding the year eighteen hundred and seventy-six, containing the names of all corporations having stock owned in any city or town in the Commonwealth; also, the excess of the market value of all the capital stock of each corporation taxed by said act over the value of its real estate and machinery; also, the whole number of shares of such corporation and the number of shares owned in this Commonwealth, specifying the number of shares owned in each city and town by parties other than insurance companies, savings banks and institutions for savings.

SECT. 3. The tax commissioner shall be authorized to require such further returns in addition to those provided for by this act, from state, city and town officers, as in his judgment may be necessary; and upon the returns herein provided and authorized, the commissioner shall proceed according to his best judgment and discretion to equalize and apportion upon the several cities and towns the number of polls, the amount of property, and the proportion of every one thousand dollars of tax, including polls at one-tenth of a mill each, which should be assessed upon each city and town; and said commissioner shall perform the duties required by this act, and report the same in tabular form, in print to the legislature, within one week from the first Monday in January in the year eighteen hundred and seventy-six.

SECT. 4. The sergeant-at-arms is directed to provide for the use of said commissioner a suitable room in the state house, and the tax commissioner is authorized to employ such clerical assistance as may be needed, for the purposes of this act, and may procure such stationery and other articles as may be required.

SECT. 5. This act shall take effect upon its passage. [*Approved June 8, 1874.*

THE EXEMPTION FROM TAXATION

OF

CHURCH PROPERTY, AND THE PROPERTY OF EDUCATIONAL, LITERARY AND CHARITABLE INSTITUTIONS.

BY CHAS. W. ELIOT,
PRESIDENT HARVARD COLLEGE.

CAMBRIDGE, December 12, 1874.

To the Commissioners of the Commonwealth, appointed "to inquire into the expediency of revising and amending the laws of the State relating to taxation and the exemptions therefrom":—

GENTLEMEN:—In accordance with a request contained in a letter of October 14, 1874, from Prof. J. H. Seelye, that I lay before your Commission my "views respecting the present exemption from taxation of property used for religious, educational and charitable purposes," I respectfully present for your consideration the following paper.

Your obedient servant,

CHARLES W. ELIOT.

The property which has been set apart for religious, educational and charitable uses is not to be thought of or dealt with as if it were private property; for it is completely unavailable for all the ordinary purposes of property, so long as the trusts endure. It is like property of a city or state which is essential for carrying on the work of the city or state, and so cannot be reckoned among the public assets; it is irrecoverable and completely unproductive. The capital is sunk, so to speak, just as the cost of a sewer or a highway is capital sunk. There is a return, both from a church or a college, and from a sewer or a highway, in the benefit secured to the community; but the money which built them is no longer to be counted as property, in the common sense. It can never again be productive, except for the purposes of the trust for which it was set apart.

When a new road is made where there was none, the State, or some individual, sacrifices the value of the land it covers, and the money spent in building the road. It also sacrifices the opportunity to tax, in the future, the improvements which might have been put upon that land if it had not been converted into a road, and all the indirect taxable benefits which might have been derived from the use for productive purposes of the land, and of the money which the road cost.

When a church, or a college, or a hospital, buys land, and erects buildings thereon, the State does not sacrifice the value of the land, or the money spent upon the buildings; private persons make these sacrifices; but the State does sacrifice, by the exemption statute, the opportunity to tax, in the future, the improvements which might have been put upon that land if it had not been converted to religious, educational or charitable uses, and all the indirect taxable benefits which might have been derived from the use for productive purposes of the land, and of the money which the buildings cost.

This is the precise burden of the exemption upon the State. Why does the State assume it? For a reason similar to, though much stronger than, its reason for building a new road, and losing that area forever for taxation. The State believes that the new road will be such a convenience to the community, that the indirect gain from making it will be greater than the direct and indirect loss. In the same way the State believes, or at least believed when the exemption statute was adopted, that the indirect gain to its treasury which results from the establishment of the exempted institutions is greater than the loss which the exemption involves. If this belief is correct in the main, though not perhaps universally and always, the exemption can hardly be properly described as a burden to the State at large.

The parallel between a sewer or a highway, on the one hand, and land and buildings of exempted institutions, on the other, may be carried a little farther with advantage. The abutters often pay a part of the cost of the sewer or the highway which passes their doors, because it is of more use to them than to the rest of the inhabitants, and the members of the religious, educational or charitable society erect their necessary buildings and pay for their land themselves. If it be granted that the religious, educational or charitable use is a public use, like the use of a sewer or a highway, there is no more reason for taxing the church, the academy or the hospital, than for annually taxing the abutters on a sewer or a highway on the cost of that sewer or on the cost of the highway and its value considered as so many feet of land, worth, like the adjoining lots, so many dollars a foot. The community is repaid for the loss of the taxable capital sunk in the sewer by the benefit to the public health, and the resulting enhancement of the value of all its territory. In like manner, it is repaid for the loss of the capital set apart for religious, educational and charitable uses, by the increase of morality, spirituality, intelligence and virtue, and the general well-being which results therefrom. To tax lands, buildings, or funds which have been devoted to religious or educational purposes, would be to divert money from the highest public use,—the promotion of learning and virtue,—to some lower public use, like the maintenance of roads, prisons or courts, an operation which cannot be expedient until too large an amount of property has been devoted to the superior use. This is certainly not the case in Massachusetts to-day. The simple reasons for the exemption of churches, colleges and hospitals from taxation are these: first, that the State needs those institutions; and secondly, that experience has shown that by far the cheapest and best way in which the State can get them is to encourage benevolent and public-spirited people to provide them by promising not to divert to inferior public uses any part of the income of the money which these benefactors devote to this noblest public use. The statute which provides for the exemption is that promise.

Exemption from taxation is not then a form of State aid, in the usual sense of those words; it is an inducement or encouragement held out by the State to private persons, or private corporations, to establish or maintain institutions which are of benefit to the State. The answer to the question,—Why should the State give encouragement, in any form, to private corporations which support churches, academies, colleges, hospitals, asylums, and similar institutions of learning, advanced education and public charity,—involves, therefore, an exposition of the public usefulness of these corporations. I say advanced education, because the lower grades of education are already provided for at the public charge, and there seems to be little disposition to question the expediency and rightfulness of this provision.

The reason for treating these institutions in an exceptional manner is, that having no selfish object in view, or purpose of personal gain, they contribute to the welfare of the State. Their function is largely a public function; their work is done, primarily, indeed, for individuals, but ultimately for the public good. It is not enough to say of churches and colleges that they contribute to the welfare of a State; they are necessary to the existence of a free State. They form and mold the public character; and that public character is the foundation of everything which is precious in the State, including even its material prosperity. To develop noble human character is the end for which States themselves exist, and civil liberty is not a good in itself, but only a means to that good end. The work of churches and institutions of education is a direct work upon human character. The material prosperity of every improving community is a fruit of character; for it is energetic, honest and sensible men that make prosperous business, and not prosperous business that makes men. Who have built up the manufactures and trade of this bleak and sterile Massachusetts? A few men of singular sagacity, integrity and courage, backed by hundreds of thousands of men and women of common intelligence and honesty. The roots of the prosperity are in the intelligence, courage and honesty. Massachusetts to-day owes its mental and moral characteristics, and its wealth, to eight generations of people who have loved and cherished Church, School and College.

The public services of these institutions can hardly need to be enlarged upon. A single sentence may be given to the utility of that class of institutions which I may be supposed to speak for—the institutions of advanced education—the academies, colleges, scientific and technical schools, professional schools and seminaries, art collections and museums of natural history. All the professions called learned or scientific are fed by these institutions; the whole school system depends upon them, and could not be maintained in efficiency without them; they foster piety, art, literature and poetry; they gather in and preserve the intellectual capital of the race, and are the storehouses of the acquired knowledge on which invention and progress depend; they enlarge the boundaries of knowledge; they maintain the standards of honor, public duty and public spirit, and diffuse the refinement, culture and spirituality without which added wealth would only be added grossness and corruption.

Such is the absolute necessity of the public work which the institutions of religion, education and charity do, that if the work were not done by these private societies, the State would be compelled to carry it on through its own agents, and at its own charge. In all the civilized world, there are but two known ways of supporting the great institutions of religion, high education and public charity. The first and commonest way is by direct annual subsidies or appropriations by government; the second way is by means of endowments. These two methods may of course be combined. An endowment, in this sense, is property, once private, which has been consecrated forever to public uses. If, in one generation, a group of people subscribe to buy a piece of land, and build a church thereon, that church is an inalienable endowment for the benefit of succeeding generations. It cannot be diverted from religious uses, or ever again become private property. If a private person bequeath fifty thousand dollars with which to maintain six free beds for Boston sick or wounded in the Massachusetts General Hospital, which is an institution supported by endowments, that beneficent act obviates forever the necessity of maintaining six beds at the Boston City Hospital, which is an institution supported by direct taxation. If, by the sacrifices of generous and public-spirited people in seven generations, Harvard University has gradually gathered property which might now be valued at five or six millions of dollars, the State of Massachusetts is thereby saved from an annual expenditure of three or four hundred thousand dollars for the purpose of maintaining the liberal arts and professions; unless, indeed, the people of the State should be willing to leave the work of the university undone. To the precise extent of the work done by the income of endowments is the State relieved of what would otherwise be its charge. If some benevolent private citizen had built with his own money the State Lunatic Hospitals, the State would have been relieved of a very considerable charge. To tax such endowments is to reduce the good work done by them, and therefore to increase the work to be done by direct appropriation of government money, unless the people are willing to accept the alternative of having less work of the kind done. If the State wants the work done, it has but two alternatives—it can do it itself, or it can encourage and help benevolent and public-spirited individuals to do it. There is no third way.

The above argument in favor of the exemption of institutions of religion, education and charity from taxation being conclusive unless it can be rebutted, I propose to consider successively the various attempts which have been made to repel or evade it.

The first objection which I propose to consider would be expressed somewhat in this fashion by one who felt it: "I admit that churches, colleges and hospitals are useful, and I do not wish to see their good work diminished; but these institutions get the benefit of schools, police, roads, street lamps, prisons and courts, and should help to support them; their friends and supporters are generous, and will more than make good what the institutions contribute to the city or town expenses." The meaning of this suggestion is just this: The body of tax-payers in a given community having, through the public spirit and generosity of a few of their number, got rid of one of their principal charges,—namely, the support of the institutions of religion, high education and charity,—propose to avoid paying their full proportion of the remaining charges for public purposes, such as schools, roads, prisons, and police. They propose, by taxing the institutions which the benevolent few established for the benefit of the whole body, to throw upon these same public-spirited and generous men an undue share of the other public charges. To state the same thing in another form: there are in the community common charges, A, B, C,

D and E; A has been provided for by a few private persons at their own cost, and the burden of other tax-payers has been to that extent lightened; thereupon the tax-payers say, Let us take part of the money which these men have given for A, and use it for meeting charges B, C, D and E. Our friends who provided for A will give some more money for that purpose, and we shall escape a part of our share of the cost of providing for B, C, D and E. It is at once apparent that this objection is both illogical and mean;—illogical, because if churches, colleges and hospitals subserve the highest public ends, there is no reason for making them contribute to the inferior public charges; and mean, because it deliberately proposes to use the benevolent affections of the best part of the community as means of getting out of them a very disproportionate share of the taxes.

The next objection to the exemption which I propose to consider is formulated as follows:—Churches, colleges and hospitals do indeed render public service; they are useful to the State; but let them be established because people feel the need of them, just as people feel the need of houses, and food, and clothes, and by all means let them support themselves; they ought not to be favored or artificially fostered. Railroads, factories and steamship lines do service to the State; but it does not follow that they ought to be fostered by direct grants of public money, or be exempt from taxation. This objection is a plausible one at first sight; but there is a gap in the argument wide enough for whole communities to fall through into ignorance and misery. For the building of railroads, factories and steamships there exists an all-sufficient motive; namely, the motive of private gain; and they ought not to be built unless there be a genuine motive of that sort. A few men can combine together to build a cotton mill whenever there seems to be a good chance to make money by so doing; and they will thus supply the community with mills. The benefit they might confer upon the State would not be a legitimate motive for building a mill in the absence of the probability of private gain. Now this motive of private gain is not only absent from the minds of men who found or endow churches, colleges or hospitals, but would be absolutely ineffective to the end of procuring such institutions. It would be impossible for three or four men to establish and carry on a university simply for the education of their own sons. Those who found and maintain hospitals have, as a rule, no personal use of them. It is an unworthy idea that a church exists for the personal profit and pleasure of its members, or a college for the private advantage of those who are educated there. A church or a college is a sacred trust, to be used and improved by its members of to-day, and to be by them transmitted to its members of to-morrow. A modern church is an active centre of diffused charity, and of public exhortation to duty. The press has enlarged the public influence of the pulpit by adding the multitude who read the printed sermon to the congregation who listen to it. The orators, poets, artists, physicians, architects, preachers and statesmen do not exercise their trained faculties simply for their own pleasure and advantage, but for the improvement and delight, or the consolation and relief, of the community. In short, they do not live for themselves, and could not if they would. To increase virtue and piety, to diffuse knowledge and foster learning, and to alleviate suffering, are the real motives for founding and maintaining churches, colleges and hospitals. The work must be done through the individuals on whom the institutions spend their efforts, but the motive of those who promote the work is the public good and the advancement of humanity. Mills, hotels, railroads and steamships, moreover, though they benefit the public, benefit them only in a material way; they provide clothing, shelter, easy transportation, and, in general, increase material well-being. People may be relied on to make themselves comfortable or wealthy, if they can; but they need every possible aid in making themselves good, or learned. The self-interest of no man, and of no association of men, would lead to the establishment of a university. The motive of private gain or benefit being wholly lacking in most cases, and feeble in all, it is to be expected that institutions of religion, high education and public charity would not be founded and maintained, except by the direct action of the State, on the one hand, or, on the other, by the benefactions of private persons encouraged by fostering legislation. This is precisely the experience of all the modern nations. The American States now do less for the institutions of religion directly than any civilized nation, and they have done wisely in completely avoiding an establishment of religion; but from the time when they ceased to support religious institutions directly they fostered them by exempting them from taxation. Institutions of high education never have been self-supporting in any country; and there is no reason whatever to suppose that they ever can be. If they were made self-supporting, they would be inaccessible to the poor, and be maintained exclusively for the benefit of the rich. The higher the plane of teaching, the more the teaching costs, and the fewer the pupils, from the nature of the case. As to the charitable corporations whose whole income is used upon the sick, blind or insane poor, the notion that they could ever be self-supporting is of course an absurdity. Hospitals and asylums which are wholly devoted to taking care of men and women of the laboring classes who have lost their health, their reason, or some of their senses, cannot be self-supporting in the nature of the case. It is an abuse of language to apply the word to them; they are inevitably supported by private benevolence, or from the government treasury, or by the combination of these two resources.

The opinion, then, that churches, colleges and charitable institutions would be established in sufficient numbers without fostering legislation, and be as well maintained taxed as untaxed, has no warrant either in sound reason or in experience. Not a bit of practical experience can be found in the civilized world to support it; and the analogy set up between these institutions of religion, education and charity, on the one hand, and establishments of trade, manufactures and transportation, on the other, is wholly inapplicable and deceptive.

I come now to the consideration of an objection to the exemption, which is local in its nature, but not on that account less worthy of careful examination. Those who urge this objection admit that the public receives great benefit from churches, colleges and hospitals; but, as these institutions necessarily have local habitations, and taxes under our laws are locally levied, they allege that the particular cities or towns in which the institutions happen to be situated bear, in loss of taxable property, the so-called burden of their exemption, while the whole State, or perhaps the whole country, shares the public benefits which accrue from them. The public burdened, it is alleged, is not the same public as the public benefited. This objection assumes, in the first place, that it is a burden to a city or town to have a lot of land within its borders occupied by an institution exempted from taxation; and this assumption is based upon the belief that, if the exempted institution did not occupy the lot, the taxable houses, or factories, or stores within the limits of the city or town would be increased by the number of houses or stores which might stand upon the exempted lot. This is a proposition which is generally quite incapable of proof, and is intrinsically improbable, but which nevertheless has, in some cases, a small basis of unimportant fact. It implies that there is an unsatisfied demand for eligible land on which to build houses, or factories, or stores, within the city or town limits; but this can be the case only in very few exceptionally situated cities, and not all the time in them, but only spasmodically in seasons of speculation or unusual activity,—and even then not over their whole area, but only in very limited portions of it. Of course the cost of the buildings which might be erected upon a lot rescued from an exempted institution is not to be counted as an additional resource for the tax-gatherer; for that amount was, under our laws, taxable somewhere before as personal property. If, in any town or city, there are houses or factories or stores enough to meet the demand for such accommodations, the town or city will gain nothing by having more buildings erected. There may be more houses or more stores, but each house or each store will be worth less. In a large city there will always be a few streets, and perhaps wharves, which are absolutely needed for business purposes. Thus, for example, it might not be expedient to have an exempted institution, which had no need of water-front, occupy a portion of a limited water-front, every yard of which was needed for commerce. It might not be expedient that a church should occupy a street corner, or an open square, in the heart of the business quarter of a growing city,—though London has not felt obliged to move St. Paul's into the country, or build upon Trafalgar Square. But such peculiar cases are to be wisely treated as the exceptions which they really are; at any rate, they cannot be made the basis of a great State's policy towards its most precious institutions,—its institutions of religion, learning and charity. As a rule, the amount of taxable property, real and personal, in a town or city is in no way diminished by the fact that a portion of its territory is exempted from taxation; and in many cases it is obvious that the taxable property is actually increased by reservations, whether natural—like small sheets of water—cr artificial,—like parks, squares, or open grounds about churches and public buildings. It is well known that, in many new towns and cities of the Western States, it was a well-recognized, and, in some cases, very successful device for raising the price of house-lots, and stimulating the speculation in land, to make a large reservation in the centre of the town for an academy or college. This is one of the reasons why there are such a multitude of colleges at the West. It is but a few years since several towns were bidding against each other to get the Massachusetts Agricultural College planted within their borders. The town of Amherst paid $50,000 for this privilege. In Boston itself, the block of land on which the buildings of the Natural History Society and the Institute of Technology stand, was given to those corporations on the condition that, if the lands surrounding the reserved area did not rise in value, in consequence of the grant, enough to cover the estimated value of the reservation itself, then the two corporations should pay the deficiency. These corporations never had to pay anything for their land. The city had just as much value in land available for taxation after the gift was made to these two exempted societies as it would have had if no such gift had been made. It cannot be maintained that the exemption of the church lots in a country town is in any possible sense a burden to the town, or that it diminishes in any way the valuation or amount of the property in the town which is available for taxation. On the contrary, every estate in the town is worth more to the occupant and to the assessor, because of the presence of those churches. The proposition that the presence, in a town or city, of exempted institutions diminishes the amount of taxable property therein is, therefore, not only incapable of proof, but is manifestly untrue in the vast majority of cases. There are, nevertheless, some cases in which a new exemption involves a real loss, though not without compensations, to the town or city from which the property was abstracted; and there are also cases in which the restoration of an exempted piece of property to taxation might be a real gain, in spite of considerable losses. When a benevolent citizen of one town gives $100,000 of personal property to an exempted institution situated in another town, the first town loses so much property which was there taxable, and the second town has the local benefit of the institution, if there be any. On the other hand, the town which loses in this case has similar chances of gaining local benefits by gifts to institutions situated within its limits from citizens of other towns. Again, it by no means follows that the citizen who gave this $100,000 would have kept it in a taxable form at his place of residence, if he had not given it to an exempted institution. Such gifts are often—perhaps generally—made out of annual earnings or sudden profits; and if the $100,000 had not been given to an exempted institution, it might have been unprofitably consumed, or lost, or given away to individuals resident elsewhere. A good deal of the personal property which now goes to churches, colleges and hospitals, would be consumed outright if it were not so saved. If the gift is made by will, instead of during life, there are more chances that the $100,000 would, in the distribution of the property, have been carried away from the testator's place of residence, at any rate. When a piece of real estate is transferred to an exempted institution for its own proper use, the local benefits of the institution, if there be any, are for the same town which gives up the taxes on the piece of real estate, and the withdrawal of that piece from productive uses probably brings some other piece into use at once, or at least sooner than would otherwise have happened. It would seem, at first sight, as if it would be clear gain to get a piece of land, once exempted, taxed again, and covered with taxable houses or stores; but there are always drawbacks on the gain. If Boston Common should be cut up and built upon, the conveniently situated houses and stores built there would cause other houses and stores, less well placed, to be vacated, or to fall in value; and the improvement of real estate in the outskirts would be arrested or checked for a time. The estates which face the Common would also fall in value. It would be a permanent gain that the business of the city would probably be more conveniently done thereafter; and this indirect gain, whatever it might be, would ultimately be represented in the taxable property of the city. In this particular instance the productiveness of Boston would doubtless be diminished by the loss of health, vigor and spirits, on the part of the inhabitants, consequent upon the loss of the healthful open area. It is, then, quite impossible to maintain that any exemption is a clear loss to the place in which it exists. With every loss there come chances of advantage. Sometimes the loss is great and the compensation small, and sometimes the advantages quite outweigh the loss. We have seen that, in the long run, there is no real loss to the State at large; and, in all probability, the local gains and losses of the various towns and cities of the Commonwealth would be found to be distributed with tolerable fairness, if the averaging period were long enough. Absolute equality in matters of taxation is unattainable.

It is important to demonstrate satisfactorily the statement just made, that great advantages often accrue to a town or city from the presence of institutions exempted from taxation, advantages which much more than offset any losses which are real. A concrete instance will best illustrate this proposition; and no better instance can be chosen than that of Harvard University, an exempted institution occupying about seventy acres of land in the city of Cambridge, which land, with the buildings thereon and their contents, is alleged by the assessors to be worth from three to four millions of dollars. This case is perhaps as strong as any on the side of the objectors to the exemption, because the exempted area is large and its value is high, and on this very account it is a case well adapted to my present purpose. In the first place, all the land which faces or adjoins the university's inclosures, is enhanced in value in consequence of that position. The open grounds of the university have the same effect on the surrounding lands which open spaces of an ornamental character always have in cities. They improve the quality and value of the whole neighborhood. Secondly, the university brings to Cambridge a large amount of personal property, which becomes taxable there. The fifty families, of which the heads are teachers in the university, possess, on the average, an amount of personal property which much exceeds the property of the average family throughout the city. A considerable number of families are always living near the university for the sake of educating their children. They come to Cambridge for this express purpose, and stay there from four to seven years, or sometimes indefinitely. Many of these families have large means; in fact, few others could afford such a temporary change of residence. Again; families of former officers and teachers in the university continue to live in Cambridge; and it is notorious that some of the largest properties taxed in the city are of this sort. Finally, families come to Cambridge to live because of the society which has gathered about the university. The amount of taxable personal property brought into ward one of Cambridge by the university in these several ways counts by millions. Accordingly, this ward is the richest ward in Cambridge, and has always been the most desirable part of the city to live in, as the character of its houses and of its population abundantly testifies. It has eighteen per cent. of the houses in Cambridge and sixteen per cent. of the polls, while it has thirty per cent. of the taxable property. The ward had no natural advantage over the rest of the city, having, to this day, its fair share of bogs, salt marshes and sandy barrens. The greater part of its surface is but a few feet above high-water mark, and nothing but the presence of the university during two hundred and forty years has made it the desirable place of residence which it is.

In still another way does the university bring taxable money to Cambridge. It collects from its students in Cambridge about $150,000 a year, adds thereto about $50,000 of the income of its personal property, and pays this large sum out as salaries and wages to people who live in Cambridge. A large portion of this sum is annually taxed by the city as the income of individuals in excess of $2,000 a year.

It is well understood that the building of a new factory in a village, or the introduction of some new industry into a town, which gives employment to a large number of respectable people, is a gain to that village or town. Whatever brings into a town a large body of respectable consumers benefits that town. Now, the university brings into Cambridge a large body of respectable consumers; there are fifty families of teachers, about fifty more unmarried officers, about one thousand students, and about one hundred janitors, mechanics, laborers, bed-makers and waiters, a fair proportion of whom have families. As the great part of these persons belong to the refined and intelligent and well-to-do class, they consume very much more than the average of the community. The money thus spent in Cambridge is mainly brought from without, for the greater part of it is either derived from the personal property of the university, or it is money brought from home by the students. If it were not for the presence of this body of consumers, the land, houses and shops of that part of Cambridge would all be worth less than they are, and the assessors would find so much less to tax.

It is a great advantage to a city to have a place of high education at its doors, just as it adds to the attractiveness and prosperity of a city to maintain good schools. Nearly one hundred Cambridge young men are now members of the university.

The grounds of the university adorn the city, and serve as protection against spreading conflagrations. They give light and air, trees, shrubs, grass and birds to a part of the city which must soon become densely populated. In the future they will serve many of the purposes of a public park, while they will be maintained without expense to the city. The buildings and collections of the university, which are becoming more and more attractive, are a source of interest and pleasure to all the people of the neighborhood. It is a curious illustration of the incidental advantages which Cambridge has reaped from the presence of the university, that printing and binding are still principal industries in the city, industries which give employment to hundreds of work-people and a large taxable capital. The business of printing was planted in Cambridge by the college, and was maintained there by the college, in spite of great difficulties, for many years.

Finally, the presence of the university gives distinction to the city. Cambridge is one of the famous spots of the country, and its citizens take pride and pleasure in its eminence.

I have taken a single notable example through which to exhibit the various advantages which a town or city may derive from the presence of one of the exempted institutions. *Mutatis mutandis*, the principles just laid down apply to almost all of them, with a force which varies with the locality, the nature of the institution, and the stage of its development. The benefits of many of the exempted charitable institutions are almost exclusively local. The direct benefits of a town's churches are largely, though not exclusively, local, and if the church buildings are beautiful, or interesting from historical associations, this indirect benefit is local too. It may not be impossible to pick out some exceptional institution of education or charity, or some single peculiarly placed church, to which these principles concerning the bearing of the exemption upon the interests of localities may not apply in their full force, or may not apply at all at a given moment; but the legislator should never be much influenced by the exceptions to general rules, or by momentary abnormal phenomena, or by the back eddies in a strong current of opinion.

We have seen that exempted institutions are considered by towns desirable acquisitions, in spite of the exemption. There is competition among them even for the state prison and the lunatic asylums; and they doubtless understand their own interests. But if the towns were allowed to tax the institutions now exempted, what a treasure would a college, or a hospital, with a large amount of personal property, be to a town! The town would have all the indirect local benefits of the institution, and the taxes on its property besides; and this unmerited addition to the property taxable in the town would correspond to no service performed, sacrifice made, or burden borne by the town.

It has been often asserted, that to exempt an institution from taxation is the same thing as to grant it money directly from the public treasury. This statement is sophistical and fallacious. It is true that the immediate effect on the public treasury is in dollars and cents the same, whether Harvard University be taxed $50,000, and then get a grant of $50,000, or be exempted from taxes to the amount of $50,000, and get no grant. The immediate effect on the budget of the university would also be the same. The proximate effects of these two methods of state action in favor of religion, education and charity are however unlike,—so unlike, indeed, that one is a safe method, while the other is an unsafe method in the long run, though it may be justifiable under exceptional circumstances. The exemption method is comprehensive, simple and automatic; the grant method, as it has been exhibited in this country, requires special legislation of a peculiarly dangerous sort, a legislation which inflames religious quarrels, gives occasion for acrimonious debates, and tempts to jobbery. The exemption method leaves the trustees of the institutions fostered untrammelled in their action, and untempted to unworthy arts or mean compliances. The grant method, as practised here, puts them in the position of importunate suitors for the public bounty, or, worse, converts them into ingenious and unscrupulous assailants of the public treasury. Finally and chiefly,—and to this point I ask special attention,—the exemption method fosters public spirit, while the grant method, persevered in, annihilates it. The State says to the public-spirited benefactor, "You devote a part of your private property forever to certain public uses; you subscribe to build a church, for example, or you endow an academy; we agree not to take a portion of the income of that property every year for other public uses, such as the maintenance of schools, prisons and highways." That is the whole significance of the exemption of any endowment from taxation. The State agrees that no part of the income of property, once private, which a former generation, or the present generation, has devoted forever to some particular public use, shall be diverted by the State to other public uses. The exemption method is emphatically an encouragement to public benefactions. On the contrary, the grant method extinguishes public spirit. No private person thinks of contributing to the support of an institution which has once got firmly saddled on the public treasury. The exemption method fosters the public virtues of self-respect and reliance; the grant method leads straight to an abject dependence upon that superior power—Government. The proximate effects of the two methods of state action are as different as well-being from pauperism, as republicanism from communism. It depends upon the form which the action of the State takes, and upon the means which must be used to secure its favor, whether the action of the State be on the whole wholesome or pernicious. The exemption is wholesome, while the direct grant is, in the long run, pernicious.

There has been, of late years, a good deal of vague declamation against endowments. We have heard much of the follies and whimseys of testators, and fearful pictures have been painted of dead hands stretched out from the cold grave to chill and oppress the living. We frequently read sneers and flings at those benefactors of the public who, living or dying, consecrate their money to religious, educational or charitable uses. In urging the abolition of the exemption, much use has been made of this sort of appeal. What is its basis? Are there any grounds whatever for jealousy of endowments? Millions of private property in this State have been devoted to public uses of religion, education and charity. These endowments are all doing good work for the present generation, and are likely to do good to many generations to come. To how many injurious or useless endowments can any one point in Massachusetts? There are persons who too hastily say that they hold Catholic churches to be injurious endowments; but it must be a very bigoted Protestant that does not admit that a Catholic church is better for a Catholic population than no church at all. Catholics would doubtless, in these days, grant as much as that for a Protestant population. The judicious legislator, when he speaks of the church, does not mean any particular church, or the churches of any particular sect; he means the sum of all the churches, the aggregate of all religious institutions, Christian, Israelite and Greek, Roman and Protestant, Congregational, Baptist, Anglican and Quaker. To legislate, directly or indirectly, either for or against any particular religious belief or worship, would be utterly repugnant to all sound American opinion and practice.

What silly fancy or absurd whim of a testator can be instanced in Massachusetts? Is anybody in this country obstructed, as to his rights, duties or enjoyments, by any endowment or foundation provided by the living or the dead? The suggestion is to the last degree ungrateful and absurd. Because there have been found in England a few endowments six or seven centuries old, which, in the changed condition of society, had come to do more harm than good, shall we on this fresh continent, in this newly organized society, distrust all endowments? Let us at least wait to be hurt before we cry out. If the time ever comes in this country when certain endowments, or classes of endowments, are found to do more harm than good to the community, legislation must then reform them, so as to prevent the harm and increase the good. We may be sure that our descendants of five centuries hence will have the sense to treat the endowments which we are establishing as England has treated some of her mediæval endowments—reconstruct them, when they need it, without destroying them. Taxation would not only be no remedy for the folly of endowments, if there were foolish endowments; but it would actually abridge the moral right of the State to interfere with mischievous endowments. Institutions which are fostered by the State through exemption from taxation must admit the ultimate right of the State to inquire into the administration of their affairs. An institution, on the other hand, which got no help from the State, and was taxed like a private person, would have a right to claim all the immunity from state inquiry into its affairs which an individual may claim. Thus the State may and should demand from every exempted institution an annual statement of its affairs which could be given to the public; but no such statement for public use could properly be demanded of an institution which paid taxes like any private citizen. Such an institution would have a moral right to the privacy which an individual is entitled to in a free country.

In this country, when one wishes to scoff at endowments, he must draw on his imagination for his facts. There is but one well-founded charge to bring against our countrymen in this matter of setting apart private property for public uses of religion, education and charity.

They scatter their gifts too widely, so that a greater number of institutions are started than can be well maintained. But the remedy for this evil is to consolidate endowments,—not to tax them. This consolidation has already begun, and will be brought about by the gradual enlightenment of public opinion on this subject. To draw a vivid picture of alleged scandals and abuses, and then propose some action of an irrelevant nature, desired for other reasons, as if it were a remedy for those scandals and abuses, is a well-known device of ingenious disputants; but it is a device which ought not to impose on clear-headed people. To prejudice the mass of the people against endowments is the part of a demagogue, for it is to induce them to act ignorantly in direct opposition to their own real interests; since endowments exist for the benefit of the great mass of the people, while they are a matter of but slight concern to the rich. The rich man does not care whether education be dear or cheap; he does not want the scholarships of a college; he does not need to send his children to a hospital; he could afford to keep a clergyman in his own family, if he cared to. It is the poor man who needs the church which others have built; the college which, because it has endowments, is able to offer his ambitious son a liberal education; the hospital which can give him, when disabled, attendance as skilful and careful as the rich man can buy. Moreover, the poor man has no direct interest in this proposed taxation of the institutions now exempted; it will not help him pay his poll-tax, nor lessen the amount of it; it will help no one but the property-holders. It is natural enough that a property-holder who has no public spirit should desire to escape his share of the charge of supporting institutions of public utility, on the ground that he feels no personal need of them. But that a man of property feels no want of institutions which are necessary to the security of the community, and does not believe in them, is no reason for excusing him from his share of the support of these institutions. The doctrine that a citizen can justly be called upon to contribute to the support of those things only which he approves, or which are of direct benefit to him, would cripple our public schools as well as our colleges, and, in fact, would destroy the basis of almost all taxation.

The Massachusetts statute about the exemption, as it is administered, guards effectually against all the real evils described by the law term "mortmain,"—a word, the translation of which seems to be such an irresistible rhetorical titbit for many who advocate taxing churches and carrying on universities by legislative grants. It is, indeed, inexpedient that religious, educational, or charitable corporations should hold large quantities of real estate for purposes of revenue; first, because experience shows that such corporate bodies do not, as a rule, improve real estate as steadily and promptly as individuals; and secondly, because the accumulation of large quantities of land in single hands, although permissible, and often rather beneficial than hurtful to the community, is an operation which needs the natural check of death and distribution among heirs. This check is wanting in the case of permanent corporations. Now, the Massachusetts statute does not exempt from taxation real estate held by religious, educational and charitable institutions for purposes of revenue. On the contrary, all such property so held by these institutions pays taxes precisely as if the pieces of property belonged to private individuals. If the Old South Church corporation owns stores, from which they derive income applicable to the purposes of their trust, those stores are taxed precisely as if they were the property of individuals. Harvard University owns a number of stores in the business part of Boston; with one exception (a store included in the exemption given by the charter of 1650), these stores are taxed just as if they belonged to an individual. If the Catholic Church undertakes to hold real estate for income, or as an investment, it has to pay taxes on such property, under the existing statute, like any private citizen. No exempted institution can hold real estate free of taxes except that which is fairly necessary for the purposes of the religious, educational or charitable trust. It would be a dishonorable evasion of the real intent of the statute to claim exemption on real estate which was bought with the intention of selling it again at a profit; and if any addition could be made to the statute which would make such a practice impossible, or would subject to penalties any institution which should be guilty of it, such an addition would be an improvement; although it is altogether likely that the offence contemplated has never, as a matter of fact, been committed. Of course, the mere fact that an institution has made a sale of exempted land is not in itself evidence of an evasion of the statute; for poverty may compel an institution to part with land which it ought, in the real interest of the trust, to keep. It is also a perfectly legitimate transaction for an exempted institution to sell one site in order to occupy another. One cause of the agitation for the abolition of the exemption has been the distrust awakened by sales of church property at large profit in the older parts of our growing cities. But these sales are perfectly legitimate. Those who believe in the public utility of churches need only to be assured that the proceeds of these advantageous sales must be invested in new churches,—that none of the property can relapse into the condition of private property. This assurance the action of the Massachusetts Courts indisputably gives. It is hard to see why these transfers of churches from more valuable to less valuable city lots should seem a grievance to anybody. Whenever a city church sells its old site for a large sum, buys a new site for a much smaller sum, and with the balance erects a handsome church, the amount of property exempted from taxation remains precisely what it was before, and the city gains an ornamental building. There is less value in the exempted land than before, but more in the building. On the whole, considering the nature of American legislation concerning testamentary dispositions and the holding and transfer of land; considering the nature and history of our ecclesiastical bodies, and the mobility of our whole social fabric, there is probably no economical evil from which an American State is so little likely to suffer as the mediæval evil of mortmain. To live in apprehension of it would be as little reasonable as for the people of Boston to live in constant dread of being overwhelmed by an eruption of lava from Blue Hill.

It has been suggested by persons who apprehend that the institutions of religion, education and charity, or some of them, will get a disproportionate and injurious development, that only a limited exemption should be allowed them, the limit to be fixed by legislation. If, however, the property of these corporations is really held and used for a high public purpose, it is hard to understand how it can be for the interest of the public to pass any laws which tend to limit the amount of that property,—at least until more property has been set aside for that purpose than can be well used. If it is inexpedient for the State to use for its common purposes—not religious or educational—any portion of the income of a church or an academy up to $5,000, why is it not also inexpedient to divert from religious or educational uses any portion of the income above $5,000? If the legislature could tell with certainty just how much property it was expedient for a church, or a college, or a hospital to have, then a limit for exempted property in each case would be natural and right; but the legislature cannot have this knowledge; and if they could acquire it for to-day, it would be outgrown to-morrow. Moreover, the circumstances and functions of the various exempted institutions are so widely different and so changeable, that each institution would necessarily have its own limit prescribed by law, and would be incessantly besieging the legislature for a change in its limit. The legislature would be forced to keep removing the limit of exemption, because in most cases there would be no logic in the limit. The more books there are in a library, the better; it would be absurd to exempt the first hundred thousand, and tax the second hundred thousand. The more good pictures, statues and engravings there are in an art museum, the better; it would be absurd to exempt a museum while it had few of these precious objects, and tax it when it got more, and so became more useful to the public. A sumptuary law to prevent the erection of beautiful churches, by taxing the excess of the value of a church above a certain moderate sum, would be singular legislation for Massachusetts. Who can tell how much money Harvard, or Amherst, or Williams could use legitimately to-day for the advantage of the State in advanced education? If one knew to-day, the knowledge would be worthless next year. The one perfectly plain fact is, that no one of the institutions of advanced education in this State has one-half the property which it could use to advantage. It would be cruel mockery to enact that a woman, who can hardly buy calico and flannel, shall not wear velvet and sable. The amount of exempted real estate which any of the exempted institutions can hold is limited by natural causes. As such real estate is, as a rule, completely unproductive, the institution will not be likely to tie up any more of its property in that form than it can help. A limit to exempted real estate has seemed desirable to some persons, because it has sometimes happened in large cities that institutions of religion, education or charity, have changed their sites with great profit; but in such cases the community gets the whole advantage of the profit in the increased work of the church, college or hospital. Moreover, such transactions imply a growing population, likely to make increasing demands upon the institutions of religion, education and charity, which, therefore, need all the new resources which the growth of population fairly brings them.

Those who advocate limiting the amount of the exempted property which may be held for a religious, educational or charitable trust, seem to forget that it is the public which is the real enjoyer of all such property, and that it is the public only which is really interested in its increase, except as gratitude, affection or public spirit may prompt individuals to share this public interest. All such trusts are gifts "to a general public use, which extends to the poor as well as the rich," to quote Lord Camden's definition of a charity in the legal sense. They are gifts for the benefit of an indefinite number of persons, by bringing their minds under the influence of religion or education, or by relieving their bodies from disease. They are trusts in the support and execution of which the whole public is concerned, on which account they are allowed, unlike private trusts, to be perpetual. Now, for the public to make laws which tend to discourage private persons from giving property to the public for its own uses, is as unwise as for the natural heir to put difficulties in the way of a well-disposed relative who is making his will. The fact that the property of these public trusts is administered by persons who are not immediately chosen or appointed by the public, obscures to some minds the essential principle that the property is really held and used for the public benefit; but the mode of administration does not alter the uses, or make the property any less property held for the public. Experience has shown that many of the religious, educational and charitable works of the community can be peacefully, frugally and wisely carried on by boards of trustees; and that method has been preferred in England and the United States. On the continent of Europe these functions are discharged by government; but, under both methods of administration, the functions are public functions. The fact that nobody has any permanent interest in the property of such trusts, except the public, is well brought out by imagining what would occur if a church, or an academy, or an insane asylum should be taxed, and nobody should come forward to pay the taxes. It is nobody's private interest to pay such taxes. The city or town could proceed to sell the church or other building belonging to the trust; but if it did so, the effect would be that a piece of property, which had been set apart for public uses, would become private property again, unless some benevolent persons should, for the love of God or the love of their neighbors, buy the property over again for its original public uses. A city might as well levy taxes on its city hall, and sell it for taxes in default of payment.

It remains to consider the effect of abolishing the exemption. No church could be maintained upon ground which would be very valuable for other purposes, and costly church edifices would be out of the question. A society whose land and building were worth $300,000 would have to pay $4,500 a year in taxes, besides all the proper expenses of a church. The burden would be intolerable. The loss to the community, in that pure pleasure which familiar objects of beauty give, would be unspeakable. The village could spare its spired wooden church as ill as the city its cathedral. Cities have learned that fine architecture in their own buildings is a justifiable luxury. On the same betterment principle handsome churches are profitable to the public as well as delightful. I say nothing of the grievous moral loss to the whole people which would result from crippling the existing churches, and making it harder to build the new ones which our growing population should have. That loss would be deep and wide-spread and lasting; but other pens than mine can better depict it. Educational institutions would be obliged to take the taxes out of the income of their personal property or out of their tuition fees. The fifty or sixty thousand dollars which the city of Cambridge would take next year from Harvard University would be deducted from the money now available for salaries of teachers. This sum represents the pay of from twelve to fifteen professors, or of a much larger number of teachers of the lower grades. Moreover, the sum thus withdrawn from teaching would annually increase with the rising value of land in Cambridge; while it can by no means be assumed that the personal property and tuition fees of the University would increase proportionally. The burden might easily become wholly unbearable. The barbarous character of the proposition to tax property devoted to educational purposes may be well brought home by specifying a few of the items of what would be the tax on Harvard University. Memorial Hall, with the two acres of land in which it stands, would be taxable for not less than $550,000 next year, and there is no telling the price per foot to which the land may rise, for it is well situated between three good streets. Eight thousand dollars would be next year's tax on that monument of pure devotion to the public good, and every year the tax would increase. Charlestown might as well be allowed to tax Bunker Hill Monument, as Cambridge to tax Memorial Hall. To commemorate the virtue of its one hundred and forty graduates and students, who died for their country in the war of the Rebellion, would cost the University the salaries of at least two professorships every year, in addition to the original cost of the land and buildings and the maintenance of the buildings. Moreover, every added picture or bust would entail an additional contribution on the part of the University to the ordinary expenses of the city of Cambridge. To place Charles Sumner's bust in the Hall would increase the annual taxes by $7.50, and to hang there the portrait of Col. Robert G. Shaw, who was killed at Fort Wagner, would give $15 a year to the city. The College Library may be freely consulted by all persons, whether connected with the University or not. With the building which contains it, this collection of books could hardly be valued at less than $300,000,—a sum very far short of its cost. There would, therefore, be a tax upon that library of perhaps $4,500 a year now; and, as about $10,000 worth of books are bought each year, the annual increase of the tax would be sure. If it is inexpedient that such a library should be exempt from taxation, how wrong it must be that cities and towns should pay all the expenses of public libraries, besides exempting them from taxation. The Observatory, an institution maintained solely for the advancement of knowledge, and having no regular income except from its endowments, is necessarily surrounded by open grounds, embracing several acres, and it must remain so protected, if good work is to be done there. The taxes on this land would eat up half the income of the Observatory now, and in a few years the whole income. The richer and more populous Cambridge became, the heavier would be the charges upon the University, for the higher would be the price of land throughout the city. It is to be observed, that the facts and illustrations used to support the proposition that institutions of religion, education and charity must be taxed, are mostly drawn from the rich towns and cities of the Commonwealth—not from the country villages. The advisability of taxing churches, colleges and hospitals, does not seem to suggest itself until a community gets very rich,—until its territory is at a great price per square foot. When Cambridge was a country village, she was glad to give the College a site for its first building.

The abolition of the exemption would reduce the service of all the institutions of advanced education in the State from 20 to 25 per cent. at present, and this diminution of efficiency would grow greater year by year. All the academies, colleges, professional schools, and scientific or technical schools, all the libraries not town libraries, all the museums of art or natural history, would see from one-fifth to one-quarter of their income diverted from education, and applied to ordinary city and town expenditures. An extravagant city or town government might at any time demand much more than one-fourth of their income. Precious institutions, which render great services to the whole State, or perhaps to the nation, would be at the mercy of a single local government.

It is impossible that a Massachusetts legislature should consent to so great a reduction in the work of the institutions of advanced education all over the State; that work is none too great now. Considering the place which Massachusetts has always claimed among her sister States in all matters of education, and which she must hold if her influence is to be maintained, it is incredible that she should seriously contemplate putting all her best institutions at such a terrible disadvantage in the race for excellence with similar institutions in the other States, where high education would remain untaxed. Of course, the direct aid of the State would be urgently invoked, and, indeed, it is obvious that the State would be compelled to assume the charges which the crippled endowments for religion, education and charity could no longer sustain; the State tax would thereby be largely increased, and the tax-payers would lose rather than gain by the change. There is but small chance that local taxes would be diminished by abolishing the exemption. Give the cities and towns of Massachusetts new resources, and instantly they will make new expenditures which will more than absorb these resources. It is the excessive expenditure of towns and cities which has been the principal cause of this extraordinary proposition to tax religion, education and charity. The assessors are driven to desperate devices for increasing the public revenue. The one real remedy for the evils, which cause the eager search for something new to tax, is reduction of expenditure; and this reduction can only be accomplished through the election of independent and courageous legislators and administrators in towns, cities, and the State at large. Whenever the people find themselves in serious difficulty, they instinctively show their fundamental reliance upon men of character by calling upon them to bring the State out of trouble. The proposition under discussion is a proposition to cripple or crush the institutions which breed men of character. It should be called a proposition to get rid of churches, to cripple colleges, to impair charities, and to extinguish public spirit. The direct intervention of the State might indeed avert some of these evils, but only at the great cost of adding to the already too numerous and too complex functions of the State, and of strengthening the vicious tendency to centralization of powers in government.

The two nations in which endowments for public uses have long existed are the two free nations of the world. In England and the United States, the method of doing public work by means of endowments managed by private corporations, has been domesticated for several centuries; and these are the only two nations which have succeeded on a great scale in combining liberty with stability in free institutions. The connection of these two facts is not accidental. The citizens of a free State must be accustomed to associated action in a great variety of forms; they must have many local centres of common action, and many agencies and administrations for public objects, besides the central agency of government. France perfectly illustrates the deplorable consequences of concentrating all powers in the hands of government. Her people have no experience in associated action, and no means of getting any. To abandon the method of fostering endowments, in favor of the method of direct government action, is to forego one of the great securities of public liberty.

The sudden abolition of the exemption would work great hardship, because of the nature of the contracts and undertakings into which the exempted institutions are accustomed to enter. Churches and colleges have been planted or built up, life salaries have been promised, wills have been made, gifts received, trusts accepted, and investments made, all on the faith of this exemption. In all the institutions of advanced instruction, for example, professors are appointed for life, and great hardships would result from the violation of that implied contract. It would have been impossible for Amherst College to accept the gift of its new Chapel, or Harvard University the gift of its Memorial Hall, except under the exemption statute. Several active churches in our cities have built chapels for the benefit of the poorer classes; they did this good work under the exemption statute, and neither would nor could otherwise have done it. In case the legislature should see fit to abolish the exemption, equity would require that taxation should fall, not on property acquired during the existence of the exemption, but only on that acquired after the exemption was repealed. The legislature of a civilized State should always set an example of scrupulous respect for every acquired right or vested interest, particularly when it is endeavoring to enact justice and equality in the distribution of public burdens.

But I trust that it is not necessary to discuss how or by what stages this exemption should be abolished. The American States, rough and rude communities as they are in some respects, still lacking many of the finer fruits of civilization, nevertheless possess in an extraordinary degree the main elements of national strength. Churches, schools and colleges were their historical foundations, and are to-day their main reliance. The general respect for religion and education, the prevalence of public spirit, the diffusion of knowledge, the common maintenance of high standards of character,—these, and not growing wealth and increasing luxury, are the things which guarantee free institutions. Massachusetts has grown to be what she is under legislation which fostered institutions of religion, high education and charity, and these institutions, with the public schools, are the very foundations of her social fabric. We must not undermine the foundations of the solid old house which our fathers so wisely built.

If abuses have crept in, let them be reformed. If institutions which are really not of a public character get exempted, cut them off; if greater publicity is desirable in regard to the condition and affairs of the institutions exempted, provide for annual published returns; if there be fear of improper sales of land, long exempted, to the private advantage of the trustees or proprietors of the moment, enact that all sales of such property shall be by order of a court, and that the court shall take cognizance of the investment of the proceeds. But while we reform the abuses, let us carefully preserve the precious uses of the exemption statute. That statute is an essential part of our existing system of taxation. It may be expedient that the whole system should be reconstructed; but the exemption of religious, educational and charitable property is certainly not the point at which the reconstruction should begin.

Let us transmit to our descendants, in long generations, the invaluable institutions of religion, education and charity, which we inherited from our fathers, and transmit them, not merely as strong and ample as ever, but multiplied, beautified and enriched by our loving care.

THE

EXEMPTION FROM TAXATION OF PROPERTY

USED FOR

RELIGIOUS, EDUCATIONAL AND CHARITABLE PURPOSES.

By FRANCIS E. ABBOT.

BOSTON, MASS., October 26, 1874.

Prof. JULIUS H. SEELYE, *Amherst College:*

MY DEAR SIR:—Inclosed please find the statement of views you were so good as to ask for the Taxation Commission. As it is unlikely that the views of the petitioners to the legislature will be fairly brought before it except through the Commission, I thank you for the justice and impartial spirit which prompted your suggestion that this paper might be embodied in the Commission's report. Though not so short as I hoped it might be, I think you will perceive how condensed it is; and many will be grateful if it can be laid in full before the legislature.

Very respectfully yours,

FRANCIS E. ABBOT.

BOSTON, October 25, 1874.

THOMAS HILLS, Esq., Boston; Prof. JULIUS H. SEELYE, Amherst; JAMES M. BARKER, Esq., Pittsfield, *Taxation Commission:*

GENTLEMEN:—In compliance with your request, contained in the letter of Professor Seelye of the 14th instant, to lay before you, in written form, such as I should be willing to have you embody in your report to the legislature, my views respecting the present exemption from taxation of property used for religious, educational, and charitable purposes, I respectfully submit the following condensed statement, which you are at liberty to employ in such manner as you may deem most useful in the discharge of your highly important and honorable function. I make it, of course, purely as an individual citizen, and do not desire for it any other consideration than such as its intrinsic truth may warrant; but I believe that I express substantially the views of the Boston Liberal League, of which I have the honor to be president, and the petition of which to the last legislature occasioned the appointment of the joint special committee whose report led to your own appointment as State Commissioners on this subject.

1. The tenth article of the first part of the Constitution of the Commonwealth of Massachusetts explicitly declares the only principle on which just taxation can rest: "Each individual of the society has a right to be protected by it in the enjoyment of his life, liberty and property, according to standing laws. He is obliged, consequently, to contribute his share to the expense of this protection." The great fundamental principle that *protection is the only just ground of taxation* is thus recognized unqualifiedly in our State Constitution, and I need not say a word to sustain it.

2. All just taxes being assessed and collected for protection alone, all expenditure of state funds should be for the same purpose. Otherwise the public money is raised under false pretences.

3. There are two modes of expending state funds at present: direct expenditure by appropriation, indirect expenditure by omission to collect actual dues, *i. e.*, exemption from taxation, which is indirect appropriation. The right to exempt presupposes the right to tax; and exemption in every case is omission to collect money actually due to the State. All property is protected (theoretically), and all property is, therefore, justly liable to pay the cost of this protection. If the State exempts any property from taxation, it does but excuse it from bearing its proportion of the burden of taxation, which burden must be borne in full by non-exempted property. The State, like a private citizen in business, must average its loss by bad debts upon its solvent or honest debtors, on pain of bankruptcy. Hence the effect of all exemption is to collect from each tax-payer more than the actual cost of his protection, for the purpose of paying back in full the taxes on all exempted property. Exemption, that is, is indirect appropriation; and, unless the money thus appropriated is spent for the public protection, *exemption is a fraud by the State committed against every tax-payer.* I mean that the State has no right to appropriate money which it has raised avowedly for protective purposes alone, whether the mode of appropriation be direct or indirect, unless protection be the exclusive object of appropriation.

4. All public funds appropriated to private parties should be solely for *services rendered* by them in securing the general protection. Appropriations or exemptions on grounds of favor, partiality, or privilege,

are not only unjust but (as I have shown) fraudulent. Nothing can be honestly paid out of the public treasury, whether directly or indirectly, except for the purpose of defraying the expenses of that protection for which, by the State Constitution, all money is paid into it; and this self-evident principle requires that the parties to whom it is paid shall have earned it by services rendered.

5. If exemption from taxation, therefore, is granted to any species of property, it should be such property alone as might, with equal justice, receive a direct appropriation. I would lay the greatest possible emphasis upon this principle. *Exemption from taxation is a violation of public faith in all cases where a direct appropriation would not be equally proper and just.*

6. For many and weighty reasons I believe that direct appropriation would be a wiser policy than exemption from taxation in all cases. The public ought to know exactly for what and to whom the public money is paid, and also to what amount; whereas the effect of exemption is to conceal these facts. Abuses and corruption always attend such concealment; which is another strong argument against exemption. The recipients of public money will be stimulated to render the required services more faithfully if they know that no such concealment is possible. Various other reasons might be enumerated.

7. At the same time, however, I admit the right of the State to exempt, rather than to appropriate, when exemption is in return for services rendered, and when direct appropriation would be equally justifiable. If public economy can be increased by exemption under these provisos, or if any other advantage can be secured by it to the State, then I should approve the exemption. But I greatly doubt whether direct appropriation is not always preferable. Even if exemption is retained, all exempted property ought to be regularly assessed, to the end that the amount of exemption may be precisely known.

8. A special board, so constituted as to insure the maximum of character and ability in its members, might be permanently organized to take cognizance of all claims for appropriation or exemption on behalf of applicant institutions, and to report them to the legislature, annually, with favorable or unfavorable recommendations, and the reasons therefor in full. If all applications were first submitted to such a board, and rigorously scrutinized, there would be little danger of the evils apprehended from "special legislation." At any rate, it should not be forgotten that exemption from taxation is special legislation as things are, and is accompanied with very great and grave

abuses. A change, as here intimated, would probably be a change for the better, at least.

9. Passing now to consider the claims of certain classes of property to exemption, I would make a broad distinction between property used for charitable or educational purposes, on the one hand, and property used for religious purposes on the other.

With reference to the former class, the State must, to some extent, support charities and schools, in order to give the protection which it is organized to secure, and to save still greater expense from neglecting them. This is universally admitted, and I need not argue the point. Charitable and educational institutions which are, in part or in whole, owned or controlled by the State have, therefore, a just claim upon the public treasury. But those in which the State has neither ownership nor control ought not, in my judgment, to receive either direct appropriation or exemption from taxation. Such aid makes unjust discrimination in favor of corporate as against private property, which is used for the very same objects; exemption, in particular, appropriates the largest amount of public money to the wealthiest and least needy of such institutions, many of which are only partially or nominally charitable or educational in their objects. Certainly no public aid, whether by direct or indirect appropriation, ought to be given to any private institution except on the ground of services rendered to the public; and whenever profession of public service is made the ground of a claim for public aid, the State should share in the control of the claimant institution, so far, at least, as to make sure that the profession shall be carried out in good faith. If any institution prefers to be under purely private management, it ought not to ask or receive either appropriation or exemption.

10. With reference to property used for religious purposes, there are conclusive reasons, in my judgment, why it should neither receive direct appropriation from the State nor be exempted from taxation to any extent.

In the first place, twenty-three of the States of the Union provide expressly in their Constitutions that no one shall be taxed for the support of any religious society of which he is not a member; and this State makes the same provision in the sixtieth chapter of the General Statutes. Referring to the time of the Revolution, it is said in Tyler's *American Ecclesiastical Law*, page 177: "All land-holders, resident and non-resident, Christian and un-Christian, were taxed [to sustain public worship], though they never saw the minister or entered the meeting-house; and all corporations holding lands within the parish were also taxed, upon the principle that, so far as the community were concerned, public religious and moral instruction was intended for the prevention of crimes, and not for the salvation of souls." I would call especial attention to the fact that the principle upon which direct taxation for the support of public worship was then justified, was the *good moral influence* of the churches in repressing crime; the identical argument now urged to justify the exemption of church property from taxation. Now, what was the sequel? In 1833 the people of this Commonwealth amended their Constitution so as to abolish this practice of direct taxation for the support of religious worship; and they thereby condemned the principle upon which the practice rested. If, then, the rule is a correct one, that tax exemption is unjustifiable wherever direct taxation and appropriation would be unjustifiable, it is clear as noon-day that the Commonwealth of Massachusetts is pledged to a principle which forbids all exemption of church property from taxation. It is to-day illegal to tax any man for the support of any religious society in which he is not a member; to exempt church property from taxation is to tax everybody for its support, whether members or non-members; and it follows that the exemption of church property violates the General Statutes as they now are, at the same time that it rests on a general principle already emphatically condemned by the amendment of the Constitution in 1833. I therefore claim that the exemption of church property from taxation, even to the smallest extent, is an illegal practice, judged by the Constitution and General Statutes as they exist to-day; and that the statutory exemption of such property is in flagrant contradiction of both. It is a practice which, if justifiable at all, justifies direct taxation for the support of the churches; but, this being declared unjustifiable in 1833, consistency and justice alike require the total cessation of church exemption.

In the second place, the exemption of church property from taxation is equivalent to a direct subsidy from the State to the Church; which is a violation of the principle, well recognized in this country, that Church and State should be totally separate. It is a subsidy which can in no way be justified under our republican institutions, until the National and State Constitutions are so amended as to recognize Christianity as the national religion. The advocates of that measure are the only ones who can consistently uphold the present exemption of the churches from taxation.

In the third place, the practice under consideration is fraught with the gravest dangers to free institutions, by fostering the accumulation of wealth in ecclesiastical hands, especially in the Roman Catholic Church. The designs of this body upon the public school system are so hostile and perilous to its very existence,—they are so open and undisguised in many localities, and have already done so much to precipitate religious dissensions of the worst character,—that the simple instinct of self-preservation ought to determine the people of Massachusetts, as of all the States, to put an end to the growth of this cancerous organism in the body-politic, so far as granting it any special privilege is concerned.

In the fourth place, the exemption of the churches from taxation presses heavily on some consciences, and ought to press heavily on all. By exempting all churches from taxation, the entire community is taxed for the support of each; that is, each tax-payer is made to contribute to the support, not only of the beliefs he himself cherishes, but also of the beliefs which contradict them. The Protestant is obliged to pay for the support of Catholicism, the Catholic for the support of Protestantism; the Christian must help support Judaism, the Jew Christianity, the free-thinker both. Whoever has a conscience against being compelled to support beliefs which he considers false and pernicious, ought to see that he is thus compelled by the exemption of the churches from taxation. The State, which he is taxed to support, to-day practically supports a host of conflicting faiths by indirect taxation of the whole people; and the consciousness of this wrong is becoming deep and widespread. In a country where conscience and thought are supposed to be free, it is a public iniquity to continue such a wrong in the light of increasing knowledge of its character; and, regardless of private opinions, all honest citizens ought to favor reform in this direction. Contrary to the General Statutes, every citizen is now forced to pay tribute to religious societies in which he is not a member; and the only way to avoid this is to tax the churches equitably at their actual market value, exempting none to any extent.

In the fifth place, the churches themselves would gain in self-respect to be no longer pensioners upon the public treasury, supported by contributions levied upon thousands who would not pay except on compulsion. What they might lose in some directions they would certainly gain in moral dignity and self-respect; nor is it likely they would lose financially in the long run, so long as their supporters retained a sincere faith in their usefulness. Many eminent divines among the various denominations, many religious journals, and an increasing number of the laity, are coming to see the justice of taxing the churches, and to favor this step. The movement to secure it is a thoroughly honest one, by no means confined to so-called "infidels," and by no means having its root in mercenary or sordid motives, as has been very inconsiderately charged by heated opponents. The motives of the Liberal League, so far as I am qualified to bear testimony on that point, are a strong love of religious liberty, a desire for justice, a wish to be relieved from a grievance which galls conscience and wounds self-respect, and a hearty devotion to the fundamental principles of republican institutions. It is not the *amount*, but the *fact*, of the tax now indirectly imposed for the support of religious societies in which they are not members, which constitutes the evil that is opposed by the Liberal League. The spirit of their petition is well expressed by Rev. Alvah Hovey, D. D., speaking with reference to "Baptist usage" in his little book entitled "Religion and the State," pages 138, 139: "It has protested, even to imprisonment, against *direct* taxation for the support of religion, but has winked at *indirect* taxation for the same purpose. It is charitable to believe that this inconsistency has not commonly been perceived; but it is now manifest to all, and the only proper course is to bring our practice as soon as possible into agreement with our theory."

11. In conclusion, may I express the hope that your honorable Commission, if unprepared to report in favor of the principle we contend for—namely, the right of American citizens to be wholly untaxed, either directly or indirectly, for the support of religious worship,—will, at least, not report in favor of a compromise, by exempting only a minimum of church property from taxation and taxing the rest? Such a course could not possibly meet the point of conscience involved; and a point of conscience is most certainly involved in the exemption of a fixed minimum of church property as much as in the present state of things. The exemption of property used for charitable and educational purposes does not wound conscience; but the exemption of church property does, and no solution of the question can possibly be final which still leaves the community taxed to never so small an amount for the support of religious worship. It is not a question of dollars, but of rights; and I earnestly hope that the Commission and the legislature will so regard it.

With high respect, I am
Very truly yours,

FRANCIS E. ABBOT,
President of the Boston Liberal League.

THE

TAXATION ONLY OF TANGIBLE THINGS.

By WILLIAM ENDICOTT, Jr.

To the Commissioners on Taxation.

Gentlemen:—I desire to call your attention to the injustice of taxing mortgages, or, indeed, any form of indebtedness for property which is also taxed. It is obviously an act of injustice to tax the same property twice, and this is practically the effect of tax upon mortgages. This is readily seen by supposing the case of a person owning a house worth $10,000 and mortgaged for $5,000. The owner is taxed for the full value of his house, $10,000, and the mortgagee is now taxed for $5,000. The value of the property in question belonging to the two parties is but $10,000, while they are now compelled by law to pay taxes upon $15,000. Here is gross injustice, and who is the sufferer? It can be easily shown, I think, that it is the owner and mortgagor of the premises who really pays both taxes. He is taxed, in the first place, upon the full value of his house, $10,000. Does he also pay the tax upon the $5,000 which he owes upon the mortgage? Unquestionably, he does. To effect the loan, he must pay such rate as will give the lender the highest NET return which he can gain from any investment of equal security, and, *in addition thereto*, the amount of the tax. For example, the only investments which are here considered equal in security to first-class city mortgages, are the bonds of the City of Boston, of the State of Massachusetts, or of the United States.

During the war, the price of the latter was low, by reason of the doubt as to the result of the war, and the payment of the debt; but since this has been dispelled, the bonds sell at prices that give the purchaser from 4½ to five per cent. per annum. (It cannot be supposed that these would be held for investment at such prices, if subject to local taxation of 1½ per centum, giving the holder a net income of but little more than three per cent.) In deciding whether he shall invest in U. S. bonds, or in a mortgage, the lender would consider that the bonds would pay him say five per cent NET, equivalent to 6½ per cent. upon a mortgage subject to a tax of 1½ per cent., and, of course, he will not make the loan at a lower rate, even upon the very best security.

In point of fact, as the bonds can easily be converted into cash at any time, while a mortgage cannot, it is not easy to borrow upon mortgage, even upon first-class property, at less than seven per cent.

It is a popular impression that the holder of U. S. bonds gains some advantage at the expense of the public, by reason of this exemption. The market price shows that this is an error, and that he pays his tax, as well as his neighbors, in loaning to the government at a rate of interest sufficiently below the market rate to cover the gain from tax exemption.

Boston Currency *Sixes*, which must be considered quite as safe as U. S. bonds, sell at about par, giving the holder who pays taxes upon them about 4½ per cent. net. Though legally subject to tax, they can be so easily kept from the sight of the tax-gatherer as to be practically, to a considerable extent, untaxable. It is probable that this facility for eluding taxation adds to the market price of the bond, and that, if they could all be found out and taxed, the price would decline so much as to give the holder about five per cent. per annum net.

These figures show conclusively that first-class Boston mortgages, than which no security can be better, command a rate of 6½ to 7 per centum only because they are taxable, and being matter of public record, cannot easily escape taxation. And that in paying these rates the borrower, in fact, pays the tax upon them.

If mortgages were exempted from taxation, therefore, the inevitable result would be that borrowers upon mortgage would be able to borrow at present rates, less about the present taxation, say from five to six per centum, as the property might be first or second class. The law of supply and demand would compel this. If lenders should demand the old rates, new capital would be attracted from other investments and underbid them.

As with mortgages, so also can it be shown that the present system of taxing book debts duplicates taxation. Suppose that A B, a wholesale dealer, owing no debts, sells to C D, upon credit, merchandise valued at $5,000. C D takes his goods home, and is forthwith taxed upon his stock, $5,000, though he owns not a dollar of it. At same time, a tax bill is sent to A B, taxing him $5,000 upon the debt of C D. Obviously, here is property of but $5,000 in value, while the taxation is for $10,000. Each pays his tax bill. As A B must make the profits of his business pay his taxes, as well as store rent and other expenses, and his competitors in business must do the same, it is evident that the business must, for a series of years, afford a profit that will pay all expenses, taxes included, and something more, otherwise it would be abandoned. A B must make his customers pay his taxes, and, as C D is one of them, buying fully his proportion of the sales of A B, it follows that C D must pay to A B sufficient profit to pay his share of A B's taxes, that is, the tax upon his own note. Thus, it will be seen that C D, having paid the tax upon his own goods, pays also the tax upon the note which he gave in settlement of his purchase. He, in turn, collects both taxes from his customers, and, in this way, almost all taxes, however imposed, ultimately fall upon consumption. It is this tendency of taxes to distribute themselves, which, as Mr. D. A. Wells has shown in his very able report to the legislature of New York, makes it of much less importance that every species of property should be taxed, than that taxation should fall certainly and equally upon whatever kinds of property may be selected for taxation.

The present system of taxing mortgages bears with especial severity upon persons of small means, struggling to become the owners of homes. Often able to give but small margins, they cannot borrow at the lowest rates, and the imposition of double taxation is a burden upon them which the community ought not to impose. The relief would be more apparent if the amount of mortgage were to be deducted from the taxable value of the mortgaged property. In my opinion, the exemption of mortgages from taxation is preferable, as (while producing the same result) it simplifies very much the assessment and collection of the tax, and also because it seems to me to be a correct principle *that a tax should be assessed upon property where it exists, and not upon the owner, wherever he may happen to live.* It is wrong that property should be doubly taxed, and it is equally unjust to those who pay taxes that any property should escape taxation. Both of these results are inevitable under the system which now obtains in this State, of endeavoring to tax, sometimes the owner, and sometimes the holder of property (situated, perhaps, thousands of miles distant, and often of so intangible a character that no one but the owner and his debtor can possibly know whether or not there is any such property in existence), by the application of a sort of thumb-screw process to the conscience of the tax-payer. The result is, as might be expected, that evasion, subterfuge, and often fraud, are resorted to in order to escape just taxation; and that conscientious persons pay not only their own taxes but that portion which the less scrupulous escape. This demoralizing influence is, to my mind, a great argument against the present system, and ought to stimulate us to seek for something better.

In a popular government it is of the first importance that the *law* should be the embodiment of *justice*. To secure the obedience of the people, it must command their respect. A tax system which taxes one man for every dollar which he possesses, and but half taxes his neighbor, who owns twice as much of the same kind of property, is not calculated to secure that man's reverence or affection. So long as you maintain such a system you must expect human ingenuity to be exhausted in finding means to evade it. As might be expected under a system of gross inequality, the tax-payer gains nothing but a loss. *Injustice never pays.* The nation deluded itself for three-quarters of a century with the idea that it gained great profit from the slave system, but the shock of war has dispelled that illusion.

Let us examine a little the effect of the tax upon city bonds. The city of Boston can borrow* upon a taxable bond at six per cent. per annum, and not less. Upon a bond, exempt from local taxation, it could undoubtedly borrow at five per cent. If all our bonds were held here and taxed, the difference should be 1½ per cent.; but, as I have said, the proportion of bonds that escape taxation, or are held out of the State, is sufficient to affect the market price equal, probably, to one-half of one per cent. per annum.

Probably not one-half of these bonds are taxed in Boston. The tax-payers pay, therefore, one per cent. per annum more interest *upon the whole debt* for the privilege of taxing *one-half* of it; and, of course, pay more in interest than they receive in taxes.

The case may be much more clearly stated by supposing that there was no market for the bonds outside of this city. In this way we get rid of one element of their present value, which tends to confuse my argument.

In such case, the city would be able to borrow upon a taxable bond at six per cent. per annum, and equally able to borrow at 4½

* I make no reference to that part of the city debt borrowed in Europe, as having no relation to the question under discussion.

per centum upon a non-taxable bond; for it would manifestly be the same thing to all those lenders who expected to pay their full city tax. But every one knows that there are many persons, really resident here, who manage to evade the whole, or a large portion of their taxes, by gaining a legal residence in other towns where their property is not known to the assessors, or by keeping their bonds from the knowledge of the assessors, sometimes by fraud, sometimes by not being known as large property-holders. Of an issue of city bonds such a I have supposed, held entirely by persons really resident here, you probably would not claim that more than two-thirds could or would be taxed in Boston. Is it not clear as the sunlight, then, that the tax-payers would pay $1\frac{1}{2}$ per cent. upon the whole loan, for the purpose of getting back $1\frac{1}{2}$ per cent. upon two-thirds of it? The city treasurer collects the whole amount of the tax, keeps two-thirds of it in the city treasury, and pays over the other third, as interest, to those of our citizens who manage to escape full taxation. And, strangely enough, the reason given for this absurd system is, that our taxation must be *just* and *equal!!!*

The same objections lie, as it seems to me, against the attempted taxation of other forms of indebtedness, railroad bonds, for example.

The Fitchburg Railroad, needing funds to lay a second track, issues a mortgage bond, and must pay about seven per cent. per annum to get the money.

The rates for doing the business of the road must be so adjusted as to yield:

1st. Operating expenses.
2d. Taxes.
3d. Repairs and improvements.
4th. Interest upon the bonded debt.
5th. A reasonable percentage upon the capital, considering all risks.

Of course, the company must first gain from the community doing business with the road whatever it has to pay for either of these items, the charge for interest quite as much as the operating expenses. The latter must, indeed, take precedence, as a railroad can do its business without paying interest or dividends, but not without locomotives.

The rate of interest upon the bonds must, as I have shown, be such as to include the tax, while, in point of fact, I doubt if one-quarter part of such bonds ever pay tax anywhere.

The result is that the public pays the tax to the road; the road pays the tax to the bondholders; one-quarter part of the bondholders pay the tax to the proper authorities, and the other three-quarters keep it themselves.

If the bonds were not taxable the corporation could borrow at 5½ to 6 per cent., and could afford to do its business at lower rates. Why should the bonds be taxed? Tax the corporation, and you have taxed all the property that it owns. Why should you tax it a second time because it owes money, when you would think it grossly unjust to do so if the road were so fortunate as to be out of debt, and therefore better able to pay double taxes?

It will, doubtless, be said that if the bonds paid less interest, the stockholders would make larger profits. Even if this were true, I see no reason in it for confiscating a part of their property under a system of double taxation, but I do not believe that it is true. The stockholders are probably as desirous now as they well can be to gain large dividends, and would make ten per cent. instead of eight, if they could. That law of the Almighty, which we call *competition*, would regulate their profits then, as now, and would allow their business to be a fairly paying one, and nothing more. If their profits became exorbitant, somebody would appear, ready to build another road near enough to spoil their business, and thus punish them for their extortion.

It is matter of marvel to watch the nice adjustment of these social forces, and note how certainly, whenever a human need, real or supposed, is felt, somebody turns up, ready to satisfy it "upon reasonable terms."

From such reflection as I have been able to give to the subject, I am satisfied that the most equitable mode is to abandon the fruitless effort to tax intangible or incorporeal property, which will be found to be only liens upon property existing somewhere in a concrete or tangible form, and to tax only visible property, real and personal, wherever it may be found. *Collect the tax from the property, and not from the owner.*

In this way all property can be taxed once, and no property taxed twice. To this tax upon property might properly be added a tax upon the franchises of corporations having valuable privileges granted by the State, as banks, trust and insurance companies, gas companies, etc. The corporation tax might be appropriated to state expenditures.

It will, doubtless, be said that this will offer a bounty to Massachusetts capital to be invested out of the State. This objection seems plausible, but I find but little force in it. That Utopia is yet to be found where the tax-gatherer is unknown, and the other States of the Union are as hard pushed as Massachusetts to find subjects for taxation.

Most investments abroad are controlled by other considerations than freedom from taxation, and often indicate a willingness to take great risks in expectation of great profits. A railroad would naturally be located where a large business, rather than a light tax, would be looked for, though the experience of recent years shows that this rule is not always followed.

If taxation is to be regarded as the price paid by property for the protection of the law, there seems little reason for imposing a tax upon property which gets no protection. What benefit does Massachusetts render to the holder of railroad shares in Wisconsin? If the Wisconsin legislature proceeds to carry out the proposed virtual confiscation of railroad property, the owner must look for protection to the Wisconsin or United States courts alone. He can get none in Massachusetts. The property is in Wisconsin, under the protection (such as it is) of Wisconsin law, and it seems proper that in Wisconsin it should be taxed.

In regard to Massachusetts manufacturing corporations, it may be said that the proposed change would impose no new tax, inasmuch as all such property within the State is now taxed, not only upon the capital invested, but upon a valuation based upon the aggregate of all the shares of such corporations raised above par by debts due for goods sold and delivered. For these debts the corporations would not then be taxed, the taxation following the property into the hands of the purchaser.

Other States would attract manufacturing capital away from Massachusetts only so far as they might exempt it from taxation, and that is equally possible under the present system, while this State can also exempt such property, if it be thought expedient to do so.

It is well known that mill property in other States, and paying taxes there, is again taxed in Massachusetts, which would be considered a gross outrage if we had not become accustomed to such abuses of the taxing power of government.

No one questions the propriety of taxing real estate where it is located, and I can see no reason why the same rule should not equally apply to personal property.

The effect of such a change upon existing rates of taxation would be much less than might be supposed.

The valuation of Boston for 1874 is:—

Real Estate, ...	$554,200,150 00
Personal Estate, ...	244,554,900 00
	$798,755,050 00

More than two thirds of the valuation being real estate.

Of the total valuation of the state, more than seventy per cent. is real estate.

You estimate that the proposed change would reduce the personal estate of Boston about one hundred millions; but, of this amount, it is probable that at least fifty millions represent mortgaged property, book debts, or other forms of property now doubly taxed, and which ought, in justice, to be relieved from taxation under the present system. The reduction of the remaining fifty millions would add about one-tenth of one per cent. to the present rate, changing it from $15.60 to $16.70 per thousand.

It should be remembered that we shall have only the same amount to raise in the aggregate, and that it is proposed only to make a slight change in the distribution of the tax. It is probable that the change would be more marked in Boston than in the rest of the State, for the reason that a larger proportion of Boston capital is invested in other States than would be the case with country investments.

As to Boston, it may be said that the sum of fifty millions represents scarcely more than the usual gain in valuation of a single year. We can well afford to sacrifice the increment of one or two years, if thereby we can have a system of taxation which shall be *reasonably* just and equal, and which can be made to fall, like the dews from heaven, upon the just and the unjust, and from which there can be no escape.

I find two reasons for not approving the plan proposed by Mr. Wells in the report before alluded to.

First. The adoption of the rental, as the sign of a man's ability to pay taxes would, I think, throw a disproportionate share of taxation upon persons of moderate means, as the rental of such persons bears a much larger proportion to their income than does that of the wealthier class.

Second. The entire exemption of personal property—even if it made no real difference to the pocket of the tax-payer—would be very likely to lead to a feeling of injustice on the part of owners and tenants of real estate, and to jealousies between these different classes of property-holders, which it is desirable to avoid.

In making your report, I beg that you will overcome the inclination to gather in everything that, rightfully or wrongfully, can possibly be taxed, and endeavor to frame a system absolutely just, however it may affect existing methods. Have faith in principles, and be willing to accept their logical results. A system that is correct in theory *must* work well in practice.

Yours, very truly,

WM. ENDICOTT, Jr.

Boston, November 24, 1874.

EXTRA-TERRITORIAL TAXATION.

By Prof. A. L. PERRY,
OF WILLIAMS COLLEGE.

WILLIAMS COLLEGE, NOV. 27, 1874.

Gentlemen of the Tax Commission:

At your request, I proceed to put down a few considerations relating to the present tax laws of Massachusetts, and relating also to the subject of taxation in general.

1. Recent decisions of the supreme court of the United States, which I have no need to cite, inasmuch as they are discussed at length in Mr. Wells's Tax Reports and elsewhere, make it necessary that the law of Massachusetts shall be changed, in so far as it enacts that "Personal estate shall, for purposes of taxation, include goods, chattels, money, and effects, *wherever they are;* ships and vessels, *at home or abroad;* money at interest, and other debts due to the persons to be taxed more than they are indebted to pay interest for; public stocks and securities; stocks in turnpikes, bridges, and moneyed corporations, *within or without the state;* the income from an annuity, and so much of the income of any individual as exceeds two thousand dollars, *but no income shall be taxed which is derived from property subject to taxation.*"

I have italicized the phrases incompatible with the letter or spirit of legal decisions of the highest authority. Massachusetts cannot legally tax personal effects "wherever they are," simply because the owner is under her jurisdiction; the effects must be under her jurisdiction also.* Ships can only be taxed at their port of registry; the domicile of the owners is a matter of indifference. Massachusetts cannot legally tax stocks in corporations organized "without the state," unless the stocks themselves—the written instruments—are under her jurisdiction and protection. It is even doubtful whether she can tax the stocks of corporations organized and located "within the state," so far as citizens of other states are *bona fide* owners of the stocks, and keep them in those states under the protection and within reach

* *Note by the Commissioners.*—The position of the author must be considered as an opinion only. No decision of the United States supreme court can be found which prohibits the taxation of any class of personal property to our citizens wherever it may be, excepting only United States securities and imported goods in the hands of the original importer.

of the process thereof. In short, the doctrine is coming to be established, even if it be not well-nigh established already, that the same rule shall apply, for purposes of taxation, to personal chattels of all kinds as to real estate. Massachusetts can tax every farm within her borders, whether the owners are resident or non-resident, because she protects every farm, and must issue process in behalf of every farm. The deeds to those farms are of no validity separate from the farms themselves. The whole value is in the *farms*, and the farms are in Massachusetts, and Massachusetts can tax every rod of land covered by a deed. It is worth while to notice that a deed is not like a piece of credit-property, like a certificate of stock,—it is like a bill of lading or a dock warrant,—it goes with the land, and has no significance independent of the land. All credit-property, on the other hand, all negotiable instruments whatever, pass from hand to hand by endorsement or delivery. Because these are bought and sold separately from that physical thing called a railroad, a manufactory, a mine, they are separate *property*, and must have a *situs* for the purposes of taxation. That *situs* is where they are for the time being, within that jurisdiction whose sheriff would be called on to recover them in case they were stolen. Their migratory habits might constitute a reason, on the ground of expediency, why they should be exempted from taxation; but, if taxed at all, they should evidently be taxed where they are, not where they are not. The true rule, accordingly, applicable to both real and personal estate, would seem to be, that the situation of the property determines the right to tax it—the right residing in that jurisdiction that protects and defends the property for the time being. Of course it follows, from this rule, that certificates of stock in corporations, although the corporations are organized and operated wholly within the state, cannot be taxed in that state, so far as they are owned and held by non-residents. This is the doctrine, perhaps it may be called the extreme doctrine, of ex-territoriality as applicable to taxation.

Probably the worst feature, both theoretically and practically, of the present tax law of Massachusetts is the clause taxing and exempting incomes. A proper and exclusive income tax, as I shall shortly show, is the only form of taxation theoretically and absolutely just; but the miserable fragment of an income tax incorporated in our law at present can be justified on no ground of principle, or even of practical fairness. It is in reality a tax on wages, but the added exemption practically restricts it to a very limited class of wages; namely, salaries of over two thousand dollars *per annum*. No income can be taxed derived from property subject to taxation; so that the merchant, for example, who manages his own capital and works in his own store, and who, consequently, both earns wages and receives profits, although the two come in together, cannot be taxed on the element of wages: that is, the fruits of his labor, because it is income derived in connection with property subject to taxation.* Practically, therefore, our income tax is only a tax on salaries, and not on wages generally; and many a man, the reward of whose *labor* is five times greater than that of a taxed salaried man, pays not a cent on the score of what is really wages. This feature of the law ought clearly to be abolished. It is in the last degree partial, inasmuch as it discriminates directly against the man who works without a capital, in favor of the man who works and earns equally with the first, but who has a capital in addition that yields him a profit besides.

2. The old Roman law gave a perfect definition of property when it defined it as "anything that can be bought and sold"—*ea res est quœ emi et vendi potest.* If we analyze the things that are actually bought and sold, we find that they all come readily into three classes; namely, material commodities, personal services, and claims or credits. Value exists in these three forms, and never did and never will exist in any other. Each of these is equally property, since each is equally bought and sold; and the state has an equal claim on all these forms of property, for the purposes of taxation. Men, moreover, can only pay their taxes out of the proceeds of something that they have sold; they can sell only commodities, services, and credits, and their ability to pay taxes is exactly measured by the returns that they get from their sales of one or other or all of these three kinds of property. All taxes, therefore, of necessity, are really taxes on sales, and a man's net income of the year is an exact gauge both of the extent of his sales and of his ability and obligation to pay taxes. In effect, every tax must be a tax on income; for how can a man pay his taxes except out of income? The fundamental question of taxation, then, and really the only question, is, whether men shall pay taxes on and out of an income carefully ascertained, or on and out of an income indirectly conjectured and loosely guessed at. It all comes to that in the end.

The division of government into nation, state, and municipality,

* *Note by the Commissioners.*—It has been the practice in many municipalities to assess merchants and manufacturers for "income from profession, trade, or employment." The right to do so has been sustained by the supreme judicial court in the case of Wilcox *v.* Middlesex, 103 Mass. 544.

while doubtless of great advantage politically, is certainly an inconvenience fiscally, because, while the nation has one system and taxes certain things, the states have different systems and tax all sorts of things, and there is sure to be much of cross-purposes and something of double taxation. It is perhaps irrelevant in a paper like this to suggest what is the best possible—because the justest and most economical—system of taxation for a country situated as this is, so much of prejudice and pride and unwillingness to bear the just proportion of burden still hedge up the way to its adoption. Nevertheless, I will suggest it, for the sake of the light it may throw upon the more specific question of taxation by the state. If the whole people should see this thing as it is, they would enact, that the municipality should ascertain every man's income for the year; that municipal, state, and national taxes should be assessed upon this income once for all; that one set of municipal officers should collect the whole and distribute to each treasury; and that all other taxes of every name should be at once abolished. There is no practical difficulty in this scheme that would not disappear before an intelligent determination to carry it out. The only objections that lie against it are drawn either from its justness, or its economy, or its political simplicity. If it be objected, that men do not know their own annual income, the answer is, that they can know and ought to know it for their own sake as well as for the sake of the government. If objection be raised to the publicity of income, the answer is, that the *state* has a *right* to know the incomes, and cannot properly adjust its burdens otherwise. Moreover, the citizens have a right to know each other's incomes, for they cannot otherwise possibly know that each is bearing his share of the public burden. If objection be raised on the score of ex-territoriality, the answer is, that these considerations cease to have any significance after the adoption of such a system, inasmuch as double taxation is now no longer possible; inasmuch as income, no matter from what quarters derived, finds its centre where the person is, and cannot be touched elsewhere. For the rest, there would be no difficulty other or greater than is now experienced under internal revenue and tariff. The central fact that will long prevent the adoption of any such just and simple system as this, is the determination of influential men and classes of men, that they will not consent, under any circumstances, to bear their full share of the public burdens. They have not been accustomed to do so, and they are not willing to begin to do so. Add to this, the pride, as between state and nation, in respect to the mutual independence of their fiscal expedients.

3. A state income tax is out of the question in Massachusetts, so long as her citizens are so largely taxed under the national internal revenue system, and so monstrously taxed under the tariff; insomuch also as so much of the property of the state is owned by non-residents and the residents own so much property in other states and derive income from that. I see no better way at present than to continue to tax, at a full valuation, all real estate, both private and corporate, within the state, and to authorize the assessors *to jump* at the personal property of every resident, according to the style of house he lives in, or other general scale of expenditure. If we are not allowed to ascertain a man's personal property through his annual income, then we must guess at it through his annual expenditures. There is no other way. The real estate is open to observation, and has a well-known current value, always proportioned to the value of the annual sales from it; while the proceeds from personal property in credits, and from the sales of personal services, can be roughly approximated by local assessors, familiar with the habits and style of living of each individual. There should be, of course, an open process of abatement in the personal property tax under the oath of the person aggrieved. I do not see, gentlemen, but that you are practically shut up to these two sources of revenue:—a definite real estate tax, and an indefinite personal property tax, subject to the limitations of the assessorial judgment and to the limitations of legal ex-territoriality. I hope that you will be able to guide the legislature to something simpler and better in the way of taxation than has been hitherto attained in this state, remembering all the while that the simplest and the best is probably, for the present, unattainable.

4. In respect to exemptions, I will only say that it seems to me that the state would virtually tax its own agencies and creations by taxing the higher educational institutions. These have been built up by the state almost as much as the common-school system itself. They stand in most intimate relations to that common-school system, and to the ongoing of the state itself. Taxes on them would not enrich the state. It would be like taking out of one pocket to put into another pocket. Besides, I do not know but that the supreme court of the United States would decide, as in the Dartmouth College case, that the colleges are the result of a contract between the private donors and their trustees, and that a law taxing them is "a law impairing the obligation of a contract."

The taxation of church property is much less objectionable. The churches are indeed just as essential to the well-being of the state, but they stand in quite a different relation to the state. They have not been built up by the state. Religion is more independent of the state than education is, or ever can be made. Church proprety can be taxed without working any harm to religion, or to the interests of the state, or without infringing the constitution of the United States, and I am rather inclined to think that it should be taxed.

With high respect, gentlemen, I remain,

Your obedient servant,

A. L. PERRY.

TAXATION OF DEPOSITS IN SAVINGS BANKS.

BY THE

COMMITTEE OF ASSOCIATED SAVINGS BANKS.

To the Honorable Board of Commissioners on the Revision of Taxation:

The Committee of Associated Savings Banks, of the State of Massachusetts, have the honor of submitting to you the following considerations upon savings banks, and the taxation of their deposits.

These institutions, while still completely fulfilling their original purpose in taking care of the savings of labor, and thereby promoting thrift and industry, have acquired a political and financial importance not less beneficent to the Commonwealth.

Thirty or forty years since, the population consisted almost entirely of persons born on the soil,—descendants of the original settlers. Property was widely distributed, and the larger portion of the inhabitants were interested in the possession of real estate. It may be said, generally, that this was a Commonwealth of farmers, bred in habits of economy and industry, of respect for law, religion and learning, and having the sense of independence and responsibility, which the possession of property is calculated to give. And from all this has risen the wealth and power and high civilization which have heretofore given character to the state.

But there has, within a generation, come a great change in population and industry. Agriculture has relatively declined, and a large Western emigration of the steady and intelligent farming population has taken place; manufacturing has become the dominant interest; natives have been drawn from the farm to the mill, and immense numbers of persons of foreign birth have also been attracted by manufacturing interests, so that now we have a very large population dependent upon wages for a livelihood, with no fixed interest in the soil and institutions of the state, except through the savings banks in which they are depositors or from which they are borrowers.

Of the total population, in 1870, of 1,457,351 souls, there were of foreign birth and extraction 626,211, which is 15,803 more than the total population in 1830, and is forty-three per cent. of the present population.

And here the savings banks step in, and, by attracting to their vaults the savings of labor, and by enabling operatives, through liberal loans, to acquire homes of their own, supply that steadiness and independence of character which comes from a sense of property, and which might otherwise be lost under the changed condition of population and employments. To the statesman it will be readily manifest how vital to the character of the state this action of savings banks becomes.

Financially, these banks have been an important factor in that development of resources and increase of wealth, which have swollen the tax valuation from $897,150,983, in 1863, to $1,763,429,990, in 1873. While the banks do not *literally* create capital, yet practically they may be said to do so. In this state they gather together, in sums from one to one thousand dollars, the petty and smaller savings and hoardings of people, which, if kept in the pockets of depositors, could give little or no aid, *as capital*, to industry, but which, in the hands of the banks, have been loaned within the state, to the extent of $160,000,000 in round numbers. These deposits, dispersed among the depositors, could constitute no available loaning fund. The overflowing waters of a river answer no purposes of navigation, but, when confined within its banks, become the highway of commerce.

This relation of the banks to the industrial enterprise of the state is of modern growth, and is too important to be ignored in any legislation concerning them.

With reference to taxation, under the present laws, the savings banks expose, to a tax of three-fourths of one per cent. per annum, the full amount of their deposits; and it is the opinion of a gentleman long conversant with the management of one of these banks, and who has been an assessor in a large town for twenty years, that a tax of one-half of one per cent. per annum would net a larger revenue than could possibly be collected from the deposits, if they were remitted to the depositors and liable to the full average taxation of the state.

A large portion of these deposits, in individual possession, would be exempt from any tax under existing laws; and, of the remainder, fully one-third would escape taxation, as it is a well-ascertained fact that, under no system yet devised by any state, can more than two-thirds of the actual value of personal property be reached for purposes of taxation. In addition to this, it should be noted that savings-banks deposits are not only taxed in the hands of the banks, but go to the production of new, tangible, taxable values on a large scale, and these values are subject to full taxation.

In 1863 the banks held $56,000,000 of deposits, with mortgage loans of $16,000,000 in round numbers. In the decade from 1863 to 1873 the deposits had increased to $202,000,000, and the mortgage loans to $100,000,000. In this decade there were erected in the state, 59,762 dwelling-houses,—nearly one-third of the whole number standing in 1863. We have no statistics as to the erection of new mills, stores, shops, barns, etc.; but the proportion of these probably exceeds that of dwelling-houses. Now, the $84,000,000 of increased mortgage-loans have been principally taken for these new structures, which would not and could not have been built without the aid obtained from the banks. It is a common practice throughout the state to arrange for savings-bank loans in anticipation of building; and it is a common saying that towns have been built up by the savings banks. Of the remaining $60,000,000 loaned within the state, a considerable sum has gone to the erection of buildings, though this sum has been borrowed upon other than real estate security.

Perhaps no more ingenious system could be devised to obtain a large revenue, than that of bringing money into sight, by inducing deposits in savings banks, where it is made effective as capital and subjected to a moderate tax, and then taxing, at the full rate, the values this money creates.

Admitting all this, it may be said that the banks can stand an increased taxation without impairing their usefulness.

Anything like equal taxation with that imposed upon property in individual possession is clearly unjust in itself; for the use of capital by savings banks is severely restricted, with a view to the safety of depositors and the keeping of capital at home. Investments are strictly limited to a few home securities and U. S. bonds. Savings banks are not free, as individuals are, to seek such investments as they may deem most profitable, either within or without the state. It is not just, therefore, that their deposits should bear the same burden of tax as free capital, unless their franchise is considered as a fair equivalent for the limitations imposed upon them.

Now, the franchise is of no value to any one, there being no capital stock and no shareholders,—the whole office of savings banks being the safe investment of deposits and the distribution of the interest to depositors.

But cannot the banks stand a tax of one per cent. per annum?

During the war, investments in U. S. bonds, and the high premiums on gold interest, gave the banks more than normal profits; and, since the war, sales of these bonds at a profit have sustained dividends to a considerable extent. Many banks now paying annual dividends of six per cent. have ceased to pay extra dividends as they formerly did, and many others must soon do the same. Should the present tax be increased, most of the banks cannot pay six per cent. annually, and the effect of reduced dividends would be a partial arrest of new deposits, and the rapid withdrawal of present deposits, particularly of that large amount which comes from other states. Capital would leave the state in quest of more profitable investment, and loans might have to be called in, and pecuniary embarrassments would follow. Either this would inevitably occur, or a higher rate of interest on loans would be demanded by the banks and have to be paid,—equally to the detriment of business interests.

The foregoing considerations, we think, fully meet any objections to the practical operation of savings banks, in attracting deposits to a certain extent, which may be classed as capital; and, if complaint should be made by some few towns on this point, it should be borne in mind that the law of this attraction probably operates with considerable uniformity throughout the state. If so, all the towns stand on nearly an equal footing in this regard. To the extent, then, of three-quarters of one per cent. per annum on all deposits, large and small, originally exempt or not exempt from taxation, coming from each town, it is released from so much state taxation, and such release, it is believed, is more than equivalent to the revenue any town could obtain by returning the deposits of its inhabitants to their respective owners. It is not claimed that inequalities here and there may not be found; but, for all practical purposes of taxation, we think this conclusion must stand.

It would, therefore, seem that the amount of the tax on savings banks, the method of its collection and application are, in the existing state of things, as nearly as is practicable, all that can be desired.

ALBERT BOWKER,
Treas. of East Boston Savings Bank.

C. J. HOLMES,
Treas. of Fall River Five Cents Sav. Bank.

JAMES ADAMS,
Pres. Warren Inst. for Savings, Charlestown.

L. MALTBY,
Treas. of Northampton Inst. for Savings.

A. H. EVANS,
Pres. of Boston Five Cents Sav. Bank.

THE MASSACHUSETTS INCOME-TAX.

By ALANSON W. BEARD, of Boston,

For Repeal of Law;

GEORGE S. PENDERGAST, of Boston,

Against Repeal of Law;

Dr. A. Z. BROWN, of Cambridge,

From Argument delivered by him before the House Committee on the Judiciary, March 21, 1873,

Against Repeal.

THE MASSACHUSETTS INCOME TAX.

By ALANSON W. BEARD, Esq., of Boston.

The income tax of Massachusetts is upon an income derived from a profession, trade, or employment. It is a special tax upon the proceeds of labor, not a general tax upon *all* income. Income from capital, whether invested in real estate or otherwise, is not included. This tax is not levied upon the income of the year in which the tax is laid, but upon the income of the previous year, no matter whether that income has been wholly spent or partly saved, to be also taxed as property on hand the first of May. The income of the previous year may have been all used up in expenses; sickness or business misfortune may entirely cut off any income the year the tax is made; but, nevertheless, the law knows no abatement. The tax is to be paid upon the money expended in the past year's house-rent, and other family expenses, whether or not there is anything earned with which to pay such expenses the present year. This is an exact statement of the theory of the Massachusetts income tax. The amount of exemption does not change the principle.

The generally accepted theory of taxation is to tax the *property* of the people equally; to tax each person for what he is really worth, that *all* may share in the public expense in proportion to their means. But this tax is on that which has passed away in expenses, or, if saved, is invested in property liable to taxation. It is not a tax upon a person's property, but upon his life, health, and capacity to work the previous year.

The theory of taxation in the laws of this state, is more to tax a person for what he has in possession, rather than on the balance he is really worth. If one has real estate or merchandise the first of May, the law makes no exemptions for debts, but taxes alike what he owns and what he owes. The income tax goes further in injustice, even, than this principle of taxing all in possession. If the income has been expended, it is taxed, though not in possession; if saved and invested in property of any kind, it is taxed twice; first, as the income which acquired the property, and then the property itself is taxed. The double taxation, arising from taxing the income of the past year, and also taxing the property in which that income has been invested, is readily seen; but that part of the income not saved, is also twice taxed.

It is an admitted principle of political economy that the consumer pays the taxes. Taxes become a part of the cost of every article produced or sold, and the price is increased thereby. The tax nominally paid by the maker and seller, is really paid by the purchaser who *finally* uses or consumes the article.

Apparently, the Sears estate, in Boston, pays a large amount of taxes to the city and state, when, really, it is not the tax-payer. The tenant first finds the tax in his rent, then it enters into the cost of that which he manufactures or sells, and is paid by his customers; and so on, till at last it reaches the *final* consumers, who really pay the tax originally assessed. He who expends five hundred dollars in a year, pays just so much tax as is involved in the production of what the expenditure is for; and he who expends five thousand dollars, is a larger tax-payer in proportion to his larger consumption. The income having been spent, he has, in spending that income, really paid, in the consumption, all proper tax upon it, and the tax upon that income is as much double, as if he saved it and invested it in taxable property.

As before said, the theory of taxation in Massachusetts statutes, seems to be the taxation of all in possession of the tax-payer, without regard to the amount owed on account of the property in possession. The income of the past year is not property in possession of the tax-payer. If he has saved anything from it, it is in property subject to tax; if he has spent it, it is not on hand, and there is no property from which to collect the tax. Taxes should be levied on property that is itself security for the tax being paid. What lien has the state on an expended income? A professional man may have had in eighteen hundred and seventy-three, an income from his profession of $25,000. He lives liberally; is educating his family, and expends the whole,—in fact has no property,—and is entirely dependent, with his family, upon the continuance of his life and health. In eighteen hundred and seventy-four the tax is levied upon this income of the past year. But health has failed and he is unable to continue in that profession upon the past income of which he is taxed. Of course, the tax cannot be collected as there is nothing to levy upon for this tax. In case of death, the result would be the same. It is a poor system of taxation that has no security for the collection of its taxes. That which is taxed should have tangible value,—something which can be seized and sold for taxes due thereon.

This special tax upon income derived from a profession, trade, or employment, is a discrimination against labor, and in favor of capital. Income from capital invested is not taxed; the capital itself is only taxed. A person may have a large amount of real estate, so situated as to require his whole time and attention, and the results of that attention be a large income over and above the interest on the capital invested. This income is not taxed. But if his investment is mercantile or manufacturing, he is taxed on his capital and his credit; and, if he makes anything above the interest, he is taxed on that profit. It is, therefore, an extra tax upon enterprise and industry, which should be favored rather than burdened. Income from capital invested in corporations, is not taxed; but a private individual or firm engaged in manufacturing, is liable to this tax, in addition to the tax upon the capital employed. It is, therefore, a discrimination in favor of corporate capital against individual enterprise.

The oppressiveness of this tax upon salaried persons is so evident as to need no illustration.

So far, I have treated this tax upon the supposition that it is carried out strictly in accordance with the letter of the law; but the practice of assessors is not alike in the different towns and cities of the state. A few years since, and this tax was only enforced in two or three of the suburbs of Boston. It is now a dead letter in many portions of the state. Each board of assessors is practically a court in itself,—making its own interpretation and its own practice. In Cambridge, Brookline and most of the suburbs of Boston, where enforced at all, the tax is levied as heretofore stated. Before Roxbury and Charlestown were annexed to Boston, the practice in those cities was the same. In some of the towns around Boston, this tax is ignored entirely, as they wish to induce the residence of mercantile and salaried men. In Boston, the practice of the assessors has been different from the letter of the law, and from that of the other places mentioned, in this respect: — that portion of the income saved and invested in property subject to taxation, is exempted. A merchant or manufacturer living in Roxbury or Charlestown finds an entirely different principle since annexation. Two equal partners, doing business in Boston,—one living in Cambridge and one in Boston,—make $20,000 in a year, and invest the gain in additional stock or other taxable property. The one living in Cambridge is taxed on $10,000 where the Boston partner goes clear. But this liberality of the Boston assessors, shows more glaringly the oppressiveness of this tax upon the junior partner, and the professional or salaried man, who have saved nothing and are taxed the same as elsewhere, on their expended income.

If the injustice of this tax is acknowledged, that should be sufficient for its abolishment, without considering its effect upon the public finances; but every effort for its repeal has been met by a clamor, from more or less of assessors, that it would not do to let go so large a source of income. It is impossible to obtain any data from assessors' returns to show how much the state derives from this source. The proportion of state tax is very small compared to other taxes paid, and the effect upon the state treasury of this tax, is hardly noticeable. From data obtained in eighteen hundred and seventy-one from U. S. Internal Revenue returns of previous years,—but which data I have mislaid, and am therefore unable to give here,—I was convinced that the state itself had never received over $30,000 in any year, provided the tax had been impartially assessed and collected. The annexation of Roxbury, Dorchester, Brighton, West Roxbury and Charlestown to Boston, has cut off very much of this tax, because of the different practice of the Boston assessors. Cambridge assesses a respectable amount in this way, especially upon that class who do business in Boston.

This tax is oppressive and unjust to individuals, and of very little benefit to the community. It is an easy way for the assessors to assess so much for income. The tax-payer of moderate means cannot afford to contest, and the rich man gets off, perhaps, easier this way, than to disclose the property he really has. Rich men who are large holders of personal property frequently neglect to give in a sworn statement, as they think their taxes will be less if they leave it to the assessors to doom them. A little effort on the part of the assessors would make these men bring in their sworn statements, and soon make up for all loss on account of doing away with this income tax.

It is said that abolishing this tax would be unjust to the small towns around Boston; that many men do business in Boston, pay taxes on their capital in Boston, and only sleep in these towns; that these are really "bed-room" towns. Where men sleep, they generally own or hire houses. The fact that these towns are convenient to Boston, for such purpose, has built them up. Every new comer adds to the taxable property, and increases the value of real estate. These men have families, who, with them, are consumers in these towns, and whose consumption builds up and supports the business of these "bed-room" towns.

Every man doing business in a city and residing in a suburban town becomes of necessity a tax-payer in that town, on his own and his family's consumption, and on the real estate he occupies.

This peculiar income tax is not in accordance with the spirit of the people or the usage of the other states; but is peculiar to this state alone. Most of the older states *have had* a tax, in some form, similar in spirit, but without exception, have repealed and reformed their laws.

To sum up: the income tax should be abolished because it is a partial tax; a tax upon a special class of incomes, the proceeds of labor, and therefore a discrimination in favor of capital, and against labor and enterprise; because it is not in accordance with the principle of the tax-payer paying on what he is actually worth; because it is in violation of the theory of taxing the citizen for all he has in his possession; because there is no present property, no security in that which is taxed, to insure the payment of the tax; because it is a tax upon the *past* life and health of the citizen; and because, under all circumstances, it is double taxation, and therefore unequal, unjust and oppressive.

INCOME FROM AN ANNUITY, AND INCOME FROM PROFESSION, TRADE OR EMPLOYMENT.

By GEO. S. PENDERGAST, Esq.,

For many years Chairman of the Assessors of Charlestown.

The assessment of income, as a specific item, I consider eminently equitable; and I think the changing the law, so as to exempt two thousand dollars thereof from assessment, instead of one thousand, was a mistake in legislation.

The theory of the law of taxation is, that taxes are assessed upon persons and property in accordance with ability to pay. The *result* of taxation is protection and privilege to the whole community, individually and collectively.

It seems to me that the law assessing income was based upon this theory, viz.: Every person who can, by his profession, trade or employment, earn or make over one thousand dollars, is better off pecuniarily than the average of his fellow-men, and, therefore, once only, he should be required to pay a tax on so much of said income as is clearly above that average. But the law, in its wisdom and conservatism, says this tax shall not be assessed by a judgment or an estimation, as other personal estate is, but it shall be upon actual results; and, therefore, it shall be upon the income of the previous year, when it is known beyond question what has been done. Objection is made to this tax on the ground that it is a tax, or an assessment, upon a person's ability. This is a mistake. It is not so. It is an assessment upon the result of his ability to earn and make, favored by condition and circumstances; and the measure thereof is the result,—a very safe and unerring measure for the past, but not in any sense, in this case, a measure for the future. Every year must be measured by the result of that same year in which the income has accrued, and the tax thereon cannot be assessed until after it has been realized. Does this tax differ materially in principle from the tax on property? For what is property, acquired and possessed, but an evidence of ability to acquire, favored by condition and circumstances?—not an evidence, perhaps, of the result of one year, but, in many instances, the result of a long series of years; or it might have been wholly the result of condition and circumstances. It might have come by inheritance, or bequest, or otherwise, without ability to acquire and make on the part of the possessor; still, the absence of the ability to acquire and make would not enhance his ability to pay a tax; and the tax on property acquired and possessed is assessed, year after year, so long as the person taxed continues to own it,—not for a single year, as income is, but for a series of years. To illustrate my idea of the equity of assessing income, let us suppose A and B are young, enterprising persons, possessing good abilities, and industrious. A chooses farming for his vocation, aud B chooses the legal profession for his. Each must paddle his own canoe, and each commences with a strong arm and determined will. A earns five thousand dollars, and invests it in a farm, at a cost of five thousand dollars. From the time he possesses it he is taxed for it annually, to say nothing of the tax on the money, which he acquires, from year to year, while earning it. B earns five thousand dollars, and he spends it all in procuring an education,—invests it in brain-work as fast as he earns it. No tax is assessed upon it, and he works and studies on until he is, so to speak, master of his profession. But the law assessing the result of his investment, is very chary of his rights. It virtually says, "Wait until there is unmistakable evidence that his investment is a good one, and only on that unmistakable evidence—viz., results—will we assess his income; and that, after we have exempted, say one thousand dollars, —a sum which places him in condition, far above the average of his fellow-men. And the result itself, of one year, shall be no measure or criterion for another year." I think any candid person must say that a law exempting one thousand dollars of the income of B, and taxing the balance, would use B more tenderly than it would A. These are extreme cases, but I think they illustrate the principle fairly. Let us suppose that the law for assessing incomes should be abolished. We will continue the cases of A and B for further illustration. B now has a professional practice which brings him in an income of ten thousand dollars a year net. He hires a good house in the town where A owns his farm, and makes his residence there,—he and his family, of say four children, to educate at the public schools. They want and receive all the common protection and privileges which the community enjoys. He gets his life insured for a large sum, so it will accrue to himself and family to the best advantage, and the balance of his large income he and his family spend in luxury and pleasure every year, leaving nothing to assess except his poll,—viz., two dollars; while A is assessed on his farm to educate the children of B; and, by assessment on the same farm, he furnishes streets, and throws around B and his family the strong protecting arm of the law to guard the safety and lives of his children, so that he may have the *privilege* of educating them,—while, perhaps, the children of A are deprived of the advantages of a good education, because A must pay for his own and the children of B also. Such a condition would place the burden very unequally and unjustly; and yet, if the law assessing incomes was abolished, similar cases in principle would not, by any means, be solitary.

Admit that this income tax is a tax on ability, and in that respect different from any other tax, why then should the law hesitate to tax it? Weighed by the standard of values,—viz., time and labor, which are the bases for all values,—it is an investment as valuable as gold itself,—it is a value which no possessor hesitates, to bring into the market before his fellow-men, for sale; and it is a highly honorable freight of rich and shining merchandise, illuminating the entire pathway of its possessor. And the law does not ask him to pay a tax, only on so much of it as he has actually sold to his fellow-men, and that only once, and then on so much only, as exceeds the sum of one thousand dollars (if the law should be amended to that effect), thereby accepting the theory that all persons have some of this ability to bring to market. But on the very equitable principle of taxing household furniture and mechanics' tools, it refrains from taxing the same until it swells above the average, and then on the excess of that average only. This investment in ability is a peculiarly advantageous one to the possessor, for in gathering a bundle of ideas and judgments for sale, it always originates new ideas and judgments and enlarges old ones, thereby, in each instance, increasing the stock to be drawn from in future. This ability is sold by all classes of men,—by the lawyer, in his opinions; by the doctor, in his prescriptions; by the minister, in his sermons; by the merchant, in his imports and consignments; by the trader, in every package of goods which he sells; by the mechanic and artisan, in every piece of their handiwork; and by the laborer, in the skill with which he wields the implements of labor. This is also indirectly, if not directly, an insurable interest or investment.

Compare the equity of the tax upon a share of corporate stock with the equity of this assessment upon income. The value of an incorporeal right or share in a corporation is determined by the assessors, for the purpose of assessment, on the first day of May—and it may be fixed above its par value—and the tax thereon is a burden upon the owner, by reason of such ownership, for one year forward from first day of May; and yet this incorporeal right may be entirely worthless before the taxable year expires. And this same contingency attaches in a degree to all visible, tangible property which is assessed. There is no more hardship by the possibility of such a contingency in the principle of assessing income, as that is fixed by what has transpired and become an unalterable result.

I trust that the legislature will take such action upon this subject as will make it sure that income, beyond the exemption, will be taxed without regard to what may have been done with it, though, to my mind, the intent and meaning of the law is now clear and explicit; and the exempting of all or a portion of it from assessment, by reason of the investment thereof, is contrary to the intent or meaning of the law, and works a hardship, and is an unjust discrimination, in many cases, in favor of the more prosperous and against the less prosperous, and has in my judgment, done more to render the law, taxing incomes, unpopular, than any other one cause.

THE INCOME TAX.

WHY IT SHOULD BE RETAINED, AND THE IMPORTANCE OF EQUALLY ENFORCING IT.

The following is substantially the argument against the repeal of the income tax, delivered March 21, 1873, before the House Committee on the Judiciary, by Dr. A. Z. Brown, one of the principal assessors of Cambridge:—

Mr. Chairman,—The law taxing income is, I think, of greater importance than is generally supposed. I will state a few facts bearing upon the question of its repeal,—this question, I understand, being under consideration at this time. The following objections against the law have been urged as reasons why it should be repealed:—

First. That the burden of the tax is borne by the middle class and poor salaried men.

Second. That it is double taxation.

Third. That the law is unequally, and never can be equally and properly, enforced.

Fourth. That it induces persons to lie.

Fifth. That it is unjust.

I propose, Mr. Chairman, to notice these objections in the order in which I have just stated them, and I think I shall be able to show that none of them are sound.

1st. Is the burden of the tax borne by the middle class, and poor salaried men?

If this is true, then the law ought to be swept from the statute book at once. But I believe it is not true when the law is properly enforced, but that, on the contrary, the tax falls upon those who are well able to bear it. To illustrate the operations of the law, I take ward two, of Cambridge, not because it is the wealthiest, but because it is the largest ward under my immediate supervision.

Residing in this ward are one thousand three hundred and seven property and income tax-payers. Of this number, three hundred and two are taxed on incomes.

The total value of personal estate and income taxed to residents of said ward is $4,316,650. Of this sum, $1,065,000 is for incomes, being about 25 per cent. of the total value of personal property taxed to residents of the ward, and between one-thirteenth and one-fourteenth of the total valuation of the ward. Deduct $28,000 for abatements from the total value of income, and there remains the sum of $1,037,-000 from which taxes are to be derived. Twenty-seven persons, nearly all of them the wealthiest residents of the ward, pay a tax on income valued at $519,400,—that is, twenty-seven of the three hundred and two individuals in this ward, taxed on incomes, pay more than the remaining two hundred and seventy-five persons,—one hundred and seventy-six of the three hundred and two are taxed on $454,600, and one hundred are taxed on $70,000.

The latter class is composed of the less favored as to property. Repeal the law, and distribute upon property the amount taxed as income, and the share that would fall to these twenty-seven wealthy individuals would be a little less than $200,000, instead of $519,000, as it now is.

These, Mr. Chairman, are important facts, and show conclusively upon what class of persons the burden falls, when the law is properly enforced, and is a complete refutation of the argument that the burden is borne by the middle class and poor salaried men.

2d. Is it double taxation?

Income is made up of earnings, profits, and certain receipts from other sources, during the year next preceding the first day of May. The law has nothing to do with the disposition which has been made of income, whether spent or invested,—it only seeks to know the amount of the income, and what is taxable. All property subject to taxation is taxable the current year, while the income tax is retrospective. It is a tax assessed upon new capital acquired or created, after one and before the next specific time of assessment, which, if not taxed as income, would not be taxed at all until it entered into the following year's valuation. It may, perhaps, be said to be a tax assessed upon a man's good fortune in having acquired or created capital, and if so, who would object to the good fortune, even if obliged to take the income tax with it?

The supreme judicial court, in a recent decision (Wilcox *vs.* County Commissioners of Middlesex, 103 Mass., 544), says, "It is the creation of capital, industry, and skill."

If the foregoing statement is correct, then the charge of double taxation is untrue.

3d. Is the law unequally, and can it be equally and properly, enforced?

There is great diversity of opinion in regard to taxing income. In some cities, the assessors assess income irrespective of what is done with it; while in others, the assessors say to the tax-payer, "If you have invested your income in property that we can tax, we will not tax you on income; but if you have spent it, or invested it where we cannot tax the investment, then we must tax you on income." This I deem to be not only contrary to law, but unjust towards those who are obliged to use their incomes in the support of their families.

The man who is able to save a portion of his income to invest, is in better condition to pay both the income tax and the tax on the investment, than he a tax on his income who has been obliged to consume all of it. These investments are made by those who are the best able to pay taxes, and whose incomes are frequently of great magnitude.

The suggestion made by some to so modify the law that the portion of income invested in taxable property should not be taxed, would, if adopted, abolish the greater portion of the income tax, and throw the burden of the remainder equally upon those of small with those who receive large incomes. A moment's consideration of the subject must convince any one of the injustice of such a law.

Not to tax income because the proceeds have been invested in taxable property, is virtually exempting income from taxation; for these same investments would be taxable the current year, if there were no income tax.

It is only necessary to state the law and facts, to show the absurdity of the rule not to tax income because it has been invested in taxable property. Income follows residence, and is taxable nowhere else; and yet the same income that is taxed to a resident, may have been invested in taxable property in a place other than the residence of the investor; and who will say that both the investment and income are not subject to taxation? And I would ask, What difference does it make whether a person invests in the town where he resides or in another town? There is no necessity of the unequal enforcement, as described above, if the law is rightly interpreted.

4th. It is said that the law is inquisitorial,—that a direct income tax induces persons to make false statements. The same objection can be urged with equal force against taxing personal property; for the assessors are no more dependent upon the tax-payer for an account of his income, than they are for an account of many kinds of personal property, such as state, county, city, town, and railroad bonds, certificates of stocks of all kinds in corporations out of the state (corporations within the state being taxed by the state), notes and mortgages, recorded where the assessors cannot readily obtain a knowledge of them. For an account of these, and of many other kinds of taxable property, the assessors are entirely dependent upon the veracity of the tax-payer. Now is it expedient to repeal the law taxing personal property merely because it is necessary to make inquiries about it, or because some one may misinform the assessors as to the amount possessed by him?

John Stuart Mill, the eminent writer on political economy, thinks the greatest objection to an income tax is that it is a "tax on conscience, and a premium on deception and improbity."

I leave others to judge whether or not this objection is satisfactorily answered. If it is not, then it seems to me there is but one course to pursue, and that is to tax nothing but what is open to and necessarily comes within the knowledge of the assessors, exempting from taxation not only income, but a large portion of personal property, thereby relieving the assessors from the unpleasant duty of inquiring after the whole taxable property belonging to a person. If this mode of taxation is preferred, then establish it by law, and let real estate bear the burden which must necessarily follow with the fact of unequal taxation.

My experience, as principal assessor in a large city for a period of twelve consecutive years, is that individuals are just as ready and honest in rendering an account of their income, as they are of any taxable property they may possess.

5th. Is the law taxing income just?

Upon justice should all laws be based. I think I have demonstrated upon what class the burden falls, when the law taxing income is properly enforced. Now, if it is right for the wealthy, for those who are the best able, for those who receive ample incomes—some of which alone amount to a fortune,—to bear this burden instead of putting an additional one upon those who are less favored as to property, then, Mr. Chairman, the law taxing income is just.

Of the one thousand three hundred and seven property and income tax-payers, to whom I have alluded, eight hundred and twenty-three are taxed on sums varying from $100 to $5,000, showing that a great majority of property-holders are persons of quite limited means. Many of them find it a hardship to pay their taxes, and can ill bear an increase. Repeal the law, and a very considerable number who are able to live in good style, and who enjoy all the benefits and privileges of our social system, which are sustained and protected by taxation, will be almost entirely relieved from its burdens. I refer to those who have no visible property, but receive ample incomes, and make such disposition of them that they cannot be taxed; and also to those who receive annuities derived from property that cannot be reached by taxation. I do not think that these individuals desire to be placed on the list of mere poll-tax payers, and if they should so desire, they ought not to be gratified.

Taxation is a necessity that cannot be got rid of, and every honorable man ought to be willing to bear his share of the burden according to his ability; and I do not understand why it is not just as fair and right to put a portion of the burden upon income, as it is to put it upon property,—why the tax on one is not as easily paid as the tax on the other. Certainly, those who receive ample incomes can pay their taxes with the least inconvenience; and if it is right to tax at all, it is right and humane to place the burden where it will be the least oppressive.

Taxation has become a heavy burden; and who, Mr. Chairman, can so well afford to bear it as those who receive large incomes? They pay their taxes out of their surplus funds, while men of small means pay them out of their living. The amount of tax is so much taken from the comforts and needs of their families. Shall this class be further oppressed?

It is well known to those who have given much attention to the subject, that real estate now bears more than its share of tax. This is so, for the reason that a large amount of personal property, in one way and another, escapes taxation. Increase the tax on real estate (which will be the case, if the income tax is abolished), and it is legislation against the middle classes, who now pay more than their proportionate share of taxes,—against those who are laboring for little homesteads for themselves and their families,—against those who hire tenements, and against the best interests of the state; for in real estate is the home, the comfort, and the well-being of a people.

To show the probable effect upon those who hire tenements, if the law taxing income is repealed, take the one hundred individuals to whom allusion has been made, who are assessed on income valued at $70,000; the amount of tax on this sum, with a rate at $12 per $1,000, would be $840; to each individual it would be $8.40. Put upon property the total amount taxed as income in the ward, which has been taken to show the operations of the law, and these same persons would have to pay, probably, three times $8.40 in increased rents, showing that even poor salaried men are better off with the law in operation than they would be to have it abolished. All that seems to be necessary to make the law just in its operations is, that it shall be equally and impartially enforced; and this is as easily done as the enforcement of any tax law.

Incomes have been and are so large that individual fortunes are built up as it were by magic; and is there any injustice in assessing these large incomes in their first stage of existence? It may be the only tax that will be assessed upon them; for, in their next stage, they may be placed beyond the reach of taxation,—large sums of money being thus disposed of.

There is a disposition on the part of some to evade taxation, in part, if no more,—they adopt the method of declaring a summer resort to be their place of residence,—they reside for a short time in some obscure town, where there is a very low rate of taxation,—they, perhaps, compound with the assessors to be assessed a certain sum,—all for the purpose of paying the least possible amount of tax.

Do these individuals realize the great injustice which, by such conduct, they inflict upon the community to which they properly belong, and in which they ought, in all honor, to pay their taxes? Do they not thus publish to the world that money is of more consequence to them than right and honor? Let such persons hang their heads with shame in the presence of those who have remained faithful to duty, and honestly paid, not only their own, but also the taxes that justly belonged to others.

It seems to me, Mr. Chairman, that from the same motive that actuates these individuals to shirk their just taxation, comes the desire to get rid of the income tax. These people wish to throw the whole burden upon fixed properties, and upon those who use them.

I believe the income tax to be as little burdensome as any tax. None feel taxation with so much hardship as those of little properties and small incomes. Make taxable all income that it is right to tax,—make the exemption sufficient; and, if the law is properly enforced, no injustice will be done, but the burden will fall upon those who are the best able to bear it. And there is no reason why it should not be properly enforced in every city and town in the Commonwealth; and the fact that it is not so enforced causes more dissatisfaction than the law itself.

The charges of double and unequal taxation which are made against the income tax will, I think, upon further examination, prove to be untrue.

If the world stood still, and nothing new were produced, then the income tax would, necessarily, be double taxation; but as there is a continuous reproduction of capital, and as capital will, at the rate of six per cent. per annum, in about twelve years reproduce itself, it is fair to assume that the income tax reaches nothing but the new capital, which is the only object sought by the law.

A lawyer gives his services in exchange for a house that was taxed the previous May. In taxing the lawyer for an income, do we tax the house? By no means; we but tax him for the value of his services, the house merely showing this value. A grocer's profits are made up of the daily earnings of his customers, and so on in other branches of trade. The products of the farm are entirely new capital. The manufacture of raw material into beautiful fabrics, and into articles of use and value, is the making of capital, which serves in exchange to make up the profits of the grocer, merchant, banker, and the so-called middleman. The erection of dwellings and other buildings, and the increased value of lands by improvements having been made, are the creation of capital. A man's thought, when producing results which can be reduced to a money value, is also the creation of capital. A man may have the good fortune to be in possession of a large amount of merchandise when a scarcity of such goods occurs,—this would give him a new capital in the enhanced value of his goods; or, if it could not be considered new capital, the income tax would reach him through his good fortune. This would operate, in some degree, to the relief of those who have been less fortunate.

Whenever any property—whether land, houses, merchandise, stocks, bonds, notes, or any other kind of property—is used in trade, and, by reason of buying and selling, a net gain is produced over and above what are the specific rents, dividends, and interest of such property, the net gain constitutes a capital which has been created by industry and skill, and is taxable as income.

The income tax touches none but those who have been blessed with good fortune; and the fact that the exemption of a certain portion of income from taxation operates more to the benefit of those receiving small incomes—just in proportion to the amount of income received—than to those receiving large incomes, is another feature of the justice and humanity of the law. Those who oppose the law taxing income—having been driven from the position that it is double taxation—now say that it is unequal taxation, and that it is intended only to "squeeze the rich," and that the rich ultimately make the poor pay the tax, by charging them higher for everything they consume.

Let us see what John Stuart Mill says upon this subject: "Nevertheless, an income tax is felt to be indispensable on our present financial system, because without it there are actually no means, recognized by existing opinion, of making the richer classes pay their just share of taxation,—a thing which cannot be done by any system of taxes on consumption yet devised." He also says: "The maxim that equal means should pay equal taxes has nothing to rest upon, unless the means intended are those which are available to pay taxes from. What forms no part of a person's means of expenditure forms no part of his means for paying taxes." What stronger evidence can be adduced to show, not only the justice, but the absolute necessity, of the income tax, if all are to be taxed according to their ability? Is not a man's income his means of expenditure? and, if so, is it not his means of paying taxes?

Those persons who possess but small means, and those means not available for expenditures, find it no easy thing to pay taxes. For this class there is no escape from taxation; with them there is no concealment; all they possess is open to, and at the mercy of, the assessors; and they are frequently in debt for what they pay taxes upon. To relieve the richer classes of the income tax—which to them is no burden, and who always have at command available means—and to distribute any portion of it upon those whose only means of expenditure consist of what is produced by daily toil, and which would come within the limits of what would be exempted by the law taxing income, would be an act that could not be justified by any law of right; neither would such an act escape the odium of unequal taxation, according to the testimony I have just cited. There must be a certain amount of money raised by taxation as a means of public expenditure, and our laws should be so framed that taxation will not oppress one class more than another.

The income tax is the least oppressive of any, because it is a tax assessed upon available means. It is a just tax, because it falls upon those who have accumulated the extra or newly-created means upon which the assessment is made, and it affords the only way yet devised, by which the burden of taxation can be equally distributed.

It may be said that some of the property taxed as income is held but a short time before it becomes taxable as property, and, therefore, the income tax is not altogether just. Precisely so may it be with property regularly assessed on the first day of May; for in a few days thereafter it may be destroyed; but this would not relieve the owner of the property so destroyed from the liability of the tax assessed upon it. We have had an illustration of this fact in the devastating fire in Boston. The question was raised that a portion of the tax ought to be abated, because the owners were deprived of the use and benefit of the property in about six months after the assessment was made; but it was decided that the assessors had no power to abate for such cause; neither could the city remit or refund any portion of the tax. So it is with articles of consumption,—they may be used up in a short time after they have been assessed; and all perishable productions are in the same condition of uncertainty as to the time they may be held after an assessment is made upon them.

To illustrate the fact more fully, that those who hire tenements are better off with the income tax in operation than they would be to have it repealed,—take a man with a salary of $3,000 per annum, who pays $600 rent for a house. The tax on the salary, after exempting $1,000, would be, at the high rate of $15 per $1,000, $30. The total amount of taxable income is about one-fourteenth of the total valuation. Now, repeal the income tax, and put upon property the amount taxed as income, and the rents should be increased about one-fourteenth to make the return to the landlord the same as now, which would increase the rent on the house $42.85 against the income tax of $30.

A gentleman who has pursued this subject with great pertinacity, both before the Senate and also before the House committee on the judiciary, stated, in his argument before the committee, that he believed the income tax to be the only just tax, provided all other taxes were abolished. I accepted his admission that the income tax was a just tax; but that it is the only just tax, I do not admit; for to tax nothing but incomes would exempt entirely from taxation millions' worth of property which produces no income, but is held only for a rise in value.

Constantine Baer, a distinguished Italian political economist, in his work on "Property and Taxation," says: "The primary requisite of just taxation is, that every one should be taxed in proportion to his means."

Mr. Mill says: "In order, therefore, to reach the whole of his means, we ought to tax his income, and also his land and capital."

I know of no more equitable way of raising a revenue than to tax all men according to their ability, whether this be a tax on real estate, on personal property, or on income, after making a suitable deduction. There is no more reason why a man's income should be exempt from taxation than there is that his real or personal estate should be.

The law taxing income, when properly enforced (as it may be), will, upon reflection, commend itself to every person who has a desire to mitigate the hardships of those who find life a hard struggle, and upon whom taxation falls with a relentless hand.

For twelve years I have enforced this law precisely as stated, and have taxed income derived from all sources, irrespective of what use has been made of it, in the same manner as other property not specially exempted by law; and my observation of its operations during that time has convinced me, more than any mere theoretical reasoning could have done, that the tax is as just and as easily borne as any, and that there is no more difficulty in applying the law taxing income, than the law taxing personal property.

DISCOUNT ON TAXES.

By ASSESSORS OF FITCHBURG,

AND

ALDEN S. BRADFORD, Assessor of Kingston.

DISCOUNT ON TAXES.

Sections 41 and 42 of chapter 11 of the General Statutes, should be repealed.

The effect of the law is a discrimination against the poor man, and in favor of the rich. The rate this year has to be 93 cents higher on $1,000, in this city, because five per cent. discount is allowed to those who can pay their taxes before a given day, while those who cannot pay have to bear the burden of twelve per cent. interest added to their taxes. The rate is announced at $20, for instance; then we turn round and take $19. A falsehood goes out to the world, and into the books of statistics, to our detriment. The law permitting towns and cities to charge a high rate of interest on taxes not paid, is a complete remedy for slowness, and the discount rule ought to be annulled. The banks and rich men, who are best able to pay taxes, derive the chief benefit from the rule.

In this city, an appropriation of $10,000, with $12,000,000 valuation, is equivalent to an increase in the rate of 83⅓ cents per $1,000. The whole amount of assessors' warrants for eighteen hundred and seventy-three was $222,259.46. Of this amount, $187,703.44 was paid previous to September sixteenth, eighteen hundred and seventy-three, and the discount allowed for prompt payment was $9,876.13. The amount of taxes abated to September fifteenth, was $725.55. This left uncollected on the sixteenth of September, $23,951.34.

The ordinance, as it stands, provides that the tax bills shall be in the hands of the treasurer and collector on the first day of September. All who voluntarily pay their taxes before the sixteenth of the month are to be allowed a discount of five per cent. on the amount thereof; after which time no discount shall be allowed, but interest shall be charged from October first, at the rate of twelve per cent. per annum until payment be made. This, considering five per cent. is allowed for fifteen days, is equivalent to one hundred and twenty per cent. per annum. The treasurer can borrow all the money he needs at seven per cent. per annum. Abolish the discount—have interest at the rate of twelve per cent. per annum, commencing October first, and it is safe to assume that seventy-five per cent. of those who take the benefit of the discount rule, will pay by that time, for the simple reason that they will not pay twelve per cent. interest when they can borrow at seven per cent. Suppose they do not pay,—the city has a lien upon the bodies of its single-poll payers, upon all real estate, and practically upon all machinery. We receive twelve per cent. interest, and can borrow at seven per cent., making a gain of five per cent. annually.

In whose favor does the discount rule work? It is safe to say that ninety per cent. of the tax-payers representing the $23,951.34 uncollected taxes on the sixteenth of September, paid less than $100 tax. From a variety of causes they did not pay before September sixteenth, and were obliged to pay 83 cents per $1,000 valuation more than those who obtained the discount. In eighteen hundred and seventy-two, the number of persons who paid taxes on property was one thousand nine hundred and seventy-three,—of these, one thousand six hundred and forty-four persons paid taxes between $2 and $100, or 83⅓ per cent. of the whole. In eighteen hundred and seventy-three, of the one thousand nine hundred and fifty-eight dwelling-houses taxed, at least one thousand five hundred were in the hands of the middle and poorer classes.

Those persons who possess but small means, and those means not available for expenditure, find it no easy thing to pay taxes. For this class, there is no escape from taxation; with them there is no concealment; all they possess is open to and at the mercy of the assessors; and they are frequently in debt for what they pay taxes upon. There must be a certain amount of money raised by taxation, as a means of public expenditure, and our laws should be so framed that taxation will not oppress one class more than another.

J. F. SIMONDS,
J. M. CARPENTER,
E. P. LORING,
Assessors of Fitchburg.

DISCOUNT ON TAXES.

Section 41 of chapter 11 of the General Statutes, authorizing towns to allow a discount for voluntary payment of taxes, has been the cause of a vast aggregate of little petty wrongs to individuals, without any corresponding advantage to the public. For example: A town votes (not a quarter of the voters, perhaps, understanding the effect of such a vote) that all taxes be made payable January first, and that a discount of ten per cent. be allowed on all taxes voluntarily paid before October first,—the reasons assigned being that the collection of taxes will be thereby facilitated, and that otherwise the treasurer might be compelled to hire money for current expenses. The result of the vote is, that a few resident tax-payers who have money at command, will, by payment of their taxes in September, virtually loan their amount to the treasurer for three months, at the rate of forty per cent. a year, at the expense of all other resident tax-payers, and to the special wrong of non-residents, who are not entitled to notice under the statute (section 25), and cannot keep posted as to the votes of the town.

Neither of the reasons named in favor of such a vote is of much weight. In the town of Kingston, for the last ten years, the taxes have been made payable October tenth. During that time they have been paid far more promptly than in previous years, when a discount was allowed; and I think that in but one of those years has the collector had occasion, on settlement, to credit himself with uncollected taxes. A rule of prompt payment, adopted and enforced in any town, will prove more potent than any allowance of discount, which, by those who do not avail themselves of its benefits, is usually deemed a warrant for postponing payment indefinitely. And, if a town needs money in advance of the taxes, it can always be had at six or seven per cent., instead of at forty. Section 41, chapter 11, is a relic of the past, not in keeping with the cash system of transacting business now in vogue.

ALDEN S. BRADFORD,
One of the Assessors of Kingston.

THE

TAXATION OF LIFE INSURANCE COMPANIES.

By BENJ. F. STEVENS,

President New England Mutual Life Insurance Company.

TAXATION OF LIFE INSURANCE COMPANIES.

To the Committee on Taxation:

GENTLEMEN:—It is not altogether possible to give, in the narrow space of an official correspondence, all the reasons that can be urged against a tax upon life-insurance companies. Those which occur to my mind have been spoken and written about scores of times. In this state, on two separate occasions (1862 and 1870), the subject was before the legislature for consideration, when exhaustive hearings were had before the appropriate committees. The subject has also received the attention of Congress, as will be stated further on.

In 1862, at a time when the sinews of war were more needed by our state than in any previous period of our history, the subject of levying a tax upon the business of life insurance was first agitated, and so great was the alarm among all classes of the community that the legislature might, in its anxiety to provide ways and means, do a great moral wrong, which would result in incalculable injury to the business, that the insurance commissioners of Massachusetts—men of understanding and capacity, who were selected for the special purpose of communication between the companies and the state—felt it to be their duty to call the attention of the legislature to the subject of taxation, especially as affecting life-insurance companies. In their seventh annual report to the legislature, dated June 20, 1862, these gentlemen—Messrs. Elizur Wright and George W. Sargent—wrote as follows:—

"In times of war, when self-preservation calls aloud for the utmost exertion, and every resource, the temptation not to neglect institutions so profitable as insurance companies are commonly supposed to be, and so full of available funds, is multiplied manifold. But we think a little careful reflection will show that insurance companies can never be wisely taxed for the general purposes of government, and that it is better not to tax them, even for the purpose of supervising their own operations, beyond the benefit which they themselves, as institutions, derive from such supervision. So far as individuals have money invested in those institutions, let them be taxed, no more and no less than if it were invested elsewhere. This does not operate to discourage, depress or embarrass the institution. But a tax laid upon the institution itself, in its corporate capacity, is only so much penalty on its corporate existence. The worst possible time to exact such a penalty, is war-time. Then, every institution specially adapted to times of peace is put to a strain. The more troublous the times, the more tenderly let us cherish the institutions which knit into one whole the structure of our industry. There seems, in regard to insurance companies of all kinds, no valid reason why every person who is in any way connected with them should not be taxed for the support of the government according to his ability as an individual, and any tax on the company after that, is in fact taxing him beyond his share, and, if he is a policy-holder, exacting a penalty on his prudence. Life-insurance companies are built up almost entirely of contracts extending over the entire life of policy-holders, or the largest part of it, and requiring small annual payments to be accumulated at compound interest, in order to pay large sums at the close of life, or at a very advanced age.

"These annual premiums are carefully calculated on certain assumptions as to future interest, the average vitality or chances of after life at given ages, and the probable expenses of managing the business. When money is invested to accumulate at compound interest, the effect of taking out at an early stage, or establishing a regular leak, even of small dimensions, becomes very surprising when we contemplate the ultimate result.

"Suppose the accumulation of a mutual life-insurance company is one million of dollars, and instead of being contented with taxing individual members according to their means, the state taxes the funds of the company one per cent. for five years, thus obtaining for the public use fifty thousand dollars. The managers of the company, afraid to drive away business by asking more of new-comers, or withholding from old policy-holders the usual facilities for keeping up their policies, very naturally proceed as if nothing had happened, their accumulation still being ample for all proximate calls. At the end of thirty years from the first imposition of this small temporary tax, their fund, then called into its full play to meet the thickening losses which belong to the mature age of the company, will, at the ordinary rate of interest, be the worse for the tax by the important sum of $241,930. The deficiency may then be found irreparable, causing the premature death of the company, and the saddest havoc and ruin among the multitude of precious hopes clustered around it.

"No state which values its future, or has any sense of the bearing upon it of these great social and prudential institutions, can willingly inflict any such injury on any life-insurance company within its jurisdiction; nor will it, by exercising any power of partial taxation upon the companies of other states, provoke retaliation upon its own."

In the same year (1862), the subject of taxing the funds of life-insurance companies was brought before Congress, and after mature consideration by both Senate and House of Representatives, was defeated. In the course of the Senate debate, Mr. Sherman, of Ohio, moved to strike out of the general tax bill all that related to life-insurance companies, because "the whole capital in life-insurance was taxed under other provisions of the bill,—that is to say, the accumulations or capital of life-insurance companies, being composed of bank, railroad, and other stocks and securities, should not pay a double tax. The most that should be done was to tax the income, but not levy a tax as an insurance company on life-insurance."

Mr. Sumner favored the proposition, and spoke as follows:—

"The business of insurance, as it seems to me, is peculiar. It differs from most others in being not strictly, if I may so say, a money-making business. I know that persons get up insurance companies in order to advance their own interests, but the primary object of the insurance office is to protect other people, particularly the poor,—it is to help the poor. I say, therefore, it is not primarily, as compared with many other businesses, a money-making business. On that account, as it seems to me, it has a title to a certain consideration. Now, what is proposed? A tax on the premiums. What are the premiums? The premiums are themselves a tax. The premiums constitute the tax which the person insured pays for his insurance; and now it is proposed to put a tax on a tax. That is the precise case. I state it in this way in order to simplify it, in order to reduce it, if I may say so, to its most naked form."

The question was asked by Mr. Chandler, of Michigan, "Why do you tax railroads on the gross receipts of their passenger earnings"? to which Mr. Dixon, of Connecticut replied:—

"I will tell you why. That money belongs to them,—it is their money. They spend a portion of it, it is true, in their incidental expenses, just as the insurance companies spend a portion of their funds in transacting their business; but that money belongs to the railroad company,—it is their fund. They do not hold it in trust for anybody. They hold it for themselves The insurance company receives money in trust—a solemn and sacred trust. There can be no more sacred trust than the fund which an insurance company receives from those who take out policies in the office. They hold it for them. They are bound to pay it all out, etc." (See Congressional Debates, 1862.)

In 1870 the subject received the attention of our own legislature, and a very full and exhaustive hearing was had before the committee on expenditures.

Hon. Elizur Wright,—who, as one of the insurance commissioners in 1862, presented his views to the legislature, which have been quoted somewhat at length,—spoke as follows (and, in order to do justice to the remarks of a very eminent authority in all matters connected with life-insurance, I append them in full).

"This bill, or any other of the kind, should be considered in the light of the elementary principles that apply to the subject of taxation.

"Every government requires pecuniary means. The proper method of acquiring these means depends upon the nature of the government, whether it exists for its own benefit or pleasure, or for the benefit of the people at large. A government which does not—with a desire to promote the greatest good—regard the interests of all, but looks simply to its own aggrandizement and pleasure, will, of course, resort to all those indirect methods of taxation which will fill its treasury with the least disturbance to individuals. It will tap the great channels of commerce, through which the products that feed and clothe the people pass on their way from producer to consumer, or the great reservoirs in which people of moderate estates combine small capitals, in order to enjoy the advantage which a large capital has over a small one in regard to productive power. In either of these methods people are made to contribute to the support of government to a certain extent, and often to an unnecessarily large extent, without their knowing it, which is a great advantage for a despotic or selfish government. For a government *of* the people and *for* the people the facility of collection is of no account compared with the consideration of equitable assessment. And here arises the question, What *is* equitable assessment? It is not assessment in the ratio of consumption, for this would not necessarily demand more from the richest than from the poorest; and the protection of the rich costs the government far more than the protection of the poor. It is not assessment in the ratio of production, for that, by raising the price of products, results largely in a tax on consumption. It is plain to see that in a community consisting of individuals all more or less rich, an equitable assessment would be in the ratio of property, of whatever kind, taken at its market value, provided the property is so used or situated as to cost the government in the same ratio for its protection. But in a community which consists of rich and poor, in which the possessions of an individual over and above his own body and soul vary from zero to millions of dollars, the *pro-rata* principle of assessment cannot hold good in expediency, if it does in abstract justice. In such a community, and especially where the acquired wealth of thousands stands either at zero or above it by not more than the consumption of a few months, there are apt to exist what are called "dangerous classes," or at least classes that might easily become dangerous. This really means that it costs the government far more to protect the large capitalists, in proportion to their capital, than the small ones. Hence the *ratio* of the tax should increase as the wealth increases. This principle has been recognized to some extent by exempting from taxation properties below a certain sum of value, and by taxing large incomes at a larger percentage than small ones. Whatever may be said of the abstract or mathematical justice of this, there can be no doubt of the expediency of it, especially so far as the *very* rich capitalists are concerned. It must be a grand object with them to protect the wealth they have acquired, or to keep as much of it as possible safely in their own possession. Hence the thing of the greatest importance to them is to annihilate the *danger* of the " dangerous classes." There is no possible way of doing this but one. It cannot be done by alms-giving, nor by increasing wages beyond the rate fixed by the relation of supply and demand, which is only another name for alms. It can only be done by encouraging and tempting the poor to become capitalists by consuming less than their wages or the net product to themselves of their own labor.

"There must be a sort of pivot of taxation somewhere, below which there should be complete exemption, or perhaps not merely that. For the men who possess more than, say $1,000, for each member of their families might wisely tax themselves to encourage the poor in saving, by adding something to their little accumulations, till they are brought up fairly into the class of capitalists, and have secured the sweet of making past labor aid the present,—a condition that is favorable to the greatest industry and the largest production.

" If these considerations have any truth in them, or any application to the present state of facts, there can be very little wisdom in taxing the savings of the poor, it being just the reverse of the statesmanship which the true interests of the rich require. A tax on savings banks, taxes about all the little savings of the poor, for they save little or nothing elsewhere, to any purpose. The only argument I can see for it is, that some of the deposits are owned by rich men. These men, of course, ought to pay a tax on such deposits, and might be made to pay it outside of the bank.

"I deem these remarks pertinent to the question of the bill, because it expressly makes the tax on savings banks the model and measure of that to be levied on life-insurance companies. But—

"1. It does not follow that because the state has a right to tax its citizens on the interests they have in life-insurance corporations as so much personal property, it can, therefore, rightly collect this tax of those corporations themselves.

"2. If the state has a right to tax the deposits of citizens in savings banks, either within or without the state, and collect the tax through the corporations, it does not follow that it can tax the reserves in life-insurance companies, and collect through the companies.

"3. The reserve in a life-insurance policy is not a savings-bank deposit in any such sense as to make it the personal property of the policy-holder, however proper and convenient it may be, for the sake of determining the liabilities of the company, to consider it so. It has been absolutely conveyed and paid to the corporation as part of the consideration for a contract or bond of indemnity, and cannot be withdrawn except according to the terms of the contract, and is, in fact, a part of the said indemnity itself; its remaining in the company *intact* is essential to the power of the corporation to fulfil its contract. Therefore, if the state, having authorized and empowered the corporation to make such a contract, without having inserted in the charter any provision for such taxation, or any premonition of it, steps in and diminishes the corporation's power to fulfil, it undoes its own work, and is, in fact, guilty of bad faith with its own creature. The corporation is bound by its policies, whatever may become of its reserves. If the state, on the plea of taxing the personal property of policy-holders resident in its limits, has taxed their reserves, the companies cannot recover of those policy-holders. What they are to pay, and what they are to receive, is fixed by the terms of their policies. The state, therefore, by this bill, does not tax the personal property of the policy-holders within its jurisdiction, but the whole company, including many persons beyond its jurisdiction, in the ratio of such personal property.

"As life-insurance, in respect of this peculiar contract, is totally different from a mere deposit of savings, the considerations above stated, seem to be fatal to the right of the state to tax the interests of its citizens therein, through the corporation. If it taxes those interests at all, it must do it *outside* of the corporations. But supposing the right of the state to tax the interest of a citizen in a life-insurance company admitted, two questions arise:—

"1. What is the measure or value of such interest?

"2. Is it expedient to tax it at all?

"*First.* As a piece of personal property, what is an individual policy-holder's interest in a life-insurance company worth? What is its money value? Plainly, taking the whole company together, and supposing its net assets equal to the net values of all its policies, this sum is the sum of all the interests, and the interest of the average policy-holder is precisely the net value of his own policy. But in taxation the state does not deal with average or abstract persons, but with flesh and blood individuals. The interest of the individual policy-holder is almost inevitably more or less, and it may be much more or much less than the net value of his policy. If he is a healthy individual, he cannot withdraw the whole net value of his policy if so disposed, but must pay a heavy surrender charge; and if he does not withdraw, the value of his policy, which, without withdrawing, he can only enjoy as a reversion, is proportionally small. Then again, if he is poor, there is a strong chance, enchanced by this very tax, that he will not be able to keep up his policy, in which case he will forfeit the whole value of it, if insured in some of the companies, and a considerable part of it, if insured in any. On the contrary, an invalid policy-holder has an interest much beyond the value of his policy, for a very obvious reason. It would, perhaps, be better for the state to abstain from a mode of taxation, which is sure to be unjust in almost every individual case, however just on the average,—all this on the supposition that the entire premiums have been paid in cash. But it is about as likely as not to be the case, that the premiums have been paid partly in notes, and then a part, if not the whole, of the reserve on the policy, will consist of the interest-bearing notes of the insured. The use to the company of the *principal* of these notes, is simply to diminish its risk to the same extent; and that is all the use to *it* of the principal of a cash deposit. But to the policy-holder the cash deposit will be valuable to his heirs at his death, while the note deposit, having answered its purposes of bearing interest to the company, and limiting its risk, will be of no value to them. Of course *it* cannot be a subject of taxation inside or outside of the company.

" *Second.* Is it expedient?

" The only persons benefited by life-insurance,—the only persons to whom it is a really profitable investment,—are those whose families, in case of their death, would be left a burden upon either private or public charity. Persons possessed of sufficient estate to leave their dependents, at death, in comfortable circumstances, do not, as a general rule, increase their estates by life-insurance; but, on the contrary, their connection with life-insurance—if such insurance is equitably managed—is a tax upon their estates for the benefit of others, who possess no other estates than their policies. At all events, this is true to such an extent, that rich men can never understandingly resort to life-insurance to escape civil taxes, unless the rate of taxation is far higher than it has ever yet been in this country.

" Now let us see what is the real work actually done and to be done by life-insurance. By the returns to the insurance commissioner of this Commonwealth, it appears that in 1868, the various companies doing more or less business in this state, paid about four thousand death-claims, amounting to $11,500,000, or, on the average, $2,875 each. Making some allowance for multiplication of policies by the same persons, in the same or different companies, the companies may be estimated to consist of half a million members, each insured to the average amount of $3,134, and having an interest in the company, considered as a savings bank, of $280. As the death-claims in 1868 averaged $257 below the average of outstanding policies, it is plain that in that year the poorer rather than the richer class of policy-holders took the benefit. Each on the average received from his company $2,618, and at the same time his own little "savings bank" deposit of $257 was withdrawn, which added to the indemnity from the company made the whole sum $2,875. But four thousand times this average result was not the whole work of 1868; five hundred thousand men were all the year kept happy in the idea—the average idea—that an estate was secured to the family in case of death, of $3,134, or at least of $2,854, in case the average self-insurance of $280 should consist of his own premium notes. Just look at the average policy-holder. He is a man with a family with whose help he could easily consume every dollar of his income. No mere savings bank could tempt him to deposit to the extent of his present life-insurance premium, for that would be no adequate provision for his family. Life-insurance tempts him to a course of saving, because it effects his great object at once,—it ties him up to that course,—it makes him a happy, energetic man, putting at once an impregnable barricade between his family and the poor-house. Here is an immense problem solved,—how to give the individual the strength of the million, and yet maintain his independence.

" Now comes (but heaven forbid it!) the great and rich and enlightened

Commonwealth of Massachusetts, casting about how to raise money to invest in railroad bonds and other lofty or profound speculation, and does not see our *average* policy-holder at all, or look into the nature and conditions of his contract at all, but does see a remarkably large pile of money (or notes counted as money) which is made up of his little pile multiplied by five hundred thousand. This is tempting As the Hibernian said to his son, going with a shillalah to Donnybrook fair, "Wherever you see a head, hit it," so it seems to have been said to some state legislatures, wherever you see a pile, make a scoop at it.

"If the capitalists and large property-holders of Massachusetts do not wish to be harassed into insane asylums, or suicide, by clamors for eight-hour laws and rise of wages, from men who will spend every additional dollar on rum and tobacco, they will, by all means, encourage all sorts of savings banks, instead of taxing them, and those of life-insurance companies especially. Supposing it admitted that the bill only contemplates a fair tax upon property which would otherwise escape taxation. It is none the less true that it is also a tax upon family affection, foresight and prudence,—upon those very qualities on which we are to depend for exemption in the future from that curse of pauperism which is always threatening to overshadow every adult and rich community. The real estate and manufacturing capital of Massachusetts, including its railroad and ordinary bank capitals, had far better bear all the present burdens of the state than to run the terrible risk of increasing those burdens by the slightest discouragement, or even neglect to encourage those institutions which promote economy, manliness, and independence in the operative classes. What if, by leaving life-insurance companies untaxed, now and then a dollar that ought to be taxed should escape taxation? The Greeks had temples, and the Jews cities of refuge, in which criminals might occasionally escape punishment. Yet they were tolerated, and even cherished, because they far more often saved the innocent from the fangs of the cruel. Nothing can be more certain than that all the revenue the state can lose by leaving life-insurance companies untaxed, will be returned to it many fold, in due time, in the improved character and increased wealth of its citizens.

"Among the large exemptions from taxation made in the General Statutes, is, all 'houses of religious worship'; this is done, undoubtedly, on the ground that the state can better afford to lose the revenue that might be derived from taxing these structures on their cost, or market value, than the influence for good which they exert on the character of the citizens. Yet it may be stated, without fear of contradiction, that these structures have absorbed twice the property they need for their purpose, and that the property which fairly ought to be taxed, being unnecessarily invested in the extravagant ornamentation of houses of worship, equals the whole amount of reserves on life-insurance policies held in Massachusetts. What these reserves amount to I have no means of ascertaining, but it would be extravagant to estimate them at more than $8,500,000, and of this sum probably nearly three millions consists of premium notes, no more taxable than good resolutions or hopes of future happiness."

I have stated as briefly as possible what occurs to my recollection as having been done in national and state legislation within the past few years, to levy a tax upon the business of life-insurance.

One good and substantial reason why life-insurance should not be taxed is, that premiums upon life-policies are not like deposits in a bank, which are subject to withdrawal at pleasure, and are the individual property of the depositor and admitted to be taxable. They are annual payments extending over the period of a man's life,—to be compounded at a moderate rate of interest,—to be returned to his heirs when a claim by death is made upon the company. These premiums pay a tax in one way or another, either as railroad, bank or other investment. To put another tax thereon is unjust, and cannot be defended even upon grounds that necessity requires the tax, for there are many other ways in which a tax can be levied than by a repletion of taxes upon the same capital. Other insurance, whether marine or against fire, is made upon a particular piece or species of property; whereas life-insurance is not a property possessed or profit expected by the insurer, but upon his own life, which is not property. The payment of premiums by the insured is, in fact, a present sacrifice, a charity, a duty to save his surviving family from want, and to the extent of his ability, to save the community from the burthen of supporting them. It is, in a very large proportion of cases, a donation consecrated to this purpose out of his hard earnings, and not out of property in possession. In very many instances men insure their lives because they have lost their property, and the only provision they can leave for their surviving families must be out of their future earnings, and it seems hard to add to this burthen which fortune has already imposed upon them.

When underwriters take risks on the credit of specific paid-up capital stock, they indemnify themselves by dividends, and when insurance is made upon specific property against fire, the insured can indemnify himself by the price at which he sells the subject, or the rent which he charges for the use of it. In case of a tax upon a mutual life-insurance company having no stock capital, the assured has no such remedy for indemnity; the tax is in effect a direct capitation tax, not being in any regular ratio or relation to the value of what is at risk, or the means of the assured to pay it. Under the present non-forfeiture law of April 10, 1861, there is little or no profit in the business of life-insurance as conducted in this state; the so-called dividends are not profit, for they are not revenue derived from investment of capital. In fact, mutual life-insurance companies require of the insured for their own security premiums greater in amount than the actual value of the risk. This places in the hands of the companies a surplus out of which to meet all exigencies, and the remainder is returned to the insured in the form of a remission of future premiums, or in any other way agreed upon. In either case the return of the surplus, called wrongly a "dividend," has nothing in common with the dividends of banks or of other joint-stock companies, which are really profits from capital invested; hence no tax on principal should be assessed upon them.

Another good and substantial reason why a life-insurance company should not be taxed in this Commonwealth is, that a very large part of the premiums are collected in other states and are there taxed,—*e. g.*, the largest part of the premiums received by the New England Mutual Life-Insurance Company, are subject to taxation as follows: In Pennsylvania, 3 per cent.; in Connecticut, 2 per cent.; in California, New York, Ohio, Illinois, and other states, a fee for valuation of policies, and in some instances a percentage upon the premiums in addition.

The portion of premiums received in this state from citizens of Massachusetts, is comparatively small. The Massachusetts companies now pay a tax to the state in the shape of a fee for valuation of policies, which helps to support the Insurance Department. The present law (see chapter 58, General Statutes) is reciprocal, and answers its purpose very well indeed.

I will not trouble you with more than an allusion to the present unfortunate condition of the finances of the country, or the decline of business, owing to the late panic and other causes; but will simply say, that life-insurance is at the same low ebb as, and partakes of, the general distress of all other kinds of business, from which it will take a long time to recover.

TABLES.

CHURCH PROPERTY EXEMPT FROM TAXATION.

Table No. 1.

Valuation of Church Property exempt from Taxation in the several Counties and Towns in the Commonwealth, showing Amount held by each Denomination in each County.

BAPTIST SOCIETIES.

Counties and Towns.	Number.	Value of Land.	Value of Buildings.	Total Value of Real Estate.	Value of Personal Estate.	Total Value of Real and Personal Estate.
Barnstable.						
Barnstable, . .	3	$350	$5,500	$5,850	$1,000	$6,850
Brewster, . .	1	-	-	1,500	-	1,500
Chatham, . .	1	-	-	3,650	-	3,650
Harwich, . .	1	-	-	1,500	-	1,500
Mashpee, . .	1	-	-	950	-	950
Orleans, . .	1	50	600	650	-	650
Sandwich, . .	1	-	-	1,250	-	1,250
Yarmouth, . .	1	-	-	1,000	-	1,000
Totals, . .	10	$400	$6,100	$16,350	$1,000	$17,350
Berkshire.						
Adams, . .	2	-	-	$36,000	-	$36,000
Cheshire, . .	1	-	-	2,000	-	2,000
Egremont, . .	1	-	-	600	-	600
Florida, . .	1	-	-	1,000	-	1,000
Hancock, . .	1	-	-	2,000	-	2,000
Hinsdale, . .	1	-	-	5,000	-	5,000
Lanesborough, .	1	-	-	3,300	$200	3,500
Lee, ...	1	-	-	5,000	-	5,000
N. Marlborough,	1	-	-	4,000	-	4,000
Pittsfield, . .	1	-	-	30,000	-	30,000
Sandisfield, . .	1	-	-	1,500	-	1,500
Savoy, . .	2	-	-	800	-	800
Tyringham, .	1	$200	-	200	-	200
Williamstown, .	1	-	-	200	-	200
Totals, . .	16	$200	-	$91,600	$200	$91,800
Bristol.						
Acushnet, . .	2	-	-	$4,350	-	$4,350
Attleborough, .	1	-	-	9,000	$1,000	10,000

BAPTIST SOCIETIES—CONTINUED.

COUNTIES AND TOWNS.	Number.	Value of Land.	Value of Buildings.	Total Value of Real Estate.	Value of Personal Estate.	Total Value of Real and Personal Estate.
BRISTOL—Con.						
Dartmouth, . .	1	-	-	$1,000	-	$1,000
Dighton, . .	1	$100	$700	800	-	800
Fall River, . .	3	68,500	75,000	143,500	-	143,500
Mansfield, . .	1	-	-	10,000	-	10,000
New Bedford, .	4	-	-	19,500	-	19,500
Norton, . .	1	50	1,500	1,550	-	1,550
Raynham, . .	1	-	-	2,500	-	2,500
Rehoboth, . .	1	-	-	1,800	-	1,800
Somerset, . .	2	-	-	17,000	-	17,000
Swanzey, . .	2	-	-	1,800	-	1,800
Taunton, . .	3	5,200	68,000	73,200	$3,800	77,000
Totals, . .	23	$73,850	$145,200	$286,000	$4,800	$290,800
DUKES.						
Edgartown, .	1	$500	$7,500	$8,000	-	$8,000
Gay Head, . .	1	-	-	700	-	700
Tisbury, . .	3	-	-	13,800	-	13,800
Totals, . .	5	$500	$7,500	$22,500	-	$22,500
ESSEX.						
Amesbury, . .	3	-	-	$18,000	-	$18,000
Andover, . .	1	$900	$12,000	12,900	-	12,900
Beverly, . .	2	-	-	14,000	-	14,000
Danvers, . .	1	-	-	6,900	-	6,900
Georgetown, .	1	500	4,000	4,500	-	4,500
Gloucester, . .	2	-	-	35,000	-	35,000
Groveland, . .	1	150	4,000	4,150	-	4,150
Haverhill, . .	5	-	-	77,050	-	77,050
Lawrence, . .	3	6,000	44,500	50,500	$6,500	57,000
Lynn, . . .	4	33,500	103,000	136,500	-	136,500
Manchester, .	1	500	4,600	5,100	600	5,700
Marblehead, .	1	-	-	12,700	-	12,700
Methuen, . .	1	-	-	7,700	2,500	10,200
Newburyport, .	2	3,300	13,000	16,300	-	16,300
Peabody, . .	1	-	-	10,000	-	10,000
Rockport, . .	1	-	-	5,000	-	5,000
Rowley, . .	1	200	5,000	5,200	-	5,200
Salem, . .	3	-	-	82,000	-	82,000
Salisbury, . .	2	-	-	17,000	-	17,000
Swampscott, .	1	-	-	12,000	-	12,000
Wenham, . .	1	-	-	2,800	-	2,800
West Newbury, .	1	-	-	1,500	-	1,500
Totals, . .	39	$45,050	$190,100	$536,800	$9,600	$546,400

BAPTIST SOCIETIES—CONTINUED.

COUNTIES AND TOWNS.	Number.	Value of Land.	Value of Buildings.	Total Value of Real Estate.	Value of Personal Estate.	Total Value of Real and Personal Estate.
FRANKLIN.						
Ashfield,	1	-	-	$1,600	-	$1,600
Bernardston,	1	-	-	3,500	-	3,500
Charlemont,	1	-	-	500	-	500
Colrain,	1	-	-	700	-	700
Conway,	1	-	-	3,500	-	3,500
Deerfield,	1	-	-	800	-	800
Greenfield,	1	$2,000	$4,000	6,000	$1,000	7,000
Leverett,	1	-	-	1,500	-	1,500
Montague,	1	-	-	1,500	-	1,500
New Salem,	1	-	-	200	-	200
Orange,	1	1,500	4,000	5,500	700	6,200
Rowe,	1	-	-	200	-	200
Shelburne,	1	-	-	9,000	-	9,000
Shutesbury,	1	-	-	2,000	-	2,000
Sunderland,	1	-	-	1,200	-	1,200
Warwick,	1	-	-	800	-	800
Wendell,	1	-	-	200	-	200
Totals,	17	$3,500	$8,000	$38,700	$1,700	$40,400
HAMPDEN.						
Agawam,	1	-	-	$2,500	-	$2,500
Chicopee,	2	-	-	10,700	-	10,700
Granville,	1	-	-	650	-	650
Holyoke,	2	$8,250	$16,200	24,450	-	24,450
Longmeadow,	1	-	-	2,650	-	2,650
Palmer,	2	-	-	7,700	-	7,700
Russell,	1	-	-	3,500	-	3,500
Southwick,	1	100	2,900	3,000	-	3,000
Springfield,	2	-	-	135,000	-	135,000
Wales,	1	-	-	1,500	$500	2,000
Westfield,	1	5,800	20,000	25,800	-	25,800
West Springfield,	1	1,000	3,000	4,000	-	4,000
Wilbraham,	1	-	-	2,200	-	2,200
Totals,	17	$15,150	$42,100	$223,650	$500	$224,150
HAMPSHIRE.						
Amherst,	1	$1,000	$5,000	$6,000	-	$6,000
Belchertown,	1	-	-	2,000	$500	2,500
Cummington,	1	-	-	500	-	500
Huntington,	1	-	-	1,500	-	1,500
Northampton,	1	-	-	12,500	500	13,000
Middlefield,	1	-	-	1,500	-	1,500
Totals,	6	$1,000	$5,000	$24,000	$1,000	$25,000

BAPTIST SOCIETIES—CONTINUED.

COUNTIES AND TOWNS.	Number.	Value of Land.	Value of Buildings.	Total Value of Real Estate.	Value of Personal Estate.	Total Value of Real and Personal Estate.
MIDDLESEX.						
Acton,	1	-	-	$4,300	-	$4,300
Arlington,	1	$4,400	$20,000	24,400	$4,000	28,400
Ashland,	1	-	-	5,000	-	5,000
Ayer,	1	-	-	6,000	-	6,000
Billerica,	2	600	11,000	11,600	10,800	22,400
Cambridge,	6	-	-	297,000	-	297,000
Chelmsford,	2	-	-	9,200	-	9,200
Everett,	1	-	-	10,000	1,000	11,000
Framingham,	2	1,200	14,000	15,200	-	15,200
Groton,	1	-	-	5,000	-	5,000
Holliston,	1	-	-	8,000	1,000	9,000
Hopkinton,	1	-	-	3,000	-	3,000
Hudson,	1	-	-	2,500	-	2,500
Lexington,	1	700	3,300	4,000	200	4,200
Littleton,	1	-	-	2,100	-	2,100
Lowell,	5	-	-	77,100	-	77,100
Malden,	2	-	-	55,000	-	55,000
Marlborough,	1	-	-	3,000	200	3,200
Medford,	1	-	-	25,000	-	25,000
Melrose,	1	-	-	25,000	-	25,000
Natick,	1	-	-	13,000	1,500	14,500
Newton,	5	-	-	51,700	2,600	54,300
Reading,	1	1,000	5,000	6,000	1,000	7,000
Reading, North,	1	-	-	3,000	-	3,000
Shirley,	1	-	-	800	200	1,000
Somerville,	2	-	-	76,000	8,500	84,500
Stoneham,	1	700	3,000	3,700	-	3,700
Tewksbury,	1	-	-	5,000	-	5,000
Townsend,	1	-	-	3,500	-	3,500
Wakefield,	1	-	-	64,000	-	64,000
Waltham,	1	-	-	12,000	-	12,000
Watertown,	1	9,900	15,000	24,900	2,000	26,900
Weston,	1	-	-	6,000	-	6,000
Winchester,	1	2,000	13,000	15,000	-	15,000
Woburn,	2	10,000	16,500	26,500	3,000	29,500
Totals,	54	$30,500	$100,800	$903,500	$36,000	$939,500
NANTUCKET.						
Nantucket,	1	-	-	$2,600	-	$2,600
NORFOLK.						
Bellingham,	1	-	-	$4,000	-	$4,000
Braintree,	1	-	-	1,300	-	1,300

BAPTIST SOCIETIES—CONTINUED.

COUNTIES AND TOWNS.	Number.	Value of Land.	Value of Buildings.	Total Value of Real Estate.	Value of Personal Estate.	Total Value of Real and Personal Estate.
NORFOLK—Con.						
Brookline, . .	1	-	-	$35,000	-	$35,000
Canton, . .	1	-	-	6,000	-	6,000
Dedham, . .	2	$550	$8,100	8,650	-	8,650
Dover, . .	1	50	600	650	-	650
Foxborough, .	1	-	-	8,200	$500	8,700
Franklin, . .	1	600	2,500	3,100	200	3,300
Holbrook, . .	1	-	-	2,000	-	2,000
Hyde Park, . .	1	11,900	13,000	24,900	3,000	27,900
Medfield, . .	1	-	-	9,000	-	9,000
Medway, . .	1	-	-	4,100	-	4,100
Needham, . .	1	800	10,000	10,800	-	10,800
Norfolk, . .	1	-	-	2,500	-	2,500
Norwood, . .	1	1,000	8,000	9,000	500	9,500
Quincy, . .	1	-	-	6,000	-	6,000
Randolph, . .	1	-	-	25,000	-	25,000
Sharon, . .	1	250	3,000	3,250	-	3,250
Stoughton, . .	1	-	-	10,000	-	10,000
Weymouth, .	1	-	-	15,700	-	15,700
Wrentham, . .	1	-	-	2,500	-	2,500
Totals, . .	22	$15,150	$45,200	$191,650	$4,200	$195,850
PLYMOUTH.						
Abington, . .	1	$500	$5,000	$5,500	-	$5,500
Carver, . .	1	-	-	800	-	800
Halifax, . .	1	-	-	600	-	600
Hanover, . .	1	100	2,500	2,600	-	2,600
Hanson, . .	1	100	5,000	5,100	-	5,100
Hingham, . .	1	-	-	6,000	-	6,000
Kingston, . .	1	-	-	3,200	$300	3,500
Marshfield, . .	2	-	-	6,000	-	6,000
Mattapoisett, .	1	-	-	2,000	-	2,000
Middleborough, .	3	2,700	15,000	17,700	2,500	20,200
Plymouth, . .	2	-	-	15,800	1,500	17,300
Rockland, . .	1	1,500	5,050	6,550	-	6,550
Scituate, . .	1	-	-	10,000	-	10,000
W. Bridgewater,	1	-	-	2,600	-	2,600
Totals, . .	18	$4,900	$32,550	$84,450	$4,300	$88,750
SUFFOLK.						
Boston, .. .	24	$802,900	$690,600	$1,493,500	-	$1,493,500
Chelsea, . .	3	-	-	108,000	$5,000	113,000
Winthrop, . .	1	-	-	12,000	-	12,000
Totals, . .	28	$802,900	$690,600	$1,613,500	$5,000	$1,618,500

BAPTIST SOCIETIES—CONCLUDED.

COUNTIES AND TOWNS.	Number.	Value of Land.	Value of Buildings.	Total Value of Real Estate.	Value of Personal Estate.	Total Value of Real and Personal Estate.
WORCESTER.						
Athol, . . .	1	$800	$4,000	$4,800	$500	$5,300
Barre, . . .	1	–	–	2,000	200	2,200
Blackstone, .	1	500	2,000	2,500	–	2,500
Bolton, . .	1	–	–	3,000	–	3,000
Brookfield, . .	1	500	6,500	7,000	–	7,000
Clinton, . .	1	2,500	13,000	15,500	–	15,500
Fitchburg, . .	1	15,000	25,500	40,500	2,500	43,000
Gardner, . .	1	500	6,000	6,500	–	6,500
Grafton, . .	3	–	–	10,050	–	10,050
Harvard, . .	1	–	–	3,000	–	3,000
Holden, . .	1	1,000	4,000	5,000	–	5,000
Leicester, . .	1	–	–	7,000	–	7,000
Leominster, .	1	1,250	3,000	4,250	–	4,250
Milford, . .	1	1,000	9,000	10,000	500	10,500
Millbury, . .	1	–	–	9,000	2,000	11,000
Northborough, .	1	–	–	7,500	–	7,500
Oxford, . .	1	–	–	2,500	–	2,500
Petersham, . .	1	–	–	3,000	–	3,000
Royalston, . .	1	500	1,500	2,000	–	2,000
Southborough, .	1	–	–	4,000	100	4,100
Southbridge, .	1	–	–	15,000	1,000	16,000
Sterling, . .	1	–	–	1,500	–	1,500
Sturbridge, .	1	–	–	4,000	–	4,000
Sutton, . .	1	–	–	4,650	400	5,050
Templeton, . .	1	–	–	5,500	–	5,500
Webster, . .	1	–	–	17,400	–	17,400
Westborough, .	1	–	–	15,000	–	15,000
West Boylston, .	1	–	–	5,500	–	5,500
Westminster, .	1	–	–	2,500	350	2,850
Winchendon, .	2	–	–	4,250	–	4,250
Worcester, . .	4	–	–	140,700	–	140,700
Totals, . .	37	$23,550	$74,500	$365,100	$7,550	$372,650

CATHOLIC SOCIETIES.

COUNTIES AND TOWNS.	Number.	Value of Land.	Value of Buildings.	Total Value of Real Estate.	Value of Personal Estate.	Total Value of Real and Personal Estate.
BARNSTABLE.						
Provincetown, .	1	–	–	$7,200	–	$7,200
Sandwich, . .	1	–	–	7,400	–	7,400
Totals, . .	2	–	–	$14,600	–	$14,600

CATHOLIC SOCIETIES—CONTINUED.

COUNTIES AND TOWNS.	Number.	Value of Land.	Value of Buildings.	Total Value of Real Estate.	Value of Personal Estate.	Total Value of Real and Personal Estate.
BERKSHIRE.						
Adams, . .	4	-	-	$78,000	-	$78,000
Cheshire, . .	1	-	-	2,500	-	2,500
Great Barrington,	1	-	-	5,000	-	5,000
Hinsdale, . .	1	-	-	4,000	-	4,000
Lee, . . .	1	-	-	7,000	-	7,000
Lenox, . .	1	-	-	4,000	-	4,000
New Marlboro', .	1	-	-	3,000	-	3,000
Pittsfield, . .	2	-	-	54,000	-	54,000
Sheffield, . .	1	-	-	250	-	250
Stockbridge, .	1	$1,200	$6,000	7,200	$1,000	8,200
W. Stockbridge, .	1	-	-	7,500	-	7,500
Williamstown, .	1	-	-	35,000	-	35,000
Totals, . .	16	$1,200	$6,000	$207,450	$1,000	$208,450
BRISTOL.						
Attleborough, .	1	-	-	$3,500	-	$3,500
Easton, . .	1	-	-	5,500	-	5,500
Fall River, . .	4	$25,300	$88,500	113,800	-	113,800
Mansfield, . .	1	-	-	3,500	-	3,500
New Bedford, .	2	-	-	52,400	-	52,400
Norton, . .	1	50	1,000	1,050	-	1,050
Taunton, . .	3	8,500	80,000	88,500	$2,500	91,000
Totals, . .	13	$33,850	$169,500	$268,250	$2,500	$270,750
ESSEX.						
Amesbury, . .	1	-	-	$75,000	-	$75,000
Andover, . .	1	$400	$3,600	4,000	-	4,000
Beverly, . .	1	-	-	3,000	-	3,000
Danvers, . .	1	-	-	11,000	-	11,000
Georgetown, .	1	150	1,000	1,150	-	1,150
Gloucester, . .	1	-	-	12,000	-	12,000
Haverhill, . .	1	-	-	16,000	-	16,000
Ipswich, . .	1	150	2,500	2,650	-	2,650
Lawrence, . .	5	49,000	243,000	292,000	$19,500	311,500
Lynn, . . .	1	20,000	40,000	60,000	-	60,000
Manchester, .	1	400	3,600	4,000	-	4,000
Marblehead, .	1	-	-	5,600	-	5,600
Nahant, . .	1	-	-	9,800	-	9,800
Newburyport, .	1	4,500	26,000	30,500	-	30,500
North Andover, .	1	-	-	3,000	200	3,200
Peabody, . .	1	-	-	35,000	-	35,000
Rockport, . .	1	-	-	3,500	-	3,500
Salem, . .	3	-	-	74,000	-	74,000
Totals, . .	24	$74,600	$319,700	$642,200	$19,700	$661,900

CATHOLIC SOCIETIES—CONTINUED.

COUNTIES AND TOWNS.	Number.	Value of Land.	Value of Buildings.	Total Value of Real Estate.	Value of Personal Estate.	Total Value of Real and Personal Estate.
FRANKLIN.						
Greenfield, . .	1	$2,000	$10,000	$12,000	$1,500	$13,500
Montague, . .	1	-	-	1,000	-	1,000
Totals, . .	2	$2,000	$10,000	$13,000	$1,500	$14,500
HAMPDEN.						
Chicopee, . .	2	-	-	$48,700	-	$48,700
Holyoke, . .	2	$17,000	$27,000	44,000	-	44,000
Monson, . .	1	500	10,000	10,500	-	10,500
Palmer, . .	1	-	-	800	-	800
Springfield, .	3	-	-	152,000	-	152,000
Westfield, . .	1	1,000	6,000	7,000	-	7,000
West Springfield,	1	500	6,000	6,500	-	6,500
Totals, . .	11	$19,000	$49,000	$269,500	-	$269,500
HAMPSHIRE.						
Amherst, . .	1	$400	$10,000	$10,400	-	$10,400
Easthampton, .	1	-	-	800	-	800
Northampton, .	1	-	-	6,000	-	6,000
South Hadley, .	1	800	13,000	13,800	-	13,800
Ware, . . .	2	1,500	20,000	21,500	-	21,500
Williamsburg, .	1	-	-	12,300	-	12,300
Totals, . .	7	$2,700	$43,000	$64,800	-	$64,800
MIDDLESEX.						
Arlington, . .	1	$4,400	$25,000	$29,400	$2,500	$31,900
Ayer, . . .	1	-	-	4,800	-	4,800
Billerica, . .	1	300	4,000	4,300	-	4,300
Cambridge, .	3	-	-	170,000	-	170,000
Chelmsford, .	1	-	-	3,000	-	3,000
Concord, . .	1	-	-	4,000	1,000	5,000
Framingham, .	2	400	9,000	9,400	-	9,400
Holliston, . .	1	-	-	5,000	-	5,000
Hopkinton, . .	1	-	-	4,500	-	4,500
Hudson, . .	1	-	-	4,800	-	4,800
Lexington, . .	1	4,000	1,000	5,000	500	5,500
Lowell, . .	5	-	-	126,900	-	126,900
Marlborough, .	2	-	-	33,000	2,500	35,500
Maynard, . .	1	-	-	6,500	-	6,500
Medford, . .	1	-	-	36,000	-	36,000
Melrose, . .	1	-	-	3,000	-	3,000
Natick, . .	2	-	-	19,000	1,500	20,500
Newton, . .	3	-	-	54,500	1,500	56,000

CATHOLIC SOCIETIES—CONTINUED.

COUNTIES AND TOWNS.	Number.	Value of Land.	Value of Buildings.	Total Value of Real Estate.	Value of Personal Estate.	Total Value of Real and Personal Estate.
MIDDLESEX—Con.						
Pepperell, . .	1	-	-	$1,000	-	$1,000
Somerville, . .	1	-	-	83,000	$2,000	85,000
Stoneham, . .	1	$750	$5,000	5,750	-	5,750
Wakefield, . .	1	-	-	19,000	-	19,000
Waltham, . .	1	-	-	25,000	-	25,000
Watertown, .	1	4,300	8,000	12,300	500	12,800
Winchester, .	1	1,500	13,000	14,500	-	14,500
Woburn, . .	1	16,500	50,000	66,500	3,500	70,000
Totals, . .	37	$32,150	$115,000	$750,150	$15,500	$765,650
NANTUCKET.						
Nantucket, . .	1	-	-	$3,000	-	$3,000
NORFOLK.						
Brookline, . .	1	-	-	$10,000	-	$10,000
Canton, . .	1	-	-	7,000	-	7,000
Dedham, . .	1	$1,550	$4,000	5,550	-	5,550
Foxborough, .	1	-	-	2,400	-	2,400
Franklin, . .	1	500	5,000	5,500	-	5,500
Hyde Park, . .	1	1,400	12,000	13,400	$1,500	14,900
Medway, . .	1	-	-	2,000	-	2,000
Norwood, . .	1	600	2,500	3,100	300	3,400
Quincy, . .	2	-	-	48,000	-	48,000
Randolph, . .	1	-	-	20,000	-	20,000
Sharon, . .	1	100	1,000	1,100	-	1,100
Stoughton, . .	2	-	-	21,000	-	21,000
Weymouth, .	3	-	-	27,400	-	27,400
Totals, . .	17	$4,150	$24,500	$166,450	$1,800	$168,250
PLYMOUTH.						
Abington, . .	1	$300	$11,000	$11,300	-	$11,300
Bridgewater, .	1	100	8,000	8,100	$1,000	9,100
Brockton, . .	1	4,000	14,000	18,000	-	18,000
E. Bridgewater, .	1	-	-	2,400	-	2,400
Plymouth, . .	1	-	-	8,000	-	8,000
Scituate, . .	1	-	-	8,000	-	8,000
Wareham, . .	1	-	-	5,000	-	5,000
Totals, . .	7	$4,400	$33,000	$60,800	$1,000	$61,800
SUFFOLK.						
Boston, . .	30	$872,000	$1,693,800	$2,565,800	-	$2,565,800
Chelsea, . .	1	-	-	85,000	$6,000	91,000
Totals, . .	31	$872,000	$1,693,800	$2,650,800	$6,000	$2,656,800

CATHOLIC SOCIETIES—CONCLUDED.

COUNTIES AND TOWNS.	Number.	Value of Land.	Value of Buildings.	Total Value of Real Estate.	Value of Personal Estate.	Total Value of Real and Personal Estate.
WORCESTER.						
Ashburnham,	1	–	–	$2,000	$500	$2,500
Athol,	1	$800	$800	1,600	–	1,600
Auburn,	1	–	–	3,000	–	3,000
Barre,	1	–	–	2,000	250	2,250
Blackstone,	1	500	2,500	3,000	–	3,000
Brookfield,	1	1,000	5,000	6,000	–	6,000
Clinton,	1	7,400	11,000	18,400	–	18,400
Douglas,	1	–	–	2,000	–	2,000
Fitchburg,	1	10,200	33,000	43,200	2,000	45,200
Gardner,	1	500	1,000	1,500	–	1,500
Grafton,	1	–	–	3,800	–	3,800
Holden,	1	1,000	2,000	3,000	–	3,000
Lancaster,	1	–	–	5,000	–	5,000
Leicester,	2	–	–	12,500	–	12,500
Leominster,	1	1,650	3,000	4,650	–	4,650
Milford,	1	2,000	60,000	62,000	1,000	63,000
Millbury,	1	–	–	4,000	250	4,250
Northbridge,	1	–	–	10,000	–	10,000
N. Brookfield,	1	1,000	6,000	7,000	–	7,000
Oxford,	1	–	–	4,000	–	4,000
Shrewsbury,	1	–	–	2,000	–	2,000
Southbridge,	2	–	–	22,000	1,000	23,000
Spencer,	1	–	–	8,000	500	8,500
Templeton,	1	–	–	3,000	–	3,000
Upton,	1	–	–	6,000	–	6,000
Warren,	2	–	–	7,000	–	7,000
Webster,	2	–	–	29,600	–	29,600
Westborough,	1	–	–	5,500	–	5,500
Winchendon,	1	–	–	500	–	500
Worcester,	5	–	–	259,400	–	259,400
Totals,	38	$26,050	$124,300	$541,650	$5,500	$547,150

CONGREGATIONAL SOCIETIES.

COUNTIES AND TOWNS.	Number.	Value of Land.	Value of Buildings.	Total Value of Real Estate.	Value of Personal Estate.	Total Value of Real and Personal Estate.
BARNSTABLE.						
Barnstable,	4	$200	$9,400	$9,600	$700	$10,300
Chatham,	1	–	–	6,200	–	6,200
Dennis,	1	–	–	2,500	–	2,500
Falmouth,	4	–	–	17,350	–	17,350
Harwich,	1	–	–	1,500	–	1,500
Orleans,	1	–	–	1,200	–	1,200
Provincetown,	1	–	–	6,300	2,000	8,300

CONGREGATIONAL SOCIETIES—CONTINUED.

COUNTIES AND TOWNS.	Number.	Value of Land.	Value of Buildings.	Total Value of Real Estate.	Value of Personal Estate.	Total Value of Real and Personal Estate.
BARNST'LE—Con.						
Sandwich,	1	-	-	$4,750	-	$4,750
Truro,	1	-	-	1,500	-	1,500
Wellfleet,	2	-	-	11,000	-	11,000
Yarmouth,	3	-	-	15,500	$4,000	19,500
Totals,	20	$200	$9,400	$77,400	$6,700	$84,100
BERKSHIRE.						
Adams,	2	-	-	$45,000	-	$45,000
Becket,	3	-	-	4,700	-	4,700
Dalton,	1	-	-	7,000	$1,500	8,500
Egremont,	1	-	-	1,500	-	1,500
Great Barrington,	2	-	-	18,500	-	18,500
Hinsdale,	1	-	-	8,000	-	8,000
Lanesborough,	1	-	-	2,600	400	3,000
Lee,	2	-	-	22,000	-	22,000
Lenox,	1	-	-	10,000	1,000	11,000
Monterey,	1	-	-	1,000	-	1,000
New Marlboro',	3	-	-	18,000	-	18,000
Otis,	1	-	-	3,350	-	3,350
Peru,	1	-	-	1,000	-	1,000
Pittsfield,	3	-	-	68,500	-	68,500
Richmond,	1	-	-	5,000	-	5,000
Sandisfield,	1	-	-	2,000	100	2,100
Sheffield,	1	-	-	6,000	-	6,000
Stockbridge,	2	$2,500	$10,500	13,000	2,300	15,300
W. Stockbridge,	2	-	-	3,700	-	3,700
Williamstown,	2	-	-	67,050	-	67,050
Windsor,	1	-	-	600	-	600
Totals,	33	$2,500	$10,500	$308,500	$5,300	$313,800
BRISTOL.						
Attleborough,	2	-	-	$15,300	$1,500	$16,800
Berkley,	1	-	-	3,000	100	3,100
Dartmouth,	1	-	-	2,700	-	2,700
Dighton,	1	$100	$600	700	-	700
Easton,	1	-	-	4,000	-	4,000
Fairhaven,	1	-	-	10,000	-	10,000
Fall River,	3	42,700	30,200	72,900	-	72,900
Freetown,	1	-	-	4,200	1,500	5,700
Mansfield,	1	-	-	15,000	-	15,000
New Bedford,	4	-	-	50,300	-	50,300
Norton,	1	100	4,000	4,100	-	4,100
Raynham,	2	-	-	4,200	-	4,200

CONGREGATIONAL SOCIETIES—CONTINUED.

COUNTIES AND TOWNS.	Number.	Value of Land.	Value of Buildings.	Total Value of Real Estate.	Value of Personal Estate.	Total Value of Real and Personal Estate.
BRISTOL—Con.						
Rehoboth,	1	-	-	$2,500	-	$2,500
Somerset,	1	-	-	7,000	-	7,000
Taunton,	5	$12,800	$76,500	89,300	$7,000	96,300
Westport,	1	-	-	4,000	-	4,000
Totals,	27	$55,700	$111,300	$289,200	$10,100	$299,300
DUKES.						
Chilmark,	1	-	-	$500	-	$500
Edgartown,	1	$500	$8,500	9,000	-	9,000
Tisbury,	1	-	-	2,500	-	2,500
Totals,	3	$500	$8,500	$12,000	-	$12,000
ESSEX.						
Amesbury,	2	-	-	$36,200	-	$36,200
Andover,	3	$2,400	$42,800	45,200	-	45,200
Beverly,	3	-	-	13,500	-	13,500
Boxford,	2	-	-	9,200	-	9,200
Bradford,	1	-	-	15,000	-	15,000
Danvers,	2	-	-	18,250	-	18,250
Essex,	1	-	-	6,000	-	6,000
Georgetown,	4	3,300	50,000	53,300	-	53,300
Gloucester,	3	-	-	25,000	-	25,000
Groveland,	1	300	6,000	6,300	-	6,300
Hamilton,	1	-	-	4,000	$500	4,500
Haverhill,	4	-	-	59,100	-	59,100
Ipswich,	3	400	13,600	14,000	700	14,700
Lawrence,	4	15,000	71,000	86,000	14,000	100,000
Lynn,	4	48,000	112,000	160,000	-	160,000
Lynnfield,	2	1,000	6,000	7,000	-	7,000
Manchester,	1	500	13,600	14,100	900	15,000
Marblehead,	3	-	-	40,000	1,200	41,200
Methuen,	1	-	-	14,000	2,500	16,500
Middleton,	1	200	3,000	3,200	-	3,200
Newbury,	2	1,800	15,400	17,200	2,650	19,850
Newburyport,	4	10,500	53,500	64,000	5,000	69,000
North Andover,	1	-	-	17,000	1,500	18,500
Peabody,	1	-	-	30,000	-	30,000
Rockport,	1	-	-	20,000	1,000	21,000
Rowley,	1	300	10,900	11,200	-	11,200
Salem,	3	-	-	82,000	-	82,000
Salisbury,	1	-	-	3,500	-	3,500
Saugus,	1	-	-	8,000	-	8,000
Swampscott,	1	-	-	10,000	-	10,000

CONGREGATIONAL SOCIETIES—CONTINUED.

COUNTIES AND TOWNS.	Number.	Value of Land.	Value of Buildings.	Total Value of Real Estate.	Value of Personal Estate.	Total Value of Real and Personal Estate.
ESSEX—Con.						
Topsfield,	1	-	-	$6,000	-	$6,000
Wenham,	1	-	-	5,300	-	5,300
West Newbury,	2	-	-	11,300	$2,300	13,600
Totals,	66	$83,700	$397,800	$914,850	$32,250	$947,100
FRANKLIN.						
Ashfield,	1	-	-	$2,500	-	$2,500
Bernardston,	1	-	-	3,000	-	3,000
Buckland,	1	-	-	1,800	-	1,800
Charlemont,	2	-	-	1,400	-	1,400
Colrain,	1	-	-	800	-	800
Conway,	1	-	-	7,000	-	7,000
Deerfield,	2	-	-	9,100	-	9,100
Erving,	1	-	-	2,000	-	2,000
Gill,	1	$200	$4,000	4,500	$500	5,000
Greenfield,	2	5,100	32,900	38,000	3,200	41,200
Hawley,	2	-	-	2,000	-	2,000
Heath,	1	-	-	400	-	400
Leverett,	1	-	-	1,200	-	1,200
Montague,	2	-	-	3,200	-	3,200
New Salem,	1	-	-	1,000	-	1,000
Northfield,	1	-	-	4,000	-	4,000
Orange,	1	2,000	10,000	12,000	3,500	15,500
Shelburne,	2	-	-	9,000	10,000	19,000
Shutesbury,	1	-	-	1,200	-	1,200
Sunderland,	1	-	-	7,000	1,000	8,000
Warwick,	1	-	-	1,200	-	1,200
Wendell,	1	-	-	800	-	800
Whately,	1	-	-	2,250	1,050	3,300
Totals,	29	$7,300	$46,900	$115,350	$19,250	$134,600
HAMPDEN.						
Agawam,	2	-	-	$5,000	-	$5,000
Blandford,	1	-	-	5,000	$3,000	8,000
Brimfield,	1	-	-	7,500	-	7,500
Chester,	2	$500	$3,500	4,000	-	4,000
Chicopee,	3	-	-	35,200	-	35,200
Granville,	2	-	-	1,050	-	1,050
Holland,	1	-	-	3,000	-	3,000
Holyoke,	2	13,100	13,500	26,600	-	26,600
Longmeadow,	2	-	-	10,850	-	10,850
Ludlow,	1	-	-	3,500	-	3,500
Monson,	1	500	25,000	25,500	-	25,500

CONGREGATIONAL SOCIETIES—CONTINUED.

COUNTIES AND TOWNS.	Number.	Value of Land.	Value of Buildings.	Total Value of Real Estate.	Value of Personal Estate.	Total Value of Real and Personal Estate.
HAMPDEN—Con.						
Montgomery,	1	-	.	$800	-	$800
Palmer,	2	-	-	13,000	-	13,000
Southwick,	1	$150	$2,850	3,000	-	3,000
Springfield,	8	-	-	284,000	-	284,000
Tolland,	1	-	-	1,200	$1,800	3,000
Westfield,	2	9,550	56,000	65,550	-	65,550
Wilbraham,	2	-	-	8,500	-	8,500
W. Springfield,	1	1,800	33,000	34,800	-	34,800
Totals,	36	$25,600	$133,850	$538,050	$4,800	$542,850
HAMPSHIRE.						
Amherst,	4	$3,700	$43,500	$47,200	-	$47,200
Belchertown,	1	-	-	4,000	$500	4,500
Chesterfield,	1	-	-	2,500	-	2,500
Cummington,	2	-	-	7,000	-	7,000
Easthampton,	2	-	-	27,400	2,800	30,200
Enfield,	1	-	-	11,500	2,000	13,500
Goshen,	1	-	-	4,000	-	4,000
Granby,	1	-	-	10,000	-	10,000
Greenwich,	1	-	-	2,000	500	2,500
Hadley,	2	1,150	20,000	21,150	-	21,150
Hatfield,	1	-	-	12,000	-	12,000
Huntington,	2	-	-	5,000	-	5,000
Middlefield,	1	-	-	2,500	-	2,500
Northampton,	4	-	-	141,000	6,000	147,000
Pelham,	1	-	-	1,500	-	1,500
Plainfield,	1	-	-	1,500	-	1,500
Prescott,	1	-	-	500	-	500
South Hadley,	3	1,200	35,000	36,200	5,000	41,200
Southampton,	1	-	-	3,000	-	3,000
Ware,	2	1,700	21,800	23,500	1,300	24,800
Westhampton,	1	-	-	3,500	-	3,500
Williamsburg,	2	-	-	26,000	-	26,000
Worthington,	1	-	-	5,000	300	5,300
Totals,	37	$7,750	$120,300	$397,950	$18,400	$416,350
MIDDLESEX.						
Acton,	1	-	-	$5,500	$500	$6,000
Arlington,	1	$5,400	$18,000	23,400	3,500	26,900
Ashby,	1	-	-	3,500	-	3,500
Ashland,	1	-	-	5,000	-	5,000

CONGREGATIONAL SOCIETIES—CONTINUED.

COUNTIES AND TOWNS.	Number.	Value of Land.	Value of Buildings.	Total Value of Real Estate.	Value of Personal Estate.	Total Value of Real and Personal Estate.
MID'LESEX—Con.						
Ayer,	1	-	-	$6,000	-	$6,000
Bedford,	1	-	-	4,500	-	4,500
Belmont,	2	-	-	22,000	-	22,000
Billerica,	1	$300	$4,300	4,600	$3,000	7,600
Boxborough,	1	-	-	500	-	500
Burlington,	1	-	-	2,500	4,000	6,500
Cambridge,	6	-	-	287,500	-	287,500
Chelmsford,	1	-	-	5,000	-	5,000
Carlisle,	1	-	-	800	-	800
Concord,	1	-	-	4,200	1,500	5,700
Dracut,	3	-	-	5,000	-	5,000
Dunstable,	1	-	-	1,000	-	1,000
Everett,	1	-	-	15,000	2,000	17,000
Framingham,	4	2,100	20,000	22,100	-	22,100
Groton,	1	-	-	8,000	-	8,000
Holliston,	1	-	-	10,000	1,000	11,000
Hopkinton,	1	-	-	12,000	4,000	16,000
Lexington,	1	1,000	7,000	8,000	500	8,500
Lincoln,	1	-	-	3,300	-	3,300
Littleton,	1	-	-	1,600	-	1,600
Lowell,	6	-	-	113,100	-	113,100
Malden,	2	-	-	67,000	-	67,000
Marlborough,	1	-	-	15,000	1,500	16,500
Maynard,	1	-	-	7,000	-	7,000
Medford,	3	-	-	62,000	-	62,000
Melrose,	1	-	-	42,000	-	42,000
Natick,	2	-	-	13,900	900	14,800
Newton,	7	-	-	180,700	11,800	192,500
North Reading,	1	-	-	2,500	-	2,500
Pepperell,	1	-	-	8,000	-	8,000
Reading,	2	5,200	29,500	34,700	9,000	43,700
Sherborn,	1	1,000	4,000	5,000	-	5,000
Shirley,	1	-	-	1,600	500	2,100
Somerville,	2	-	-	67,000	7,500	74,500
Stoneham,	1	13,000	6,000	19,000	-	19,000
Sudbury,	1	-	-	4,000	-	4,000
Tewksbury,	1	-	-	8,000	-	8,000
Townsend,	1	-	-	6,000	1,000	7,000
Tyngsborough,	1	-	-	4,100	-	4,100
Wakefield,	1	-	-	21,000	-	21,000
Waltham,	1	-	-	38,000	-	38,000
Watertown,	1	4,500	12,000	16,500	1,200	17,700
Wayland,	1	-	-	5,000	-	5,000
Westford,	1	-	-	4,000	-	4,000
Wilmington,	1	200	10,750	10,950	1,000	11,950

CONGREGATIONAL SOCIETIES—CONTINUED.

COUNTIES AND TOWNS.	Number.	Value of Land.	Value of Buildings.	Total Value of Real Estate.	Value of Personal Estate.	Total Value of Real and Personal Estate
MID'LESEX—Con.						
Winchester, .	1	$10,000	$30,000	$40,000	-	$40,000
Woburn, . .	2	18,800	55,200	74,000	$5,000	79,000
Totals, . .	80	$61,500	$196,750	$1,331,050	$59,400	$1,390,450
NANTUCKET.						
Nantucket, . .	1	-	-	$6,000	-	$6,000
NORFOLK.						
Braintree, . .	2	-	-	$35,500	-	$35,500
Brookline, . .	1	-	-	80,000	-	80,000
Canton, . .	1	-	-	6,000	-	6,000
Cohasset, . .	1	-	-	7,500	$700	8,200
Dedham, . .	1	$2,750	$12,000	14,750	-	14,750
Dover, . .	1	50	1,000	1,050	-	1,050
Foxborough, .	1	-	-	15,250	1,000	16,250
Franklin, . .	2	1,050	27,000	28,050	4,100	32,150
Holbrook, . .	2	-	-	21,000	-	21,000
Hyde Park, . .	1	15,400	10,000	25,400	3,000	28,400
Medfield, . .	1	-	-	5,000	-	5,000
Medway, . .	3	-	-	18,200	3,600	21,800
Milton, . .	2	-	-	17,000	-	17,000
Needham, . .	3	2,300	26,000	28,300	-	28,300
Norfolk, . .	1	-	-	2,000	-	2,000
Norwood, . .	2	800	3,300	4,100	500	4,600
Quincy, . .	1	-	-	28,000	-	28,000
Randolph, . .	1	-	-	20,000	-	20,000
Sharon, . .	1	500	5,000	5,500	-	5,500
Stoughton, . .	1	-	-	13,000	-	13,000
Walpole, . .	1	1,000	15,000	16,000	1,000	17,000
Weymouth, . .	5	-	-	86,100	8,100	94,200
Wrentham, . .	1	-	-	8,000	2,000	10,000
Totals, . .	36	$24,850	$99,300	$485,700	$24,000	$509,700
PLYMOUTH.						
Abington, . .	3	$2,100	$22,000	$24,100	-	$24,100
Bridgewater, .	2	1,050	14,500	15,550	$2,200	17,750
Brockton, . .	3	17,000	44,000	61,000	-	61,000
Carver, . .	1	100	1,750	1,850	-	1,850
Duxbury. . .	1	150	3,000	3,150	350	3,500
E. Bridgewater, .	1	-	-	3,100	-	3,100
Halifax, . .	1	-	-	2,500	-	2,500
Hanover, . .	2	200	6,000	6,200	-	6,200
Hanson, . .	1	50	5,000	5,050	-	5,050

CONGREGATIONAL SOCIETIES—Continued.

Counties and Towns.	Number.	Value of Land.	Value of Buildings.	Total Value of Real Estate.	Value of Personal Estate.	Total Value of Real and Personal Estate.
Plymouth—Con.						
Hingham, . .	1	–	–	$4,000	–	$4,000
Kingston, . .	1	–	–	3,300	–	3,300
Lakeville, . .	1	–	–	2,300	–	2,300
Marion, . .	1	–	–	5,000	$500	5,500
Marshfield, . .	2	–	–	9,000	–	9,000
Mattapoisett, .	1	–	–	8,000	–	8,000
Middleborough, .	3	$1,700	$22,000	23,700	5,700	29,400
Plymouth, . .	5	–	–	17,400	2,250	19,650
Plympton, . .	1	100	2,500	2,600	–	2,600
Rockland, . .	1	3,000	15,150	18,150	–	18,150
Scituate, . .	1	–	–	4,500	–	4,500
Wareham, . .	2	–	–	8,700	–	8,700
Totals, . .	35	$25,450	$135,900	$229,150	$11,000	$240,150
Suffolk.						
Boston, . .	23	$739,000	$1,070,000	$1,809,000	–	$1,809,000
Chelsea, . .	2	–	–	115,000	$15,000	130,000
Revere, . .	1	–	–	6,000	–	6,000
Totals, . .	26	$739,000	$1,070,000	$1,930,000	$15,000	$1,945,000
Worcester.						
Ashburnham, .	2	–	–	$11,000	$3,100	$14,100
Athol, . . .	1	$1,000	$5,000	6,000	1,000	7,000
Auburn, . .	1	–	–	5,000	–	5,000
Barre, . . .	1	–	–	6,000	1,000	7,000
Blackstone, . .	1	1,000	2,000	3,000	–	3,000
Boylston, . .	1	500	5,500	6,000	–	6,000
Brookfield, . .	1	1,500	11,500	13,000	–	13,000
Charlton, . .	1	–	–	3,500	–	3,500
Clinton, . .	1	3,000	15,000	18,000	–	18,000
Dana, . . .	1	–	–	2,400	–	2,400
Douglas, . .	2	–	–	8,000	–	8,000
Dudley, . .	1	–	–	2,000	–	2,000
Fitchburg, . .	2	24,000	64,000	88,000	8,000	96,000
Gardner, . .	1	800	8,200	9,000	–	9,000
Grafton, . .	1	–	–	6,100	–	6,100
Hardwick, . .	2	–	–	23,000	–	23,000
Harvard, . .	1	–	–	4,000	–	4,000
Holden, . .	1	–	–	3,000	–	3,000
Hubbardston, .	1	–	–	2,500	–	2,500
Lancaster, . .	1	–	–	5,000	–	5,000
Leicester, . .	1	–	–	15,000	–	15,000
Leominster, .	1	8,200	30,000	38,200	–	38,200

CONGREGATIONAL SOCIETIES—Concluded.

Counties and Towns.	Number.	Value of Land.	Value of Buildings.	Total Value of Real Estate.	Value of Personal Estate.	Total Value of Real and Personal Estate.
Wor'ster—Con.						
Lunenburg,	1	-	-	$5,000	-	$5,000
Milford,	1	$5,000	$27,500	32,500	$2,000	34,500
Millbury,	2	-	-	14,200	2,400	16,600
New Braintree,	1	-	-	6,500	-	6,500
Northborough,	1	-	-	10,500	-	10,500
Northbridge,	1	-	-	21,000	-	21,000
North Brookfield,	2	9,000	16,000	25,000	2,000	27,000
Oakham,	1	-	-	6,000	-	6,000
Oxford,	1	-	-	5,000	-	5,000
Paxton,	1	100	4,000	4,100	-	4,100
Petersham,	1	-	-	2,000	-	2,000
Phillipston,	1	50	5,000	5,050	-	5,050
Princeton,	1	-	-	6,000	-	6,000
Royalston,	2	2,000	6,000	8,000	-	8,000
Rutland,	1	100	3,000	3,100	-	3,100
Shrewsbury,	1	-	-	5,000	1,300	6,300
Southborough,	2	-	-	16,200	1,700	17,900
Southbridge,	1	-	-	10,000	800	10,800
Spencer,	1	-	-	12,000	3,000	15,000
Sterling,	1	-	-	1,500	-	1,500
Sturbridge,	1	-	-	5,000	-	5,000
Sutton,	1	-	-	3,000	1,000	4,000
Templeton,	1	-	-	4,500	-	4,500
Upton,	1	-	-	10,000	-	10,000
Uxbridge,	1	500	10,000	10,500	100	10,600
Warren,	2	-	-	5,000	100	5,100
Webster,	1	-	-	7,000	-	7,000
Westborough,	1	-	-	20,000	-	20,000
West Boylston,	1	-	-	7,200	-	7,200
West Brookfield,	1	-	-	3,500	-	3,500
Westminster,	1	-	-	3,500	300	3,800
Winchendon,	1	-	-	5,850	-	5,850
Worcester,	7	-	-	322,900	-	322,900
Totals,	70	$56,750	$212,700	$884,300	$27,800	$912,100

EPISCOPAL SOCIETIES.

Barnstable.						
Falmouth,	1	-	-	$3,500	-	$3,500

EPISCOPAL SOCIETIES—CONTINUED.

COUNTIES AND TOWNS.	Number.	Value of Land.	Value of Buildings.	Total Value of Real Estate.	Value of Personal Estate.	Total Value of Real and Personal Estate.
BERKSHIRE.						
Adams,	1	-	-	$20,000	-	$20,000
Great Barrington,	2	-	-	16,500	-	16,500
Lanesborough,	1	-	-	3,000	$1,000	4,000
Lee,	1	-	-	5,000	-	5,000
Lenox,	1	-	-	6,000	-	6,000
Pittsfield,	1	-	-	17,000	-	17,000
Sheffield,	1	-	-	1,000	-	1,000
Stockbridge,	1	$1,000	$4,000	5,000	1,000	6,000
Williamstown,	1	-	-	2,500	-	2,500
Totals,	10	$1,000	$4,000	$76,000	$2,000	$78,000
BRISTOL.						
Attleborough,	1	-	-	$8,000	$300	$8,300
New Bedford,	1	-	-	8,600	-	8,600
Swanzey,	1	-	-	3,000	-	3,000
Taunton,	2	$5,000	$80,000	85,000	5,000	90,000
Totals,	5	$5,000	$80,000	$104,600	$5.300	$109,900
ESSEX.						
Amesbury,	1	-	-	$6,000	-	$6,000
Andover,	1	$500	$8,000	8,500	-	8,500
Beverly,	1	-	-	3,000	-	3,000
Danvers,	1	-	-	4,800	-	4,800
Gloucester,	1	-	-	6,000	-	6,000
Groveland,	1	300	7,000	7,300	-	7,300
Haverhill,	1	-	-	10,000	-	10,000
Ipswich,	1	200	5,000	5,200	-	5,200
Lawrence,	2	4,500	23,000	27,500	$4,500	32,000
Lynn,	2	7,000	8,000	15,000	-	15,000
Marblehead,	1	-	-	5,500	-	5,500
Newburyport,	1	1,500	13,000	14,500	14,000	28,500
Salem,	2	-	-	43,000	-	43,000
Totals,	16	$14,000	$64,000	$156,300	$18,500	$174,800
FRANKLIN.						
Ashfield,	1	-	-	$1,800	-	$1,800
Greenfield,	1	$2,500	$8,500	11,000	$1,500	12,500
Totals,	2	$2,500	$8,500	$12,800	$1,500	$14,300

EPISCOPAL SOCIETIES—CONTINUED.

COUNTIES AND TOWNS.	Number.	Value of Land.	Value of Buildings.	Total Value of Real Estate.	Value of Personal Estate.	Total Value of Real and Personal Estate.
HAMPDEN.						
Chicopee, . .	1	-	-	$500	-	$500
Holyoke, . .	1	$4,100	$10,000	14,100	-	14,100
Springfield, .	1	-	-	25,000	-	25,000
W. Springfield, .	1	1,000	3,000	4,000	-	4,000
Totals, . .	4	$5,100	$13,000	$43,600	-	$43,600
HAMPSHIRE.						
Amherst, . .	1	$800	$20,000	$20,800	-	$20,800
Northampton, .	1	-	-	7,000	$500	7,500
Totals, . .	2	$800	$20,000	$27,800	$500	$28,300
MIDDLESEX.						
Cambridge, .	4	-	-	$114,500	-	$114,500
Chelmsford, .	1	-	-	1,000	-	1,000
Framingham, .	1	$300	$6,000	6,300	-	6,300
Lincoln, . .	1	-	-	2,150	-	2,150
Lowell, . .	2	-	-	75,950	-	75,950
Malden, . .	1	-	-	13,000	-	13,000
Medford, . .	1	-	-	35,000	-	35,000
Melrose, . .	1	-	-	4,500	-	4,500
Newton, . .	2	-	-	99,000	$13,300	112,300
Pepperell, . .	1	-	-	4,000	-	4,000
Somerville, .	2	-	-	25,500	2,000	27,500
Waltham, . .	1	-	-	7,000	-	7,000
Woburn, . .	1	1,200	6,000	7,200	500	7,700
Totals, . .	19	$1,500	$12,000	$395,100	$15,800	$410,900
NORFOLK.						
Brookline, . .	2	-	-	$70,000	-	$70,000
Dedham, . .	1	$1,850	$25,000	26,850	-	26,850
Hyde Park, . .	1	16,750	3,000	19,750	$1,500	21,250
Quincy, . .	1	-	-	14,000	-	14,000
Weymouth, .	1	-	-	3,000	-	3,000
Wrentham, . .	1	-	-	5,000	-	5,000
Totals, . .	7	$18,600	$28,000	$138,600	$1,500	$140,100
PLYMOUTH.						
Bridgewater, .	1	$400	$7,000	$7,400	$1,000	$8,400
Hanover, . .	1	200	3,000	3,200	-	3,200
Plymouth, . .	1	-	-	2,000	350	2,350
Totals, . .	3	$600	$10,000	$12,600	$1,350	$13,950

EPISCOPAL SOCIETIES—CONCLUDED.

COUNTIES AND TOWNS.	Number.	Value of Land.	Value of Buildings.	Total Value of Real Estate.	Value of Personal Estate.	Total Value of Real and Personal Estate.
SUFFOLK.						
Boston, . .	16	$695,300	$328,300	$1,023,600	-	$1,023,600
Chelsea, . .	1	-	-	14,000	$1,000	15,000
Totals, . .	17	$695,300	$328,300	$1,037,600	$1,000	$1,038,600
WORCESTER.						
Blackstone, .	1	$300	$1,800	$2,100	-	$2,100
Fitchburg, . .	1	20,000	26,000	46,000	$2,500	48,500
Leicester, . .	1	-	-	2,500	-	2,500
Milford, . .	1	1,000	5,500	6,500	500	7,000
Oxford, . .	1	-	-	10,000	-	10,000
Southborough, .	1	-	-	8,000	1,000	9,000
Sutton, . .	1	-	-	3,000	500	3,500
Webster, . .	1	-	-	6,000	-	6,000
Worcester, . .	1	-	-	20,300	-	20,300
Totals, . .	9	$21,300	$33,300	$104,400	$4,500	$108,900

METHODIST SOCIETIES.

COUNTIES AND TOWNS.	Number.	Value of Land.	Value of Buildings.	Total Value of Real Estate.	Value of Personal Estate.	Total Value of Real and Personal Estate.
BARNSTABLE.						
Barnstable, . .	3	$100	$1,800	$1,900	-	$1,900
Chatham, . .	1	-	-	6,200	-	6,200
Dennis, . .	3	-	-	3,500	-	3,500
Falmouth, . .	3	-	-	5,400	-	5,400
Harwich, . .	3	-	-	1,800	-	1,800
Orleans, . .	1	50	1,200	1,250	-	1,250
Provincetown, .	2	-	-	36,500	$6,000	42,500
Sandwich, . .	5	-	-	10,050	-	10,050
Truro, . .	2	-	-	4,000	-	4,000
Wellfleet, . .	1	-	-	8,000	-	8,000
Yarmouth, . .	3	-	-	5,800	-	5,800
Totals, . .	27	$150	$3,000	$84,400	$6,000	$90,400
BERKSHIRE.						
Adams, . .	2	-	-	$55,000	-	$55,000
Cheshire, . .	1	-	-	1,500	-	1,500
Dalton, . .	1	-	-	8,000	$500	8,500
Egremont, . .	1	-	-	1,200	-	1,200
Gt. Barrington, .	3	-	-	5,500	-	5,500
Lanesborough, .	1	-	-	800	-	800
Lee, . . .	3	-	-	5,800	-	5,800

METHODIST SOCIETIES—CONTINUED.

COUNTIES AND TOWNS.	Number.	Value of Land.	Value of Buildings.	Total Value of Real Estate.	Value of Personal Estate.	Total Value of Real and Personal Estate.
BERKSH.—Con.						
Lenox, . .	1	-	-	$2,000	-	$2,000
N. Marlborough,	1	-	-	3,000	-	3,000
Pittsfield, . .	1	-	-	50,000	-	50,000
Savoy, . .	1	-	-	500	-	500
Sheffield, . .	2	-	-	6,500	-	6,500
Tyringham, .	1	-	-	5,000	-	5,000
W. Stockbridge, .	1	-	-	1,500	-	1,500
Williamstown, .	1	-	-	15,000	-	15,000
Totals, . .	21	-	-	$161,300	$500	$161,800
BRISTOL.						
Acushnet, . .	2	-	-	$6,000	-	$6,000
Attleborough, .	1	-	-	9,400	$500	9,900
Berkley, . .	1	-	-	1,800	100	1,900
Dartmouth, .	1	-	-	600	-	600
Dighton, . .	2	$400	$6,000	6,400	-	6,400
Easton, . .	2	-	-	2,500	-	2,500
Fairhaven, . .	1	-	-	5,000	-	5,000
Fall River, . .	5	34,500	50,000	84,500	-	84,500
Mansfield, . .	1	-	-	2,000	-	2,000
New Bedford, .	4	-	-	51,500	-	51,500
Norton, . .	1	50	1,000	1,050	-	1,050
Rehoboth, . .	1	-	-	1,200	-	1,200
Seekonk, . .	1	-	-	5,000	-	5,000
Somerset, . .	2	-	-	17,000	-	17,000
Taunton, . .	3	4,100	36,000	40,100	1,500	41,600
Westport, . .	1	-	-	2,500	-	2,500
Totals, . .	29	$39,050	$93,000	$236,550	$2,100	$238,650
DUKES.						
Chilmark, . .	1	-	-	$1,500	-	$1,500
Edgartown, .	1	$1,000	$16,000	17,000	-	17,000
Tisbury, . .	2	-	-	14,500	-	14,500
Totals, . .	4	$1,000	$16,000	$33,000	-	$33,000
ESSEX.						
Andover, . .	1	$100	$2,750	$2,850	-	$2,850
Beverly, . .	1	-	-	4,000	-	4,000
Danvers, . .	1	-	-	7,400	-	7,400
Essex, . . .	1	-	-	2,500	-	2,500
Gloucester, . .	3	-	-	17,500	-	17,500
Groveland, . .	1	150	4,000	4,150	-	4,150

METHODIST SOCIETIES—Continued.

Counties and Towns.	Number.	Value of Land.	Value of Buildings.	Total Value of Real Estate.	Value of Personal Estate.	Total Value of Real and Personal Estate.
Essex—Con.						
Haverhill,	2	-	-	$55,000	-	$55,000
Ipswich,	1	$200	$7,000	7,200	$1,500	8,700
Lawrence,	6	7,100	41,500	48,600	6,500	55,100
Lynn,	7	27,500	73,000	100,500	-	100,500
Marblehead,	1	-	-	6,400	-	6,400
Methuen,	1	-	-	5,200	800	6,000
Nahant,	1	-	-	4,400	-	4,400
Newbury,	1	-	-	2,000	-	2,000
Newburyport,	2	2,000	13,500	15,500	-	15,500
North Andover,	1	-	-	3,000	100	3,100
Peabody,	1	-	-	13,000	-	13,000
Rockport,	1	-	-	7,500	-	7,500
Salem,	2	-	-	26,000	-	26,000
Salisbury,	2	-	-	11,000	-	11,000
Saugus,	2	-	-	10,000	-	10,000
Swampscott,	1	-	-	10,000	-	10,000
Topsfield,	1	-	-	6,200	-	6,200
Totals,	41	$37,050	$141,750	$369,900	$8,900	$378,800
Franklin.						
Bernardston,	1	-	-	$1,500	-	$1,500
Buckland,	2	-	-	4,500	-	4,500
Charlemont,	1	-	-	600	-	600
Colrain,	2	-	-	1,300	-	1,300
Conway,	1	-	-	5,500	-	5,500
Deerfield,	1	-	-	2,000	-	2,000
Gill,	1	$300	$1,500	1,800	$300	2,100
Greenfield,	1	1,000	500	1,500	200	1,700
Heath,	1	-	-	1,800	-	1,800
Leyden,	1	-	-	1,500	-	1,500
Montague,	1	-	-	1,000	-	1,000
New Salem,	1	-	-	700	-	700
Rowe,	1	-	-	500	-	500
Shutesbury,	1	-	-	800	-	800
Totals,	16	$1,300	$2,000	$25,000	$500	$25,500
Hampden.						
Agawam,	1	-	-	$2,000	-	$2,000
Blandford,	1	-	-	1,800	-	1,800
Chester,	1	$200	$1,800	2,000	-	2,000
Chicopee,	2	-	-	12,100	-	12,100
Holyoke,	1	3,100	10,000	13,100	-	13,100
Longmeadow,	1	-	-	2,600	-	2,600

METHODIST SOCIETIES—CONTINUED.

COUNTIES AND TOWNS.	Number.	Value of Land.	Value of Buildings.	Total Value of Real Estate.	Value of Personal Estate.	Total Value of Real and Personal Estate.
HAMPDEN—Con.						
Ludlow,	1	-	-	$2,500	-	$2,500
Monson,	1	$300	$6,000	6,300	-	6,300
Montgomery,	1	-	-	700	-	700
Palmer,	1	-	-	3,800	-	3,800
Russell,	1	-	-	3,500	-	3,500
Southwick,	1	100	1,900	2,000	-	2,000
Springfield,	5	-	-	212,000	-	212,000
Wales,	1	-	-	1,500	-	1,500
Westfield,	2	10,650	8,000	18,650	-	18,650
Wilbraham,	3	-	-	29,000	-	29,000
Totals,	24	$14,350	$27,700	$313,550	-	$313,550
HAMPSHIRE.						
Amherst,	1	$100	$500	$600	-	$600
Belchertown,	1	-	-	4,000	$500	4,500
Easthampton,	1	-	-	7,400	-	7,400
Enfield,	1	-	-	5,000	-	5,000
Northampton,	2	-	-	13,000	500	13,500
Pelham,	1	-	-	1,500	-	1,500
South Hadley,	1	200	3,000	3,200	-	3,200
Southampton,	1	-	-	2,000	-	2,000
Ware,	1	500	6,000	6,500	-	6,500
Williamsburg,	1	-	-	6,200	-	6,200
Worthington,	1	-	-	2,500	100	2,600
Totals,	12	$800	$9,500	$51,900	$1,100	$53,000
MIDDLESEX.						
Ashland,	1	-	-	$5,000	-	$5,000
Cambridge,	4	-	-	46,000	-	46,000
Dracut,	1	-	-	800	-	800
Everett,	1	-	-	7,500	$1,000	8,500
Framingham,	2	$1,900	$5,500	7,400	-	7,400
Holliston,	1	-	-	2,000	500	2,500
Hopkinton,	1	-	-	6,000	-	6,000
Hudson,	1	-	-	7,000	-	7,000
Lowell,	4	-	-	59,100	-	59,100
Malden,	3	-	-	95,000	-	95,000
Marlborough,	1	-	-	4,000	500	4,500
Maynard,	1	-	-	2,400	-	2,400
Medford,	2	-	-	52,500	-	52,500
Melrose,	1	-	-	20,000	-	20,000
Natick,	1	-	-	14,000	-	14,000
Newton,	5	-	-	60,700	3,200	63,900

METHODIST SOCIETIES—CONTINUED.

COUNTIES AND TOWNS.	Number.	Value of Land.	Value of Buildings.	Total Value of Real Estate.	Value of Personal Estate.	Total Value of Real and Personal Estate.
MID'LESEX—Con.						
Reading, . .	1	$2,400	$3,500	$5,900	$700	$6,600
Somerville,. .	4	-	-	33,900	500	34,400
Stoneham, . .	1	2,500	12,000	14,500	-	14,500
Stow, . . .	1	-	-	3,100	-	3,100
Sudbury, . .	1	-	-	2,000	-	2,000
Townsend, . .	1	-	-	6,000	50	6,050
Wakefield, . .	1	-	-	22,500	-	22,500
Waltham, . .	1	-	-	18,000	-	18,000
Watertown, .	1	3,900	6,500	10,400	500	10,900
Wayland, . .	2	-	-	9,000	-	9,000
Westford, . .	1	-	-	5,000	-	5,000
Weston, . .	1	-	-	3,500	-	3,500
Woburn, . .	1	5,000	20,000	25,000	1,400	26,400
Totals, . .	47	$15,700	$47,500	$548,200	$8,350	$556,550
NANTUCKET.						
Nantucket, . .	1	-	-	$4,500	-	$4,500
NORFOLK.						
Braintree, . .	1	-	-	$3,500	-	$3,500
Brookline, . .	1	-	-	15,000	-	15,000
Cohasset, . .	1	-	-	2,500	$100	2,600
Dedham, . .	1	$350	$2,000	2,350	-	2,350
Franklin, . .	1	800	12,000	12,800	1,500	14,300
Hyde Park, .	1	6,000	12,000	18,000	500	18,500
Medway, . .	1	-	-	3,600	-	3,600
Quincy, . .	2	-	-	10,500	-	10,500
Randolph, . .	1	-	-	1,000	-	1,000
Stoughton, . .	2	-	-	13,000	-	13,000
Walpole, . .	1	500	5,000	5,500	500	6,000
Weymouth, .	1	-	-	16,500	3,000	$19,500
Totals, . .	14	$7,650	$31,000	$104,250	$5,600	$109,850
PLYMOUTH.						
Brockton, . .	2	$3,100	$17,000	$20,100	-	$20,100
Carver, . .	1	-	-	1,000	-	1,000
Duxbury, . .	2	350	6,000	6,350	$600	6,950
E. Bridgewater, .	1	-	-	4,300	-	4,300
Hingham, . .	1	-	-	4,000	-	4,000
Hull, . .	1	-	-	500	-	500
Marion, . .	1	-	-	2,000	200	2,200
Marshfield, . .	1	-	-	3,000	-	3,000
Middleborough, .	3	700	9,000	9,700	1,600	11,300

METHODIST SOCIETIES—CONTINUED.

COUNTIES AND TOWNS.	Number.	Value of Land.	Value of Buildings.	Total Value of Real Estate.	Value of Personal Estate.	Total Value of Real and Personal Estate.
PLYMOUTH—Con.						
Pembroke, . .	1	$100	$2,500	$2,600	-	$2,600
Plymouth, . .	5	-	-	7,500	$1,200	8,700
Rockland, . .	1	300	4,000	4,300	-	4,300
Scituate, . .	1	-	-	6,000	-	6,000
South Scituate, .	1	-	-	2,000	-	2,000
Wareham, . .	1	-	-	3,500	-	3,500
W. Bridgewater,	1	-	-	3,200	-	3,200
Totals, . .	24	$4,550	$38,500	$80,050	$3,600	$83,650
SUFFOLK.						
Boston, . .	19	$367,200	$433,000	$800,200	-	$800,200
Chelsea, . .	2	-	-	60,500	$6,000	66,500
Winthrop, . .	1	-	-	14,000	-	14,000
Totals, . .	22	$367,200	$433,000	$874,700	$6,000	$880,700
WORCESTER.						
Ashburnham, .	1	-	-	$20,000	$3,000	$23,000
Athol, . .	2	$1,150	$6,550	7,700	1,000	8,700
Barre, . .	1	-	-	2,500	500	3,000
Blackstone, .	2	600	3,600	4,200	-	4,200
Brookfield, . .	1	1,000	8,000	9,000	-	9,000
Charlton, . .	1	-	-	2,500	-	2,500
Clinton, . .	1	1,500	8,000	9,500	-	9,500
Douglas, . .	1	-	-	2,000	-	2,000
Dudley, .	1	-	-	1,000	-	1,000
Fitchburg, . .	2	6,500	11,200	17,700	1,800	19,500
Gardner, . .	1	600	2,400	3,000	-	3,000
Grafton, . .	1	-	-	2,000	-	2,000
Hubbardston, .	1	-	-	3,000	-	3,000
Leicester, . .	2	-	-	4,000	-	4,000
Leominster, .	1	2,450	20,000	22,450	-	22,450
Lunenburg, .	1	-	-	3,000	-	3,000
Mendon, . .	1	-	-	1,500	-	1,500
Milford, . .	1	1,500	10,000	11,500	700	12,200
Millbury, . .	1	-	-	4,000	500	4,500
Northbridge, .	1	-	-	2,000	-	2,000
N. Brookfield, .	1	500	3,000	3,500	-	3,500
Oxford, . .	1	-	-	7,000	-	7,000
Phillipston, .	1	50	500	550	-	550
Princeton, . .	1	-	-	3,100	-	3,100
Royalston, . .	1	500	1,500	2,000	-	2,000
Shrewsbury, .	1	-	-	5,000	800	5,800
Southbridge, .	1	-	-	12,000	500	12,500

METHODIST SOCIETIES—Concluded.

Counties and Towns.	Number.	Value of Land.	Value of Buildings.	Total Value of Real Estate.	Value of Personal Estate.	Total Value of Real and Personal Estate.
Wor'ster—Con.						
Spencer,	1	-	-	$8,000	$1,500	$9,500
Templeton,	1	-	-	4,000	-	4,000
Warren,	1	-	-	4,000	100	4,100
Webster,	2	-	-	15,300	-	15,300
Westborough,	1	-	-	8,500	-	8,500
West Boylston,	1	-	-	5,000	-	5,000
West Brookfield,	1	-	-	2,000	-	2,000
Winchendon,	1	-	-	2,850	-	2,850
Worcester,	6	-	-	163,300	-	163,300
Totals,	46	$16,350	$74,750	$378,650	$10,400	$389,050

UNITARIAN SOCIETIES.

Counties and Towns.	Number.	Value of Land.	Value of Buildings.	Total Value of Real Estate.	Value of Personal Estate.	Total Value of Real and Personal Estate.
Barnstable.						
Barnstable,	1	-	-	$4,500	$600	$5,100
Brewster,	1	-	-	2,000	-	2,000
Sandwich,	1	-	-	4,700	-	4,700
Totals,	3	-	-	$11,200	$600	$11,800
Bristol.						
Dighton,	1	$200	$1,000	$1,200	-	$1,200
Easton,	2	-	-	4,000	-	4,000
Fairhaven,	1	-	-	6,000	-	6,000
Fall River,	1	$12,300	12,000	24,300	-	24,300
Mansfield,	1	-	-	3,000	-	3,000
New Bedford,	1	-	-	40,000	-	40,000
Norton,	1	100	4,000	4,100	-	4,100
Taunton,	1	10,000	55,000	65,000	$4,000	69,000
Totals,	9	$22,600	$72,000	$147,600	$4,000	$151,600
Dukes.						
Tisbury,	1	-	-	$3,000	-	$3,000
Essex.						
Beverly,	1	-	-	$5,000	-	$5,000
Danvers,	1	-	-	8,500	-	8,500
Gloucester,	1	-	-	16,000	-	16,000
Haverhill,	1	-	-	11,000	-	11,000
Lawrence,	1	$2,000	$14,000	16,000	$2,500	18,500

UNITARIAN SOCIETIES—CONTINUED.

COUNTIES AND TOWNS.	Number.	Value of Land.	Value of Buildings.	Total Value of Real Estate.	Value of Personal Estate.	Total Value of Real and Personal Estate.
ESSEX—Con.						
Lynn,	1	$6,000	$8,000	$14,000	-	$14,000
Lynnfield,	1	500	1,500	2,000	-	2,000
Newburyport,	1	7,000	14,000	21,000	$5,000	26,000
North Andover,	1	-	-	5,000	700	5,700
Peabody,	1	-	-	18,000	-	18,000
Salem,	4	-	-	134,000	-	134,000
Totals,	14	$15,500	$37,500	$250,500	$8,200	$258,700
FRANKLIN.						
Bernardston,	1	-	-	$5,000	-	$5,000
Greenfield,	1	$3,000	$6,000	9,000	$1,500	10,500
New Salem,	1	-	-	400	-	400
Northfield,	1	-	-	6,000	-	6,000
Rowe,	1	-	-	600	-	600
Warwick,	1	-	-	1,600	-	1,600
Whately,	1	-	-	1,250	200	1,450
Totals,	7	$3,000	$6,000	$23,850	$1,700	$25,550
HAMPDEN.						
Chicopee,	1	-	-	$5,600	-	$5,600
Springfield,	1	-	-	150,000	-	150,000
Totals,	2	-	-	$155,600	-	$155,600
HAMPSHIRE.						
Northampton,	1	-	-	$16,000	$1,000	$17,000
Ware,	1	$1,000	$13,000	14,000	7,000	21,000
Totals,	2	$1,000	$13,000	$30,000	$8,000	$38,000
MIDDLESEX.						
Arlington,	1	$15,200	$20,000	$35,200	$3,500	$38,700
Ashby,	1	-	-	3,500	-	3,500
Ayer,	1	-	-	9,200	-	9,200
Bedford,	1	-	-	5,500	-	5,500
Billerica,	1	500	8,000	8,500	3,000	11,500
Cambridge,	3	-	-	87,000	-	87,000
Carlisle,	1	-	-	2,000	600	2,600
Concord,	1	-	-	7,000	3,000	10,000
Framingham,	1	500	6,000	6,500	-	6,500
Groton,	1	-	-	7,000	-	7,000
Lexington,	1	1,500	16,000	17,500	2,200	19,700
Lincoln,	1	-	-	2,650	-	2,650

UNITARIAN SOCIETIES—CONTINUED.

COUNTIES AND TOWNS.	Number.	Value of Land.	Value of Buildings.	Total Value of Real Estate.	Value of Personal Estate.	Total Value of Real and Personal Estate.
Littleton,	1	-	-	$3,000	-	$3,000
Lowell,	2	-	-	15,500	-	15,500
Marlborough,	1	-	-	15,000	$2,000	17,000
Medford,	1	-	-	25,000	-	25,000
Melrose,	1	-	-	4,500	-	4,500
Natick,	1	-	-	7,500	800	8,300
Newton,	3	-	-	45,500	2,000	47,500
Pepperell,	1	-	-	5,000	-	5,000
Sherborn,	1	$400	$5,000	5,400	-	5,400
Shirley,	1	-	-	2,500	1,000	3,500
Somerville,	1	-	-	35,000	5,000	40,000
Stoneham,	1	3,500	20,000	23,500	-	23,500
Stow,	1	-	-	3,400	-	3,400
Sudbury,	1	-	-	4,000	-	4,000
Townsend,	1	-	-	2,000	-	2,000
Tyngsborough,	1	-	-	4,500	-	4,500
Waltham,	1	-	-	25,000	-	25,000
Watertown,	1	17,400	13,000	30,400	1,500	31,900
Wayland,	1	-	-	6,000	-	6,000
Westford,	1	-	-	4,000	-	4,000
Weston,	1	-	-	8,000	-	8,000
Winchester,	1	2,000	18,000	20,000	-	20,000
Woburn,	1	7,000	35,000	42,000	7,300	49,300
Totals,	40	$48,000	$141,000	$528,250	$31,900	$560,150
NANTUCKET.						
Nantucket,	1	-	-	$7,000	$1,000	$8,000
NORFOLK.						
Brookline,	1	-	-	$20,000	-	$20,000
Canton,	1	-	-	5,000	-	5,000
Cohasset,	1	-	-	5,000	$1,000	6,000
Dedham,	2	$5,000	$16,000	21,000	-	21,000
Dover,	1	100	2,000	2,100	-	2,100
Medfield,	1	-	-	5,000	-	5,000
Milton,	1	-	-	18,000	-	18,000
Needham,	2	1,100	5,000	6,100	-	6,100
Quincy,	1	-	-	38,000	-	38,000
Sharon,	1	1,000	4,000	5,000	-	5,000
Walpole,	1	1,000	12,000	13,000	1,000	14,000
Totals,	13	$8,200	$39,000	$138,200	$2,000	$140,200

UNITARIAN SOCIETIES—CONTINUED.

COUNTIES AND TOWNS.	Number.	Value of Land.	Value of Buildings.	Total Value of Real Estate.	Value of Personal Estate.	Total Value of Real and Personal Estate.
PLYMOUTH.						
Bridgewater, .	1	$2,000	$12,000	$14,000	$2,000	$16,000
Duxbury, . .	1	100	3,500	3,600	600	4,200
E. Bridgewater, .	1	-	-	5,000	-	5,000
Hingham, . .	3	-	-	40,000	-	40,000
Kingston, . .	1	-	-	6,200	500	6,700
Marshfield, . .	1		-	3,000	-	3,000
Pembroke, . .	1	100	5,000	5,100	1,000	6,100
Plymouth, . .	1	-	-	12,000	1,800	13,800
Scituate, . .	1	-	-	9,000	-	9,000
South Scituate, .	1	-	-	5,000	600	5,600
W. Bridgewater,	1	-	-	5,700	-	5,700
Totals, . .	13	$2,200	$20,500	$108,600	$6,500	$115,100
SUFFOLK.						
Boston, . .	27	$1,199,700	$1,005,700	$2,205,400	-	$2,205,400
Chelsea, . .	1	-	-	12,000	$1,000	13,000
Revere, . .	1	-	-	6,000	-	6,000
Totals, . .	29	$1,199,700	$1,005,700	$2,223,400	$1,000	$2,224,400
WORCESTER.						
Athol, . .	1	$1,200	$3,000	$4,200	$200	$4,400
Barre, . .	1	-	-	5,000	1,500	6,500
Berlin, . .	1	-	-	4,000	-	4,000
Bolton, . .	1	-	-	6,000	-	6,000
Brookfield, . .	1	1,000	12,000	13,000	-	13,000
Clinton, . .	1	2,000	11,000	13,000	-	13,000
Fitchburg, . .	1	24,000	20,800	44,800	4,000	48,800
Grafton, . .	1	-	-	5,400	-	5,400
Harvard, . .	1	-	-	3,000	-	3,000
Hubbardston, .	1	-	-	5,000	-	5,000
Lancaster, . .	1	-	-	10,000	-	10,000
Leicester, . .	1	-	-	4,000	600	4,600
Leominster, .	1	7,600	15,000	22,600	-	22,600
Mendon, . .	1	-	-	3,500	-	3,500
Milford, . .	1	600	6,000	6,600	600	7,200
Northborough, .	1	-	-	14,000	-	14,000
Petersham, . .	1	-	-	5,000	400	5,400
Sterling, . .	1	-	-	5,000	-	5,000
Sturbridge, . .	1	-	-	5,000	-	5,000
Templeton, . .	1	-	-	15,000	-	15,000
Upton, . .	1	-	-	12,000	-	12,000

UNITARIAN SOCIETIES—CONCLUDED.

COUNTIES AND TOWNS.	Number.	Value of Land.	Value of Buildings.	Total Value of Real Estate.	Value of Personal Estate.	Total Value of Real and Personal Estate.
WO'STER—Con.						
Uxbridge, . .	1	$500	$10,000	$10,500	$100	$10,600
Westborough, .	1	-	-	9,000	-	9,000
Winchendon, .	1	-	-	18,350	-	18,350
Worcester, . .	2	-	-	93,600	-	93,600
Totals, . .	26	$36,900	$77,800	$337,550	$7,400	$344,950

UNIVERSALIST SOCIETIES.

COUNTIES AND TOWNS.	Number.	Value of Land.	Value of Buildings.	Total Value of Real Estate.	Value of Personal Estate.	Total Value of Real and Personal Estate.
BARNSTABLE.						
Chatham, . .	1	-	-	$5,200	-	$5,200
Orleans, . .	1	$50	$1,200	1,250	-	1,250
Provincetown, .	1	-	-	6,800	$2,000	8,800
Wellfleet, . .	1	-	-	1,000	-	1,000
Yarmouth, . .	1	-	-	2,000	-	2,000
Totals, . .	5	$50	$1,200	$16,250	$2,000	$18,250
BERKSHIRE.						
Adams, . .	2	-	-	$25,000	-	$25,000
Cheshire, . .	1	-	-	1,200	-	1,200
Totals, . .	3	-	-	$26,200	-	$26,200
BRISTOL.						
Attleborough, .	1	-	-	$5,000	$1,200	$6,200
New Bedford, .	1	-	-	5,400	-	5,400
Swanzey, . .	1	-	-	1,500	-	1,500
Taunton, . .	1	$2,000	$6,000	8,000	1,000	9,000
Totals, . .	4	$2,000	$6,000	$19,900	$2,200	$22,100
ESSEX.						
Amesbury, . .	1	-	-	$3,000	-	$3,000
Beverly, . .	1	-	-	4,000	-	4,000
Danvers, . .	1	-	-	8,500	-	8,500
Essex, . .	1	-	-	5,000	-	5,000
Gloucester, . .	3	-	-	35,500	-	35,500
Haverhill, . .	2	-	-	16,550	-	16,550
Lawrence, . .	1	$3,500	$23,000	26,500	$3,500	30,000
Lynn, . .	2	25,000	110,000	135,000	-	135,000
Marblehead, .	1	-	-	10,700	-	10,700

UNIVERSALIST SOCIETIES—CONTINUED.

COUNTIES AND TOWNS.	Number.	Value of Land.	Value of Buildings.	Total Value of Real Estate.	Value of Personal Estate.	Total Value of Real and Personal Estate.
ESSEX—Con.						
Methuen,	1	-	-	$3,100	$500	$3,600
Newburyport,	1	$2,000	$9,000	11,000	-	11,000
Peabody,	1	-	-	13,000	-	13,000
Rockport,	2	-	-	15,500	-	15,500
Salem,	1	-	-	25,000	-	25,000
Salisbury,	1	-	-	4,000	-	4,000
Saugus,	1	-	-	3,000	-	3,000
Totals,	21	$30,500	$142,000	$319,350	$4,000	$323,350
FRANKLIN.						
Ashfield,	1	-	-	$300	-	$300
Bernardston,	1	-	-	2,000	-	2,000
Leyden,	1	-	-	500	-	500
Orange,	2	$1,100	$9,800	10,900	$1,400	12,300
Shelburne,	1	-	-	5,000	-	5,000
Totals,	6	$1,100	$9,800	$18,700	$1,400	$20,100
HAMPDEN.						
Chicopee,	1	-	-	$3,000	-	$3,000
Granville,	1	-	-	600	-	600
Springfield,	1	-	-	54,000	-	54,000
Westfield,	1	$800	$1,500	2,300	-	2,300
Totals,	4	$800	$1,500	$59,900	-	$59,900
HAMPSHIRE.						
Cummington,	1	-	-	$2,500	-	$2,500
MIDDLESEX.						
Acton,	1	-	-	$4,500	-	$4,500
Arlington,	1	$2,700	$12,000	14,700	$3,000	17,700
Cambridge,	3	-	-	52,000	-	52,000
Everett,	1	-	-	6,200	700	6,900
Lexington,	1	400	7,100	7,500	2,000	9,500
Lowell,	2	-	-	36,500	-	36,500
Malden,	1	-	-	40,000	-	40,000
Marlborough,	1	-	-	8,000	500	8,500
Medford,	1	-	-	13,000	-	13,000
Melrose,	1	-	-	8,000	-	8,000

UNIVERSALIST SOCIETIES—CONTINUED.

COUNTIES AND TOWNS.	Number.	Value of Land.	Value of Buildings.	Total Value of Real Estate.	Value of Personal Estate.	Total Value of Real and Personal Estate.
MID'SEX—Con.						
Newton,	1	-	-	$19,500	$500	$20,000
North Reading,	1	-	-	1,500	-	1,500
Shirley,	1	-	-	8,000	2,000	10,000
Somerville,	1	-	-	42,000	5,000	47,000
Townsend,	1	-	-	2,000	-	2,000
Tyngsborough,	1	-	-	2,700	-	2,700
Wakefield,	1	-	-	18,000	-	18,000
Totals,	20	$3,100	$19,100	$284,100	$13,700	$297,800
NORFOLK.						
Canton,	1	-	-	$4,000	-	$4,000
Foxborough,	1	-	-	5,400	$800	6,200
Franklin,	1	$800	$25,000	25,800	4,500	30,300
Norwood,	1	1,000	14,000	15,000	1,000	16,000
Quincy,	1	-	-	8,000	-	8,000
Stoughton,	1	-	-	13,000	-	13,000
Weymouth,	3	-	-	19,600	2,800	22,400
Wrentham,	1	-	-	2,000	-	2,000
Totals,	10	$1,800	$39,000	$92,800	$9,100	$101,900
PLYMOUTH.						
Abington,	1	$300	$6,000	$6,300	-	$6,300
Brockton,	1	5,000	15,000	20,000	-	20,000
Halifax,	1	-	-	500	-	500
Hingham,	1	-	-	4,000	-	4,000
Marion,	1	-	-	2,500	$200	2,700
Mattapoisett,	1	-	-	5,000	-	5,000
Plymouth,	1	-	-	6,000	1,000	7,000
South Scituate,	1	-	-	3,500	400	3,900
Totals,	8	$5,300	$21,000	$47,800	$1,600	$49,400
SUFFOLK.						
Boston,	6	$136,100	$183,000	$319,100	-	$319,100
Chelsea,	1	-	-	54,000	$4,000	58,000
Totals,	7	$136,100	$183,000	$373,100	$4,000	$377,100
WORCESTER.						
Charlton,	1	-	-	$3,500	-	$3,500
Dana,	1	-	-	1,600	-	1,600
Fitchburg,	1	$5,000	$6,500	11,500	$1,000	12,500
Gardner,	1	500	7,000	7,500	-	7,500

UNIVERSALIST SOCIETIES—CONCLUDED.

COUNTIES ANE TOWNS.	Number.	Value of Land.	Value of Buildings.	Total Value of Real Estate.	Value of Personal Estate.	Total Value of Real ana Personal Estate.
WO'STER—Con.						
Hardwick, . .	1	-	-	$2,200	-	$2,200
Milford, . .	1	$1,200	$15,000	16,200	$1,000	17,200
Oxford, . .	1	-	-	3,500	-	3,500
Southbridge, .	1	-	-	12,000	1,000	13,000
Warren, . .	1	-	-	4,000	500	4,500
Webster, . .	1	-	-	8,700	-	8,700
Westminster, .	1	-	-	2,300	350	2,650
Worcester, . .	1	-	-	61,700	-	61,700
Totals, . .	12	$6,700	$28,500	$134,700	$3,850	$138,550

ALL OTHER SOCIETIES.

COUNTIES ANE TOWNS.	Number.	Value of Land.	Value of Buildings.	Total Value of Real Estate.	Value of Personal Estate.	Total Value of Real ana Personal Estate.
BARNSTABLE.						
Barnstable,. .	2	$300	$10,500	$10,800	$600	$11,400
Dennis, . .	1	-	-	600	-	600
Eastham, . .	1	-	-	100	-	100
Falmouth, . .	1	-	-	2,100	-	2,100
Harwich, . .	2	-	-	2,500	-	2,500
Sandwich, . .	1	-	-	2,250	-	2,250
Truro, . .	1	-	-	1,200	-	1,200
Yarmouth, . .	3	-	-	12,200	-	12,200
Totals, . .	12	$300	$10,500	$31,750	$600	$32,350
BERKSHIRE.						
Adams, . .	1	-	-	$9,000	-	$9,000
Alford, . .	1	-	-	2,000	-	2,000
Pittsfield, . .	1	-	-	2,500	-	2,500
Lee, . . .	1	-	-	3,000	-	3,000
Mt. Washington,	1	-	-	3,000	-	3,000
Savoy, . .	1	-	-	100	-	100
Totals, . .	6	-	-	$19,600	-	$19,600
BRISTOL.						
Acushnet, . .	2	-	-	$1,000	-	$1,000
Attleborough, .	2	-	-	7,000	$500	7,500
Dartmouth,. .	9	-	-	7,400	-	7,400
Dighton, . .	2	$200	$1,300	1,500	-	1,500
Fairhaven, . .	2	-	-	2,800	-	2,800
Fall River, . .	6	34,350	42,300	76,650	-	76,650
Freetown, . .	5	-	-	7,150	-	7,150

ALL OTHER SOCIETIES—CONTINUED.

COUNTIES AND TOWNS.	Number.	Value of Land.	Value of Buildings.	Total Value of Real Estate.	Value of Personal Estate.	Total Value of Real and Personal Estate.
BRISTOL—Con.						
Mansfield,	3	-	-	$6,200	-	$6,200
New Bedford,	12	-	-	63,600	-	63,600
Rehoboth,	3	-	-	3,000	-	3,000
Somerset,	1	-	-	4,000	-	4,000
Swanzey,	1	-	-	6,000	-	6,000
Taunton,	3	$2,300	$11,400	13,700	$300	14,000
Westport,	9	-	-	12,200	-	12,200
Totals,	60	$36,850	$55,000	$212,200	$800	$213,000
ESSEX.						
Amesbury,	1	-	-	$4,000	-	$4,000
Gloucester,	1	-	-	300	-	300
Groveland,	1	$100	$500	600	-	600
Lawrence,	3	3,000	10,550	13,550	$1,950	15,500
Lynn,	2	15,000	8,000	23,000	-	23,000
Nahant,	1	-	-	12,000	-	12,000
Newburyport,	3	8,500	31,000	39,500	33,000	72,500
Peabody,	1	-	-	800	-	800
Rockport,	1	-	-	5,000	-	5,000
Salem,	2	-	-	20,000	-	20,000
Salisbury,	2	-	-	2,200	-	2,200
Swampscott,	1	-	-	2,500	-	2,500
West Newbury,	1	-	-	1,500	-	1,500
Totals,	20	$26,600	$50,050	$124,950	$34,950	$159,900
FRANKLIN.						
Deerfield,	1	-	-	$2,800	-	$2,800
New Salem,	1	-	-	400	-	400
Orange,	1	$50	$600	650	$200	850
Totals,	3	$50	$600	$3,850	$200	$4,050
HAMPDEN.						
Blandford,	1	-	-	$1,500	-	$1,500
Brimfield,	3	-	-	1,550	-	1,550
Chicopee,	1	-	-	1,050	-	1,050
Holyoke,	1	-	-	2,000	-	2,000
Ludlow,	1	-	-	2,500	-	2,500
Springfield,	3	-	-	125,000	-	125,000
Westfield,	1	$1,500	$5,000	6,500	-	6,500
Wilbraham,	1	-	-	1,300	-	1,300
Totals,	12	$1,500	$5,000	$141,400	-	$141,400

ALL OTHER SOCIETIES—CONTINUED.

COUNTIES AND TOWNS.	Number.	Value of Land.	Value of Buildings.	Total Value of Real Estate.	Value of Personal Estate.	Total Value of Real and Personal Estate.
HAMPSHIRE.						
Northampton, .	3	-	-	$4,000	-	$4,000
Pelham, . .	1	-	-	2,550	-	2,550
Prescott, . .	2	-	-	350	-	350
Totals, . .	6	-	-	$6,900	-	$6,900
MIDDLESEX.						
Cambridge, .	1	-	-	$7,500	-	$7,500
Chelmsford, .	2	-	-	4,500	-	4,500
Everett, . .	1	-	-	700	-	700
Hudson, . .	1	-	-	7,000	-	7,000
Lowell, . .	1	-	-	6,700	-	6,700
Melrose, . .	1	-	-	2,000	-	2,000
Newton, . .	1	-	-	9,500	-	9,500
Reading, . .	3	$3,000	$14,200	17,200	$3,600	20,800
Shirley, . .	1	-	-	1,000	-	1,000
Somerville, . .	1	-	-	2,000	-	2,000
Waltham, . .	1	-	-	15,000	-	15,000
Woburn, . .	1	350	2,000	2,350	150	2,500
Totals, . .	15	$3,350	$16,200	$75,450	$3,750	$79,200
NANTUCKET.						
Nantucket, . .	1	-	-	$800	-	$800
NORFOLK.						
Braintree, . .	1	-	-	$20,000	-	$20,000
Brookline, . .	2	-	-	45,000	-	45,000
Foxborough, .	1	-	-	1,100	-	1,100
Norfolk, . .	1	-	-	500	-	500
Quincy, . .	1	-	-	1,500	-	1,500
Totals, . .	6	-	-	$68,100	-	$68,100
PLYMOUTH.						
Abington, . .	1	$600	$5,500	$6,100	-	$6,100
Bridgewater, .	1	1,000	10,000	11,000	$1,500	12,500
Brockton, . .	2	8,800	14,500	23,300	-	23,300
Carver, . .	2	100	2,200	2,300	-	2,300
E. Bridgewater, .	1	-	-	3,200	-	3,200
Hingham, . .	1	-	-	1,500	-	1,500
Marion, . .	1	-	-	1,000	100	1,100
Mattapoisett, .	2	-	-	2,000	-	2,000
Pembroke, . .	1	50	500	550	-	550
Plymouth, . .	2	-	-	3,500	500	4,000

ALL OTHER SOCIETIES—CONCLUDED.

COUNTIES AND TOWNS.	Number.	Value of Land.	Value of Buildings.	Total Value of Real Estate.	Value of Personal Estate.	Total Value of Real and Personal Estate.
PLYMOUTH—Con.						
Rochester, . .	1	-	-	$3,100	-	$3,100
Wareham, . .	2	-	-	2,500	-	2,500
Totals, . .	17	$10,550	$32,700	$60,050	$2,100	$62,150
SUFFOLK.						
Boston, . .	18	$240,100	$249,000	$489,100	-	$489,100
Chelsea, . .	2	-	-	9,500	$500	10,000
Totals, . .	20	$240,100	$249,000	$498,600	$500	$499,100
WORCESTER.						
Athol, . . .	1	$500	$1,500	$2,000	-	$2,000
Blackstone, .	2	500	2,000	2,500	-	2,500
Bolton, . .	1	-	-	2,000	-	2,000
Charlton, . .	2	-	-	1,100	-	1,100
Harvard, . .	1	-	-	1,500	-	1,500
Leicester, . .	1	-	-	150	-	150
Northbridge, .	1	-	-	500	-	500
Southbridge, .	1	-	-	15,000	$1,000	16,000
Sutton, . .	1	-	-	1,550	-	1,550
Uxbridge, . .	1	100	500	600	-	600
Westborough, .	1	-	-	3,000	-	3,000
West Boylston, .	2	-	-	4,000	-	4,000
Worcester, . .	3	-	-	26,400	-	26,400
Totals, . .	18	$1,100	$4,000	$60,300	$1,000	$61,300

NOTE.—Of these (all others) there are,—

Eighteen Second Advent Societies, with a valuation of	$55,900
Thirty-two Societies of Friends, with a valuation of	106,850
Three Societies of Jews, with a valuation of	40,000
Six Lutheran Societies, with a valuation of	68,500
Nine Presbyterian Societies, with a valuation of	271,750
Two Societies of Shakers, with a valuation of	2,500
Fourteen Swedenborgian Societies (New Jerusalem), with a valuation of .	208,900
One hundred and twelve Societies which could not be credited to any of the denominations enumerated in the foregoing tables, with a valuation of	593,450
Total amount, ...	$1,347,850

The assessors of Eastham, in Barnstable County; Clarksburg, in Berkshire County, and Monroe, in Franklin County, report no churches.

No return could be obtained from the assessors of Melrose; the amounts were therefore made up from other sources, and are not official.

TABLE No 2.

Recapitulation, by Counties, showing Amount of Church Property exempt from Taxation, held by each Denomination in the Commonwealth.

BAPTIST SOCIETIES.

COUNTIES.	Number.	Value of Land.	Value of Buildings.	Total Value of Real Estate.	Value of Personal Estate.	Total Value of Real and Personal Estate.
Barnstable,	10	$400	$6,100	$16,350	$1,000	$17,350
Berkshire,	16	200	-	91,600	200	91,800
Bristol,	23	73,850	145.200	286,000	4,800	290,800
Dukes,	5	500	7,500	22,500	-	22,500
Essex,	39	45,050	190,100	536,800	9,600	546,400
Franklin,	17	3,500	8,000	38,700	1,700	40,400
Hampden,	17	15,150	42,100	223,650	500	224,150
Hampshire,	6	1,000	5,000	24,000	1,000	25,000
Middlesex,	54	30,500	100,800	903,500	36,000	939,500
Nantucket,	1	-	-	2,600	-	2,600
Norfolk,	22	15,150	45,200	191,650	4,200	195,850
Plymouth,	18	4,900	32,550	84,450	4,300	88,750
Suffolk,	28	802,900	690,600	1,613,500	5,000	1,618,500
Worcester,	37	23,550	74,500	365,100	7,550	372,650
Totals,	293	$1,016,650	$1,347,650	$4,400,400	$75,850	$4,476,250

CATHOLIC SOCIETIES.

COUNTIES.	Number.	Value of Land.	Value of Buildings.	Total Value of Real Estate.	Value of Personal Estate.	Total Value of Real and Personal Estate.
Barnstable,	2	-	-	$14,600	-	$14,600
Berkshire,	16	$1,200	$6,000	207,450	$1,000	208,450
Bristol,	13	33,850	169,500	268,250	2,500	270,750
Essex,	24	74,600	319,700	642,200	19,700	661,900
Franklin,	2	2,000	10,000	13,000	1,500	14,500
Hampden,	11	19,000	49,000	269,500	-	269,500
Hampshire,	7	2,700	43,000	64,800	-	64,800
Middlesex,	37	32,150	115,000	750,150	15,500	765,650
Nantucket,	1	-	-	3,000	-	3,000
Norfolk,	17	4,150	24,500	166,450	1,800	168,250
Plymouth,	7	4,400	33,000	60,800	1,000	61,800
Suffolk,	31	872,000	1,693,800	2,650,800	6,000	2,656,800
Worcester,	38	26,050	124,300	541,650	5,500	547,150
Totals,	206	$1,072,100	$2,587,800	$5,652,650	$54,500	$5,707,150

CONGREGATIONAL SOCIETIES.

Counties.	Number.	Value of Land.	Value of Buildings.	Total Value of Real Estate.	Value of Personal Estate.	Total Value of Real and Personal Estate.
Barnstable, .	20	$200	$9,400	$77,400	$6,700	$84,100
Berkshire, .	33	2,500	10,500	308,500	5,300	313,800
Bristol, . .	27	55,700	111,300	289,200	10,100	299,300
Dukes, . .	3	500	8,500	12,000	-	12,000
Essex, . .	66	83,700	397,800	914,850	32,250	947,100
Franklin,. .	29	7,300	46,900	115,350	19,250	134,600
Hampden, .	36	25,600	133,850	538,050	4,800	542,850
Hampshire, .	37	7,750	120,300	397,950	18,400	416,350
Middlesex, .	80	61,500	196,750	1,331,050	59,400	1,390,450
Nantucket, .	1	-	-	6,000	-	6,000
Norfolk, . .	36	24,850	99,300	485,700	24,000	509,700
Plymouth, .	35	25,450	135,900	229,150	11,000	240,150
Suffolk, . .	26	739,000	1,070,000	1,930,000	15,000	1,945,000
Worcester, .	70	56,750	212,700	884,300	27,800	912,100
Totals, . .	499	$1,090,800	$2,553,200	$7,519,500	$234,000	$7,753,500

EPISCOPAL SOCIETIES.

Counties.	Number.	Value of Land.	Value of Buildings.	Total Value of Real Estate.	Value of Personal Estate.	Total Value of Real and Personal Estate.
Barnstable, .	1	-	-	$3,500	-	$3,500
Berkshire, .	10	$1,000	$4,000	76,000	$2,000	78,000
Bristol, . .	5	5,000	80,000	104,600	5,300	109,900
Essex, . .	16	14,000	64,000	156,300	18,500	174,800
Franklin,. .	2	2,500	8,500	12,800	1,500	14,300
Hampden, .	4	5,100	13,000	43,600	-	43,600
Hampshire, .	2	800	20,000	27,800	500	28,300
Middlesex, .	19	1,500	12,000	395,100	15,800	410,900
Norfolk, . .	7	18,600	28,000	138,600	1,500	140,100
Plymouth, .	3	600	10,000	12,600	1,350	13,950
Suffolk, . .	17	695,300	328,300	1,037,600	1,000	1,038,600
Worcester, .	9	21,300	33,300	104,400	4,500	108,900
Totals, . .	95	$765,700	$601,100	$2,112,900	$51,950	$2,164,850

METHODIST SOCIETIES.

Counties.	Number.	Value of Land.	Value of Buildings.	Total Value of Real Estate.	Value of Personal Estate.	Total Value of Real and Personal Estate.
Barnstable, .	27	$150	$3,000	$84,400	$6,000	$90,400
Berkshire, .	21	-	-	161,300	500	161,800
Bristol, . .	29	39,050	93,000	236,550	2,100	238,650
Dukes, . .	4	1,000	16,000	33,000	-	33,000
Essex, . .	41	37,050	141,750	369,900	8,900	378,800
Franklin, .	16	1,300	2,000	25,000	500	25,500

METHODIST SOCIETIES—CONCLUDED.

COUNTIES.	Number.	Value of Land.	Value of Buildings.	Total Value of Real Estate.	Value of Personal Estate.	Total Value of Real and Personal Estate.
Hampden, .	24	$14,350	$27,700	$313,550	-	$313,550
Hampshire, .	12	800	9,500	51,900	$1,100	53,000
Middlesex, .	47	15,700	47,500	548,200	8,350	556,550
Nantucket, .	1	-	-	4,500	-	4,500
Norfolk, . .	14	7,650	31,000	104,250	5,600	109,850
Plymouth, .	24	4,550	38,500	80,050	3,600	83,650
Suffolk, . .	22	367,200	433,000	874,700	6,000	880,700
Worcester, .	46	16,350	74,750	378,650	10,400	389,050
Totals, . .	328	$505,150	$917,700	$3,265,950	$53,050	$3,319,000

UNITARIAN SOCIETIES.

COUNTIES.	Number.	Value of Land.	Value of Buildings.	Total Value of Real Estate.	Value of Personal Estate.	Total Value of Real and Personal Estate.
Barnstable, .	3	-	-	$11,200	$600	$11,800
Bristol, . .	9	$22,600	$72,000	147,600	4,000	151,600
Dukes, . .	1	-	-	3,000	-	3,000
Essex, . .	14	15,500	37,500	250,500	8,200	258,700
Franklin, . .	7	3,000	6,000	23,850	1,700	25,550
Hampden, .	2	-	-	155,600	-	155,600
Hampshire, .	2	1,000	13,000	30,000	8,000	38,000
Middlesex, .	40	48,000	141,000	528,250	31,900	560,150
Nantucket, .	1	-	-	7,000	1,000	8,000
Norfolk, . .	13	8,200	39,000	138,200	2,000	140,200
Plymouth, .	13	2,200	20,500	108,600	6,500	115,100
Suffolk, . .	29	1,199,700	1,005,700	2,223,400	1,000	2,224,400
Worcester, .	26	36,900	77,800	337,550	7,400	344,950
Totals, . .	160	$1,337,100	$1,412,500	$3,964,750	$72,300	$4,037,050

UNIVERSALIST SOCIETIES.

COUNTIES.	Number.	Value of Land.	Value of Buildings.	Total Value of Real Estate.	Value of Personal Estate.	Total Value of Real and Personal Estate.
Barnstable, .	5	$50	$1,200	$16,250	$2,000	$18,250
Berkshire, .	3	-	-	26,200	-	26,200
Bristol, . .	4	2,000	6,000	19,900	2,200	22,100
Essex, . .	21	30,500	142,000	319,350	4,000	323,350
Franklin, . .	6	1,100	9,800	18,700	1,400	20,100
Hampden, .	4	800	1,500	59,900	-	59,900
Hampshire, .	1	-	-	2,500	-	2,500
Middlesex, .	20	3,100	19,100	284,100	13,700	297,800
Norfolk, . .	10	1,800	39,000	92,800	9,100	101,900
Plymouth, .	8	5,300	21,000	47,800	1,600	49,400

UNIVERSALIST SOCIETIES—CONCLUDED.

COUNTIES.	Number.	Value of Land.	Value of Buildings.	Total Value of Real Estate.	Value of Personal Estate.	Total Value of Real and Personal Estate.
Suffolk, . .	7	$136,100	$183,000	$373,100	$4,000	$377,100
Worcester, .	12	6,700	28,500	134,700	3,850	138,550
Totals, . .	101	$187,900	$451,100	$1,395,300	$41,850	$1,437,150

ALL OTHER SOCIETIES.

COUNTIES.	Number.	Value of Land.	Value of Buildings.	Total Value of Real Estate.	Value of Personal Estate.	Total Value of Real and Personal Estate.
Barnstable, .	12	$300	$10,500	$31,750	$600	$32,350
Berkshire, .	6	–	–	19,600	–	19,600
Bristol, . .	60	36,850	55,000	212,200	800	213,000
Essex, . .	20	26,600	50,050	124,950	34,950	159,900
Franklin, . .	3	50	600	3,850	200	4,050
Hampden, .	12	1,500	5,000	141,400	–	141,400
Hampshire, .	6	–	–	6,900	–	6,900
Middlesex, .	15	3,350	16,200	75,450	3,750	79,200
Nantucket, .	1	–	–	800	–	800
Norfolk, . .	6	–	–	68,100	–	68,100
Plymouth, .	17	10,550	32,700	60,050	2,100	62,150
Suffolk, . .	20	240,100	249,000	498,600	500	499,100
Worcester, .	18	1,100	4,000	60,300	1,000	61,300
Totals, . .	196	$320,400	$423,050	$1,303,950	$43,900	$1,347,850

NOTE.—The first and second columns of *values* in the above tables are the aggregates of partial returns, as some assessors did not return lands and buildings separately. The third column shows the total amount of real estate held.

Table No. 3.

Recapitulation by Counties, showing Amount of Church Property exempt from Taxation held by all Denominations in the Commonwealth.

Counties.	Baptist.		Catholic.		Congregational.		Episcopal.	
	No.	Amount.	No.	Amount.	No.	Amount.	No.	Amount.
Barnstable,	10	$17,350	2	$14,600	20	$84,100	1	$3,500
Berkshire,	16	91,800	16	208,450	33	313,800	10	78,000
Bristol,	23	290,800	13	270,750	27	299,300	5	109,900
Dukes,	5	22,500	–	–	3	12,000	–	–
Essex,	39	546,400	24	661,900	66	947,100	16	174,800
Franklin,	17	40,400	2	14,500	29	134,600	2	14,300
Hampden,	17	224,150	11	269,500	36	542,850	4	43,600
Hampshire,	6	25,000	7	64,800	37	416,350	2	28,300
Middlesex,	54	939,500	37	765,650	80	1,390,450	19	410,900
Nantucket,	1	2,600	1	3,000	1	6,000	–	–
Norfolk,	22	195,850	17	168,250	36	509,700	7	140,100
Plymouth,	18	88,750	7	61,800	35	240,150	3	13,950
Suffolk,	28	1,618,500	31	2,656,800	26	1,945,000	17	1,038,600
Worcester,	37	372,650	38	547,150	70	912,100	9	108,900
Totals,	293	$4,476,250	206	$5,707,150	499	$7,753,500	95	$2,164,850

TABLE No. 3.—*Church Property exempt from Taxation*—Continued.

COUNTIES.	METHODIST.		UNITARIAN.		UNIVERSALIST.		ALL OTHERS.		TOTAL.	
	No.	Amount.	No.	Amount.	No.	Amount.	No.	Amount.	No.	Amount.
Barnstable,	27	$90,400	3	$11,800	5	$18,250	12	$32,350	80	$272,350
Berkshire,	21	161,800	–	–	3	26,200	6	19,600	105	899,650
Bristol,	29	238,650	9	151,600	4	22,100	60	213,000	170	1,596,100
Dukes,	4	33,000	1	3,000	–	–	–	–	13	70,500
Essex,	41	378,800	14	258,700	21	323,350	20	159,900	241	3,450,950
Franklin,	16	25,500	7	25,550	6	20,100	3	4,050	82	279,000
Hampden,	24	313,550	2	155,600	4	59,900	12	141,400	110	1,750,550
Hampshire,	12	53,000	2	38,000	1	2,500	6	6,900	73	634,850
Middlesex,	47	556,550	40	560,150	20	297,800	15	79,200	312	5,000,200
Nantucket,	1	4,500	1	8,000	–	–	1	800	6	24,900
Norfolk,	14	109,850	13	140,200	10	101,900	6	68,100	125	1,433,950
Plymouth,	24	83,650	13	115,100	8	49,400	17	62,150	125	714,950
Suffolk,	22	880,700	29	2,224,400	7	377,100	20	499,100	181	11,240,200
Worcester,	46	389,050	26	344,950	12	138,550	18	61,300	256	2,874,650
Totals.	328	$3,319,000	160	$4,037,050	101	$1,437,150	196	$1,347,850	1,879	$30,242,800

NOTE.—See note, page 533.

LITERARY AND SCIENTIFIC INSTITUTIONS.

Table No. 4.

Valuation of Property of Literary and Scientific Institutions exempt from Taxation, arranged by Counties and Towns.

Name of Institution.	Value of Land.	Value of Buildings.	Value of Real Estate.	Value of Personal Estate.	Total Value of Real and Personal Estate.
Barnstable County.					
Barnstable:					
Percival Fund for Schools, .	-	-	-	$2,000	
Sturgis Library, . . .	$500	$3,000	$3,500	17,500	
					$23,000
Dennis:					
Liberty Hall, ...	-	-	600	-	
Union Hall, ...	-	-	500	-	
Concert Hall, ...	-	-	800	-	
Worden Hall, ...	-	-	1,500	-	
Carlton Hall, ...	-	-	1,000	-	
					4,400
Falmouth:					
Lawrence Academy, . .	-	-	2,150	10,300	12,450
Yarmouth:					
Yarmouth Library Ass'n, .	-	-	7,000	1,000	
S. Yarmouth Library Ass'n, .	-	-	-	500	
W. Yarmouth Library Ass'n,	-	-	-	200	
					8,700
Berkshire County.					
Lenox:					
Charles Sedgwick Library, .	-	-	6,000	3,000	
Lenox Academy Association,	-	-	2,000	2,000	
					13,000
New Marlborough:					
S. Berkshire Institute, . .	-	-	8,000	1,000	9,000
Pittsfield:					
Trustees of the Berkshire Athenæum, . . .	-	-	4,000	4,000	8,000
Stockbridge:					
Stockbridge Library Ass'n, .	-	-	7,000	3,600	
Williams Academy, . .	-	-	-	1,600	
					12,200
Williamstown:					
Williams College Corp'n, .	-	-	212,000	288,000	500,000

TABLE No. 4—Continued.

NAME OF INSTITUTION.	Value of Land.	Value of Buildings.	Value of Real Estate.	Value of Personal Estate.	Total Value of Real and Personal Estate.
BRISTOL COUNTY.					
New Bedford:					
Friends' Academy,	-	-	$16,000	$2,000	
New Bedford Lyceum,	-	-	-	3,200	$21,200
Norton:					
Wheaton Female Seminary,	$5,000	$40,000	45,000	5,000	50,000
Taunton:					
Bristol Academy,	5,000	15,000	20,000	1,300	21,300
DUKES COUNTY.					
Gosnold:					
Anderson School,	-	-	19,700	-	19,700
Tisbury:					
Dukes County Academy,	-	-	5,500	-	
Seamen's Free Read'g Room,	-	-	300	-	5,800
ESSEX COUNTY.					
Andover:					
Trustees of Phillips Academy,	-	-	222,100	518,150	
Abbott Female Seminary,	-	-	25,600	-	765,850
Bradford:					
Bradford Female Seminary,	-	-	140,000	-	140,000
Danvers:					
Peabody Institute,	6,000	12,000	18,000	65,450	83,450
Groveland:					
Merrimac Academy,	150	1,150	1,300	-	1,300
Lawrence:					
St. Mary's Literary and Scientific Institution,	6,000	3,000	9,000	1,000	10,000
Marblehead:					
Marblehead Academy,	-	-	3,500	2,900	6,400
Newbury:					
Dummer Academy,	-	-	13,500	6,750	20,250
Newburyport:					
Putnam Free School,	5,000	25,000	30,000	50,000	
Library,	4,000	10,000	14,000	-	94,000

TABLE No. 4—Continued.

NAME OF INSTITUTION.	Value of Land.	Value of Buildings.	Value of Real Estate.	Value of Personal Estate.	Total Value of Real and Personal Estate.
ESSEX COUNTY—Con.					
Salem:					
Plummer Hall and Athe'um,	-	-	$50,000	$10,000	
Peabody Acad. of Science, .	-	-	22,000	100,000	
					$182,000
FRANKLIN COUNTY.					
Ashfield:					
Academy, ...	-	-	1,200	-	
Library, ...	-	-	-	1,200	
					2,400
Bernardston:					
Powers Institute, . . .	-	-	10,000	-	
Cushman Library, . . .	-	-	-	5,000	
					15,000
Conway:					
Conway Academy, . .	-	-	1,500	-	1,500
Deerfield:					
Deerfield Academy, . .	-	-	3,150	10,000	13,150
Greenfield:					
Prospect Hill School, . .	-	-	15,000	1,000	
Greenfield Library Associa'n,	-	-	-	6,000	
					22,000
New Salem:					
New Salem Academy, . .	-	-	5,200	8,000	13,200
Shelburne:					
Arms Academy Fund, . .	-	-	2,500	34,000	
Arms Library, ...	-	-	-	4,600	
Shelburne Academy, . .	-	-	3,000	350	
					44,450
HAMPDEN COUNTY.					
Blandford:					
Taggart School Fund, . .	-	-	-	2,500	2,500
Brimfield:					
Hitchcock Free High School,	-	-	4,500	40,000	44,500
Holyoke:					
St. Jerome's School Ass'n, .	-	-	43,500	-	43,500
Monson:					
Monson Academy, . .	-	-	4,800	25,000	29,800

TABLE No. 4—Continued.

NAME OF INSTITUTION.	Value of Land.	Value of Buildings.	Value of Real Estate.	Value of Personal Estate.	Total Value of Real and Personal Estate.
HAMPDEN CO.—Con.					
Springfield:					
City Library Association, .	-	-	$95,000	$45,000	$140,000
Westfield:					
Athenæum, ...	$2,000	$6,000	8,000	-	8,000
Wilbraham:					
Wesleyan Academy, . .	-	-	124,500	2,000	126,500
HAMPSHIRE COUNTY.					
Amherst:					
Amherst College,* . .	8,500	254,500	263,000	550,000	813,000
Easthampton:					
Williston Seminary, . .	2,700	85,050	87,750	35,400	123,150
Hatfield:					
Smith Academy, . . .	-	-	20,000	55,000	75,000
Northampton:					
Trustees Smith College, .	-	-	35,000	230,000	
Clarke Institute, . . .	-	-	70,000	235,000	570,000
South Hadley:					
Ladies' Seminary, . . .	7,000	113,000	120,000	-	120,000
Southampton:					
Sheldon Academy, . .	-	-	1,500	1,700	3,200
MIDDLESEX COUNTY.					
Ashby:					
Watutic Academy and Hall, .	-	-	1,000	-	1,000
Billerica:					
Howe School, ...	600	7,000	7,600	21,000	
Trust Fund for Sing'g Sch'ls,	-	-	-	1,400	30,000
Cambridge:					
Harvard College and Agassiz Museum,†	-	-	3,391,000	3,000,000	
Prot. Episcopal Theological Seminary, ...	-	-	175,000	-	6,566,000
Concord:					
Concord Free Pub. Library, .	-	-	52,000	10,000	62,000

* See Report, p. 177. † See Boston.

TABLE No. 4—Continued.

NAME OF INSTITUTION.	Value of Land.	Value of Buildings.	Value of Real Estate.	Value of Personal Estate.	Total Value of Real and Personal Estate.
MIDDLESEX CO.—Con.					
Groton:					
Lawrence Academy,	-	-	$28,000	$37,000	$65,000
Lowell:					
Middlesex Mechanic Ass'n,	-	-	8,000	-	8,000
Medford:					
Tufts College,†	$65,000	$101,000	166,000	*	166,000
Newton:					
Newton Free Library,	-	-	40,000	10,000	
Laselle Female Seminary,	-	-	38,000	3,000	
Newton Theological Institute,	-	-	142,600	254,000	
West Newton English Classical School,	-	-	46,000	1,000	
					534,600
Pepperell:					
Pepperell Academy,	-	-	1,000	-	1,000
Sherborn:					
Sawin Academy and Dowse High School,	2,000	-	2,000	-	
Dowse Fund,	-	-	-	5,000	
					7,000
Somerville:					
Tufts College,‡	24,000	-	24,000	-	24,000
Waltham:					
New Church School,	-	-	25,000	-	25,000
Westford:					
Westford Academy,	-	-	4,000	20,000	24,000
Woburn:					
Warren Academy,	7,000	15,000	22,000	5,000	27,000
NANTUCKET COUNTY.					
Nantucket:					
Coffin School,	-	-	4,000	30,000	
Athenæum,	-	-	4,100	2,000	
					40,100

* Assessors of Medford unable to ascertain the amount of personal estate.

† See Somerville. ‡ See Medford.

TABLE No. 4—Continued.

NAME OF INSTITUTION.	Value of Land.	Value of Buildings.	Value of Real Estate.	Value of Personal Estate.	Total Value of Real and Personal Estate.
NORFOLK COUNTY.					
Foxborough:					
Memorial Hall Library, .	-	-	$6,000	-	
Boyden Library, . . .	-	-	-	$1,000	
					$7,000
Franklin:					
Dean Academy, . . .	-	-	148,500	162,800	311,300
Medway:					
Dean Library Association, .	-	-	2,500	500	3,000
Milton:					
Trustees of Milton Academy,	-	-	12,000	-	12,000
Needham:					
Wellesley College, . .	-	-	416,250	-	416,250
Quincy:					
Woodward Trustee Fund, .	-	-	-	61,000	
Adams Temple and School Fund, ...	$5,000	$20,000	25,000	-	
Coddington School Fund, .	2,000	-	2,000	-	
					88,000
Weymouth:					
Pratt School Fund, . .	-	-	-	5,800	5,800
Wrentham:					
Day's Academy, . . .	-	-	800	500	1,300
PLYMOUTH COUNTY.					
Bridgewater:					
Bridgewater Academy,. .	-	-	12,000	1,000	13,000
Duxbury:					
Partridge Academy, . .	100	2,800	2,900	24,400	27,300
Hanover:					
Hanover Academy, . .	200	2,300	2,500	-	2,500
Hingham:					
Derby Academy, . . .	-	-	3,000	27,000	30,000
Marion:					
Taber Institute, . . .	-	-	8,000	1,300	9,300

TABLE No. 4—Continued.

NAME OF INSTITUTION.	Value of Land.	Value of Buildings.	Value of Real Estate.	Value of Personal Estate.	Total Value of Real and Personal Estate.
PLYMOUTH CO.—Con.					
Middleborough:					
Peirce Academy, . . .	-	-	$6,000	$13,000	
Pratt Free School, . . .	$100	$2,500	2,600	25,000	
					$46,600
Rockland:					
Rockland Library Assoc'n, .	-	-	-	1,000	1,000
West Bridgewater:					
Howard Fund, . . .	-	-	2,500	127,000	129,500
SUFFOLK COUNTY.					
Boston:					
American Educational Ass'n,	4,400	5,000	9,400	-	
Boston Athenæum, . .	175,000	125,000	300,000	-	
Boston Acad'y of Notre Dame,	75,000	40,000	115,000	-	
Boston Catholic College, .	104,000	100,000	204,000	-	
Boston University School of Medicine, ...	45,000	40,000	85,000	-	
Eliot School Fund, . .	6,000	3,000	9,000	-	
Harvard College,* . .	532,500	118,800	651,300	-	
Homœopathic Hospital, .	5,000	6,000	11,000	-	
Industrial School, . . .	11,300	10,000	21,300	-	
Jewish School, . . .	11,300	4,700	16,000	-	
Mass. Medical College, . .	18,900	32,000	50,900	-	
Proprietors Nat'l History Soc. and Inst. of Technology, .	616,500	323,000	939,500	-	
Sisters of Notre Dame, .	78,600	74,500	153,100	-	
St. Joseph's School, . .	-	2,000	2,000	-	
St. Mary's Female School, .	30,000	30,000	60,000	-	
Trustees Fellowes' Athen'um,	14,300	25,000	39,300	-	
Trustees Latin School, . .	17,000	4,000	21,000	-	
Trust's Museum of Fine Arts,	286,000	20,000	306,000	-	
Warren Museum, . . .	3,800	2,000	5,800	-	
					2,999,600
WORCESTER COUNTY.					
Ashburnham:					
Cushing Academy, . .	-	-	90,000	100,000	190,000
Dudley:					
Nichols Academy, . . .	100	6,500	6,600	-	6,600
Leicester:					
Leicester Academy, . .	-	-	10,000	20,000	30,000

* See Cambridge—Middlesex County.

TABLE No. 4—Concluded.

NAME OF INSTITUTION.	Value of Land.	Value of Buildings.	Value of Real Estate.	Value of Personal Estate.	Total Value of Real and Personal Estate.
WORCESTER CO.—Con.					
Milford:					
Farmers' Club,	-	-	$500	-	$500
Southborough:					
St. Mark's School for Boys,	-	-	18,000	$3,500	21,500
Southbridge:					
French Catholic School,	-	-	3,000	-	
Library,	-	-	12,000	5,000	
					20,000
Worcester:					
Worcester Co. Free Institute of Industrial Science,	-	-	159,400	40,000	
American Antiquarian Soc'y,	-	-	35,400	45,000	
Worcester Academy,	-	-	60,000	2,000	
College of the Holy Cross,	-	-	133,500	4,500	
St. John's Catholic School,	-	-	13,000	-	
Oread Institute,	-	-	37,700	6,000	
					536,500
Total,	. .	. .	. .	. .	*$16,712,100

* See Report, p. 177.

BENEVOLENT AND CHARITABLE INSTITUTIONS.

Table No. 5.

Valuation of Property of Benevolent and Charitable Institutions exempt from Taxation, arranged by Counties and Towns.

Name of Institution.	Value of Land.	Value of Buildings.	Value of Real Estate.	Value of Personal Estate.	Total Value of Real and Personal Estate.
Barnstable County.					
Falmouth:					
Marine Lodge,	–	–	$950	–	
St. Luke's Benevolent Soc'y,	–	–	2,000	–	
					$2,950
Truro:					
Truro Benevolent Society,	–	–	–	$1,000	1,000
Wellfleet:					
Marine Benevolent Society,	–	–	–	2,800	2,800
Bristol County.					
Fall River:					
Children's Home,	$3,300	$5,000	8,300	–	8,300
New Bedford:					
New Bedford Port Society,	–	–	10,000	5,600	
Ladies' Branch of New Bedford Port Society,	–	–	–	17,000	
Orphans' Home,	–	–	3,000	27,000	
N. Bedford Reform and Relief Association,	–	–	1,600	3,000	
St. Joseph's Hospital,	–	–	14,000	–	
					81,200
Taunton:					
Old Ladies' Home,	1,000	4,000	5,000	3,000	8,000
Dukes County.					
Gay Head:					
Ladies' Sewing Society,	–	–	600	–	600
Essex County.					
Beverly:					
Liberty Masonic Ass'n,*	–	–	4,000	–	
Trust's Franklin Div. S. of T.,	–	–	–	3,000	
					7,000
Gloucester:					
Female Charitable Society for Relief of the Poor,	–	–	2,500	–	
Fisherman's Aid Society,	–	–	2,500	–	
					5,000

* Returned as exempt, but generally considered as taxable.

TABLE No. 5—Continued.

NAME OF INSTITUTION.	Value of Land.	Value of Buildings.	Value of Real Estate.	Value of Personal Estate.	Total Value of Real and Personal Estate.
ESSEX COUNTY—Con.					
Haverhill:					
Orphans' Home, . . .	-	-	$2,500	-	$2,500
Lawrence:					
Orphan Asylum, . . .	$1,500	$24,000	25,500	$1,500	27,000
Marblehead:					
Female Humane Society, .	-	-	-	300	
Pickett Fund, . . .	-	-	1,200	6,900	
					8,400
Newburyport:					
St. John's Lodge,*. . .	-	-	-	500	
St. Mark's Lodge,* . .	-	-	-	500	
King Cyrus Chapter,* . .	-	-	-	400	
Quascacunquen Lodge,* .	-	-	-	3,000	
Merrimack Encampment,* .	-	-	-	1,000	
Howard Benevolent Society,	-	-	-	4,000	
Old Ladies' Home, . .	1,000	4,000	5,000	25,000	
Merrimac Humane Society, .	-	-	-	8,000	
Newburyport Marine Soc'y, .	500	2,500	3,000	40,000	
					90,400
Peabody:					
Jordan Lodge,* . . .	-	-	-	2,250	
Female Benevolent Society, .	-	-	-	650	
Charitable Tenement Ass'n, .	-	-	3,500	-	
					6,400
Rockport:					
Young Men's Christian Ass'n,	-	-	2,500	-	
Granite Lodge I. O. of O. F.,*	-	-	2,500	1,300	
Bay Flint I. O. of R.,* . .	-	-	-	400	
					6,700
Salem:					
Old Ladies' Home, . .	-	-	8,000	50,000	
Children's Friend and Seaman's Orphan Association,	-	-	8,000	20,000	
Sisters of Charity, . .	-	-	22,000	-	
Salem Marine Society, . .	-	-	-	39,000	
					147,000
West Newbury:					
Trustees of Hill Fund, . .	-	-	-	1,800	1,800
FRANKLIN COUNTY.					
Northfield:					
Alexander Fund, . . .	-	-	-	1,000	1,000

* Returned as exempt, but generally considered as taxable.

TABLE No. 5—Continued.

NAME OF INSTITUTION.	Value of Land.	Value of Buildings.	Value of Real Estate.	Value of Personal Estate.	Total Value of Real and Personal Estate.
HAMPDEN COUNTY.					
Springfield:					
Home for Friendless Women,	-	-	$5,000	-	
Home for Friendless Child'n.	-	-	16,000	-	
					$21,000
West Springfield:					
Trustees of Fund Money for Home Missions, . .	-	-	3,900	-	3,900
MIDDLESEX COUNTY.					
Billerica:					
Trust Fund for Relief of the Poor, ...	-	-	-	$13,000	13,000
Lowell:					
St. Peter's School and Orphan Asylum, ...	-	-	8,600	-	
Mission School, . . .	-	-	-	300	
St. John's Hospital, . .	-	-	23,000	-	
Old Ladies' Home, . .	-	-	10,000	-	
Sisters of Notre Dame, .	-	-	42,000	-	
Lowell Hospital Association,	-	-	23,100	-	
					107,000
Newton:					
Pine Farm School for Boys, .	-	-	10,000	-	
Boston Children's Aid Soc., .	-	-	9,000	-	
					19,000
Sherborn:					
Widows' and Orphans' Fund,	-	-	-	3,000	3,000
Somerville:					
Mass. General Hospital and McLean Asylum,* . .	-	-	1,650,000	25,000	1,675,000
NORFOLK COUNTY.					
Dedham:					
Temporary Asylum for Discharged Female Convicts,	-	-	7,400	250	
St. Mary's School and Asylum,	$3,500	$5,000	8,500	-	
					16,150
Quincy:					
National Sailors' Home, .	13,000	20,000	33,000	1,500	
Sailors' Snug Harbor, . .	15,000	25,000	40,000	500	
					75,000

* See Boston.

TABLE No. 5—Continued.

NAME OF INSTITUTION.	Value of Land.	Value of Buildings.	Value of Real Estate.	Value of Personal Estate.	Total Value of Real and Personal Estate.
NORFOLK COUNTY—Con.					
Stoughton:					
Rising Star Lodge,*	-	-	-	$2,000	
Royal Arch Chapter,*	-	-	-	2,000	
I. O. of O. F.,*	-	-	-	3,000	
					$7,000
PLYMOUTH COUNTY.					
Duxbury:					
Masonic Corner Stone Lodge,*	-	-	$1,550	-	
Mattakeeset Lodge I. O. of O. F.,*	-	-	1,250	-	
					2,800
SUFFOLK COUNTY.					
Boston:					
American Unitarian Ass'n,	$20,000	$10,000	30,000	-	
American Congrega'l Ass'n,	-	-	161,000	-	
Assoc'n for the Protection of Orphan and Destitute Children,	100,000	65,000	165,000	-	
Assoc'n for Relief of Aged and Indigent Females,	70,000	70,000	140,000	-	
Boston Female Asylum,	136,800	22,000	158,800	-	
Boston Lying-in Hospital,	6,000	8,000	14,000	-	
Boston Wesleyan Assoc'n,	-	-	150,000	-	
Boston Young Men's Christian Association,	-	-	45,000	-	
Boston Young Women's Ch. Association,	18,500	50,300	68,800	-	
Bunker Hill Monument Ass'n,	248,000	-	248,000	-	
Carney Hospital,	33,300	30,000	63,300	-	
Channing Home,	6,500	7,500	14,000	-	
Children's Friend Society,	21,700	38,000	59,700	-	
Children's Mission,	29,000	8,000	37,000	-	
Church Home for Orphans,	37,000	18,000	55,000	-	
Consumptives' Home,	153,800	43,000	196,800	-	
Home for Aged Men,	22,500	40,000	62,500	-	
House of Angel Guardian,	43,300	30,000	73,300	-	
House of the Good Samaritan,	12,000	8,000	20,000	-	
House of the Good Shepherd,	-	-	102,000	-	
Infants' Home Association,	4,900	1,500	6,400	-	
Little Sisters of the Poor,	42,000	40,000	82,000	-	
Martin Luther Orph's' Home,	30,300	6,000	36,300	-	
Mass. Asylum for Idiotic Children,	17,600	20,000	37,600	-	

* Returned as exempt, but generally considered as taxable.

TABLE No. 5—Concluded.

NAME OF INSTITUTION.	Value of Land.	Value of Buildings.	Value of Real Estate.	Value of Personal Estate.	Total Value of Real and Personal Estate.
SUFFOLK COUNTY—Con.					
Boston—Con.					
Mass. Charitable Mechanic Association,	-	-	$144,000	-	
Mass. Eye and Ear Infirmary,	$78,000	$40,000	118,000	-	
Mass. General Hospital,*	750,000	250,000	1,000,000	-	
Mass. Infant Asylum,	8,600	-	8,600	-	
Mt. Hope Home of Boston North End Mission,	8,000	11,500	19,500	-	
N. E. Hospital for Women and Children,	41,500	60,000	101,500	-	
N. E. Moral Reform Society,	5,700	6,300	12,000	-	
Old Colored Ladies' Home,	6,700	4,000	10,700	-	
Old Ladies' Home,	6,000	7,000	13,000	-	
Penitent Female Refuge Soc.,	17,900	30,000	47,900	-	
Perkins Instit'n for the Blind,	118,700	84,500	203,200	-	
St. Joseph's Home,	2,300	3,500	5,800	-	
St. Joseph's Temp'ry Home,	4,200	9,800	14,000	-	
Sts. Peter and Paul Asylum,	18,500	45,000	63,500	-	
St. Vincent Orphan Asylum,	61,700	90,000	151,700	-	
Temporary Home for Destitute Children,	27,000	13,000	40,000	-	
Trustees Winchester Home,	13,500	45,000	58,500	-	
Winchester Home,	9,700	17,500	27,200	-	
Young Women's Christian Association,	34,000	12,000	46,000	-	
					$4,111,600
WORCESTER COUNTY.					
Uxbridge:					
Solomon's Temple Lodge of Masons,†	-	-	2,000	$300	2,300
Worcester:					
Home for Aged Females,	-	-	20,000	2,000	
Worcester Children's Friend Society,	-	-	21,100	1,000	
					44,100
Total,	. .	. .	. .	. .	$6,503,900

* See Somerville—Middlesex County.

† Returned as exempt, but generally considered as taxable.

AGRICULTURAL SOCIETIES.

Table No. 6.

Valuation of Property of Agricultural Societies exempt from Taxation, arranged by Counties and Towns.

Name of Institution.	Value of Land.	Value of Buildings.	Value of Real Estate.	Value of Personal Estate.	Total Value of Real and Personal Estate.
Barnstable County.					
Barnstable:					
Barnstable County Society, .	$500	$3,500	$4,000	-	$4,000
Berkshire County.					
Adams:					
Hoosac Valley Society, . .	-	-	8,000	-	8,000
Gt. Barrington:					
Housatonic Society, . .	-	-	10,000	-	10,000
Pittsfield:					
Berkshire Society, . . .	-	-	3,000	-	3,000
Bristol County.					
Swanzey:					
Agricultural Library Ass'n, .	-	-	1,000	$500	1,500
Taunton:					
Bristol County Society, . .	27,500	21,000	48,500	1,500	
Bristol Co. Central Society, .	2,500	15,000	17,500	500	68,000
Dukes County.					
Tisbury:					
Martha's Vineyard Ag. Hall,	-	-	3,000	1,000	4,000
Essex County.					
Topsfield:					
Essex Society, ...	3,000	1,000	4,000	-	4,000
Franklin County.					
Charlemont:					
Deerfield Valley Society, .	-	-	2,000	-	2,000
Greenfield:					
Franklin County Society, .	-	-	8,000	1,500	9,500

TABLE No. 6—Continued.

NAME OF INSTITUTION.	Value of Land.	Value of Buildings.	Value of Real Estate.	Value of Personal Estate.	Total Value of Real and Personal Estate.
HAMPDEN COUNTY.					
Blandford:					
Union Society, . . .	-	-	$2,900	-	$2,900
Palmer:					
Eastern Hampden Society, .	-	-	5,000	$200	5,200
Springfield:					
Hampden County Society, .	-	-	75,000	-	75,000
HAMPSHIRE COUNTY.					
Amherst:					
Hampshire Society, . .	$1,000	$500	1,500	-	1,500
Middlefield:					
Highland Society, . . .	-	-	2,000	-	2,000
Northampton:					
Hampshire, Franklin and Hampden Society, . .	-	-	10,000	-	10,000
MIDDLESEX COUNTY.					
Concord:					
Middlesex Society, . .	-	-	15,000	-	15,000
Framingham:					
Middlesex South Society, .	-	-	2,500	-	2,500
Hudson:					
Middlesex West Society, .	-	-	3,000	-	3,000
Lowell:					
Middlesex North Society, .	-	-	22,000	-	22,000
Newton:					
Newton Society, . . .	-	-	-	1,000	1,000
NANTUCKET COUNTY.					
Nantucket:					
Nantucket Society, . .	-	-	800	-	800
NORFOLK COUNTY.					
Hyde Park:					
Agricultural Fair Ground, .	10,000	-	10,000	-	10,000

TABLE No. 6—Concluded.

NAME OF INSTITUTION.	Value of Land.	Value of Buildings.	Value of Real Estate.	Value of Personal Estate.	Total Value of Real and Personal Estate.
NORFOLK COUNTY—Con.					
Weymouth:					
Agricult'l and Industrial Soc.,	-	-	$4,000	$1,000	$5,000
PLYMOUTH COUNTY.					
Bridgewater:					
Plymouth County Society, .	-	-	24,200	1,500	25,700
Hingham:					
Hingham Agricultural and Horticultural Society, .	-	-	34,600	4,600	39,200
Marshfield:					
Marshfield Agricultural and Horticultural Society, .	-	-	11,350	1,000	12,350
WORCESTER COUNTY.					
Athol:					
Worcester North-West Soc'y,	$2,500	$2,500	5,000	500	5,500
Barre:					
Worcester West Society, .	-	-	6,000	1,200	7,200
Fitchburg:					
Worcester North Society, .	-	-	12,200	150	12,350
Lunenburg:					
Worcester North Society, .	-	-	1,000	-	1,000
Milford:					
Worcester South-East Soc'y,	-	-	8,200	300	8,500
Sturbridge:					
Worcester South Society, .	-	-	12,800	1,500	14,300
Worcester:					
Worcester County Society, .	-	-	85,300	-	85,300
Total, ...	. .	. .	. .	. .	$481,300

RECAPITULATION BY COUNTIES AND TOWNS.

Table No. 7.

Showing the aggregate Amount of Valuation exempt from Taxation, as the Property of Literary, Scientific, Benevolent and Charitable Institutions and Agricultural Societies, in each County.

Counties and Towns.	Literary and Scientific Institutions.	Benevolent and Charitable Institutions.	Agricultural Societies.	Total.
Barnstable County.				
Barnstable, ...	$23,000	-	$4,000	$27,000
Dennis, ...	4,400	-	-	4,400
Falmouth, ...	12,450	$2,950	-	15,400
Truro, ...	-	1,000	-	1,000
Wellfleet, ...	-	2,800	-	2,800
Yarmouth, ...	8,700	-	-	8,700
Total, ...	$48,550	$6,750	$4,000	$59,300
Berkshire County.				
Adams, ...	-	-	$8,000	$8,000
Great Barrington, . .	-	-	10,000	10,000
Lenox, ...	$13,000	-	-	13,000
New Marlborough, . .	9,000	-	-	9,000
Pittsfield, ...	8,000	-	3,000	11,000
Stockbridge, . . .	12,200	-	-	12,200
Williamstown, . . .	500,000	-	-	500,000
Total, ...	$542,200	-	$21,000	$563,200
Bristol County.				
Fall River, ...	-	$8,300	-	$8,300
New Bedford, . . .	$21,200	81,200	-	102,400
Norton, ...	50,000	-	-	50,000
Swanzey, ...	-	-	$1,500	1,500
Taunton, ...	21,300	8,000	68,000	97,300
Total, ...	$92,500	$97,500	$69,500	$259,500
Dukes County.				
Gay Head, ...	-	$600	-	$600
Gosnold, ...	$19,700	-	-	19,700
Tisbury, ...	5,800	-	$4,000	9,800
Total, ...	$25,500	$600	$4,000	$30,100

TABLE No. 7—Continued.

COUNTIES AND TOWNS.	Literary and Scientific Institutions.	Benevolent and Charitable Institutions.	Agricultural Societies.	Total.
ESSEX COUNTY.				
Andover,	$765,850	-	-	$765,850
Beverly,	-	$7,000	-	7,000
Bradford,	140,000	-	-	140,000
Danvers,	83,450	-	-	83,450
Gloucester,	-	5,000	-	5,000
Groveland,	1,300	-	-	1,300
Haverhill,	-	2,500	-	2,500
Lawrence,	10,000	27,000	-	37,000
Marblehead,	6,400	8,400	-	14,800
Newbury,	20,250	-	-	20,250
Newburyport,	94,000	90,400	-	184,400
Peabody,	-	6,400	-	6,400
Rockport,	-	6,700	-	6,700
Salem,	182,000	147,000	-	329,000
Topsfield,	-	-	$4,000	4,000
West Newbury,	-	1,800	-	1,800
Total,	$1,303,250	$302,200	$4,000	$1,609,450
FRANKLIN COUNTY.				
Ashfield,	$2,400	-	-	$2,400
Bernardston,	15,000	-	-	15,000
Charlemont,	-	-	$2,000	2,000
Conway,	1,500	-	-	1,500
Deerfield,	13,150	-	-	13,150
Greenfield,	22,000	-	9,500	31,500
New Salem,	13,200	-	-	13,200
Northfield,	-	$1,000	-	1,000
Shelburne,	44,450	-	-	44,450
Total,	$111,700	$1,000	$11,500	$124,200
HAMPDEN COUNTY.				
Blandford,	$2,500	-	$2,900	$5,400
Brimfield,	44,500	-	-	44,500
Holyoke,	43,500	-	-	43,500
Monson,	29,800	-	-	29,800
Palmer,	-	-	5,200	5,200
Springfield,	140,000	$21,000	75,000	236,000
Westfield,	8,000	-	-	8,000
West Springfield,	-	3,900	-	3,900
Wilbraham,	126,500	-	-	126,500
Total,	$394,800	$24,900	$83,100	$502,800

TABLE No. 7—Continued.

COUNTIES AND TOWNS.	Literary and Scientific Institutions.	Benevolent and Charitable Institutions.	Agricultural Societies.	Total.
HAMPSHIRE COUNTY.				
Amherst,*	$813,000	-	$1,500	$814,500
Easthampton,	123,150	-	-	123,150
Hatfield,	75,000	-	-	75,000
Middlefield,	-	-	2,000	2,000
Northampton,	570,000	-	10,000	580,000
South Hadley,	120,000	-	-	120,000
Southampton,	3,200	-	-	3,200
Total,	$1,704,350	-	$13,500	$1,717,850
MIDDLESEX COUNTY.				
Ashby,	$1,000	-	-	$1,000
Billerica,	30,000	$13,000	-	43,000
Cambridge,	6,566,000	-	-	6,566,000
Concord,	62,000	-	$15,000	77,000
Framingham,	-	-	2,500	2,500
Groton,	65,000	-	-	65,000
Hudson,	-	-	3,000	3,000
Lowell,	8,000	107,000	22,000	137,000
Medford,	166,000	-	-	166,000
Newton,	534,600	19,000	1,000	554,600
Pepperell,	1,000	-	-	1,000
Sherborn,	7,000	3,000	-	10,000
Somerville,	24,000	1,675,000	-	1,699,000
Waltham,	25,000	-	-	25,000
Westford,	24,000	-	-	24,000
Woburn,	27,000	-	-	27,000
Total,	$7,540,600	$1,817,000	$43,500	$9,401,100
NANTUCKET COUNTY.				
Nantucket,	$40,100	-	$800	$40,900
NORFOLK COUNTY.				
Dedham,	-	$16,150	-	$16,150
Foxborough,	$7,000	-	-	7,000
Franklin,	311,300	-	-	311,300
Hyde Park,	-	-	$10,000	10,000
Medway,	3,000	-	-	3,000
Milton,	12,000	-	-	12,000
Needham,	416,250	-	-	416,250
Quincy,	88,000	75,000	-	163,000
Stoughton,	-	7,000	-	7,000
Weymouth,	5,800	-	5,000	10,800
Wrentham,	1,300	-	-	1,300
Total,	$844,650	$98,150	$15,000	$957,800

* See Report, p. 177.

TABLE No. 7—Concluded.

Counties and Towns.	Literary and Scientific Institutions.	Benevolent and Charitable Institutions.	Agricultural Societies.	Total.
Plymouth County.				
Bridgewater,	$13,000	-	$25,700	$38,700
Duxbury,	27,300	$2,800	-	30,100
Hanover,	2,500	-	-	2,500
Hingham,	30,000	-	39,200	69,200
Marion,	9,300	-	-	9,300
Marshfield,	-	-	12,350	12,350
Middleborough,	46,600	-	-	46,600
Rockland,	1,000	-	-	1,000
West Bridgewater,	129,500	-	-	129,500
Total,	$259,200	$2,800	$77,250	$339,250
Suffolk County.				
Boston,	$2,999,600	$4,111,600	-	$7,111,200
Worcester County.				
Ashburnham,	$190,000	-	-	$190,000
Athol,	-	-	$5,500	5,500
Barre,	-	-	7,200	7,200
Dudley,	6,600	-	-	6,600
Fitchburg,	-	-	12,350	12,350
Leicester,	30,000	-	-	30,000
Lunenburg,	-	-	1,000	1,000
Milford,	500	-	8,500	9,000
Southborough,	21,500	-	-	21,500
Southbridge,	20,000	-	-	20,000
Sturbridge,	-	-	14,300	14,300
Uxbridge,	-	$2,300	-	2,300
Worcester,	536,500	44,100	85,300	665,900
Total,	$805,100	$46,400	$134,150	$985,650

RECAPITULATION BY COUNTIES.

Table No. 8.

Showing the aggregate Amount of Valuation exempt from Taxation, as the Property of Literary, Scientific, Benevolent and Charitable Institutions, and Agricultural Societies.

COUNTIES.	Literary and Scientific Institutions.	Benevolent and Charitable Institutions.	Agricultural Societies.	Total.
Barnstable County, .	$48,550	$6,750	$4,000	$59,300
Berkshire County, . .	542,200	-	21,000	563,200
Bristol County, . .	92,500	97,500	69,500	259,500
Dukes County, . .	25,500	600	4,000	30,100
Essex County, . .	1,303,250	302,200	4,000	1,609,450
Franklin County, . .	111,700	1,000	11,500	124,200
Hampden County, . .	394,800	24,900	83,100	502,800
Hampshire County, .	1,704,350	-	13,500	1,717,850
Middlesex County,. .	7,540,600	1,817,000	43,500	9,401,100
Nantucket County,. .	40,100	-	800	40,900
Norfolk County, . .	844,650	98,150	15,000	957,800
Plymouth County, .	259,200	2,800	77,250	339,250
Suffolk County, . .	2,999,600	4,111,600	-	7,111,200
Worcester County,. .	805,100	46,400	134,150	985,650
Total, . . .	$16,712,100*	$6,508,900	$481,300	$23,702,300

Note.—The foregoing tables are as complete as can be made under the present system of returning property exempted from taxation. There are, no doubt, some mistakes in denominations of societies, as in many instances it was difficult to tell where they should be placed; and this was especially true of the Orthodox and Unitarian societies, both being returned as Congregational: so also touching Liberal societies, some were claimed by the Unitarians, some by the Universalists, and many were not credited to any denomination, in all of which cases we have placed them under the head of "all others."

In regard to the personal property of the churches, institutions and societies, it was not returned with any uniformity, but so far as returns of amounts were received, they are incorporated in the tables.

* See Report, p. 177.

Table No. 9.

STATEMENT showing the Amounts distributed to Towns and Cities for the year 1874, under the Corporation and Bank Tax Acts, and each Town's Share of a State Tax of the total Amount so distributed.

TOWNS.	Corporation Tax.	Bank Tax.	Total Tax.	Share of State Tax of $1,000.	Share of State Tax of $2,055,800.
Abington,*	$488.695	$2,666.269	$3,154.964	$3 54	$7,277.532
Acton,	566.511	541.478	1,107.989	79	1,624.082
Acushnet,	259.852	926.776	1,186.628	50	1,027.900
Adams,	3,991.337	3,411.222	7,402.559	4 98	10,237.884
Agawam,	245.113	933.686	1,178.799	75	1,541.850
Alford,	–	221.714	221.714	22	452.276
Amesbury,	783.417	2,890.457	3,673.874	2 13	4,378.854
Amherst,	635 934	2,710.511	3,346.445	2 22	4,563.876
Andover,	8,331.158	8,048.315	16,379.473	2 31	4,748.898
Arlington,	1,880.182	2,557.706	4,437.888	2 53	5,201.174
Ashburnham,	434.147	228.908	663.055	81	1,665.198
Ashby,	199.814	399.320	599.134	43	883 994
Ashfield,	–	282.856	282 856	46	945.668
Ashland,	436.429	151.609	588.038	95	1,953.010
Athol,	528.984	1,011.183	1,540.167	1 63	3,350.954
Attleborough,	1,728.645	1,739.024	3,467.669	2 22	4,563.876
Auburn,	42 511	294.313	336.824	41	842.878
Ayer,	171.953	61.988	233.941	72	1,480.176
Barnstable,	2,898.384	4,947.477	7,845.861	2 09	4,296.622
Barre,	403.827	2,640.602	3,044.429	1 34	2,754.772
Becket,	–	326.287	326.287	44	904.552
Bedford,	72.643	244.241	316.884	41	842.878
Belchertown,	141.709	609.865	751.574	89	1,829.662
Bellingham,	8.822	227.567	236.389	44	904.552

Belmont,	$2,960.940	$3,515.867	$6,476.807	$1 60	$3,239.280
Berkley,	36.030	256.153	292.183	27	555.066
Berlin,	214.467	291.588	506.055	37	760.646
Bernardston,	154.563	563.875	718.438	37	760.646
Beverly,	6,940.760	7,643.626	14,584.386	4 03	8,284.874
Billerica,	1,492.777	2,446.975	3,939.752	1 07	2,199.706
Blackstone,	716.224	422.697	1,138.921	1 77	3,638.766
Blandford,	.248	172.701	172.949	42	863.436
Bolton,	685.610	419.454	1,105.064	45	925.110
Boston,	355,434.741	293,766.105	649,200.846	401 06	824,499.148
Boxborough,	53.850	55.599	109.449	19	390.602
Boxford,	10.253	347.090	357.343	55	1,130.690
Boylston,	62.014	264.627	326.641	39	801.762
Bradford,	730.715	2,130.415	2,861.130	85	1,747.430
Braintree,	1,046.551	2,165.837	3,212.388	1 70	3,494.860
Brewster,	969.207	1,163.300	2,132.507	57	1,171.806
Bridgewater,	4,360.184	3,403.996	7,764.180	1 69	3,474.302
Brimfield,	147.552	1,029.626	1,177.178	54	1,110.132
Brookfield,	431.596	753.620	1,185.216	1 00	2,055.800
Brookline,	30,907.104	16,798.814	47,705.918	12 13	24,936.854
Buckland,	4.771	142.991	147.762	58	1,192.364
Burlington,	22.415	197 152	219.567	35	719.530
Cambridge,	26,357.929	30,412.695	56,770.624	29 29	60,214.382
Canton,	1,410.528	2,693.099	4,103.627	1 95	4,008.810
Carlisle,	26.014	72.280	98.294	27	555.066
Carver,	585.676	574.343	1,160.019	46	945.668
Charlemont,	9.293	190.830	200.123	34	698.972
Charlton,	208.900	550.161	759 061	80	1,644.640
Chatham,	52.318	2,171.947	2,224.265	85	1,747.430
Chelmsford,	1,287.512	2,057.911	3,345.423	1 23	2,528.634
Chelsea,	2,903.878	4,696.738	7,600.616	8 78	18,049.924

* See Rockland, part of Abington at time of apportionment of tax.

Statement showing the Amounts distributed to Towns and Cities—Continued.

TOWNS.	Corporation Tax.	Bank Tax.	Total Tax.	Share of State Tax of $1,000.	Share of State Tax of $2,055,800.
Cheshire,	$4.126	$615.193	$619.319	$0 69	$1,418.502
Chester,	.325	39.498	39.823	44	904.552
Chesterfield,	-	281.527	281.527	33	678.414
Chicopee,	1,948.879	1,841.867	3,790.746	3 51	7,215.858
Chilmark,	186.551	221.402	407.953	25	513.950
Clarksburg,	-	-	-	21	431.718
Clinton,	2,262.238	1,695.180	3,957.418	2 22	4,563.876
Cohasset,	1,143.161	1,217 142	2,360.303	1 30	2,672.540
Colrain,	112.598	235.104	347.702	57	1,171.806
Concord,	3,890.604	2,242.520	6,133.124	1 57	3,227.606
Conway,	7.877	1,083.386	1,091.263	65	1,336.270
Cummington,	62.560	12.194	74.754	33	678.414
Dalton,	1,364.433	928.305	2,292.738	74	1,521.292
Dana,	-	108.889	108.889	25	513.950
Danvers,	673.129	4,111.073	4,784.202	2 20	4,522.760
Dartmouth,	1,779.983	2,776.632	4,556.615	1 63	3,350.954
Dedham,	2,449.585	6,591.238	9,040.823	3 23	6,640.234
Deerfield,	263.934	1,644.076	1,908.010	1 19	2,446.402
Dennis,	1,500.492	2,475.699	3,976.191	1 22	2,508.076
Dighton,	373.252	1,035.570	1,408.822	69	1,418.502
Douglas,	160.141	162.408	322.549	81	1,665.198
Dover,	96.971	271.503	368.474	30	616.740
Dracut,	141.215	1,040.528	1,181.743	1 00	2,055.800
Dudley,	127.430	132.709	260.139	83	1,706 314
Dunstable,	330.542	387.589	718.131	24	493.392
Duxbury,	1,067.297	2,439.459	3,506.756	96	1,973.568
East Bridgewater,	1,336.653	1,173.805	2,510.458	1 07	2,199.706
Eastham,	279.792	388.438	668.230	21	431.718

Easthampton,	$3,787.032	$2,265.729	$6,052.761	$1 95	$4,008.810
Easton,	7,841.947	6,628.157	14,470.104	2 02	4,152.716
Edgartown,	733.535	1,390.404	2,123.939	88	1,809.104
Egremont,	72.106	149.872	221.978	43	883.994
Enfield,	888.072	1,238.379	2,126.451	53	1,089.574
Erving,	15.728	10.862	26.590	24	493.392
Essex,	159.482	1,546.813	1,706.295	71	1,459.618
Everett,	828.364	721.713	1,550.077	1 44	2,960.352
Fairhaven,	643.360	3,646.475	4,289.835	1 22	2,508.076
Fall River,	16,269.013	21,610.093	37,879.106	18 08	37,168.864
Falmouth,	3,833.773	4,277.026	8,110.799	1 01	2,076.358
Fitchburg,	15,762.170	4,835.411	20,597.581	7 62	15,665.196
Florida,	–	–	–	27	555.066
Foxborough,	184.822	476.297	661.119	1 15	2,364.170
Framingham,	2,712.348	5,952.350	8,664.698	2 68	5,509.544
Franklin,	209.935	1,185.853	1,395.788	1 15	2,364 170
Freetown,	469.523	1,696.196	2,165.719	61	1,254.038
Gardner,	822.503	2,335.566	3,158.069	1 41	2,898.678
Gay Head,	–	–	–	02	41.116
Georgetown,	120.579	293.944	414.523	75	1,541.850
Gill,	45.058	227.688	272.746	35	719.530
Gloucester,	2,630.394	12,684.156	15,314.550	5 82	11,964.756
Goshen,	3.900	8.189	12.089	13	267.254
Gosnold,	–	–	–	10	205.580
Grafton,	830.199	2,890.308	3,720.507	1 51	3,104.258
Granby,	80.430	536.402	616 832	41	842.878
Granville,	5.496	124.290	129.786	42	863.436
Great Barrington,	2,215.921	1,596.670	3,812.591	3 17	6,516.886
Greenfield,	1,572.552	3,793.719	5,366.271	1 75	3,597.650
Greenwich,	–	256.650	256.650	26	534.508
Groton,	6,403.561	1,774.277	8,177.838	1 15	2,364.170
Groveland,	27.875	359.306	387.181	67	1,377.386
Hadley,	141.450	1,247.752	1,389.202	1 09	2,240.822

Statement showing the Amounts distributed to Towns and Cities—Continued.

TOWNS.	Corporation Tax.	Bank Tax.	Total Tax.	Share of State Tax of $1,000.	Share of State Tax of $2,055,800.
Halifax,	$67.702	$132.636	$200.338	$0.27	$555.066
Hamilton,	27.926	342.912	370.838	38	781.204
Hancock,	101.439	260.522	361.961	35	719.530
Hanover,	1,026.054	1,099.211	2,125.265	75	1,541.850
Hanson,	336.148	565.693	901.841	45	925.110
Hardwick,	478.389	1,139.429	1,617.818	88	1,809.104
Harvard,	808.332	1,220.169	2,028.501	74	1,521.292
Harwich,	291.040	1,292.503	1,583.543	99	2,035.242
Hatfield,	109.120	1,720.105	1,829.225	1 07	2,199.706
Haverhill,	2,366.596	9,890.297	12,256.893	6 92	14,226.136
Hawley,	–	8.189	8.189	18	370.044
Heath,	3.377	11.464	14.841	24	493.392
Hingham,	3,303.616	3,351.370	6,654.986	2 32	4,769.456
Hinsdale,	780.466	53.569	834.035	70	1,439.060
Holbrook,	1,982.521	8,076.666	10,059.187	86	1,767.988
Holden,	55.053	307.138	362.191	74	1,521.292
Holland,	–	1.530	1.530	12	246.696
Holliston,	150.719	2,438.404	2,589.123	1 41	2,898.678
Holyoke,	5,556.087	6,095.140	11,651.227	4 72	9,703.376
Hopkinton,	189.556	2,195.635	2,385.191	1 65	3,392.070
Hubbardston,	92.014	385.716	477.730	69	1,418.502
Hudson,	135.306	242.258	377.564	1 14	2,343.612
Hull,	55.482	198.559	254.041	17	349.486
Huntington,	169.162	104.578	273.740	44	904.552
Hyde Park,	635.415	935.470	1,570.885	3 34	6,866.372
Ipswich,	1,455.388	930.370	2,385.758	1 34	2,754.772
Kingston,	3,032.604	3,114.297	6,146.901	97	1,994.126
Lakeville,	302.187	571.792	873.979	46	945.668

Lancaster,	$1,940.532	$1,920.736	$3,861.268	$1 44	$2,960.352
Lanesborough,	48.126	155.722	203.848	59	1,212.922
Lawrence,	4,273.628	7,643.494	11,917.122	13 13	26,992.654
Lee,	857.949	1,357.506	2,215.455	1 37	2,816.446
Leicester,	1,452.117	3,027.359	4,479.476	1 48	3,042.584
Lenox,	271.471	1,122.034	1,393.505	1 04	2,138.032
Leominster,	2,230.788	3,045.351	5,276.139	2 18	4,481.644
Leverett,	20.152	82.564	102.716	31	637.298
Lexington,	512.603	737.164	1,249.767	1 50	3,083.700
Leyden,	.055	199.104	199.159	19	390.602
Lincoln,	534.748	965.558	1,500.306	49	1,007.342
Littleton,	383.435	162.944	546.379	52	1,069.016
Longmeadow,	879.840	3,337.883	4,217.723	82	1,685.756
Lowell,	21,998.798	29,780.489	51,779.287	19 29	39,656.382
Ludlow,	13.275	–	13.275	39	801.762
Lunenburg,	240.407	428.390	668.797	56	1,151.248
Lynn,	3,870.830	14,279.615	18,150.445	15 29	31,433.182
Lynnfield,	207.303	932.883	1,140.186	48	986.784
Malden,	3,633.217	872.377	4,505.594	4 34	8,922.172
Manchester,	297.087	1,139.240	1,436.327	86	1,767.988
Mansfield,	737.726	386.523	1,124.249	76	1,562.408
Marblehead,	2,122.188	4,144.616	6,266.804	2 87	5,900.146
Marion,	1.545	840.708	842.253	37	760.646
Marlborough,	246.212	2,643.187	2,889.399	2 59	5,324.522
Marshfield,	789.382	445.506	1,234.888	68	1,397.944
Mashpee,	1.206	–	1.206	08	164.464
Mattapoisett,	1,046.346	568.385	1,614.731	50	1,027.900
Maynard,	312.552	69.499	382.051	75	1,541.850
Medfield,	710.929	1,256.191	1,967.120	60	1,233.480
Medford,	3,083.160	4,486.554	7,569.714	4 08	8,387.664
Medway,	552.592	2,038.096	2,590.688	1 33	2,734.214
Melrose,	1,235.575	637.444	1,873.019	1 83	3,762.114
Mendon,	161.781	378.316	540.097	53	1,089.574

Statement showing the Amounts distributed to Towns and Cities—Continued.

TOWNS.	Corporation Tax.	Bank Tax.	Total Tax.	Share of State Tax of $1,000.	Share of State Tax of $2,055,800.
Methuen,	$2,173.283	$1,030.550	$3,203.833	$1 50	$3,083.700
Middleborough,	2,499.027	1,284.876	3,783.903	1 92	3,947.136
Middlefield,	9.160	6.160	15.320	31	637.298
Middleton,	61.564	170.071	231.635	35	719.530
Milford,	2,125.331	3,478 242	5,603.573	3 94	8,099.852
Millbury,	266.032	1,361.827	1,627.859	1 56	3,207.048
Milton,	6,613.475	6,188.610	12,802.085	3 21	6,599.118
Monroe,	-	-	-	06	123.348
Monson,	1,075.854	2,599.651	3,675.505	1 07	2,199.706
Montague,	363.457	1,590.829	1,954.286	88	1,809.104
Monterey,	5.815	149.183	154.998	26	534.508
Montgomery,	-	-	-	13	267.254
Mount Washington,	-	-	-	08	164.464
Nahant,	17,252.166	10,303.155	27,555.321	3 01	6,187.958
Nantucket,	3,007.864	4,078.923	7,086.787	1 71	3,515.418
Natick,	602.697	2,692.165	3,294.862	2 48	5,098.384
Needham,	3,335.475	1,664.814	5,000.289	2 09	4,296.622
New Ashford,	-	-	-	08	164.464
New Bedford,	27,213.356	36,703.780	63,917.136	16 14	33,180.612
New Braintree,	.916	389.599	390.515	40	822.320
New Marlborough,	74.739	231.283	306.022	74	1,521.292
New Salem,	27,100	172.010	199.110	32	657.856
Newbury,	340.758	2,300.649	2,641.407	61	1,254.038
Newburyport,	5,787.943	15,571.013	21,358.956	5 98	12,293.684
Newton,	18,539.628	18,880.700	37,420.328	11 77	24,196.766
Norfolk,	18.202	374.484	392.686	39	801.762
North Andover,	1,129.579	2,882.956	4,012.535	1 53	3,145.374
North Bridgewater,	1,084.367	1,866.154	2,950.521	3 01	6,187.958

North Brookfield,	$532.951	$231.198	$764.149	$1 41	$2,898.678
North Reading,	127.380	104.106	231.486	41	842.878
Northampton,	5,913.732	9,126.140	15,039.872	5 09	10,464.022
Northborough,	1,229.393	1,432.141	2,661.534	89	1,829.662
Northbridge,	7,034.179	1,372.314	8,406.493	1 43	2,939.794
Northfield,	379.820	656.908	1,036.728	65	1,336.270
Norton,	144.601	751.400	896.001	65	1,336.270
Norwood,	335.212	1,002.094	1,337.306	86	1,767.988
Oakham,	10.039	25.995	36.034	31	637.298
Orange,	1,640.520	245.450	1,885.970	99	2,035.242
Orleans,	369.173	1,391.502	1,760.675	50	1,027.900
Otis,	.124	64.320	64.444	30	616.740
Oxford,	1,277.942	864.803	2,142.745	1 05	2,158.590
Palmer,	126.922	363.510	490.432	1 16	2,384.728
Paxton,	3.818	114.303	118.121	27	555.066
Peabody,	2,290.574	10,734.261	13,024.835	3 92	8,058.736
Pelham,	–	4.009	4.009	19	390.602
Pembroke,	131.673	432.347	564.020	53	1,089.574
Pepperell,	1,031.772	526.081	1,557.853	88	1,809.104
Peru,	–	29.260	29.260	16	328.928
Petersham,	112.061	436.493	548.554	56	1,151.248
Phillipston,	43.766	145.447	189.213	25	513.950
Pittsfield,	3,398.571	9,148.071	12,546.642	5 92	12,170.336
Plainfield,	241.061	130.051	371.112	23	472.834
Plymouth,	5,283.018	7,696.456	12,979.474	2 74	5,632.892
Plympton,	59.184	139.631	198.815	27	555.066
Prescott,	–	14.032	14.032	18	370.044
Princeton,	152.251	476.308	628.559	66	1,356.828
Provincetown,	1,653.883	4,111.539	5,765.422	1 64	3,371.512
Quincy,	3,581.011	5,740.258	9,321.269	3 53	7,256.974
Randolph,	2,085.885	7,369.972	9,455.857	1 57	3,227.606
Raynham,	2,057.561	1,779.164	3,836.725	84	1,726.872
Reading,	566.706	741.024	1,307.730	1 28	2,631.424

Statement showing the Amounts distributed to Towns and Cities—Continued.

TOWNS.	Corporation Tax.	Bank Tax.	Total Tax.	Share of State Tax of $1,000.	Share of State Tax of $2,055,800.
Rehoboth,	$1.683	$163.383	$165.066	$0 65	$1,336.270
Revere,	220.452	108.742	329.194	71	1,459.618
Richmond,	–	17.115	17.115	44	904.552
Rochester,	171.284	148.919	320.203	42	863.436
Rockland,*	349.900	1,142.643	1,492.543	–	*
Rockport,	1,383.682	3,251.445	4,635.127	1 36	2,795.888
Rowe,	1.953	72.338	74.291	18	370.044
Rowley,	87.072	252.382	339.454	44	904.552
Royalston,	103.588	1,533.794	1,637.382	63	1,295.154
Russell,	44.665	49.122	93.787	23	472.834
Rutland,	1.188	38.608	39.796	41	842.878
Salem,	18,855.714	35,255.878	54,111.592	16 19	33,283.402
Salisbury,	390.999	2,249.772	2,640.771	1 49	3,063.142
Sandisfield,	5.815	27.720	33.535	46	945.668
Sandwich,	470.921	1,272.997	1,743.918	1 17	2,405.286
Saugus,	89.451	496.939	586.390	1 04	2,138.032
Savoy,	–	38.525	38.525	25	513.950
Scituate,	671.837	1,004.330	1,676.167	91	1,870.778
Seekonk,	3.320	44.206	47.526	44	904.552
Sharon,	131.491	530.376	661.867	62	1,274.596
Sheffield,	777.194	265.394	1,042.588	99	2,035.242
Shelburne,	721.596	990.882	1,712.478	75	1,541.850
Sherborn,	398.340	721.868	1,120.208	65	1,336.270
Shirley,	1,493.757	389.480	1,883.237	66	1,356.828
Shrewsbury,	328.350	368.328	696.678	81	1,665.198
Shutesbury,	.906	50.264	51.170	19	390.602
Somerset,	1,127.185	973.264	2,100.449	76	1,562.408
Somerville,	4,232.070	5,279.348	9,511.418	8 98	18,461.084

South Hadley,	$1,511.385	$1,394.455	$2,905.840	$1 37	$2,816.446
South Scituate,	1,189.885	1,910.989	3,100.874	76	1,562.408
Southampton,	–	253.213	253.213	46	945.668
Southborough,	222.357	944.306	1,166.663	99	2,035.242
Southbridge,	773.577	1,834.420	2,607.997	1 85	3,803.230
Southwick,	.434	542.962	543.396	53	1,089.574
Spencer,	577.101	1,106.347	1,683.448	1 64	3,371.512
Springfield,	38,355.450	21,976.656	60,332.106	19 16	39,389.128
Sterling,	732.150	980.385	1,712.535	88	1,809.104
Stockbridge,	4,235.060	2,511.809	6,746.869	1 64	3,371.512
Stoneham,	223.455	161.731	385.186	1 81	3,720.998
Stoughton,	1,119.428	1,555.157	2,674.585	1 88	3,864.904
Stow,	226.261	75.676	301.937	56	1,151.248
Sturbridge,	173.677	433.803	607.480	78	1,603.524
Sudbury,	751.886	623.890	1,375.776	71	1,459.618
Sunderland,	120.703	142.467	263.170	35	719.530
Sutton,	38.617	468.712	507.329	94	1,932.452
Swampscott,	1,582.879	2,291.729	3,874.608	1 38	2,837.004
Swanzey,	221.818	650.652	872.470	52	1,069.016
Taunton,	16,367.242	16,434.219	32,801.461	10 50	21,585.900
Templeton,	517.900	2,019.822	2,537.722	98	2,014.684
Tewksbury,	753.649	825.808	1,579.457	68	1,397.944
Tisbury,	603.280	546.527	1,149.807	59	1,212.922
Tolland,	–	63.312	63.312	23	472.834
Topsfield,	136.657	590.300	726.957	56	1,151.248
Townsend,	52.889	1,170.269	1,223.158	71	1,459.618
Truro,	48.836	403.359	452.195	33	678.414
Tyngsborough,	363.088	119.088	482.176	25	513.950
Tyringham,	305.103	102.564	407.667	23	472.834
Upton,	48.571	439.591	488.162	71	1,459.618
Uxbridge,	754.560	1,671.051	2,425.611	1 34	2,754.772

* See Abington.

Statement showing the Amounts distributed to Towns and Cities—Concluded.

TOWNS.	Corporation Tax.	Bank Tax.	Total Tax.	Share of State Tax of $1,000.	Share of State Tax of $2,055,800.
Wakefield,	$10,932.985	$2,240.647	$13,173.632	$2 29	$4,707.782
Wales,	96.156	7.721	103.877	31	637.298
Walpole,	346.783	1,420.294	1,767.077	98	2,014.684
Waltham,	11,183.876	4,494.850	15,678 726	5 42	11,142.436
Ware,	1,831.018	1,722.680	3,553.698	1 38	2,837.004
Wareham,	1,283.025	1,692.920	2,975.945	98	2,014.684
Warren,	519.564	345 307	864.871	1 14	2,343.612
Warwick,	34.681	198.221	232.902	25	513.950
Washington,	–	15.400	15.400	23	472.834
Watertown,	3,681.048	2,542.080	6,223.128	3 17	6,516 886
Wayland,	309.873	560.115	869.988	55	1,130.690
Webster,	9,127.406	165.672	9,293.078	1 77	3,638.766
Wellfleet,	527.644	1,034.896	1,562.540	74	1,521.292
Wendell,	27.342	–	27.342	18	370.044
Wenham,	79.652	1,011.730	1,091.382	39	801.762
West Boylston,	760.109	206.064	966.173	89	1,829.662
West Bridgewater,	399.802	843.584	1,243.386	67	1,377.386
West Brookfield,	222.279	512.056	734.335	67	1,377 386
West Newbury,	216.952	1,727.732	1,944.684	86	1,767.988
West Springfield,	2,029.050	2,730.220	4,759.270	1 49	3,063.142
West Stockbridge,	129.464	107.792	237.256	75	1,541.850
Westborough,	376.739	2,267.761	2,644.500	1 53	3,145.374
Westfield,	3,168.415	5,457.773	8,626.188	3 73	7,668.134
Westford,	831.351	800.207	1,631.558	83	1,706.314
Westhampton,	8.624	212.189	220.813	30	616.740
Westminster,	188.093	371 357	559.450	71	1,459.618
Weston,	2,683.935	2,154.034	4,837.969	87	1,788.546
Westport,	358.279	1,739.178	2,097.457	1 14	2,343.612

Weymouth,	$2,127.123	$11,011.140	$13,138.263	$3 99	$8,202.642
Whately,	31.621	928.270	959.891	58	1.192.364
Wilbraham,	116.558	385.314	501.872	74	1,521.292
Williamsburg,	337.168	1,619.280	1,956.448	1 11	2,281.938
Williamstown,	133 254	725.720	858.974	1 25	2,569.750
Wilmington,	30.878	98.102	128.980	39	801.762
Winchendon,	806.762	2,329.937	3,136.699	1 51	3,104.258
Winchester,	1,814.671	948.798	2,763.469	2 18	4,481.644
Windsor,	–	14.683	14.683	26	534.508
Winthrop,	47.543	278.098	325.641	35	719.530
Woburn,	2,395.003	7,863.066	10,258.069	5 26	10,813.508
Worcester,	46,744.746	27,014.720	73,759.466	25 51	52,443.458
Worthington,	–	–	–	32	657.856
Wrentham,	534.088	997.295	1,531.383	89	1,829.662
Yarmouth,	1,268.508	3,818.059	5,086.567	1 14	2,343.612
Totals,	$980,765.787	$1,075,100.592	$2,055,866.379	–	$2,055,800.000

Table No. 10.

Towns in which, in 1873, the Poll Tax exceeded Two Dollars, and the Rate of Tax upon Property in such Towns.

Counties and Towns.	Number of Polls.	Whole sum rais'd on Polls.	Tax on each Poll.	Rate of Tax on Property.
Barnstable County.				
Eastham,	166	$382 00	$2 30	$27 00
Berkshire County.				
Dalton,	326	828 00	2 54	8 10
Florida,	350	868 00	2 48	28 00
Hancock,	172	588 00	3 42	9 00
Hinsdale,	502	1,255 00	2 50	15 20
Lanesborough,	408	881 00	2 18	11 30
Sandisfield,	326	987 00	3 03	22 60
Savoy,	176	440 00	2 50	19 50
Washington,	156	562 00	3 60	19 00
Essex County.				
Groveland,	529	1,307 00	2 47	13 60
Methuen,	954	2,385 00	2 50	16 60
Franklin County.				
Buckland,	475	1,204 00	2 53	19 70
Charlemont,	260	689 00	2 65	22 10
Erving,	255	676 00	2 65	19 10
Monroe,	43	170 00	4 00	32 00
Orange,	860	2,322 00	2 70	22 80
Warwick,	229	618 00	2 70	25 00
Hampden County.				
Blandford,	257	771 00	3 00	16 50
Chester,	368	1,023 00	2 78	18 20
Hampshire County.				
Cummington,	261	687 00	2 63	13 60
Worthington,	242	640 00	2 64	11 00
Middlesex County.				
Acton,	464	1,178 00	2 54	12 60
Ashland,	704	1,676 00	2 38	17 20
Bedford,	255	765 00	3 00	13 60
Billerica,	454	1,362 00	3 00	11 00
Chelmsford,	664	1,660 00	2 50	15 00
Concord,	684	2,360 00	3 45	11 70
Everett,	857	2,999 00	3 50	13 30

Towns whose Poll Tax exceeded Two Dollars, etc.—Continued.

COUNTIES AND TOWNS.	Number of Polls.	Whole sum rais'd on Polls.	Tax on each Poll.	Rate of Tax on Property.
MIDDLESEX COUNTY—Con.				
Groton,	459	$1,056 00	$2 30	$10 00
Hopkinton,	1,101	2,785 00	2 53	17 80
Lincoln,	217	759 00	3 50	13 70
Malden,	2,307	7,498 00	3 25	15 40
Medford,	1,736	6,944 00	4 00	13 90
Reading,	827	2,324 00	2 81	15 60
Stoneham,	1,340	3,015 00	2 25	16 30
Stow,	280	714 00	2 55	8 90
Wakefield,	1,960	4,900 00	2 50	18 50
Woburn,	2,900	9,454 00	2 26	15 70
NORFOLK COUNTY.				
Weymouth,	2,684	8,052 00	3 00	14 00
PLYMOUTH COUNTY.				
Duxbury,	664	1,660 00	2 50	17 60
Hanover,	405	930 00	2 30	16 50
Middleborough,	1,329	3,495 00	2 63	14 30
West Bridgewater,	467	938 00	2 01	11 70
WORCESTER COUNTY.				
Ashburnham,	593	1,868 00	3 15	22 00
Athol,	1,149	3,447 00	3 00	14 30
Barre,	672	2,016 00	3 00	14 60
Bolton,	291	829 00	2 85	16 00
Dana,	209	608 00	2 91	19 10
Douglas,	628	1,570 00	2 50	13 70
Dudley,	578	1,387 00	2 40	18 00
Gardner,	1,186	3,036 00	2 56	18 70
Hardwick,	539	1,482 00	2 75	16 90
Harvard,	347	937 00	2 72	13 50
Hubbardston,	415	1,245 00	3 00	17 00
Leicester,	680	1,938 00	2 85	10 50
Leominster,	1,365	3,303 00	2 43	15 80
Northborough,	359	1,055 00	2 94	16 40
North Brookfield,	1,170	3,101 00	2 65	13 30
Petersham,	294	882 00	3 00	13 20
Phillipston,	181	507 00	2 80	17 00
Royalston,	350	1,036 00	2 87	16 40
Rutland,	275	742 00	2 70	16 00
Southborough,	488	1,220 00	2 50	13 50
Templeton,	760	2,014 00	2 65	21 30
Uxbridge,	661	1,818 00	2 75	11 50
Westminster,	470	1,443 00	3 07	21 30
Winchendon,	968	2,604 00	2 69	18 40

Table No. 11.

List of Towns in which National Banks are located, with the Rate of Taxation in each Town, at which the Shares of the Banks therein were assessed on their Market Value, deducting Real Estate, under Act of 1873, chap. 315; and the Whole Value of the Shares as taxed.

TOWNS.	Rate of Tax.		Taxable Value.	
	1873.	1874.	1873.	1874.
Abington,	$12 80	$16 40	$201,990	$204,750
Adams,	27 00	20 00	699,500	699,500
Amesbury,	15 00	15 00	180,000	178,500
Amherst,	17 00	18 00	180,000	187,500
Andover,	12 50	12 50	282,500	282,500
Ashburnham,	-	21 00	-	50,000
Athol,	14 30	13 90	198,000	204,500
Attleborough,	13 30	12 50	119,000	119,000
Barnstable,	12 00	10 00	116,000	116,000
Barre,	14 60	16 31	172,500	172,500
Beverly,	15 00	12 40	250,000	250,000
Boston,	12 80	15 60	60,165,444	65,759,164
Brighton,	9 10	15 60*	603,400	*
Cambridge,	13 50	12 50	1,080,000	1,059,500
Canton,	9 20	10 00	287,500	295,000
Charlestown,	15 20	15 60*	956,000	*
Chelsea,	17 50	19 00	328,380	319,000
Chicopee,	17 30	15 20	195,000	195,000
Concord,	11 70	12 05	113,000	118,000
Clinton,	23 50	17 50	228,500	236,000
Conway,	15 00	14 50	159,000	159,000
Danvers,	14 40	18 60	200,000	200,000
Dedham,	13 50	13 50	375,000	375,000
Easthampton,	17 80	15 00	207,000	205,000
Easton,	10 00	10 33	378,000	390,000
Edgartown,	15 20	13 20	125,000	125,000
Fairhaven,	15 50	16 50	240,000	240,000
Fall River,	13 00	12 80	3,118,440	3,085,300
Falmouth,	10 40	10 00	108,000	110,000
Fitchburg,	16 60	18 50	712,500	740,000
Framingham,	14 00	14 00	264,000	270,000
Franklin,	17 00	17 00	115,000	115,000
Gardner,	18 70	22 90	113,000	113,000
Gloucester,	20 00	21 00	781,500	777,000
Grafton,	16 40	18 50	210,000	210,000

* Included in Boston.

List of Towns having National Banks, etc.—Continued.

TOWNS.	Rate of Tax.		Taxable Value.	
	1873.	1874.	1873.	1874.
Great Barrington, . .	$8 60	$8 60	$280,000	$280,000
Greenfield, ...	19 00	13 50	709,940	686,000
Harwich, ...	18 50	17 00	330,000	345,000
Haverhill, ...	20 00	17 50	1,058,600	1,122,200
Hingham, ...	14 00	15 00	212,000	166,000
Holliston, ...	16 30	16 80	166,500	165,000
Holyoke, ...	15 50	21 20	478,700	468,700
Hopkinton, ...	17 80	18 20	187,500	187,500
Lancaster, ...	14 00	8 50	278,000	278,600
Lawrence, ...	16 00	16 20	827,500	987,500
Lee, ...	17 30	17 50	240,000	240,000
Leicester, ...	10 50	9 85	218,000	224,000
Leominster, ...	15 80	15 50	110,000	165,000
Lowell,.	16 90	15 90	3,054,580	2,936,500
Lynn, ...	18 40	16 80	1,245,000	1,271,000
Malden, ...	15 40	14 80	100,000	100,000
Marblehead,. . . .	20 00	13 80	262,296	259,200
Marlborough, . . .	20 00	22 50	240,000	240,000
Methuen, ...	16 60	13 23	115,000	115,000
Milford, ...	20 00	17 70	312,500	312,500
Millbury, ...	13 50	15 25	230,000	224,000
Monson, ...	14 00	14 40	162,495	162,495
Montague, ...	15 00	16 50	90,000	210,000
Nantucket, ...	12 50	12 50	250,000	250,000
Natick, ...	16 50	20 50	-	103,000
New Bedford, . . .	16 20	16 20	4,068,500	4,180,500
Newburyport, . . .	20 40	19 00	1,008,960	1,034,500
Newton, ...	14 50	13 00	224,500	220,000
Northampton, . . .	21 00	12 50	1,470,000	1,475,000
Northborough, . . .	16 40	13 50	112,000	112,000
Northbridge, . . .	11 50	7 00	120,000	125,000
Oxford,.	15 00	15 00	122,000	127,000
Peabody, ...	17 00	18 00	539,000	535,000
Pittsfield, ...	12 50	12 50	955,000	955,000
Plymouth, ...	16 40	14 40	547,500	547,250
Provincetown, . . .	21 00	21 00	263,000	267,000
Quincy, ...	17 00	15 00	408,990	412,500
Randolph, ...	13 00	14 00	350,000	370,000
Rockport, ...	21 00	15 50	173,490	172,500
Salem, ...	18 00	16 50	2,517,990	2,564,000
Salisbury, ...	13 50	13 00	135,000	135,000
Shelburne, ...	16 50	16 00	165,000	165,000
Southbridge, . . .	14 50	14 50	174,750	177,750
Springfield, ...	16 00	16 50	3,441,880	3,452,230
Stockbridge, . . .	8 60	9 30	300,000	286,000
Taunton, ...	15 00	15 00	1,765,000	1,913,000
Townsend, ...	30 50	14 00	113,500	98,500
Uxbridge, ...	11 50	13 89	120,000	125,000

List of Towns having National Banks, etc.—Concluded.

TOWNS.	Rate of Tax.		Taxable Value.	
	1873.	1874.	1873.	1874.
Wakefield,	$18 50	$18 60	$120,000	$115,000
Waltham,	11 00	15 50	156,000	155,000
Ware,	21 00	20 00	476,000	475,500
Wareham,	18 00	18 10	108,500	108,446
Watertown,	12 00	13 50	-	92,000
Westborough,	15 50	15 00	120,000	125,000
Westfield,	15 00	17 00	528,000	540,000
Weymouth,	14 00	14 30	633,500	648,000
Winchendon,	18 40	12 50	172,500	172,500
Woburn,	15 70	15 80	354,990	369,000
Worcester,	17 40	16 80	2,898,000	2,953,500
Wrentham,	12 00	12 10	127,500	127,500
Yarmouth,	11 20	10 00	677,250	703,500
Totals,	. .	. .	$110,090,065	$115,094,585

TABLE No. 12.

Aggregates of Polls, Property, Taxes, etc., as returned by the Assessors of the several Cities and Towns to the Secretary of the Commonwealth, for the Years 1861 to 1874, inclusive.

YEARS.	Total number of polls.	Total tax on polls.	Total value of personal estate.	Total value of real estate.	Total tax for state, county, city and town purposes, including highway tax.	Total valuation.	Total number of dwelling-houses.	Total number of horses.	Total number of cows.	Total number of sheep.	Total number of acres of land taxed in the state.	Average ratio per $1,000.
1861, . .	280,885	$455,333 93	$309,397,669	$552,087,749	$7,600,501 28	$861,547,583	178,194	88,299	149,090	81,110	4,062,035	$8 82
1862, . .	276,443	564,796 17	315,311,213	543,669,113	8,605,511 19	858,987,326	178,450	87,478	151,756	137,478	4,397,363	10 02
1863, . .	275,758	567,360 85	343,500,267	553,650,716	10,599,097 22	897,150,983	183,528	89,228	158,905	150,922	4,383,103	11 81
1864, . .	281,220	574,274 11	324,584,847	577,298,256	12,876,850 59	901,883,103	185,232	91,862	155,043	160,513	4,410,805	14 28
1865, . .	287,655	607,528 95	386,079,955	605,761,946	16,800,332 07	991,841,901	185,005	89,750	145,801	160,997	4,431,554	16 94
1866, . .	306,993	641,413 36	430,272,298	651,043,703	15,694,039 07	1,081,316,001	190,439	95,154	145,914	157,588	4,426,000	14 51
1867, . .	315,742	664,120 00	457,728,296	708,165,117	19,104,074 79	1,165,893,413	195,388	97,244	144,561	137,352	4,429,954	16 39
1868, . .	332,759	696,179 00	469,775,322	750,723,617	16,056,193 00	1,220,498,939	200,267	99,978	151,141	140,359	4,412,186	13 16
1869, . .	337,043	722,088 00	503,085,988	838,083,415	20,007,863 00	1,341,069,403	207,027	103,113	155,830	112,047	4,461,574	14 92
1870, . .	357,339	767,734 00	516,089,535	901,037,841	21,922,569 00	1,417,127,376	214,371	107,198	161,185	87,061	4,438,549	15 47
1871, . .	374,079	782,753 00	506,154,883	991,196,803	22,063,946 00	1,497,351,686	224,333	112,782	162,172	65,565	4,447,087	14 74
1872, . .	396,784	825,250 00	565,294,622	1,131,305,347	22,911,883 00	1,696,599,969	233,787	116,719	158,304	58,534	4,453,968	13 50
1873, . .	408,131	854,250 00	537,388,751	1,226,041,239	25,153,399 00	1,763,429,990	243,290	123,290	151,033	55,642	4,451,137	14 26
1874, . .	414,800	875,486 00	542,292,402	1,289,308,763	28,700,605 00	1,831,601,165	249,738	127,601	147,359	50,228	4,467,066	15 67

REVENUE FROM INDIRECT TAXES.

Table No. 13.

Showing the Receipts from 1860 to 1874 inclusive, from Licenses, Fees, Confiscated Liquors, Taxes on Sales, and State Police, of the State of Massachusetts.

Years,	1860.	1861.	1862.	1863.	1864.	1865.	1866.	1867.
Hawkers and Pedlers' Licenses, G.S. ch. 50,	$171 00	$216 00	$286 00	$155 00	$631 15	$4,372 00	$3,000 00	$15,580 00
Secretary's Fees, G. S. ch. 14,	286 06	224 96	458 95	1,622 71	3,953 83	2,679 86	3,854 95	2,747 32
Supreme Judicial Court, G. S. ch. 121,	1,576 23	914 90	676 90	533 90	435 10	381 70	444 60	423 70
Superior Court, G. S. ch. 176,	9,180 37	3,015 89	1,130 70	-	-	-	-	-
Fees for Commissions, Acts 1862, ch. 109,	-	-	1,490 00	4,330 00	2,695 00	6,490 00	4,300 00	2,480 00
Courts of Insolvency, G. S. ch. 118,	20,641 00	21,984 52	32,652 00	18,736 63	12,157 00	8,759 50	8,047 96	8,019 00
Insurance Licenses, Acts 1867, ch. 267,	-	-	-	-	-	-	-	5,935 50
Confiscated Liquors, G. S. ch. 86, Acts 1869, ch. 415,	-	-	-	-	-	-	-	3,796 13
Tax on Sales of Liquors, Acts 1868, ch. 141,	-	-	-	-	-	-	-	-
Liquor Licenses, Acts 1868, ch. 141,	-	-	-	-	-	-	-	-
Corporation Fees, Acts 1870, ch. 224,	-	-	-	-	-	-	-	-
State Police Fees, &c., Acts 1862, ch. 27; Acts 1865, ch. 249; Acts 1871, ch. 394,	-	-	-	-	-	-	-	-
Totals,	$31,854 66	$26,356 27	$36,694 55	$25,378 24	$19,872 08	$22,683 06	$19,647 51	$38,981 65

Receipts from Licenses, Fees, Confiscated Liquors, etc.—Continued.

Years,	1868.	1869.	1870.	1871.	1872.	1873.	1874.	Total.
Hawkers and Pedlers' Licenses, G.S. ch. 50,	$11,253 00	$14,104 00	$2,600 00	$12,563 00	$14,292 00	$22,848 00	$44,567 63	$146,638 78
Secretary's Fees, G. S. ch. 14,	685 09	480 63	3,274 85	1,347 15	133 83	134 85	586 40	22,471 44
Supreme Judicial Court, G. S. ch. 121,	490 20	423 80	577 60	421 80	514 90	511 10	503 50	8,829 93
Superior Court, G. S. ch. 176,	-	-	-	-	-	-	-	13,326 96
Fees for Commissions, Acts 1862, ch. 109,	5,550 00	6,080 00	3,500 00	8,180 30	6,905 00	7,125 00	7,875 00	67,000 30
Courts of Insolvency, G. S. ch. 118,	3,859 50	2,411 00	472 00	648 00	71 00	3,579 00	435 00	142,373 11
Insurance Licenses, Acts 1867, ch. 267,	9,534 71	16,850 00	16,491 50	15,902 33	19,385 41	20,957 16	16,122 99	121,179 60
Confiscated Liquors, G. S. ch. 86, Acts 1869, ch. 415,	3,858 92	-	15 90	786 77	4,338 93	13,805 31	19,793 08	46,395 04
Tax on Sales of Liquors, Acts 1868, ch. 141,	15,773 05	37,775 05	-	174 28	-	-	-	53,722 38
Liquor Licenses, Acts 1868, ch. 141,	118,200 00	2,675 00	-	-	-	-	-	120,875 00
Corporation Fees, Acts 1870, ch. 224,	-	-	-	4,569 25	10,222 15	9,161 80	9,695 21	33,648 41
State Police Fees, etc., Acts 1862, ch. 27; Acts 1865, ch. 249; Acts 1871, ch. 394,	-	849 91	3,661 06	2,599 52	9,905 94	18,849 20	18,156 48	54,022 11
Totals,	$169,204 47	$81,649 39	$30,592 91	$47,092 40	$65,769 16	$96,971 42	$117,735 29	$830,483 06

REVENUE FROM TAXES ON CORPORATIONS.

TABLE No. 14.

Statement showing the Receipts from 1860 to 1874, from Taxes upon Banks, National Bank Shares, Savings Banks, Insurance Companies, Manufacturing Companies, and Coal and Mining Companies.

YEARS,	1860.	1861.	1862.	1863.	1864.	1865.	1866.	1867.
Bank Tax, G. S. ch. 57, § 89; Acts 1865, ch. 283; 1868, ch. 349; 1871, ch. 390; 1872, ch. 321; 1873, ch. 315,	$646,004 46	$660,396 67	$654,022 50	$646,728 89	$630,729 06	$284,975 14	$20,508 00	-
Annual and Semi-Annual Insurance Taxes, G. S. ch. 58; Acts 1862, ch. 222; 1864, ch. 208; 1867, ch. 267; 1868, ch. 165 and 283; 1873, ch. 141,	4,152 15	3,710 71	111,021 79	88,181 36	128,301 59	201,163 34	177,670 20	$201,544 13
Tax on Savings Banks, Acts 1862, ch. 224; 1868, ch. 315,	-	-	228,683 21	400,080 01	452,399 29	364,591 36	311,848 33	361,889 35
Tax on Massachusetts Hospital Life Insurance Company, Acts 1862, ch. 224; 1865, ch. 283,	-	-	-	34,032 54	-	-	-	-
Dividend Tax on Foreign Stockholders, Acts 1863, ch. 233,*	-	-	-	13,529 39	41,378 08	58 66	-	-
Tax on Corporations, Acts 1864, ch. 208; 1865, ch. 283,	-	-	-	-	676,489 69	361,144 84	314,391 63	259,101 74
Tax on Coal and Mining Companies, Acts 1864, ch. 208; 1865, ch. 283,	-	-	-	-	34,191 52	76,763 51	32,234 30	21,371 99
Totals,	$650,156 61	$664,107 38	$993,727 50	$1,182,552 19	$1,963,489 23	$1,288,696 85	$856,652 46	$843,907 21

* The amounts under this head were refunded, the law having been declared unconstitutional.

Statement showing the Receipts from Taxes upon Banks, etc.—Continued.

YEARS, ...	1868.	1869.	1870.	1871.	1872.	1873.	1874.	TOTAL.
Bank Tax, G. S. ch. 57, § 89; Acts 1865, ch. 283; 1868, ch. 349; 1871, ch. 390; 1872, ch. 321; 1873, ch. 315, ...	$30,667 49	$197,489 10	$181,798 41	$311,312 41	$134,822 98	$207,209 57	$217,964 58	$4,824,629 26
Annual and Semi-Annual Insurance Taxes, G. S., ch. 58; Acts 1862, ch. 222; 1864, ch. 208; 1867, ch. 267; 1868, ch. 165 and 283; 1873, ch. 141,	163,324 71	148,775 94	138,306 72	116,160 73	103,346 57	203,389 87	168,748 25	1,957,798 06
Tax on Savings Banks, Acts 1862, ch. 224; 1868, ch. 315, ...	570,065 86	771,998 10	927,254 91	1,097,332 13	1,329,709 89	1,454,719 46	1,550,500 99	9,821,072 89
Tax on Mass. Hosp. Life Ins. Co., Acts 1862, ch. 224; 1865, ch. 283, .	-	112,061 61	78,349 05	81,816 73	86,104 01	87,022 50	89,129 31	568,515 75
Dividend Tax on Foreign Stockholders, Act 1863, ch. 233,* . . .	-	-	-	-	-	-	-	54,966 13
Tax on Corporat'ns, Acts 1864, ch. 208; 1865, ch. 283, ...	297,653 50	364,423 54	347,593 24	360,988 98	368,869 45	330,927 21	330,032 32	4,011,616 14
Tax on Coal and Mining Companies, Acts 1864, ch. 208; 1865, ch. 283, .	22,081 56	15,911 12	8,899 02	8,190 52	7,877 43	7,182 09	5,294 65	239,997 71
Totals, . . .	$1,083,793 12	$1,610,659 41	$1,682,201 35	$1,975,801 50	$2,030,730 33	$2,290,450 70	$2,361,670 10	$21,478,595 94

* The amounts under this head were refunded, the law having been declared unconstitutional.

TABLE NO. 15.

Showing the Assessments and Distribution of Franchise Taxes assessed by the Tax Commissioner on Corporations, from 1865 to 1874, under Chapter 283, Acts of 1865.

YEARS.	Aggregate Valuation of Corporate Stocks.	Value of Corporate Real Estate and Mach'ry, assessed in Towns and Cities.	Aggregate Excess on which a Tax was laid.	Rate of Tax laid by Commissioners.	Whole Amount of Taxes assessed upon Corporat'ns on General List.	Part of General List due to Cities and Towns.	Balance of General List retained by Commonwealth.	Assessm'ts on Coal, Mining, Quarry'g and Oil Co's.	Total Am't accruing to Commonwealth from General List and Coal, Mining, Quarrying and Oil Companies.
1865,	$146,790,966 74	$70,184,722 00	$79,941,570 77	$17 56	$1,421,303 37	$1,060,158 53	$361,144 84	$76,763 51	$437,908 35
1866,	162,930,885 69	76,957,843 00	88,015,274 91	14 83	1,305,267 13	990,875 50	314,391 63	32,234 30	346,625 93
1867,	165,641,943 00	86,943,662 00	85,141,784 00	16 67	1,419,304 99	1,160,203 25	259,101 74	21,371 99	280,473 73
1868,	181,178,768 00	92,328,430 00	90,986,786 00	13 12	1,211,853 45	914,199 95	297,653 50	22,081 56	319,735 06
1869,	193,742,799 00	100,801,756 00	95,167,745 00	15 52	1,477,003 00	1,112,579 46	364,423 54	15,911 12	380,334 66
1870,	199,041,268 00	106,977,292 00	92,063,976 00	15 43	1,425,241 05	1,077,647 81	347,593 24	8,899 02	356,492 26
1871,	215,729,044 00	114,520,389 00	101,208,665 00	14 83	1,501,936 62	1,140,947 64	360,988 98	8,190 52	369,179 50
1872,	239,547,157 03	134,789,879 00	104,757,278 03	14 53	1,522,122 05	1,153,252 60	368,869 45	7,877 43	376,746 88
1873,	233,437,610 86	156,200,129 00	90,938,561 07	14 49	1,317,699 12	986,771 91	330,927 21	7,182 09	338,109 30
1874,	235,021,537 75	166,712,730 08	84,775,750 50	15 51	1,314,871 47	984,839 15	330,032 32	5,294 65	335,326 97

TABLE NO. 16.

Total taxable Property of the Commonwealth from 1863 to 1874 inclusive.

YEARS.	Property returned by Local Assessors.	Deposits in Savings Banks.	Corporate Excess above Real Estate and Machinery.	Total.	Increase.
1863,	$897,150,983 00	$56,883,828 00	None.	$954,034,811 00	–
1864,	901,883,103 00	62,557,604 30	$100,991,412 22	1,065,432,119 52	$111,397,308 52
1865,	991,841,901 00	59,936,482 52	79,941,570 77	1,131,719,954 29	66,287,834 77
1866,	1,081,316,001 00	67,732,264 31	88,015,184 91	1,237,063,450 22	105,343,495 93
1867,	1,165,893,413 00	80,431,583 71	85,522,968 02	1,331,847,964 73	94,784,514 51
1868,	1,220,498,939 00	94,838,336 54	92,326,758 60	1,407,664,034 14	75,816,069 41
1869,	1,341,069,403 00	112,119,016 64	95,167,745 25	1,548,356,164 89	140,692,130 75
1870,	1,417,127,376 00	135,745,097 54	92,063,976 00	1,644,936,449 54	96,580,284 65
1871,	1,496,678,258 00	163,704,077 54	101,208,665 00	1,761,591,000 54	116,654,551 00
1872,	1,696,599,969 00	184,797,313 92	104,757,278 03	1,986,154,560 95	224,563,560 41
1873, including bank shares,	1,794,216,110 69	202,195,343 70	90,938,561 07	2,087,350,015 46	101,195,454 51
1874, including bank shares,	1,862,170,677 57	217,452,120 84	84,775,750 50	2,164,398,584 91	77,048,533 45
Increase during 11 years,	. . . . .	. . . . .	. . . . .	. . . . .	$1,210,363,737 91

Table No. 17.

Towns which have Decreased in Valuation since 1861, taken from Returns of Assessors to the Secretary of the Commonwealth.

Counties and Towns.	Number of Polls.				Valuation.			
	1861.	1865.	1869.	1873.	1861.	1865.	1869.	1873.
Barnstable County.								
Brewster,	327	302	313	274	$640,816	$755,729	$728,405	$603,100
Eastham,	206	207	191	166	202,935	206,477	219,803	187,305
Orleans,	431	449	420	381	534,102	528,016	536,704	433,224
Sandwich,	830	852	876	783	1,524,000	1,426,400	1,391,900	1,342,250
Truro,	449	396	349	318	387,939	366,784	285,941	286,694
Yarmouth,	591	553	574	539	1,753,798	1,228,673	1,366,629	1,351,689
Berkshire County.								
Alford,	138	124	113	114	319,528	316,989	315,289	295,667
Hancock,	177	183	196	172	474,745	459,448	477,958	447,460
Monterey,	196	184	176	172	305,222	303,879	287,293	258,752
Peru,	129	126	108	120	208,266	199,500	197,816	175,798
Tyringham,	167	155	136	139	294,111	318,540	301,759	272,495
Washington,	245	154	164	156	299,622	263,503	277,633	276,679
Windsor,	208	190	189	160	296,854	275,549	313,188	249,533
Bristol County.								
Acushnet,	290	294	273	267	744,750	635,150	667,200	579,400
Dartmouth,	817	821	798	759	2,659,060	2,308,300	2,213,150	1,733,900
Fairhaven,	781	673	713	693	2,936,800	1,665,100	1,657,900	1,326,700
Freetown,	361	326	332	317	824,151	700,949	725,071	620,498

Norton,	447	415	434	437	$835,500	$814,250	$818,620	$774,875
Raynham,	405	364	442	414	1,008,231	948,996	1,038,050	986,040
Rehoboth,	477	466	442	445	798,145	779,335	790,066	787,446
Swansea,	338	322	318	312	770,250	705,500	636,925	644,575
Westport,	688	692	668	683	1,652,050	1,451,350	1,464,600	1,459,000
DUKES COUNTY.								
Chilmark,	164	156	144	161	552,241	321,551	316,435	275,855
Tisbury,	450	441	438	427	897,995	677,583	685,165	688,719
ESSEX COUNTY.								
Boxford,	252	218	221	228	647,404	685,630	779,860	627,035
Essex,	488	442	429	424	928,882	886,546	912,738	856,857
Newbury,	335	286	277	329	812,335	819,791	830,635	738,264
Wenham,	257	210	245	240	528,725	461,186	487,275	497,300
FRANKLIN COUNTY.								
Ashfield,	355	355	336	324	598,740	614,759	560,096	526,390
Bernardston,	242	232	234	238	456,354	471,648	475,982	354,935
Hawley,	197	192	176	163	173,146	156,481	168,714	162,842
Heath,	159	143	160	148	240,250	238,179	243,336	202,132
Leyden,	117	127	116	112	258,634	273,931	256,249	204,734
Monroe,	53	52	49	43	63,074	74,853	78,116	54,275
New Salem,	282	275	271	259	337,516	330,850	333,700	309,990
Shutesbury,	196	164	162	160	224,403	273,970	214,970	187,700
Wendell,	166	148	139	155	214,966	204,167	202,120	199,397
HAMPDEN COUNTY.								
Blanford,	333	302	284	257	511,902	514,515	533,900	467,250
Brimfield,	353	337	344	326	635,232	696,365	685,862	633,932
Granville,	368	345	342	300	457,969	552,523	470,762	423,016
Montgomery,	98	96	102	86	158,287	164,010	163,793	145,392

Towns which have Decreased in Valuation since 1861—Continued.

COUNTIES AND TOWNS.	Number of Polls.				Valuation.			
	1861.	1865.	1869.	1873.	1861.	1865.	1869.	1873.
Hampshire County.								
Belchertown,	698	696	614	587	$1,064,043	$1,112,296	$1,142,283	$1,034,267
Chesterfield,	225	222	224	208	373,276	377,977	404,859	373.123
Goshen,	110	104	101	91	152,100	153,584	160,514	136,552
Granby,	261	236	239	223	490,267	492,715	574,723	475,065
Hatfield,	348	359	389	402	1,257,724	1,550,888	1,509,335	1,255,071
Plainfield,	191	180	168	152	229,990	246,740	267,300	212,120
Prescott,	162	141	136	133	226,950	214,754	217,291	202,970
Worthington,	268	240	239	242	389,583	371,341	380,181	360,394
Middlesex County.								
Ashby,	312	286	297	265	543,829	485,423	531,085	474,317
Boxborough,	103	118	101	97	256,047	217,446	237,736	239,517
Dunstable,	143	143	138	133	393,789	326,338	300,021	302,578
North Reading,	326	262	274	269	565,029	502,772	509,042	464,192
Stow,	408	356	464	280	734,495	890,512	956,753	726,317
Sudbury,	436	452	545	329	1,081,474	1,064,065	1,335,675	1,018,132
Tyngsborough,	179	143	151	189	303,790	275,748	299,631	298,565
Nantucket County.								
Nantucket,	1,403	1,092	1,023	815	3,291,161	1,984,998	2,027,359	2,364,282
Norfolk County.								
Wrentham,	704	675	753	562	1,244,001	1,216,221	1,448,449	1,188,603

PLYMOUTH COUNTY.								
Duxbury,	712	628	636	664	$1,099,850	$947,850	$1,027,975	$1,089,340
East Bridgewater,	889	794	821	864	1,252,195	1,030,276	1,143,042	1,230,214
Halifax,	213	213	195	176	371,961	358,112	346,848	305,104
Hanson,	344	300	346	352	538,327	466,155	478,147	503,389
Lakeville,	339	317	331	293	584,503	509,910	521,242	528,384
Marion,	235	245	272	228	515,850	430,929	490,465	426,067
Plympton,	255	227	222	200	307,013	292,033	311,961	283,214
Rochester,	324	317	297	284	527,654	480,466	486,844	474,572
South Scituate,	422	400	443	463	930,938	796,709	826,514	895,550
WORCESTER COUNTY.								
Bolton,	360	377	284	291	579,453	627,668	539,864	510,752
Mendon,	317	296	300	318	688,297	680,850	708,038	646,979
New Braintree,	198	186	162	165	543,105	529,248	582,990	496,205
Royalston,	400	356	356	350	783,065	773,086	818,631	712,468

TABLE NO. 18.

STATEMENT showing the Collections of Tax on Incomes by the United States in Massachusetts, during the continuance of the U. S. Income Tax from 1862 to 1872, with the several rates imposed and amounts collected under each.

FOR YEARS ENDING JUNE 30,	1863.	1864.	1865.	1866.	1867.	1868.
Exceeding $600 per annum and not exceeding $10,000, 3 per cent.,	$241 10	$868,617 52	$878,583 49	-	-	-
Exceeding $10,000 per annum, 5 per ct.,	834 31	1,014,298 47	1,278,422 81	-	-	-
From property in the United States owned by any citizen of the same, residing abroad, 5 per cent.,	-	6,472 73	5,574 81	-	-	-
From interest on securities of the United States, 1½ per cent.,	4 36	16,942 04	23,900 37	-	-	-
Exceeding $600 per annum and not exceeding $5,000, 5 per cent.,	-	-	2,522 69	$2,507,163 90	$3,954,426 94	-
Exceeding $5,000 per annum, on excess over $5,000, 10 per cent.,	-	-	2,915 66	4,254,579 69	3,871,928 13	-
Bank dividends and addition to surplus funds, 5 per cent.,	-	-	-	8 00	511,755 38	$468,619 99
Bank profits not divided or added to surplus, 5 per cent.,	-	-	1,011 49	2,212 29	70,159 91	128,676 30
Canal companies' dividends, interest on bonds, and addition to surplus funds, 5 per cent.,	-	-	-	-	324 16	-
Insurance companies' dividends, and addition to surplus funds, 5 per cent.,	-	-	20 50	-	69,063 29	74,297 37
Railroad companies' dividends, interest on bonds, and addition to surplus funds, 5 per cent,	-	-	-	-	371,937 57	376,782 55

Salaries of United States officers, 5 per cent.,	–	–	–	–	–	–
Turnpike companies' dividends, interest on bonds, and addition to surplus funds, 5 per cent.,	–	–	$34 75	–	$157 91	$63 15
Income of 1863, special duty on, 5 per cent.,	–	–	–	$15,606 06	–	–
Income exceeding $1,000, 5 per cent.,	–	–	–	–	–	4,060,590 29
Bank dividends and undistributed profits, 5 per cent.,	–	–	–	–	–	–
Incomes exceeding $2,000, 2½ per cent.,	–	–	–	–	–	–
Bank dividends and undistributed profits, 2½ per cent,	–	–	–	–	–	–
Canal companies' dividends, interest on bonds, and undistributed profits, 2½ per cent.,	–	–	–	–	–	–
Insurance companies' undistributed profits and dividends, 2½ per cent.,	–	–	–	–	–	–
Railroad companies' dividends, undistributed profits and interest on bonds, 2½ per cent.,	–	–	–	–	–	–
Totals,	$1,079 77	$1,906,330 76	$2,192,986 57	$6,779,569 94	$8,849,753 29	$5,109,029 65

Statement showing the Collections of Tax on Incomes, etc.—Concluded.

For Years ending June 30,	1869.	1870.	1871.	1872.	Totals.
Exceeding $600 per annum and not exceeding $10,000, 3 per cent.,	-	-	-	-	$1,747,442 11
Exceeding $10,000 per annum, 5 per ct.,	-	-	-	-	2,293,555 59
From property in the United States owned by any citizen of the same, residing abroad, 5 per cent.,	-	-	-	-	12,047 54
From interest on securities of the United States, 1½ per cent.,	-	-	-	-	40,846 77
Exceeding $600 per annum and not exceeding $5,000, 5 per cent.,	-	-	-	-	6,464,113 53
Exceeding $5,000 per annum, on excess over $5,000, 10 per cent.,	-	-	-	-	8,129,423 48
Bank dividends and addition to surplus funds, 5 per cent.,	-	-	-	-	980,383 37
Bank profits not divided or added to surplus, 5 per cent.,	-	-	-	-	202,059 99
Canal companies' dividends, interest on bonds, and addition to surplus funds, 5 per cent.,	-	$5,783 75	-	-	6,107 91
Insurance companies' dividends, and addition to surplus funds, 5 per cent.,	$118,928 94	121,428 39	$7,415 15	-	391,153 64
Railroad companies' dividends, interest on bonds, and addition to surplus funds, 5 per cent.,	449,830 46	596,046 67	287,535 64	-	2,082,132 89
Salaries of United States officers, 5 per ct.,	-	-	-	-	-
Turnpike companies' dividends, interest on bonds, and addition to surplus funds, 5 per cent.,	94 74	63 15	-	-	413 70

Income of 1863, special duty on, 5 per cent.,	–	–	–	–	$15,606 06
Income exceeding $1,000, 5 per cent.,	$2,643,123 17	$3,195,353 54	$909,827 60	–	10,808,894 60
Bank dividends and undistributed profits, 5 per cent.,	615,920 65	587,245 74	43,110 00	–	1,246,276 39
Incomes exceeding $2,000, 2½ per cent.,	–	–	540,921 36	$1,678,719 41	2,219,640 77
Bank dividends and undistributed profits, 2½ per cent.,	–	–	91,680 10	336,254 98	427,935 08
Canal companies' dividends, interest on bonds, and undistributed profits, 2½ per cent.,	–	–	1,025 65	2,201 92	3,227 57
Insurance companies' undistributed profits and dividends, 2½ per cent.,	–	–	3,781 94	52,075 07	55,857 01
Railroad companies' dividends, undistributed profits and interest on bonds, 2½ per cent.,	–	–	26,511 48	473,729 54	500,241 02
Totals,	$3,827,897 96	$4,505,921 24	$1,911,808 92	$2,542,980 92	$37,627,359 02

Table No. 19.

Statement showing the Collections on Legacies, Distributive Shares, and Successions to Real Estate, by the United States, in the State of Massachusetts, under the Internal Revenue Laws, in force from 1862 to October 1, 1870, with the several rates imposed and collections under each.

Years ending June 30,	1863.	1864.	1865.	1866.	1867.	1868.	1869.	1870.	1871.	Totals.
Collections on Legacies and Distributive Shares.										
To parent or child, brother or sister, 75 cts. per $100,	$9,219 17	$42,802 15	-	-	-	-	-	-	-	$52,021 32
Lineal issue or ancestor, brother or sister, $1 per $100,	-	-	$55,003 97	$108,071 90	$117,190 19	$130,110 79	$118,741 40	$94,038 35	$106,462 10	729,618 70
Nephew or niece, $1.50 per $100,	6,122 39	11,138 17	-	-	-	-	-	-	-	17,260 56
Descendant of brother or sister, $2 per $100,	-	-	12,572 10	34,365 53	20,543 89	12,716 45	16,356 82	29,028 26	44,412 32	169,995 37
Uncle, aunt or cousin, $3 per $100,	290 68	5,931 51	-	-	-	-	-	-	-	6,222 19
Great uncle or aunt or 2d cousin, 1863 and 1864; uncle or aunt or descendant of same, since 1864, $4 per $100,	-	-	15,864 66	6,383 00	2,982 26	9,033 93	1,144 16	4,922 13	12,537 46	52,867 60
Stranger in blood, 1863 and 1864; great uncle or aunt or descendant of same, since 1864, $5 per $100,	14,044 44	39,826 97	6,121 54	3,161 61	1,228 10	1,605 48	16,199 73	1,252 55	1,284 00	84,724 42
Stranger in blood, since 1864, $6 per $100,	-	-	18,999 34	17,576 63	53,967 75	50,307 96	27,445 25	75,738 20	127,434 77	371,469 90
Total Collections on Legacies,	$29,676 68	$99,698 80	$108,561 61	$169,558 67	$195,912 19	$203,774 61	$179,887 36	$204,979 49	$292,130 65	$1,484,180 06

Collections on Successions to Real Estate.										
Lineal issue, or ancestor, $1 per $100,	-	-	$2,574 98	$15,328 34	$27,217 40	$69,267 34	$84,241 50	$60,157 78	$46,954 80	$305,742 14
Brother or sister, or descendant of same, $2 per $100,	-	-	2,281 03	7,163 11	9,942 56	10,337 70	12,017 87	16,839 23	12,690 60	71,272 10
Uncle or aunt, or descendant of same, $4 per $100,	-	-	1,148 00	380 47	391 22	1,052 64	5,036 60	983 52	1,498 40	10,490 85
Great uncle or aunt, or descendant of same, $5 per $100,	-	-	-	50 00	30 00	55 90	115 00	305 00	60 00	615 90
Stranger in blood, $6 per $100,	-	-	2,598 27	2,324 53	5,345 08	10,312 19	10,224 27	21,112 39	10,174 54	62,091 27
Total Collections on Successions,	-	-	$8,602 28	$25,246 45	$42,926 26	$91,025 77	$111,635 24	$99,397 92	$71,378 34	$450,212 26
Total Collections on Legacies, as above,	$29,676 68	$99,698 80	108,561 61	169,558 67	195,912 19	203,774 61	179,887 36	204,979 49	292,130 65	1,484,180 06
Total Collections on Legacies, Distributive Shares and Successions,	$29,676 68	$99,698 80	$117,163 89	$194,805 12	$238,838 45	$294,800 38	$291,522 60	$304,377 41	$363,508 99	$1,934,392 32

AN INDEX BY TOPICS.